Windows NT v4 Workstation Administration

Wave Technologies International, Inc.
MNT4-COR3-7072A

Windows NT v4.0 Workstation Administration
MNT4-COR3-7072A
©1988-1997 Wave Technologies International, Inc.
All rights reserved.

Printed in the United States of America. No part of this book may be used or reproduced in any form or by any means, or stored in a database or retrieval system, without prior written permission of the publisher. Making copies of any part of this book for any purpose other than your own personal use is a violation of United States copyright laws. For information, contact Wave Technologies International, Inc., 10845 Olive Blvd., Suite 250, St. Louis, MO 63141.

This book is sold as is, without warranty of any kind, either express or implied, respecting the contents of this book, including, but not limited to, implied warranties for the book's quality, performance, merchantability, or fitness for any particular purpose. Neither Wave Technologies International, Inc., nor its dealers or distributors shall be liable to the purchaser or any other person or entity with respect to any liability, loss, or damage caused or alleged to be caused directly or indirectly by this book.

Trademarks:

Trademarks and registered trademarks of products mentioned in this book are held by the companies producing them. Use of a term in this book should not be regarded as affecting the validity of any trademark or service mark.

The Wave logo is a registered trademark of Wave Technologies International, Inc., St. Louis, Missouri.

Copyright of any screen captures in this book are the property of the software's manufacturer.

Mention of any products in this book in no way constitutes an endorsement by Wave Technologies International, Inc.

ETI, Inc. a subsidiary of Wave Technologies International, Inc. is an independent entity from Microsoft Corporation, and not affiliated with Microsoft corporation in any manner. This publication may be used in assisting students to prepare for a Microsoft Certified Professional Exam. Neither Microsoft corporation, its designated review company, nor ETI, Inc., a subsidiary of Wave Technologies International, Inc. warrants that use of this publication will ensure passing the relevant Exam. Microsoft is either a registered trademark or trademark of Microsoft Corporation in the United States and/or other countries.

ISBN: 1-884486-21-5

10 9 8 7 6 5 4 3 2 1

Contents

Introduction 1
    Overview 1
    Course Purpose 1
    Course Goals 3

Chapter 1—Installation 5
    Objectives 6
    Pre-Test Questions 6
    Introduction 7
    Comparison of Windows Operating Systems 8
    Preparation for Windows NT Installation 15
    Installing Windows NT Workstation 31
    Automating Installation 47
    System Access 60
    Summary 70
    Post-Test Questions 71

Chapter 2—User and Group Management 73
    Objectives 74
    Pre-Test Questions 74
    Introduction 75
    Local Security 76
    User and Group Account Management 80
    Security Events 106
    Summary 117
    Post-Test Questions 118

Chapter 3—Advanced User Management — 119

- Objectives 120
- Pre-Test Questions 120
- Introduction 121
- Introduction to Domains 121
- Security Management 128
- Introduction to Profiles and Policies 135
- Summary 153
- Post-Test Questions 153

Chapter 4—Peripheral Management — 155

- Objectives 156
- Pre-Test Questions 156
- Introduction 157
- Control Panel Utilities 158
- Using the Event Viewer 179
- Introduction to Printers 182
- Summary 202
- Post-Test Questions 203

Chapter 5—Configuration Management — 205

- Objectives 206
- Pre-Test Questions 206
- Introduction 207
- System Management 208
- Additional Control Panel Utilities 218
- Introduction to the Registry 234
- Summary 250
- Post-Test Questions 250

Chapter 6—Disk and File Management — 253

- Objectives 254
- Pre-Test Questions 254
- Introduction 255
- Using Disk Administrator 256
- Resource Management 264
- Introduction to Windows NT Explorer and Access Security 268
- Summary 285
- Post-Test Questions 286

Chapter 7—Application Management — 287

- Objectives 288
- Pre-Test Questions 288
- Introduction 289
- Introduction to the Windows NT Application Environment 290
- Applications Supported By Windows NT 308
- Properties of MS-DOS Applications 320
- Managing Data Transfers 333
- Introduction to DCOM 339
- Summary 349
- Post-Test Questions 350

Chapter 8—Network Management — 351

- Objectives 352
- Pre-Test Questions 352
- Introduction 353
- Network Configuration 354
- Examining Network Services 378
- Resource Sharing and Access 385
- Summary 400
- Post-Test Questions 401

Chapter 9—Advanced Networking — 403
- Objectives — 404
- Pre-Test Questions — 404
- Introduction — 405
- NetWare Services for Windows NT — 405
- Introduction to Remote Access Service — 412
- Introduction to the Internet — 427
- Summary — 445
- Post-Test Questions — 445

Chapter 10—Ongoing Maintenance — 447
- Objectives — 448
- Pre-Test Questions — 448
- Introduction — 449
- Review of Windows NT Installation — 449
- Maintenance Issues — 463
- Troubleshooting — 474
- Remote Management — 484
- Summary — 487
- Post-Test Questions — 488

Appendix A — Answers to Pre-Test and Post-Test Questions — 489
- Chapter 1 — 489
- Chapter 2 — 491
- Chapter 3 — 492
- Chapter 4 — 493
- Chapter 5 — 493
- Chapter 6 — 494
- Chapter 7 — 495
- Chapter 8 — 495
- Chapter 9 — 496
- Chapter 10 — 497

Appendix B — Sample Answer File — 499

Glossary — 501

Index — 573

SELF STUDY

Introduction

OVERVIEW

Wave Technologies International, Inc., develops, markets, and delivers training and instructional products related to sophisticated information technologies, including LANs, WANs, telecommunications systems, advanced operating systems, and client-server systems.

This technical training program is comprised of several different media and delivery tools. Each is used for its optimum instructional and practical value. The training manuals present key knowledge, concepts, and procedures. These books can be used anywhere, anytime; and are an excellent technical reference library. They serve both as a primary learning tool and reinforcement after initial training has been completed. The videos provide visual walk throughs of important technical concepts. A picture can often "be worth a thousand words." The *Challenge! Interactive* is an excellent tool to reinforce learning and to prepare for the certification exams. For a more powerful elements, refer to Getting Started in the MCSE Self-Study Program.

Each of these elements is part of a powerful, flexible learning system that is unique in the marketplace. Our "multiple media" learning philosophy is designed to help individuals and organizations improve their knowledge, skills and performance.

COURSE PURPOSE

This course is designed to help you prepare to install, configure, and support Windows NT Workstation v4.0. It assumes that you have some prior experience working with Windows-family products, especially Windows 95. It does not assume that you have any prior experience working with Windows NT products.

The course takes you through basic skills you will need to understand and are likely to employ on a day-to-day basis. Your training materials include this manual, with both written lessons and suggested hands-on exercises, a companion video tape, and Wave's *Challenge! Interactive*, which will help you judge your understanding of the material.

This course is designed to meet all published criteria for Microsoft's Implementing and Supporting Windows NT Workstation v4.0 examination, exam number 70-73. However, the materials in this manual go beyond simple test preparation. It is designed to give you the firm foundation you need to use, manage, and support Windows NT Workstation.

It is important to realize that Windows NT Workstation does not exist in a vacuum. You need to understand not only how Windows NT Workstation works, but also how it works in relation to different network environments. This course is designed to give you that broad-based understanding.

To complete the exercises in this manual, you will need a system that meets the following minimum requirements:

- 80486 (or above) microprocessor
- 16+ MB RAM
- 120+ MB hard disk space
- VGA or better monitor
- Mouse or other pointing device
- Network adapter and cabling
- CD-ROM

For some of the exercises, you will need access to a Windows NT domain and a Novell NetWare server. If these are not available, you should still complete the remaining exercises in this manual.

You will also need to provide a Windows NT Workstation v4.0 installation CD.

Whenever possible, it is strongly suggested that the exercises in this manual be completed on a network set up specifically for training. If you will be attaching to a live network, you should review all of the exercises with your Network Administrator.

NOTICE:

The exercises in this self-study product are designed to be used on a system that is designated for training purposes ONLY. Practicing the exercises on a LAN or workstation that is used for other purposes may cause configuration problems, which will require a reinstallation and/or restoration from a tape backup of the original configuration. Please keep this in mind when working through the exercises.

COURSE GOALS

This self-study course will provide you with the information you need to complete the following:

- List the Windows NT Workstation v4.0 installation requirements.
- Install Windows NT Workstation v4.0.
- Use selected Control Panel utilities to configure Windows NT Workstation.
- Create and test multiple hardware configurations.
- Create and test user definitions.
- Create and test group definitions.
- Define and test user profiles.
- Define and test system and user policies.
- Compare and contrast FAT and NTFS file systems.
- Create an NTFS disk partition.
- Establish and test local access permissions.
- Enable auditing.
- Describe the features of the Remote Access Server client.
- Describe the features of Client Service for NetWare.
- List the application types supported by Windows NT.
- Identify common system bottlenecks.

This self study manual has a corresponding videotape that we encourage you to watch first. In it you will see the basic concepts of Window NT in action, delivered in a format focused on high learner retention and easy note-taking. Afterwards you will have a solid grasp of the fundamentals to start the manual.

Scenario-based Learning

This self study manual uses a number of scenario-based learning exercises. In these, you are presented with a situation similar to those you are likely to encounter in day-to-day support and management. You will be provided with the information you need and asked to determine a best solution. A suggested solution is provided for each in Appendix A at the back of the self study manual.

These exercises are being used to supplement hands-on practice and to help get you started thinking critically about practical applications. In some cases, they have been used as a replacement for hands-on practice for scenarios where it would be especially difficult to emulate a real-word situation.

It is important that you take the time to work through the scenario based exercises. These are an important supplement to the training materials and are meant to reinforce the text information in your manual.

CHAPTER 1

Installation

MAJOR TOPICS

Objectives	6
Pre-Test Questions	6
Introduction	7
Comparison of Windows Operating Systems	8
Preparation for Windows NT Installation	15
Installing Windows NT Workstation	31
Automating Installation	47
System Access	60
Summary	70
Post-Test Questions	71

OBJECTIVES

At the completion of this chapter, you will be able to:

- Compare and contrast current members of the Windows family.
- List and describe features and benefits of Windows NT.
- Describe the basic features of the Windows NT interface.
- List the installation requirements for Windows NT Server and Windows NT Workstation.
- List and describe the options for launching Windows NT Setup.
- Describe potential concerns when upgrading an existing system to Windows NT.
- Given configuration parameters, install Windows NT Workstation.
- Briefly describe the Windows NT boot process.
- Log onto a Windows NT Workstation station.
- List and describe common logon failures.
- Use the Security dialog to protect a station from unauthorized access.
- Shut down a system.

PRE-TEST QUESTIONS

The answers to these questions are in Appendix A at the end of this manual.

1. What is the memory requirement for installing Windows NT v4.0 on an x86 platform?

   ....

   ....

2. You are attempting to install Windows NT Workstation from a network installation source. You discover that the diskette drive is bad. What can you run and still be able to complete the installation?

   ....

   ....

3. What file system should you use as your destination if you want to be able to dual-boot between Windows NT Workstation and MS-DOS?

    ....

    ....

4. At default, what protocol selections are available for installation?

    ....

    ....

5. What is the file that is used to build the operating system selection menu during startup?

    ....

    ....

INTRODUCTION

Windows NT is Microsoft's answer to the most demanding end-user and network server requirements. Your concern should be more than implementation, however, but proper implementation of Windows NT Workstation and Windows NT Server.

This chapter is designed to help you make critical implementation decisions, focusing on those relating to installation. It opens with a brief comparison of Windows family operating systems, moving then to the features and benefits of Windows NT. This will help you determine the potential roles for Windows NT in your organizational environment.

The chapter next goes into a detailed look at installation. This starts with a list of installation requirements for Intel x86-based and RISC-based platforms. You will also be provided with guidelines for selecting your installation destination, the method of launching installation, and upgrading existing operating systems. This is followed by a detailed look at the installation process. Windows NT Workstation and Windows NT Server installation steps are covered separately. While there is a good deal of redundancy during these discussions, you should find it helpful when using this manual as a reference.

The chapter ends with an overview of system access. Logon procedures are briefly discussed, with a more detailed discussion of users and access to come later in the course. You will also see some ways of protecting a station from unauthorized access.

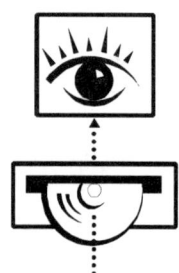

Stop now and view the following video presentation on the Interactive Learning CD-ROM:
    Windows NT v4.0 Workstation Administration Overview
    Windows NT v4.0 Workstation Administration
    Why Windows NT Workstation

COMPARISON OF WINDOWS OPERATING SYSTEMS

This section will present a brief history and summary of Microsoft Windows' products. It will also present features and benefits of Windows NT Server from an administrative standpoint. The following are topics discussed within this section:

- Windows Family
- Windows NT Features
- Windows NT Server Features
- Windows 95 User Interface
- Where Does It Fit?
- Why Not Windows 95?

Familiarity with these products will provide you with an understanding of the benefits of Windows NT versus other Windows products along with how the products relate in a network environment. This information will also enable you to determine why Windows NT is more suitable for your work environment as opposed to another product as opposed to Windows 95 alone.

Windows Family

Microsoft has designed the Windows family to meet computing needs ranging from stand-alone, through small local area networks (LAN), to wide-area enterprise networking. Family members that you are likely to see in current use include:

- Windows

    The oldest member of the Windows family, Microsoft Windows brought mass market acceptance of a PC-based graphic user interface (GUI). Windows runs in a 16-bit environment and has limited built-in support for networking. Microsoft no longer sells this product.

- Windows for Workgroups

    Network support was one of the major focuses of Windows for Workgroups. While still a 16-bit product, it does provide some 32-bit code support. Network support is significantly improved when compared to Windows, but still somewhat limited. Microsoft no longer sells this product, but a large number of Windows for Workgroups systems are still in use.

- Windows 95

    Sold as a true 32-bit operating system, Windows 95 still carries some 16-bit legacy code for support of older applications. Despite this, Windows 95 is a much more robust and stable product than earlier Windows versions. It is designed primarily for the "average" end-user desktop. Significant areas of improvement include a redesigned user interface, Plug and Play support, and drastically improved network support.

- Windows NT Workstation

    Now in its third major revision, Windows NT Workstation now includes the Windows 95 user interface. Designed to meet demanding end-user requirements, its scaleable design actually makes it a good choice for the average end-user as well, assuming that minimum hardware requirements are met.

- Windows NT Server

    Designed as the platform on which to build your network or as an addition to an existing network, NT Server has the ability to support the smallest LAN up to the largest enterprise. It is also the operating system platform for Microsoft's BackOffice product family, including SQL Server, Exchange Server, and Systems Management Server.

A large number of Windows and Windows for Workgroups users have opted, thus far, not to upgrade to newer members of the operating system family. For many, it is simply a case that the 16-bit Windows products meet their needs and they see no reason to upgrade. For others, they are unable to meet the minimum hardware requirements for system upgrade.

Windows NT Features

Windows NT Workstation and Windows NT Server share a number of common features. These include:

- 32-bit operating system

    Windows NT is a true 32-bit operating system. Your system starts up and runs in Windows NT.

- Hardware platform support

    You have the choice of selecting the hardware platform to best meet your operational requirements. Windows NT supports x86-based and RISC-based platforms.

- Preemptive multitasking

    The operating system retains control over system activity, sharing available processor time between the processes running.

- Security

    Windows NT meets C2 security specifications. A valid username and password is required for logon and resource access. Permissions can be set on a user-by-user basis or by groups of users.

- Application support

    In addition to native applications written to the Win32 API set, Windows NT supports a wide variety of 16-bit Windows and MS-DOS applications.

- Network support

    Windows NT can be used to build your network or as powerful additions to an existing network environment.

- Internet/Intranet support

    Windows NT ships with Microsoft's Internet Explorer and other Internet support tools. Implementation of a corporate Intranet is significantly simplified.

- Microsoft Exchange

    Microsoft Exchange client installs during Windows NT Setup. It provides support for both Microsoft Mail and Internet Mail.

In addition, many of the familiar utilities have been improved and enhanced with this latest release.

Windows NT Server Features

There are some additional features that are specific to Windows NT Server. Although they are not part of Windows NT Workstation, a summary is presented here to help you understand how NT Server differs from NT Workstation. These include:

- Microsoft networking

    Windows NT Server includes a fully integrated network operating system. The network model is based on the concepts developed over years of experience with LAN Manager and earlier Windows NT releases.

- NetWare support

    Windows NT supports utilities specifically designed to support existing NetWare networks. Gateway Service for NetWare lets an NT Server act as a gateway between Microsoft clients and NetWare servers. The NetWare Migration utility lets you migrate users and data from one or more NetWare servers to one or more NT Servers. Additional services that may be purchased for use with NT Server include File and Print Services for NetWare and NetWare Directory Services. File and Print sharing for NetWare gives NetWare clients access to NT Server resources. NetWare Directory Services gives you a way of managing your NetWare servers from a central location.

- Advanced fault tolerance

    Windows NT Server provides support for disk mirroring, disk duplexing, and disk striping with parity. This gives you the ability to not only protect your data, but also to allow users to keep working (often uninterrupted) when a disk failure occurs.

- Internet and TCP/IP support

    The TCP/IP support utilities have been improved and enhanced. Windows NT now includes support for a DNS (Domain Naming System) server. Microsoft Internet Information Server (IIS) can be installed at the same time as NT Server, or later after installation. Windows NT Server also ships with Microsoft's FrontPage, an easy to use HTML page editor.

Windows 95 User Interface

If you are familiar with earlier releases of Windows NT, perhaps the most obvious change is the user interface. Windows NT now uses the Windows 95 user interface. This makes for a much more powerful and flexible desktop, making it easy for users to customize their working environment to meet their needs.

This course assumes that you are already at least somewhat familiar with the Windows 95 interface. The following is an overview of some key points:

- Taskbar and Start menu

    Rather than appearing as desktop icons, minimized applications are displayed on the taskbar, which can be easily moved to any screen border. The Start menu, which replaces the Program Manager (with additional enhancements) is fully customizable.

- Windows Explorer

    Performing the same function as the File Manager in other products, the Windows Explorer is much more powerful and flexible than its predecessor.

- Property sheets

    Devices, utilities, files, and other operating system objects all have property sheets, simplifying the process of customizing your configuration.

- Shortcuts

    Shortcuts give you access to executables and data files while protecting the originals from accidental deletion.

- Pop-up menus

    Right-click (click with mouse button 2, the right button on a right-handed mouse) almost anywhere and you get a pop-up menu. The menus are context sensitive, giving you choices appropriate to the selected object.

While it might take some time to adjust to the new environment, the Windows 95 desktop is easy to use.

Where Does It Fit?

It's a good idea to spend some time planning where you are going to implement Windows-family products in your organization. It is unlikely that you would install Windows NT Workstation for all of your end-users. Despite its end-user interface, it's unlikely that you would provide Windows NT Server at any individual's desktop, except for a few very special cases. So, how do they all fit together?

Use Windows 95 or Windows NT Workstation to support "average" end-users. They will meet application support and network access requirements for most users.

Use Windows NT Workstation:

- As a stable, powerful platform for power users.
- As a means of sharing a workstation between users while providing a custom environment matched to individual needs.
- As a secure workstation for sensitive applications and data files.
- To provide additional resources to an existing network.

Use Windows NT Server:

- As a base for resource intensive client/server applications.
- As a platform for building a stable, secure LAN.
- To provide shared resources to users while maintaining centralized control over access permissions.
- To enhance existing networks.
- As a base for Internet/Intranet implementation.

These are, of course, just general suggestions. Where Windows-family products fit for you will depend on your business requirements.

Why Not Windows 95?

There is an obvious overlap between users who could be supported by Windows 95 and Windows NT Workstation. How do you decide which to use?

Installation requirements are an obvious difference. Windows 95 requires, at minimum, an 80386 processor, 40 MB of disk space, and 8 MB of RAM. Windows NT requires an 80486 processor, 120 MB of disk space, and 12 MB or more of RAM.

There are some features currently supported by Windows 95 that are not supported under Windows NT. These include:

- Support for MS-DOS device drivers.
- Support for Win16 device drivers.
- Plug and Play technology support.
- Fax support through the messaging client.
- Built-in Microsoft Network (MSN) client software.

Plug and Play, Fax, and Microsoft Network (MSN) support are planned for future releases of Windows NT. This doesn't mean to imply that Windows 95 is the sure winner. There are several Windows NT features that are not supported by Windows 95, including:

- Preemptive multitasking for Win16 applications.
- Support for IBM Presentation Manager (to v1.3) and POSIX applications.
- RISC processor support.
- Scaleable multiprocessor support configurations.
- NTFS file system and automatic failure recovery.

You will need to weigh these factors carefully when making your implementation decisions.

PREPARATION FOR WINDOWS NT INSTALLATION

This section will present some thoughts you may want to consider prior to installing Windows NT. These key issues may determine whether you are able to install Windows NT on the machines available. In order to begin installation, you will first need to determine what hardware capabilities are available for installation itself. Also presented is a discussion on configuring multiple-boot systems. The following are topics discussed within this section:

- About Installation
- Installation Requirements
- Installation Destination
- Installation Options
- WINNT/WINNT32
- Boot Installation
- WINNT/WINNT32

- WINNT/WINNT32 Without Diskettes
- RISC Installation
- Upgrade Notes
- Dual-boot Configuration
- Upgrading Windows v3.x
- Special Configurations
- Dual-Boot After Install
- Triple-Boot System
- Enabling MS-DOS Startup
- Installation Overview

These guidelines will prepare you for installing Windows NT for the very first time or as an upgrade. Also available to you are various methods to begin installation, hardware configuration issues, and system settings. This information is pertinent to the ease of installing Windows.

About Installation

The importance of a clean installation cannot be over-emphasized. Bad choices during installation can mean less than optimal performance and could mean having to reinstall the operating system at some future date.

Concerns and considerations when preparing for installation include:

- System role

    Determine what role the system will play in your network. The primary domain controller must be installed before any backup domain controllers. Clients and additional servers may be installed at any time and added to the domain later.

- Minimum installation requirements

    Make sure that all systems meet at least the minimum installation requirements. It will be a waste of effort to install Windows NT on a system that does not meet these requirements. Even if you can get Windows NT to run, it will likely be both slow and unstable.

- Operational requirements

    Minimum requirements are exactly that, what you must have to install and launch the operating system. Your operational requirements are likely to be greater and will be somewhat dependent on the applications you plan to run.

Careful planning will result in more reliable systems and a more dependable network environment.

Installation Requirements

Minimum installation requirements are somewhat dependent on the destination platform. They are, at minimum:

- Processor

    Windows supports Intel x86 (80486 or above), MIPS R4x00, Digitial Alpha, and PowerPC. Windows NT Workstation supports up to two processors. Windows NT Server supports up to four RISC processors out of the box, with vendor-specific versions supporting up to 32 processors.

- Hard disks

    One or more hard disks are required. Windows NT Workstation requires at least 117 MB on x86 and 124 MB on RISC-based systems. Windows NT Server requires 148 MB on x86 and 158 on RISC-based systems.

- CD-ROM

    A CD-ROM is required for all installations not run over the network. Default x86 installations also require a 3-1/2 inch High-density floppy disk drive.

- Memory

    You must have at least 12 MB of RAM installed on x86 systems with 16 MB being the suggested minimum. RISC-based systems require at least 32 MB of RAM.

- Display

    A VGA (or higher resolution) display and adapter are **required**.

Suggested additional hardware includes:

- Pointing device

    Despite the graphic nature of the interface, a pointing device is **not an** installation requirement. You are likely to find, however, that it is **difficult** to work using a GUI interface without some type of pointing device.

- Network adapter

    While not required, most installations of Windows NT Workstation and Server are in network environments. In order to use the **network, some type** of network communications device is required, normally a **network adapter**.

Any additional hardware should be installed before setting up Windows NT, if at all possible.

Installation Destination

Disk and file system support is discussed in detail later in the course. However, some mention needs to be made as to how supported file systems relate to your installation decisions.

Windows NT supports two file systems. The FAT file system is supported **not only by** Windows NT, but by MS-DOS, DOS Windows, Windows 95, and OS/2 as well. NTFS is supported by Windows NT only, but provides enhanced security and a higher built-in fault tolerance level. NTFS also supports file compression on a per-file basis.

You will need to use FAT:

- If you want to dual-boot with another operating system.
- If you want to be able to use FAT file utilities.
- If you want to install on a RISC-based system.

It is not required to put all of the operating system files on a FAT partition when installing on a RISC-based system. You will be required, however, to set up a small (at least 2 MB) FAT partition for the initial boot files.

You will need to use NTFS:

- If security is an overwhelming concern.
- If you don't want to allow local access after booting from another operating system.

One possible compromise is to install the operating system files on a FAT file partition, then set up one or more NTFS partitions for all of your remaining files.

Installation Options

A number of options are provided for starting and running your installation:

- Boot from installation diskettes (or CD) and install.

  This is the default method and the preferred method for installation on x86 systems. Microsoft suggests using this installation method whenever possible. If your BIOS supports Bootable CD-ROM format, you can boot directly from the CD-ROM to run Setup.

- Run WINNT or WINNT32 from the CD or network server.

  This method supports installation with or without diskettes. At default, boot diskettes will be created and the installation files copied to your hard disk when you start the installation. Optionally, you can have the startup files copied to your local hard disk.

- Install directly from CD.

  If you currently have Windows 95 or Windows NT v4.0 installed on your system, the CD will autorun when inserted and prompt you with an installation selection. This method will be described in more detail during the discussion about upgrades.

- SETUPLDR

    Run SETUPLDR to install Windows NT on a RISC platform. RISC setup requires installation directly from a local CD-ROM.

Choose a method that best meets your needs and available hardware.

WINNT/WINNT32

Before looking at installation methods in detail, some mention needs to be made of WINNT and WINNT32. These programs let you install Windows NT from an unsupported CD-ROM configuration or network server.

Run WINNT if your current operating system is MS-DOS, 16-bit Windows, or Windows 95. Run WINNT32 if the system is currently running a version of Windows NT. The options supported are as follows:

/s:sourcpath	This allows you to specify the source path for the installation files.
/i:inf_files	This is the filename of the Setup information file, defaulting to DOSNET.INF. Specify the filename only, without path information.
/t:drive	This is the drive to which you want temporary files written. Otherwise, Setup will select the drive automatically.
/w	This switch allows you to run WINNT from a DOS session in Windows.
/f	This switch will not verify the files copied to the boot floppies.
/c	The Setup boot floppies will not be checked to determine if they have enough space.
/x	Use this option so that Setup will not create boot floppies. Use this option if you already have boot floppies available.
/b	This allows you to run the upgrade as a floppy-less operation. System files are copied to the hard disk instead of to the floppy.
/ox	Installation boot floppies are created, but installation files are not copied to the hard disk.

/u	Use this option to upgrade without prompting for user intervention. All options are taken from the settings in the previous Windows NT version.
/u:script	This specifies a script file, or answer file, for unattended installation. Installation settings are taken from the script file rather than prompting for user intervention.
/udf:id[UDF_file]	This specifies the identifier to be used when you wish to replace sections of the script file with user or system specific information. If a file is not specified, Setup will prompt for a diskette and look for a file named $UNIQUE$.UDF.
/r:directory	Specify an additional directory from the installation source directory tree for installation. You must use additional /r switches to specify multiple directories.
/rx:directory	This specifies that the optional directory is to be copied to the hard disk during installation.
/e:command	The specified command will be executed after the graphic portion of installation is complete.

Boot Installation

This is the method recommended by Microsoft. It directly supports most x86 systems, and provides the best alternate support for:

- HALs (hardware application layers)
- System timing
- Third-party device drivers

It does require a high density floppy disk drive (or bootable CD-ROM BIOS) and a supported CD-ROM configuration. Finding a supported CD-ROM is less of a problem with the wider base of hardware support under Windows NT v4.0. To start the installation:

- Boot from the Setup Startup diskette (or CD-ROM).
- When prompted, replace the Startup diskette with diskette #2 and press `ENTER`.

This will take you to the Welcome screen. At this point, Setup follows a common path except that you will be prompted to change diskettes one additional time.

If your setup diskettes become lost or damaged, you can run WINNT /OX or WINNT32 /OX to create a new set of diskettes.

WINNT/WINNT32

Even though Windows NT v4.0 does support a greater variety of CD-ROM drives and adapters than earlier versions, you may still encounter an unsupported CD-ROM. If you have several systems to install, you may find it more convenient to copy the installation source files to a network server and install across the network. WINNT and WINNT32 support both of these installation options.

Microsoft considers this the next best choice for installation. When you run WINNT or WINNT32:

- Setup prompts for three blank formatted diskettes.

    These will be used to create the installation diskettes. These are not identical to the standard installation diskettes. They will use the local hard disk rather than local CD-ROM as an installation source.

- Setup will copy the installation file set to your hard disk.

    You need to be able to access the network server or CD-ROM at this point, but will not need access when you run setup. Depending on the speed of your hard disk or network connection, this can take several minutes.

When you are ready to run the installation:

- Boot from the Setup Startup diskette.
- When prompted, replace the Startup diskette with diskette #2 and press `ENTER`.

From this point on, Setup proceeds normally. You will need access to the installation media, either CD-ROM or network server, should you want to add Windows NT components or change device drivers later.

WINNT/WINNT32 Without Diskettes

This is the least reliable installation method supported by Microsoft, but may be necessary in some circumstances. It can sometimes allow you to install Windows NT when conflicts or timing errors prevent you from running your installation from diskette. You can use either a CD-ROM or network server as your source. To launch the installation, run:

- WINNT /B

    Run WINNT from MS-DOS. You must use the /W switch as well to launch WINNT from an MS-DOS prompt under Windows. The command will run directly in a Windows 95 command prompt.

- WINNT32 /B

    Run WINNT32 if upgrading or reinstalling on an existing Windows NT system.

When you start the installation:

- Setup-specific startup files are copied to the hard disk.
- The installation file set is copied to the hard disk.

You will be prompted to restart after the files have copied. After restart, Setup will proceed normally.

RISC Installation

Installation to a RISC-based computer requires a local CD-ROM as the installation source. To start the installation place the installation CD-ROM in the CD-ROM drive and boot your system.

If "Install Windows NT from CD-ROM" appears on the ARC screen, then all you need to do is choose that selection and Setup will run automatically. Otherwise, you will need to:

- Choose "Run A Program" from the menu.
- Type the following and press **ENTER**:

    cd:*system*\setupldr

Replace *system* with the appropriate directory. On some systems, you will have to supply a full device name rather than "cd:". You will need to refer to system documentation to determine the proper format.

Setup will run the same from this point on as when setting up x86-based systems.

Upgrade Notes

You can use any of the installation methods to upgrade existing systems to Windows NT v4.0. Through upgrade, you can:

- Migrate current Windows or Windows for Workgroups settings.
- Migrate current Windows NT configuration settings.
- Migrate existing program groups and applications.
- Change server role or domain membership.

In order to upgrade an existing Windows or Windows NT system, allow Windows NT v4.0 to install into the current Windows directory. When deciding whether or not to upgrade a system, there are a few points to keep in mind. These include:

- Windows dual-boot requirements

    If you install Windows NT to the existing Windows v3.1 or Windows for Workgroups v3.11 directory, you will still be able to boot MS-DOS and launch Windows. You will also have the option when logging onto Windows NT to migrate your Windows settings.

- Windows NT dual-boot requirements

    If you upgrade the existing Windows NT operating system, you will not be able to choose between booting Windows NT or the original operating system. Install Windows NT in a separate directory to support dual-boot, leaving the original Windows NT installation available for startup.

- Existing files

    You will lose any custom (user) files that have been added below the Windows NT directory if you reinstall to the Windows NT directory.

- No Windows 95 Upgrade

    You cannot upgrade from Windows 95 to Windows NT. They must be installed in separate directories. You will have the option of booting either Windows 95 or Windows NT.

In most cases, you won't need to provide dual-boot capabilities for servers. You may, however, for workstations. One reason is to support MS-DOS and Windows applications that won't run under Windows NT.

Dual-boot Configuration

You may encounter situations where it is preferable to have both Windows NT Workstation and another operating system available on the same machine. This can be accomplished through a dual-boot or multi-boot configuration.

Dual-boot configuration is automatic if there is another operating system present on the machine when you install Windows NT. During Windows NT Setup, the Primary Boot Sector is copied into BOOTSECT.DOS. It is then replaced with the Windows NT Primary Boot Sector. The BOOT.INI file is created to give you access to different Windows NT configurations and to that original Primary Boot Sector. When you launch Windows NT, you will be prompted to select the operating system to use for startup.

Currently, automatic dual-boot configuration is supported for:

- MS-DOS
- Windows v3.1
- Windows for Workgroups v3.11
- Windows 95
- OS/2 v1.1 (and v1.3)

Depending on how it was installed, some OS/2 v2.x installations may work, but Microsoft does not provide support for that configuration.

Upgrading Windows v3.x

When upgrading Windows v3.1 or Windows for Workgroups v3.11, you have the option of installing Windows NT to the existing Windows directory. This allows for migration of existing Windows information. As each user logs on at the workstation, he or she will be prompted to migrate the Windows information, setting up the start menu to include the programs configured in the Windows Program Manager. Otherwise, it will be necessary to set everything up separately under Windows NT.

Special Configurations

There are some special configurations and situations about which you should be aware. These include:

- Setting up dual-boot after Windows NT installation
- Triple-boot with Windows NT/Window95/MS-DOS
- Multi-boot including OS/2

Each of these will be given special attention.

Dual-Boot After Install

Here's the situation. You installed Windows NT on a new system. After installation, you discover that you also need to boot the system as an MS-DOS machine. Short of starting all over again, is there anything that you can do?

Preparation for Windows NT Installation

You have the ability to add dual-boot capabilities after installation. To do this, you are going to need:

- MS-DOS installation files.
- Windows NT installation diskettes.
- The Emergency Repair diskette created during installation.

The first step is to install MS-DOS on the system. You can do this from diskettes or from a network copy of the operating system installation files. This will replace the Windows NT boot sector with the MS-DOS boot sector and copy the MS-DOS files to the hard disk.

Next, you need to restore the Windows NT boot sector and create a new BOOTSECT.DOS file. Boot the system from the Windows NT Workstation installation diskette (diskette #1) and switch to diskette #2 when prompted. At the "Welcome to Setup" screen, press **R** to go into Emergency Repair procedures.

You will be prompted as follows:

```
[X]   Inspect registry files
[X]   Inspect startup environment
[X]   Verify Windows NT System files
[X]   Inspect boot sector
      Continue (perform selected tasks)
```

You need to clear all but the last selection, so that the only action being performed is boot sector inspection. Highlight "Continue (perform selected tasks)" and press **ENTER**. You will be prompted for Setup diskette #3, then for the Emergency Repair diskette.

> *WARNING!*
> *You must have a copy of the current system's Emergency Repair diskette to complete this procedure.*

Setup will inspect the boot sector, recreate BOOTSECT.DOS, and restore the Windows NT boot sector. You will be prompted with the message:

- Setup has completed repairs.
- If there is a floppy diskette inserted in drive A:, remove it.
- Press **ENTER** to restart your computer.

At this point, you will be able to select to start up with either Windows NT or MS-DOS. If you also need Windows v3.1 or Windows for Workgroups v3.11, you can start up in MS-DOS and install either, as appropriate.

Triple-Boot System

A system configured for triple-boot gives you the option of starting up the system using:

- MS-DOS

    Perform a standard MS-DOS installation. Optionally, you may also install Windows v3.1 or Windows for Workgroups v3.11.

- Windows 95

    Windows 95 should be installed as a "clean" install. This means that if the system already has a copy of Windows or Windows for Workgroups installed, Windows 95 should be installed in a separate directory.

- Windows NT

    Install Windows NT using the standard procedures for installation on a system having Windows 95 already installed.

    NOTE: *It is strongly suggested that the operating systems be installed in the order listed above.*

You will be able to select Windows NT or Windows 95 directly from the boot loader menu. To launch MS-DOS:

- Select to launch Windows 95 and press **ENTER**.
- Press **F4** or **F8** to boot MS-DOS.

F5 bypasses Windows 95 startup and boots you directly into MS-DOS. **F8** takes you to the Windows 95 Startup menu, from which you can run "Select Previous version of MS-DOS" to boot MS-DOS.

If you're not careful about your installation procedures, or if you find out about the need for a triple-boot system after the fact, you may find that you have some extra work ahead of you. If Windows 95 was installed in an existing Windows partition, you will need to enable MS-DOS startup. If Windows NT was installed before Windows 95, you will need to boot MS-DOS and install Windows 95.

Enabling MS-DOS Startup

If you installed Windows 95 in an existing Windows directory, rather than running a clean install, you will need to modify the MSDOS.SYS file to enable MS-DOS startup. Add the following to the [Options] section of the MSDOS.SYS file:

    BootMulti = 1

You will need to clear the Read Only and Hidden attributes before editing the file, then set the attributes back on when you are through making the change.

Upgrade Scenarios

Suggested solutions to these scenarios are provided in Appendix A at the end of the manual.

Upgrade: Scenario One

You have been tasked with upgrading a set of network clients. The systems are currently running Windows for Workgroups. You need to upgrade the systems to a 32-bit operating system to support a new application, preferably Windows NT. You want to retain current Windows settings. The systems are configured as follows:

- Five 80386 systems with 32 MB RAM and 500 MB disk space available.
- Five 80486 systems with 42 MB RAM and 750 MB disk space available.

What are your suggestions for upgrading the systems?

....

....

Upgrade: Scenario Two

You have seven systems currently running Windows 95. All are Pentium-based with at least 32 MB RAM and at least 500 MB disk space available. You want to upgrade the systems to Windows NT, but want to retain the option of booting Windows 95, if necessary. What is the easiest way to handle this situation?

....

....

Installation Overview

No matter which method you choose for installation, or what your chosen destination, there are common features to any installation.

- Text mode

    During the text-based portion of the installation, you will be prompted to make your initial installation decisions. These include the destination disk partition and directory. Unless running an upgrade installation, you will also be prompted to verify your system hardware list.

- Graphics mode

    After completing the text-based portion and copying initial operating system files, you are taken to the graphic-based portion of installation. The Setup Wizard launches, which steps you through the installation process with easy-to-understand prompts and available online help.

On the following pages, Windows NT is discussed in detail. By the nature of the installation process, there is a great deal of duplication between the discussions.

INSTALLING WINDOWS NT WORKSTATION

This section will present step-by-step procedures for installation. Each of these steps has been defined for you. The Installation Wizard will prompt you to select choices ranging from system and hardware configurations to components necessary for Windows NT Workstation to work efficiently within your environment. The following are topics discussed in this section:

- Welcome to Installation
- Mass Storage Detection
- Client Licensing
- Hardware Configuration
- Workstation Destination
- Partition Options
- Final Preparations
- Graphic Mode
- Workstation Information
- Select Components
- Workstation Networking
- Network Adapter Selection
- Network Selections
- Network Prompts
- Workgroup/Domain Selection
- Completing Workstation Installation
- About Server Installation
- Installation Troubleshooting

The Installation Wizard provides you with automated and easy to follow installation. By understanding each component within the Wizard, you will be able to make the most appropriate selections your system. This will help ensure that your system will run in an efficient manner. Also, you may notice that the installation procedures for both Windows NT Workstation and Windows NT Server seem identical. However, it is important to note that there are some key differences between the two.

Welcome To Installation

The different installation sources converge with the Welcome to Setup screen. The Welcome screen prompts you with your initial options:

F1   Press **F1** to display a short overview of the installation process and general instructions. It also warns you as to information you will need to know to complete setup, such as your network adapter's configuration settings.

ENTER   This will take you into the Setup program and allow you to install Windows NT Workstation.

R   Pressing **R** takes you into the emergency repair sequence. Emergency repair lets you test critical operating system file integrity, replace files, and restore your configuration. Emergency repair is discussed in more detail later in the course.

F3   You can press **F3** at any time to abort the text portion of the installation. Depending on how you initiated Setup, you may need to manually delete some files from your hard disk.

Assuming you want to install Windows NT Workstation, you would press **ENTER** at this time.

Mass Storage Detection

You are next prompted about mass storage detection. You will not be prompted to search for mass storage devices if you ran WINNT /B (or WINNT32 /B) to launch the installation. You have the option of letting Windows NT detect for mass storage devices, such as CD-ROM drives and SCSI adapters, or select the drivers to install manually. Press **ENTER** for automatic detection or **S** to skip detection.

NOTE: *If you started your installation from diskette, you will be prompted at this time for Windows NT Workstation Setup Disk #3.*

Setup will load a series of drivers and test for mass storage devices, including SCSI and IDE CD-ROM devices, as well as some of the more popular proprietary devices. Any devices found will be listed. You can:

- Press **S** to specify additional devices.
- Press **ENTER** to accept the list as is.
- Press **F3** to exit.

If you press **S**, you will need a manufacturer's drivers diskette for any devices you wish to install.

Setup will load any required drivers and file systems. An announcement will display if any of your disk devices have more than 1,024 cylinders. This is not an error, but more an informative message to let you know that your hard disk may have a higher capacity than available through its current configuration.

Client Licensing

The license agreement displays next. In earlier versions, Microsoft handled licensing much more casually than in the current product releases.

You must scroll through all pages of the license agreement before you will be allowed to continue your installation. Press **PAGE DOWN** to scroll through the agreement. After scrolling through:

- Press **F8** to agree.
- Press **ESC** to exit if you do not agree to the license agreement.
- Press **PAGE UP** to scroll back up through the agreement.

Licensing and license management are covered in more detail later in the course.

During workstation installation, you are only required to agree with the license agreement before installation can continue. You are required to select the license option, either by server or by seat, during server installation.

Hardware Configuration

Setup has determined that your computer contains the following hardware and software components.

```
Computer:           Standard PC
Display:            Auto Detect
Keyboard:           XT, AT, or Enhanced Keyboard (83-104 keys)
Keyboard Layout:    US
Pointing Device:    Microsoft Serial Mouse
No Changes:         The above list matches my computer.
```

If you want to change any item in the list, press the UP or DOWN ARROW key to move the highlight to the item you want to change. Then press **ENTER** to see alternatives for that item.

When all of the items in the list are correct, move the highlight to

"The above list matches my computer" and press **ENTER**.

Setup will prompt you with the detected hardware configuration. The example above is representative of what you will see. In most cases, you will be able to accept the list as is. Before pressing **ENTER** to continue, however, review the list carefully. Make sure that the selections are accurate.

For example, if your mouse became unplugged before you started the installation, you wouldn't see it listed. This is much easier to correct now, than to let Windows NT install without a mouse and then try to navigate the GUI interface with the keyboard while you attempt to install the proper driver.

> NOTE: *This screen will not be displayed when upgrading from an earlier version of Windows NT.*

Workstation Destination

If this is an upgrade installation, you will be prompted with the existing directory as a destination. If you select to upgrade an existing Windows or Windows NT installation, your installed applications will be migrated for you. However, you will lose the ability to run Windows separately. Press **ENTER** to accept the destination or **N** to select a different destination.

Installing Windows NT Workstation

If this is a new installation, or if you press **N** when prompted to install to the existing Windows directory, you will be provided with a list of available hard disks and configured partitions. You can also modify your disk partitions from this screen:

- Highlight your destination and press **ENTER** to accept an existing partition or unpartitioned space.
- Highlight your destination and press **C** to create a new partition in unpartitioned space.
- Highlight a partition and press **D** to delete the partition.

Make your selection as appropriate.

You will not be prompted to select a partition when upgrading and installing the files to an existing directory.

Partition Options

Your next prompt will depend on your installation method and destination. Setup will echo your selected destination and prompt you to select a partition option:

- Format the partition using the FAT file system.

    This is only available after launching installation from diskette or installing to other than your boot partition. Any data in the partition will be lost.

- Format the partition using the NTFS file system.

    This is only available after launching installation from diskette or installing to other than your boot partition. Any data in the partition will be lost.

- Convert the partition to the NTFS partition.

    The selected partition will be converted to NTFS. Even if configured for dual-boot, you will no longer be able to boot MS-DOS or Windows 95 from the partition. This selection is not available when installing on unpartitioned space.

- Leave current file system intact (no changes).

    The destination partition will not change. This selection is not available when installing on unpartitioned space.

Highlight your selection and press **ENTER**. If you highlighted either format choice, the partition will be formatted at this time.

Final Preparations

You will also be prompted for your destination directory, defaulting to:

    \WINNT

Press **ENTER** to accept or press **BACKSPACE** to type in a different directory. The directory will be created if it does not already exist. You won't see this prompt if you are installing to an existing Windows directory.

Setup will prompt you to check your hard disks for corruption. Press **ENTER** to perform the check, or **ESC** to skip the check. This check can be a lengthy procedure.

Next, Setup will build a list of files to be copied and begin copying files to the hard disk. Even though CD-ROM or network source (WINNT/WINNT32) installation copied all of the files to a temporary directory, you will still see this copy occur. It is copying files into what will be the Windows NT directory after installation.

Finally, you are prompted to remove any diskettes or CD-ROM and press **ENTER** to restart the system. This is the end of the text-based portion of the installation.

Graphic Mode

If installing from CD-ROM, you will be prompted to reinsert your CD-ROM before you can complete installation. You also have the option of picking an alternate source.

This takes you into the Setup Wizard. The first screen prompts that Setup is going to gather information about your system. This is similar to the plug and play prompt for Windows 95, however, Windows NT is not designed to make this check.

When you press **ENTER** or click on **Next**, Setup will create the destination directory and prompt you to select Setup Options. You may choose from:

- Typical

    Most user requirements are met by the typical installation. This normally requires the least amount of interaction during installation.

- Portable

    This option installs the features and services most appropriate to portable (laptop) computing, while keeping disk space requirements to a minimum.

- Compact

    Minimizing disk space used is the primary focus on this setup option. Only the files needed to set up and run Windows NT Workstation are installed.

- Custom

    The custom installation option gives you the most complete control over the installation process, letting you select the components and services to be installed.

Even if you select other than the Custom installation method, you will still be given the chance to select the optional components to be installed.

Through most of the installation, the Setup Wizard provides both **Next** and **Back** buttons. This allows you to go back to correct a selection made in error, if necessary.

Workstation Information

You will need to provide your name and organization. Be careful entering this information. Windows NT Setup does not prompt you to verify the information. You will also be prompted for your CD Key. This information is located on the back of the CD-ROM packaging.

You must also give your system a unique name. The name may be up to 15 characters with no embedded spaces. This will be used as your system's NetBIOS name, the name by which it is known for Microsoft networking. You must provide a system name, no matter what networking environment is going to be used as a final destination.

The system administrator account is created automatically during setup. You will be prompted to supply a password for this account. Use a password that you can easily remember.

Setup will let you leave the password prompt blank. This is not, however, suggested. Leaving the Administrator's password blank could quickly lead to compromised system security.

You must also decide whether or not you want to create an emergency repair diskette at this time. The emergency repair diskette gives you a way of recovering from many types of system failures. If you choose not to create one at this time, you can run the RDISK utility at any time after installation to create one.

Select Components

During custom installation, you are taken directly to a prompt asking you to select the custom components to be installed. If you chose any of the other installation options such as Typical, you are prompted as to whether or not you want to make these selections. If you answer **Yes** to the prompt, you are taken to the same set of choices. Component categories are:

- Accessibility Options

    These options allow you to configure a system to make it easier for physically challenged users to navigate and use the Windows NT interface.

- Accessories

    These are the standard accessories, such as the Calculator and Clipboard viewer. This is also where you select whether or not to install desktop wallpapers, alternate mouse pointers, and screen savers.

- Communications

    You can choose to install Chat, HyperTerminal, and the Phone Dialer through this selection.

- Games

    Though not a default selection except on upgrade, you can install Freecell, Minesweeper, Solitaire, and a new Pinball game.

- Multimedia

    This contains both the sound schemes and multimedia utility selections.
- Windows Messaging

    This allows you to install Internet Mail, Microsoft Mail, and Windows Messaging. Internet Mail installation also requires Windows Messaging.

The space required and space available are displayed near the bottom of the dialog for your reference. Make your selections carefully. Once you start installing network components, you will be unable to back up to this point again, though you may add or remove components after installation.

Workstation Networking

The Setup Wizard is now ready to install Windows NT Networking. Once you start network installation, you will not be able to back up beyond this point.

When configuring network support, you must first make your connection option selections. They are:

- Do not connect this computer to a network at this time.

    You have the option of installing the network driver and connecting later.
- This computer will participate on a network.

    You can install the system as "Wired to the network", "Remote access to the network", or both.

Choosing "Remote access to the network" will automatically install the Remote Access Service (RAS) client. RAS client installation and configuration are covered later in this course.

Network Adapter Selection

Choosing "Wired to the network" will bring up the Network Adapter dialog. This dialog has two selection buttons:

Start Search	Click on Start Search to have Setup attempt to detect your network adapter for you.
Select from list	Click on Select from list to display a list of supported adapters. This dialog will also let you install a driver from a manufacturer's disk.

Make your choice, then select the adapter for which you want to install drivers. Up to four adapters may be configured.

> *NOTE:* *Only the first network adapter will be auto-detected.*

Network Selections

You must next decide on your protocol selections. The following are provided in the default dialog:

- TCP/IP (default)
- NWLink IPX/SPX Compatible Transport
- NetBEUI Protocol

Also available for installation are:

- AppleTalk Protocol
- DLC Protocol
- Point-To-Point Tunneling Protocol
- Streams Environment

Depending on the services installed, TDP/IP and NWLink are typical defaults.

Place a check next to each protocol you wish to install. Network protocols and guidelines for their selection are discussed later in the course.

Network services are displayed next. These are somewhat dependent on your other selections. Typical default selections are:

- RPC Configuration
- NetBIOS Interface
- Workstation
- Server

Click on the dialog's **Select from list** button to view other available services. If installing a workstation to be part of an existing Novell NetWare network, this is the point at which you would choose to install Client Services for NetWare. The next dialog simply tells you that Setup is going to install your selected components.

Network Prompts

You will be prompted to verify your adapter settings. For most adapters, you can leave these set as detected. If installing TCP/IP, you will be prompted as to whether or not you plan to use DHCP. This is a method by which your station can automatically receive a TCP/IP host address from a server. Click on **Yes** for DHCP or **No** to manually configure your address.

> NOTE: *TCP/IP configuration, DHCP, and manual TCP/IP configuration are discussed in detail later in the course.*

You are given the option of disabling any bindings you wish. Bindings are a means of attaching a network driver or service to a network adapter. Windows NT is able to bind multiple protocols to a single network adapter. Bindings are discussed later in the course.

At this point, Setup is ready to start the network so that you can make the rest of your configuration selections.

Workgroup/Domain Selection

You will be prompted with your computer name and membership options:

- Workgroup

    The workgroup selection allows you to join an existing workgroup or start a new workgroup. Workgroup membership may be changed at any time.

- Domain

    To join a domain, you must be able to communicate with the primary domain controller. You must also have an account on the domain for your system. You must either create an account, or have had an account created for the machine in advance. If you select to create an account, you must know the username and password for a user with the ability to add workstations to the domain.

Workgroup and domain configurations are discussed later in the course.

You will not be able to back up after completing this dialog, though you can change network configuration values, add or remove adapters, and make other changes as necessary after installation.

Completing Workstation Installation

The next dialog informs you that the Setup Wizard is ready to finish the installation. You are prompted to select your time zone. You can also set system time and date from this dialog.

You will be prompted with the detected display. You can make changes to the Color Palette, Desktop area, Font Size, and Refresh Frequency. Be sure to test the settings before accepting them. You can also change settings later, if you wish to do so.

If the test bitmap displays properly, click on **Yes**, then on **OK**, then **OK** again to accept the settings. Setup will begin its final file copies and configure your system to run Windows NT. It will also save your system's configuration to the hard disk. If you choose to create an Emergency Repair diskette, you will be prompted to create the diskette.

Finally, you will be prompted to restart your system. Setup is complete!

About Server Installation

Windows NT Server installation prompts and Wizard screens are almost identical to those you see when installing NT Workstation. "Almost" is the key word. You need to watch carefully during installation so that you don't get caught by the differences. These include:

- Different wording to the licensing agreement

    This is during the text portion and does not impact the installation procedures.

- No prompt for Setup Options

    You are not prompted to choose a Setup option, such as Typical or Custom.

- Server role prompt

    You will be prompted to choose the roll that your server will play in the network. A server may be installed as a primary domain controller, backup domain controller, or stand-alone server.

- License mode

    You must choose the license mode for your server. In the case of Per Server licensing, you must also specify the number of Client Access Licenses.

You may see other differences, depending on the options you select during installation.

Installation Troubleshooting

Sometimes installations will fail. It could be that it hangs somewhere early in the process, takes your final boot to the dreaded blue screen, or potentially anywhere else in the process. Sometimes you make mistakes in the way you answer a prompt. It may even be something as simple as the system coming unplugged.

As with any troubleshooting process, you should start with the most obvious potential causes. Quite often, they will turn out to be at fault. Recovery procedures will depend on what you determine to be the cause.

Start by checking for the obvious:

- Check the installation CD-ROM to verify that it does not appear physically damaged.
- Make sure that the system meets all minimum installation requirements.
- Check the hardware, especially controllers and BIOS levels, against the hardware compatibility list.
- Check all system hard disks for virus infection.
- Run hardware diagnostics to verify that the machine is running properly.

If installation is aborted due to power loss or reset, restart the machine. If you were early in the Setup Wizard, Setup can often recover itself.

Exercise 1-1

During this exercise, you will install Windows NT Workstation v4.0. This exercise assumes that you are installing by booting from diskette. Refer to the installation discussion in this manual if you are starting your installation using a different method.

You should have at least one small area (10 MB or more) of unpartitioned disk space on your hard disk. This is required for later exercises. It is also required that you have a copy of MS-DOS on your hard disk.

1. Place your Windows NT Workstation diskette in the diskette drive and restart your system. You should also have the installation CD-ROM in your CD-ROM drive at this time.
2. When prompted, replace the diskette with Windows NT Workstation Setup Disk #2 and press **ENTER**.
3. When the "Welcome to Setup" screen displays, press **ENTER**.
4. Press **ENTER** to have Setup detect mass storage devices.
5. Remove diskette #2, place diskette #3 in the drive, and press **ENTER**.
6. Verify the device list and press **ENTER**.
7. When the Licensing Agreement displays, press **PAGE DOWN** until you reach the bottom of the agreement, then press .

8. Verify your hardware list and press **ENTER**.

   NOTE: *This screen may not display if you already have Windows installed.*

9. If prompted to install to \WINDOWS, press **N**. You will not see this prompt if you do not have Windows installed on your system.

10. Select drive C: as your destination and press **ENTER**.

11. Highlight "Leave the current file system intact (no changes) and press **ENTER** to restart the computer.

12. Accept the default directory (\WINNT) and press **ENTER**.

13. When prompted to perform an examination of your hard disks, press **ESC**.

14. There will be a delay while the installation files are copied to your hard disk. After the complete is complete, remove the diskette and press **ENTER**.

15. When the "Windows NT Setup" dialog appears, click on **Next**.

16. Click on the "Custom" option button, then on **Next**.

17. Type your name and company name in the "Name" and "Organization" prompts, then click on **Next**.

18. Type in the CD key value from the back of the installation media packaging, then click on **Next**.

19. Enter a computer name of your choosing.

    NOTE: *If you are connected to a network, check with your network administrator for a unique computer name.*

20. Leave the password prompts blank and click on **Next**.

21. When prompted to create an Emergency Repair Disk, leave the "Yes" prompt selected and click on **Next**.

22. When prompted to select components, click on the checkbox for "Games".

23. Click on **Next**.

24. Click on **Next** to continue to network installation.

46 Chapter 1 — Installation

25. Leave the selections at default. "This computer will participate on a network" and "Wired to the network" should both be selected. Click on **Next**.
26. Click on **Start Search**.

    NOTE: *This assumes that you have a network adapter installed. If not, click on **Select from list** and install "3Com503" to allow you to see network utilities. You cannot complete some of the later exercises without a network adapter.*

27. Verify that the correct adapter is listed and click on **Next**.
28. TCP/IP is selected at default. Click to select NWLink and NetBEUI, then click on **Next**.
29. At the "Network Services" prompt, click on **Next**.
30. Click on **Next** to continue.
31. If prompted, verify your adapter settings and click on **Continue**.
32. When prompted to participate in DHCP, click on **No**.

    WARNING!
    If attached to an operational network, verify with your Network Administrator before making any configuration selections and use your administrator's guidelines for addressing.

33. Unless told otherwise by your Network Administrator, fill in the IP address prompts as given below:

    ```
    IP Address      200.200.200.200
    Subnet Mask     255.255.255.0
    ```

34. Click on **OK**.
35. Leave the bindings at default and click on **Next**.
36. Click on **Next**.
37. Enter the following as your workgroup name and click on **Next**.

    ```
    WAVESS
    ```

38. Click on **Finish**.
39. Click on the drop-down list and select your time zone.
40. Click on **Close**.
41. Click on **OK**.
42. Leave the screen settings at default and click on **Test**.
43. Click on **OK**.

44. After the test, click on **Yes**.
45. Click on **OK** to clear the message dialog, then on **OK** to clear the Display Properties dialog.
46. Place a diskette in drive A: when prompted and click on **OK**.
47. Remove the diskette when prompted and press **ENTER** to restart your system.
48. Press **ENTER** to accept the default restart selection.
49. After restart, press **CTRL** **ALT** **DEL**.
50. Press **ENTER** to log on.
51. Click on **Close**. This will clear the Welcome screen.

AUTOMATING INSTALLATION

This section will present the methods for automating Windows NT installations. We will take a detailed look at each method by outlining various procedures that are available to you. The following are topics discussed within this section:

- Installation and Implementation
- Network Installation Source
- Unattended Installation
- Answer Files and UDFs
- About Answer Files
- About UDF Files
- Automating Application Setup
- Difference Files
- Applying the Difference
- Using SMS
- Ready to Go!

Instead of installing Windows NT manually on each machine, there are ways to automate consistent, reliable installs. Choosing which is best for you will depend on your environment, your available systems, and perhaps available hardware.

Installation and Implementation

Up to now, most of the discussion has focused on single installations. While this may be appropriate for initial test or extremely small networks, you are going to want to streamline and, as much as possible, automate the process when installing or updating larger numbers of workstations.

Ways to accomplish this include:

Network installation source	A network installation source makes the setup files readily available. Not only does this make it easier when installing Windows NT Workstation, it also provides easy access when adding or changing drivers or services.
Unattended installation	You can create files to answer Setup's prompts for you, letting you run completely unattended installations. Optionally, you can have an answer file supplying responses for most of the prompts, but have setup prompt the user for other information.
Automated application installation	You can use one system as your template, and from that, automatically install and configure applications on other systems having the same configuration.
Using Systems Management Server (SMS)	SMS not only lets you "push" Windows NT Workstation installations across the network, it also tracks status information so you can check to see which systems have been upgraded.

There is, of course, no one best solution that covers all possible situations. You will determine which, if any, of these are appropriate to your requirements. You will likely find the best solution is to use one or more of these options.

Network Installation Source

If you have a network, you will probably find it to your advantage to set up a network installation source. You will need to create a directory on a server and share the directory to the network. In this case, the term server applies to any system capable of sharing a directory to the network.

You may also need to create a OEM directory and its subdirectories beneath the shared directory. These directories will be used to store components, files, and applications for installation that are not included with Windows NT. A file named Cmdlines.txt will be placed beneath the directory. This file contains instructions for installing files in other \OEM subdirectories. These are:

\$OEM$\$$ Files used to replace or supplement systems files are placed in subdirectories of this directory.

\OEM\TEXTMODE

       Create subdirectories beneath this directory to store hardware-dependent files loaded during the text mode portion of Setup.

\OEM\NET   Create subdirectories beneath this directory to hold network component files. These can include files such as protocols, adapter drivers, and network services.

\OEM*drive_id*   Replace *drive_id* with an actual drive id (C, D, and so on) on the destination computer. Place application files and directories, as well as any other files you want copied to the destination drive, under this directory.

These additional directories are only required if you specify in your answer (unattended script) file to replace the standard installation files if automatically installing applications.

The \OEM\ directory can also include a Cmdlines.txt file, listing commands to be executed after setup runs. The file can include multiple command lines, each enclosed in double quotes.

Unattended Installation

Unattended installation lets you automate the installation process when you have a moderate number of installations, typically up to 50 or so. It would be used for larger implementations if you do not have SMS available.

During an unattended installation, Setup gets answers for its prompts from:

> Unattended answer file (UNATTEND.TXT)
>> An answer file can provide the answers for prompts during Setup's text mode, or during both text mode and graphic mode. The default filename is UNATTEND.TXT, but a different file name may be specified. This is a standard text file, divided into sections containing configuration parameters.
>
> Uniqueness database file ($UNIQUE.UPF)
>> The UDF extends the capabilities of the unattended answer file, letting you set parameters based on an id specified when you run WINNT or WINNT32. If there are sections in the answer file having the same name as sections in the UDF, the parameters in the UDF file are used.

You are not required to use a UDF when running unattended installations, but use of a UDF is appropriate in most situations. You can launch an unattended installation manually, or modify the logon file to have the installation start automatically. You can also launch the installation from a batch file. One advantage of this is that you could e-mail the batch file to your users. When they open the batch file, Setup executes.

An unattended answer file and UDF can be created with any text editor. The Microsoft Press Windows NT Workstation 4.0 Resource Kit includes a sample answer file you can edit to meet your requirements and a utility to help you generate answer files.

Answer Files and UDFs

You can think of the answer file as providing the general configuration guidelines and the UDF allowing for individual customization by machine or user. You would create a separate answer file for each general set of configuration parameters. For example, you would likely have separate answer files by:

- Hardware platform
- Geographic location
- Division or job type

Use the /u option switch when running WINNT or WINNT32 to specify that you are using an answer file.

These would then be supplemented by one or more UDF. You can set up separate sections for each UDF id within a single UDF file, or create multiple UDF files. The UDF file lets you set machine or user-specific information such as user name, machine name, and so forth.

Use the /udf option switch when running WINNT or WINNT32 to specify the unique id and UDF path and filename. If the UDF filename is not specified, the user (or person initiating the installation) will be prompted for a diskette containing the file during the graphic portion of setup. Setup will then look for a file with the default UDF filename, $Unique$.udf. This means that you would have to supply a diskette with the UDF file for each user.

About Answer Files

Though a detailed discussion of answer file contents is beyond the scope of this course, a short overview might be helpful. The answer file is formatted in sections. Each section will contain keys (parameters) followed by values, using the format:

```
[section_name]
key1 = value
key2 = value
```

The following sections are supported:

[Unattended] These keys define text mode Setup behavior. Keys in this section are only supported in the answer file. They cannot be replaced by UDF file values.

[OEMBootFiles] During an x86 install, the OEM\OEMFILES\TXTSETUP.OEM file and any files listed in that file must be listed in this section. Keys in this section are only supported in the answer file. They cannot be replaced by UDF file values.

[MassStorageDrivers] This section is used to specify SCSI device drivers. Keys in this section are only supported in the answer file. They cannot be replaced by UDF file values.

[KeyboardDrivers] Keyboard drivers are specified in this section. Keys in this section are only supported in the answer file. They cannot be replaced by UDF file values.

[PointingDeviceDrivers]
The drivers for the mouse or other pointing device are specified in this section. Keys in this section are only supported in the answer file. They cannot be replaced by UDF file values.

[OEM_Ads] This section lets you identify a custom banner, logo, and bitmap to display during GUI-mode setup. Keys in this section are also supported in UDF files.

[DisplayDrivers] Display drivers are specified in this section. Keys in this section are also supported in UDF files.

[Display] This section sets display settings, which may also be specified as UDF keys.

[DetectedMassStorage]
: You can use this section to force Setup to recognize and install a mass storage device even if not present when setup is run. Keys in this section are only supported in the answer file. They cannot be replaced by UDF file values.

[GuiUnattended]
: This section defines GUI-mode Setup behavior. Keys in this section may be specified here or in a UDF file.

[UserData]
: User and computer specific information, such as user name, is defined in this section. These values may also be defined in a UDF file.

[LicenseFilePrintData]
: This section is only used with NT Server installations and supplies license information. Keys in this section are also supported in UDF files.

[Network]
: Network settings are defined in this section. If not present, networking is not installed. UDF key values are also recognized for network settings.

[Modem]
: This section defines whether or not a modem is installed on the system. Keys in this section may be specified here or in a UDF file.

You may also see additional sections. Some key values can point to additional sections to provide detail configuration information, which you would need to add to the answer file. A key value followed by a blank value means that the default value should be used.

About UDF Files

UDF files use the same general format as answer files. A UDF file is a standard text file, divided into sections with keys and values below each section. The first section, [UniqueIds] contains the list of id values supported by the file, followed by the UDF sections to be referenced when the id has been specified. Section names must match valid answer file sections, in the format:

```
[UniqueIds]
    id1 = section, section, …
    id2 = section, …
    id3 = section, …
```

UDF file values take precedence over answer file values. You can include replacements for answer file sections, or even include valid sections that are not present in the answer file.

Unlike the answer file, a blank key value will cause the user to be prompted for information, rather than using the default value for that key.

Automating Application Setup

You have the ability to set up applications on destination workstations while running an unattended installation. Since you will often have a typical application set, common applications to be installed on all of your workstations, this can further simplify the installation process.

To install applications during unattended setup:

- Prepare snapshot and difference files to identify the applications to be installed.
- Create a subdirectory below the \$OEM$\$$ directory containing the installing files for each application.
- Modify UNATTEND.TXT (or your unattended answer file) to include the following in the [Unattended] section:

    ```
    OemPreinstall = Yes
    ```

- Modify the CMDLINES.TXT file under \OEM\ to apply the applications or apply the applications any time after installation.

You can use a UDF file to set custom answers by user or by group. The Sysdiff utility is used to create the snapshot file, create the difference file, and to apply the applications to the destination systems. These procedures can be used to install applications on NT Workstation or NT Server.

Difference Files

The SYSDIFF utility creates the files you need to support automated installation of a set of applications. You will need to set up one system to act as the model for the other systems being installed. It must use the same hardware platform (such as Intel x86) as the rest of the systems you are setting up. Install Windows NT and then run:

```
sysdiff /snap [/log:log_file] snapshot_file
```

The *log_file* is only used if you want to create an optional log when running sysdiff. The *snapshot_file* argument is required and will contain the snapshot of the system.

Next, install the applications that you want to distribute to your destination systems. Then run:

```
sysdiff /diff [/c:title] [/log:log_file] snapshot_file
    diff_file
```

The *title* argument gives the difference package a title. Use *log_file* if you want to log operations. The *snapshot_file* is the file you created earlier, before installing the applications. The *diff_file* is the filename to which the differences should be written. Both the snapshot and difference files are required arguments.

You can run the following to dump a copy of the difference file in a form you can read, letting you review its contents:

```
sysdiff /dump diff_file dump_file
```

All of these arguments are required. The output will be written to the file named as *dump_file*.

Applying the Difference

You have three options for applying the differences after installation, thereby installing the applications. These are:

- Execute sysdiff /apply through the OEM\Cmdlines.txt file.
- Run sysdiff /apply from a command line after installation.
- Create an .INF file and apply the file through OEM\Cmdlines.txt.

The syntax for running sysdiff is:

```
sysdiff /apply /m [/log:log_file] diff_file
```

The /m option causes the per-user profile structure, changes such as new Start menu entries, to be copied to the default user profile rather than the user currently logged on. By doing this, the profile information will be applied each time a new user logs on. Replace *diff_file* with the path and filename for the difference file you created.

To execute from a command line, run the command as given. If you are adding the command to the CMDLINES.TXT file, enclose the entire string in double quotes.

If you want to have the changes applied as an .INF file, you must first create the file, using the syntax:

```
sysdif /inf /m [/u] diff_file oem_root
```

As before, the /m applies changes to the default user profile. The optional /u command switch causes the .INF file to be generated as Unicode instead of ANSI. The *diff_file* is the path and filename to the difference file you created earlier, and *oem_root* identifies the directory beneath which OEM is located. The same filename will be used as the original difference file, except that it will now have an .INF extension.

Copy the file to the OEM\Textmode directory. To invoke the .INF file, add the following to the CMDLINES.TXT file:

```
"rundll32 syssetup.SetupInfObjectInstallAction section 128
    inf"
```

The *section* argument identifies the section being applied and *inf* identifies the .INF file.

Using SMS

In an existing client/server environment with SMS already implemented, you can use SMS to install and configure Windows NT. This method is typically suggested when a large number of systems (50 or more) are involved.

One advantage of SMS is that you can query your system database to quickly determine which, if any, systems can support Windows NT Workstation. Define the query based on the minimum installation criteria and any other limits you wish to set.

Installation is supported in much the same way as other software installations. One or more SMS Package Definitions Files (PDFs) are created to control the installation. These can be run as push installations, initiated by the SMS server, or pull installations, initiated by the user.

SMS will also track installation success or failure. This gives you an easy way to check on each system and see what, if any, errors occurred during installation.

Unattended Scenarios

Proposed solutions to these scenarios are provided in Appendix A at the end of the manual.

Unattended Scenario One

You are installing new systems for the entire inside sales group, a total of 12 systems. The systems are configured as follows:

- Pentium
- 24 MB RAM
- 2 GB disk space as two 1 GB hard disks

The systems will become NT Workstation clients as part of an existing NT Server domain. MS-DOS and Microsoft network client files are already installed on all of the systems. You want to keep the system configurations consistent, except for obvious exceptions such as machine name.

You already have a share point (shared directory) set up with a subdirectory containing the Windows NT Workstation installation files. What is most likely the easiest way to install these systems?

....

....

Unattended Scenario Two

Refer to Unattended Scenario One. You've installed Windows NT Workstation on all of the systems and verified that they are working properly. You have configured and tested electronic mail on all systems. You are now ready to install applications.

All of the machines will be running the same set of applications. You want to set up so that the users can quickly and easily install all of the applications, but with a minimum of user interaction.

What do you suggest?

....

....

Ready to Go!

Now you're ready to launch, run, and use Windows NT. The startup process and recovery from startup errors is covered in some detail later in the course. For now, the discussion will be limited to a quick overview:

    Boot record load   The Windows NT boot record loads, then locates and loads NTLDR.

NTLDR	This is the NT loader file, which clears the screen, places the processor into 32-bit flat memory mode, and locates the BOOT.INI file. This is a sophisticated loader file that supports the FAT and NTFS file systems. This file is flagged as system, read-only, and hidden to avoid accidental erasure.
BOOT.INI	The BOOT.INI file is a text file containing the information used to build the operating system selection menu. It will contain the selection list, optional selections, and timeout value. The file must be located in the root directory of the same drive as NTLDR.
Selection menu	The selection menu is built from the information in the BOOT.INI file. The user can make a selection from the menu, or wait the timeout period, at which point the default selection will be loaded. If Windows NT is selected, the hardware detection program and Windows NT kernel will be loaded. If a different operating system is selected, a file named BOOTSECT.DOS is loaded into memory and executed. BOOTSECT.DOS contains the boot record for the partition's original operating system. The same filename is used whether booting DOS or OS/2.
Hardware detection	NTDETECT.COM is only used on Intel x86. It builds a hardware list which is then passed back to NTLDR. This information will be written into the Registry. NTDETECT emulates the hardware information gathered during the ARC POST routine stored in ARC firmware on RISC-based systems.
Kernel load	The Windows NT kernel, NTOSKRNL.EXE, is loaded into memory and executed. This is the initial Windows NT module. The kernel receives the hardware information collected by NTDETECT or from the ARC firmware.

Low-level loads	The hardware abstraction layer (HAL) is the first operating system module that is loaded by the kernel. It will also load the Registry System hive. The System hive receives the hardware list and contains information on device drivers to load and the order for starting services.
Kernel initialization	It is easy to tell when kernel initialization occurs. This is the point when the screen turns blue. If initialization is successful, a CHKDSK is run on all hard disk partitions and the Windows NT signature, the initial logo screen, is displayed.
Driver initialization	The kernel will continue loading device drivers and launching services, using information stored in the System hive. Should errors occur, system recovery is determined by the ErrorControl value stored in the Registry with the device driver.

The final step is to display the Welcome dialog. Press **CTRL** **ALT** **DEL** to display the Logon dialog. Additional device drivers to be loaded and services to be launched will be determined according to the user account used for logon.

SYSTEM ACCESS

This section will explain the fundamentals of the Windows NT Workstation security system. You will also learn how to troubleshoot logon failures. The following are topics discussed within this section:

- Logging On
- The Logon Process
- Logon Failures
- Windows NT Desktop
- Protecting Your Station
- Logging Off
- Shut Down
- Removing Windows NT

As security is an important issue within this environment, it is beneficial to develop a routine for starting and ending a Windows NT session. By understanding these concepts, you will be able to show end users the added benefits of this feature.

Logging On

Before you can see any type of end user interface and before you can do anything on the system, you must log onto the system. Logging on requires a valid user account name and password. Passwords are case-sensitive in Windows NT. If you are part of a Windows NT Server domain, you will have the choice between logging onto the domain or your local system only. Your user account determines your level of access, to available programs, to available applications, and so on.

> *NOTE: Logging on to a system that is part of a Windows NT Server domain simultaneously logs you on to both the local station and the domain.*

The user account and password you enter are validated against an internal database of valid users. If it verifies correctly, you are given access to the system. If not, you will receive a warning message telling you to make sure that the information was entered correctly.

The Logon dialog also gives you the option of shutting down your system. Shut down is discussed later in this chapter.

The Logon Process

Windows NT uses a layered architecture design. The lower the layer, the more rigid the design and control. As you move up through the layers, control becomes more open and flexible.

When you press **CTRL** **ALT** **DEL** to display the logon dialog, the security subsystem is activated. This key sequence is used since it generates a system interrupt. By requiring an interrupt before you can logon, your system is better protected against viral infection.

When you enter your username and password, this information is passed to the security reference monitor where the account name and password are checked against an internal database for verification. The security reference monitor will also build a list of user access credentials called an access token and pass it back to the security subsystem.

Your logon attempt must be validated by a domain controller before you can access domain resources. Both Primary and Backup domain controllers can validate logon attempts. Each Backup domain controller carries a copy of the domain control database, listing all of the domain account information.

Logon Failures

Logon failures are relatively common. Luckily, the cause can often be traced to a simple error. Common causes include:

- Forgotten password

    If a user forgets his or her password, the administrator will have to assign a new password to the account. There is no way to view a user's password.

- Incorrectly typed password

    Windows NT uses case-sensitive passwords. Have the user check the `CAPS LOCK` to see if it is set correctly.

- Expired/disabled account

    The account must be enabled by the administrator before it can be used for logon.

- Expired password

    Users are warned before a password expires. If the password is allowed to expire, the administrator will have to enter a new password for the user.

- Locked workstation

    If a workstation is locked, it must be unlocked by the user or an administrator before it can be used for logon. You can also clear a lock by shutting down and restarting the system.

- Invalid access time

    You can set valid logon times for any user. Users will not be allowed to logon at any other time. To allow logon, the administrator must change the time restriction on the user account. Otherwise, the user must wait for a valid logon time.

When trying to log on to a workstation that is part of a Windows NT Server domain, it could be a domain logon problem, rather than a local logon problem. The same possible causes apply, as well as domain-specific possibilities, such as:

- Incorrect domain

    You are attempting to log onto the wrong domain in a multidomain environment.

- Local username and password

    You attempted logon with a username and password local to your system rather than a domain username and password.

Logon errors do not report the specific cause, making it harder for someone to bypass the security system.

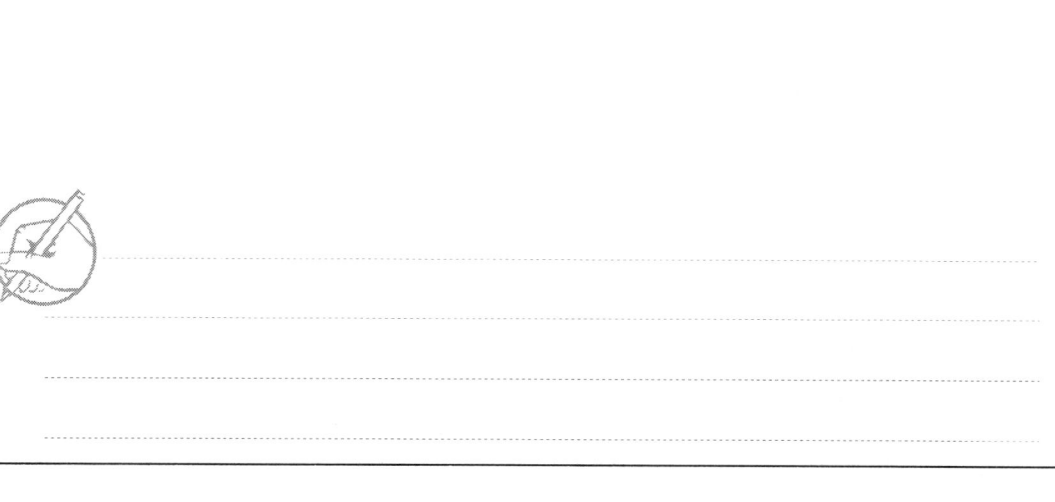

Windows NT Desktop

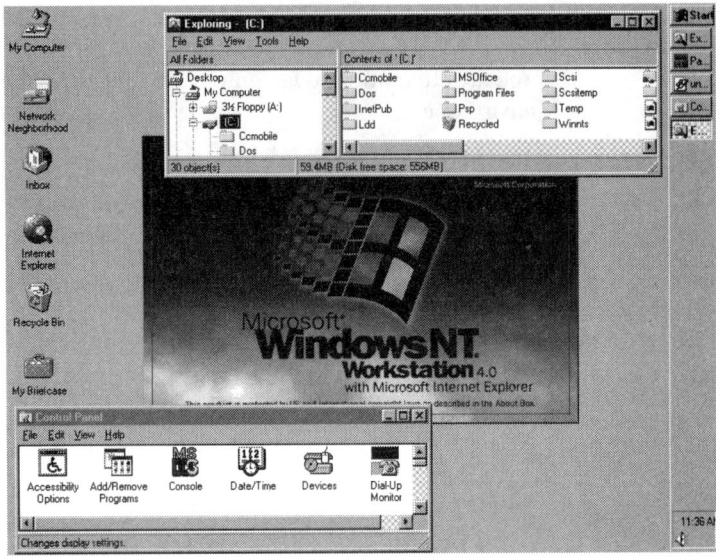

The graphic above shows a typical Windows NT Desktop. At default, the end-user has complete control over his or her desktop. It is possible to set restrictions so that users cannot make permanent changes to the desktop, and to limit what desktop features available the to the end user.

The taskbar can be moved to any screen border for convenience. It can be customized to only display as the mouse pointer moves to the border on which it is located. At default, the taskbar is always displayed in the foreground ("on top").

Protecting Your Station

Whenever you are working on a Windows NT system, you need to be in the habit of "thinking secure." Any time you leave your desk, you provide an opportunity for unauthorized access to your system. If you are attached to a network, the potential for data loss or theft becomes even greater. Windows NT provides a number of ways for protecting your workstation and its data from unauthorized access. These include:

- Lock
- Logoff
- Shutdown

System Access

Each time you leave your system, it should be protected by one of these methods. There is a Windows NT Security dialog window you call at any time you're working in Windows NT. Just press `CTRL` `ALT` `DEL`.

This displays a security dialog with six choices:

Lock Workstation	Workstation is locked, but no files are closed. Press `CTRL` `ALT` `DEL` and enter your password to unlock the workstation.
Change Password	Change your password. You must know the current password to enter a new password. You can only change the password for the current user.
Logoff	Logoff the system and return to the initial Windows NT screen.
Task Manager	The Task Manager is displayed. The Task Manager lets you switch to or end a task, view information about system processes, and view performance statistics.
Shut Down	This is the same as executing the Shut Down command from the Start menu.
Cancel	Close the dialog windows and return to the desktop without performing any action.

Locking your workstation is usually the best choice if you are leaving the system for a short time. All system activities continue running, including all applications, which will continue any background processing.

Logging Off

As long as a user remains logged on at your system, anyone can access system files and possibly delete or damage critical information. When you logoff the system, you end the current user's session. The system returns to the Welcome dialog, and no one can locally access system resources without a valid user account and password.

When you log off from the system, the operating system remains active. All background services provided by your system continue running. However, all application sessions are ended.

You can also shut down through the **Start** menu. Run **Shut Down**, click to select "Close all programs and log on as a different user", and click on **Yes**.

Shut Down

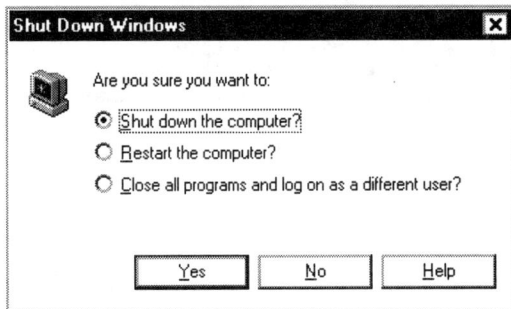

Shut down halts operating system activity. This includes ending any background services and shared resources. It is important to always shut down before turning off a system. Shut down:

- Exits applications and closes application sessions.
- Closes open data files.
- Stops active services.
- Writes any buffered data in memory to disk.

You can execute shutdown from the security dialog or run **Shut Down** from the taskbar **Start** menu. You can select:

- Shut down the computer?

    The system is shut down and a dialog box is displayed telling you it is safe to turn off your computer. The dialog box contains a **Restart** button to restart your system.

- Restart the computer?

    The system is shut down, but immediately restarts, taking you to the Welcome dialog.

- Close all programs and log on as a different user?

    The system will exit all user applications, log the user off, and display the Welcome dialog.

Shut down warns you if any applications do not respond to the End Task request. You have the option to wait for the task to complete, force the task to end (and possibly lose any unsaved data), or cancel Shut down.

Implementation Scenario

You've been tasked with upgrading all network systems capable of supporting Windows NT Workstation. Your network includes eight Windows NT Servers that have already been upgraded to NT v4.0, and close to 1,000 additional systems that include a mix of configurations and Microsoft Windows family operating systems. There are also three laptop systems that are used as RAS clients by technical support personnel when they have to go to remote office locations.

While not time critical, you would like to get the systems upgraded as soon as possible. Unfortunately, it would be unlikely that many of your users would be able to run a Windows NT installation, or even remember to initiate an automated installation.

The network is running TCP/IP. Host IP addresses are being assigned by DHCP on all systems capable of acting as DHCP clients. You set up Systems Management Server about nine months ago and have been using it for network management. The primary SMS site is local to you. There is a secondary set up at each remote location.

Describe, in general terms, how you would manage Windows NT Workstation implementation. A proposed solution is provided in Appendix A at the end of the manual.

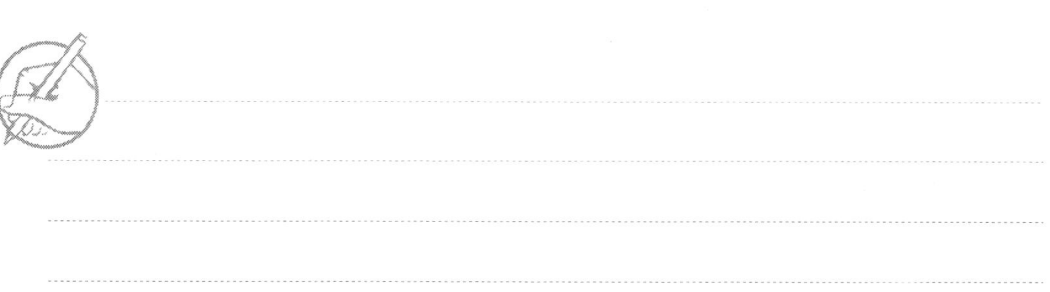

Removing Windows NT

You may find it necessary to uninstall Windows NT, going back to the system's original operating system. In case of MS-DOS systems, you can easily return the system to booting only DOS. To do this:

- Boot your system from an MS-DOS diskette.
- Use the ATTRIB command to remove the system, hidden, and read-only attributes from NTDETECT.COM and NTLDR.
- Remove the system attribute from BOOT.INI.
- Delete BOOT.INI, NTDETECT.COM, and NTLDR.
- Run the SYS command to transfer MS-DOS system files to the hard disk.

    SYS C:

- Restart the system and test.

After starting your system, you can delete the Windows NT directories and the virtual memory paging file (PAGEFILE.SYS). NT directories include the installation destination directory and any other directories created for optional components. Do not delete these directories if they contain any files that you may need later.

If you install Windows NT Workstation to the \WINDOWS directory, you can delete \WINDOWS\SYSTEM32 and its subdirectories to remove the majority of the NT files.

Exercise 1-2
Optional Exercise

This optional exercise is provided to give you a quick tour of the Windows NT interface. You can complete this exercise from working group's Windows NT Station or either domain controller.

1. Start your system and boot Windows NT.
2. When the Welcome dialog displays, press **CTRL ALT DEL** to call the Logon dialog.
3. If not already displayed, enter Administrator as the username and type in the password specified during installation.
4. Double-click on the My Computer icon. It should be located near the upper left of your screen.

5. Right-click (click once with mouse button 2) on Drive C:, then click with mouse button 1 on **Properties**.

   This displays your hard disk properties dialog.

6. Click on the **Cancel** button near the bottom of the dialog.

7. Right-click on the **Control Panel** icon, then click on **Create Shortcut**.

8. You will receive a warning dialog that Windows cannot create a shortcut here and ask if the shortcut should be created on the desktop. Click on **Yes**.

9. Close the My Computer window by clicking on **File/Close**.

10. Double-click on the Shortcut to Control Panel icon on the desktop. The Control Panel should launch.

11. Close the Control Panel.

12. Click once to select the Shortcut to Control Panel icon and press **DEL**.

13. When prompted to confirm the deletion, click on **Yes**. This will move the shortcut to the Recycle Bin but not affect the original program.

14. Double-click on the Recycle Bin. You should see Shortcut to Control Panel listed.

15. Run **Empty Recycle Bin** from the **File** menu. When prompted to verify your action, click on **Yes**.

16. Close the Recycle Bin.

17. Click with mouse button 2 (right-click on a right-handed mouse) on the Control Panel icon in the My Computer window, drag the icon to the desktop, and select **Create Shortcut(s) Here** from the pop-up menu.

18. Double-click on the Shortcut to Control Panel icon and verify that the Control Panel launches.

19. Close the Control Panel.

20. Click on the icon title area for the Shortcut to Control Panel icon, type the following, and press **ENTER**:

    ```
    Launch Control Panel
    ```

21. Close the My Computer window.

22. Click on the **Start** button on the taskbar.

23. Move the pointer to **Programs**.

24. Move the pointer to **Windows NT Explorer** and click to launch Windows NT Explorer.

    NOTE: Menu selections will commonly be described using a slashed format during the course. For example, the selection made in steps 22, 23, and 24 would be described as: *Start/Programs/Windows NT Explorer*

25. Browse down through the folders list and locate the Control Panel folder. Click on the Control Panel folder to list available utilities. The Control Panel folder should be located near the bottom of the list.

26. Right-click on Console, then click on Open. This displays the Console Windows Properties property sheets dialog.

27. Right-click on the time display on the taskbar and run Task Manager. This displays the Task Manager dialog.

    You should see the Exploring - Control Panel task running.

28. Click on the Performance tab. This displays CPU usage and memory usage.

29. Close the Console Windows Properties dialog and the Windows Explorer. You should see a small spike in CPU usage.

30. Close the Task Manager.

SUMMARY

During this chapter, you were introduced to the following:

- Windows product family
- Windows NT features and benefits
- Windows 95 user interface
- Minimum installation requirements
- Installation destination guidelines
- Installation options
- WINNT/WINNT32
- Upgrade procedures
- Installation text mode
- Setup Wizard

- Client licensing
- Workgroup/domain selections
- Server roles
- Startup overview
- Logging on
- Windows NT desktop
- Logoff/Shut down
- Removing Windows NT

During the next chapter, you will be introduced to user and group management fundamentals.

POST-TEST QUESTIONS

The answers to these questions are in Appendix A at the end of this manual.

1. What is the key combination to call the Security menu?

   ....

   ....

2. You have an Intel x86 system with two 1 GB hard disks and an internal CD-ROM. You are currently running MS-DOS. You cannot read the Windows NT boot diskettes. You suspect a problem with the floppy disk drive but do not have time to replace it. How can you install Windows NT Workstation?

   ....

   ....

3. What is the WINNT32 option switch to create setup boot diskettes?

   ....

   ....

4. You are installing Windows NT Workstation on a Windows for Workgroups system. You want to be able to boot MS-DOS or Windows NT after installation. What file system should you use on the destination partition, if installing Windows NT to the boot partition?

   ....

   ....

5. A machine name may have up to _____ characters.

   ....

   ....

6. During startup, what file is loaded by the boot loader?

   ....

   ....

CHAPTER 2

User and Group Management

MAJOR TOPICS

Objectives 74

Pre-Test Questions 74

Introduction 75

Local Security 76

User and Group Account Management 80

Security Events 106

Summary 117

Post-Test Questions 118

OBJECTIVES

At the completion of this chapter, you will be able to:

- Create and modify user accounts.
- List selected guidelines for creating user accounts.
- Create and modify group accounts.
- List and describe the default system accounts.
- List the default rights and abilities for default system accounts.
- View and modify system account policies.
- Set up and view audit information.
- Use the Event Viewer to view Security log information.

PRE-TEST QUESTIONS

The answers to these questions are in Appendix A at the end of this manual.

1. Assuming that Windows NT Workstation was installed at C:\WINNT, what is the default path to user logon scripts?

   ....

   ....

2. What field is present when editing user properties that is not present when creating a new user?

   ....

   ....

3. A workstation local group can belong to what other types of groups?

   ....

   ....

4. When setting account policies, what is the significance of specifying a minimum password age?

   ....

   ....

5. What utility lets you view the contents of the security log?

   ....

   ....

INTRODUCTION

Security is one of the major selling points of Windows NT. Most of NT's security is based around user and group account information. User logon is your first line of protection. Access rights to system resources are set according to user account and group membership. User account management is a common part of ongoing domain management.

This chapter will investigate Windows NT security by looking at user and group account management. You'll see how to create, modify, and delete user and group accounts. You'll also assign group membership to selected users. You will also spend some time with the default groups and their rights and abilities on the workstation.

This chapter will also look at system-wide policies. These policies determine password requirements, user and group rights, and security auditing settings. This chapter will cover account policies and user rights. Auditing is covered later in this chapter.

It's important to keep in mind that this chapter will focus on local security, security affecting the local workstation. Windows NT Workstation security is built around a network model, drawing largely from Microsoft LAN Manager. When working with individual workstations, that broad network model is brought down to a single system. It can sometimes be a little confusing, because network security for both domains and workgroups is based on this same model. The user and group management procedures presented in this chapter apply to Windows NT Workstation and to Windows NT Server when installed as an additional server.

LOCAL SECURITY

This section will present the importance of maintaining security on Windows NT systems. Procedures for maintaining security have been outlined for you. The following are topics discussed within this section:

- User Basics
- Account Guidelines
- A Word on Passwords
- Windows NT Security
- C2 Level Security

Many of the utilities within Windows NT have built-in features for maintaining security. Security is one of the added features of Windows NT. Administrators need to relay the importance of making security a part of the average end user's daily routine.

User Basics

We need to spend some time talking about users and user management. As you've already seen, you must have a valid user account and password to log on at a Windows NT Workstation machine. Two users are created during NT Setup:

- Administrator

    The Administrator has unlimited rights on the local system. You can create other administrator accounts on the system under different names.

- Guest

    The guest username is for guest access to the shared system resources.

You can create additional user accounts as necessary for system management. You can change the name of an existing user account without modifying other account information. Windows NT identifies each account through a unique ID which remains unchanged for the life of the account.

If a user account is deleted, all security information for that user is lost and must be re-entered. Even if the user is recreated with the same username, it will have a different security ID (SID). The security ID is a unique value identifying the user to the system. Internally, all security information for the user is tracked by the user's SID.

Account Guidelines

Since user accounts are your first line of security, exercise care in creating them:

- Limit the number of users.

    Provide user accounts for only those persons who have a valid reason for system access. Each user should be given a unique user account.

- Strictly limit the number of administrators.

    Since administrators have nearly unlimited access to the system, each administrator you create is a potential security risk.

- Limit administrator use.

    Only log on as an administrator when you are performing duties requiring that level of access. You should also have a standard user account you use for normal logon.

- Assign only those access rights the user must have to perform his or her duties.

    Use rights assignments to restrict access to critical or confidential files.

- Set and enforce password standards.

  Set and publish policies concerning passwords. Since there is no way to directly view a user's password, you have to assume that policies are being followed.

User definitions become even more critical in a network environment, since logging on gives access to both local and shared resources.

A Word on Passwords

An important issue in user management is the selection of good passwords. Since users in most cases set their own passwords, you need to provide them with guidelines that you hope will be followed.

- Always require passwords.

  By leaving a username unprotected, you are asking for trouble. You should give the user account an initial password when it is created and require the user to change the password after the first logon.

- Change passwords on a regular basis.

  It's normally suggested that passwords be changed every 30 to 60 days. More often than that can become inconvenient; less often, and you may be defeating the purpose of forcing password changes.

- Don't use easily guessed passwords.

  Children's names, spouse names, pet names, and such make bad passwords. If someone knows you well, it won't take long for them to guess your password.

- Use nonsense words and special characters.

  Common words with special characters leading, following, or embedded are hard to guess. So are nonsense words or words that have been purposely misspelled.

- Don't leave passwords displayed in an obvious location.

  It's not uncommon to find passwords in desk drawers, taped under keyboards, even posted on display screens. Emphasize to your users the importance of keeping passwords secret. In some companies, disclosure of a password is grounds for termination.

Good passwords go a long way toward helping to ensure access security.

Windows NT Security

One of the key benefits of Windows NT Workstation is its built-in security. The Windows NT security system is based on:

- User and group definitions.

    User names and passwords control primary access security and the logon process. Some security features can be more easily managed at a group level than at a user level.

- Domain-wide definitions.

    You can make domain wide definitions regarding password parameters and security policies.

- Permission assignments.

    Access to local and shared data files is determined according to permissions assigned to a user or group.

- Security tracking.

    You have the ability to track security events such as logons and logoffs, and store them in a file for later viewing and analysis.

The real strength of a security system lies not in what's there, but how it is used. Domain-wide security is discussed in the following chapter.

C2 Level Security

Much of the Windows NT security system design comes from C2 level security compliance. C2 level security is a United States Department of Defense definition. C2 level requirements include:

- User point of access control through a unique user name and password.
- Resource access control with access limits set by user or group. Access control must be both inclusive and exclusive.

- Protected memory management restricting memory contents from access until released by the controlling process (program).
- Security event audits with access to audit contents restricted to administrators.
- Identification of user performing actions appearing in a security audit.
- Protection against outside influence and tampering of operating system or system files.

C2 level security features are fully implemented when the NTFS file system is used.

USER AND GROUP ACCOUNT MANAGEMENT

This section will introduce user and group management. Here, you will learn how to create, delete, and modify users and groups via the User Manager administrative tool. Properties available for configuration of each user and group will also be outlined in detail. System-wide account policies will also be introduced and defined for you.

- User and Group Management
- User Manager
- Creating Users
- User Environmental Profile
- Dialin
- Changing User Definitions
- Changing Multiple Users' Properties
- Users and Groups
- Workstation Local Groups
- Creating Local Groups
- Managing Local Groups
- Adding Group Members
- Default Workstation Groups
- Account Policies
- User Rights Policy
- Standard Rights

The above listed topics will outline how to manage users and groups in a Windows NT environment. While reading through this section, try to imagine how you would be able to apply this to your work environment in order to run a network system efficiently.

User and Group Management

![User Manager screenshot showing Username list with Administrator, FMiller, Guest, JMiller, NButter, TTick and Groups list with Administrators, Backup Operators, Guests, Power Users, Replicator, Users]

The User Manager tool is your user and group management utility for Windows NT Workstation. Located in the **Start/Programs/Administrative Tools** menu, it allows you to create, delete, and modify user definitions. User Manager for Domain is used for user and group management on Windows NT Server, including systems configured as additional servers. When you launch the User Manager, currently defined users and groups are displayed. You can create additional users and groups, or view, modify, or delete existing entries. User Manager is also used when setting system-wide policies. You can set account, user rights, and audit policies.

User Manager

The **User** menu contains the user management commands. They are:

New User	This selection creates domain user accounts.
New Local Group	This selection creates a domain local group account.
Copy	Information from a selected user or group is copied to create a new account. The user (or group) account name, full name, and password are not copied.
Delete	The selected users or groups are deleted. Once deleted the accounts may be recreated, but account information cannot be recovered.
Rename	This selection lets you rename a user account. The selection is not available for group accounts.
Properties	Use this selection to display detailed user or group account information.
Exit	Use this selection to exit User Manager.

In a Windows NT server domain environment, the username is used for a simultaneous local and network logon. Local workstation user definitions cannot be used for domain logon. Domain users must be defined through User Manager for Domains and are tracked by the domain controllers.

The **Policies** menu selections are:

Account	This selection lets you set account password policies for all user accounts. Account policies include the minimum password age, maximum password age, minimum password length, and password uniqueness.
User Rights	This selection lets you view and modify rights assignments for users and groups.
Audit	Use this selection to set up auditing for this computer (Workstation).

The **Options** menu contains these selections:

Confirmation   This acts as a double-check when you are making changes to user and group accounts.

Save Settings on Exit
                  When checked, the user's local profile is updated with the latest desktop information.

Font   This choice allows you to pick a different display font for your viewing pleasure.

Creating Users

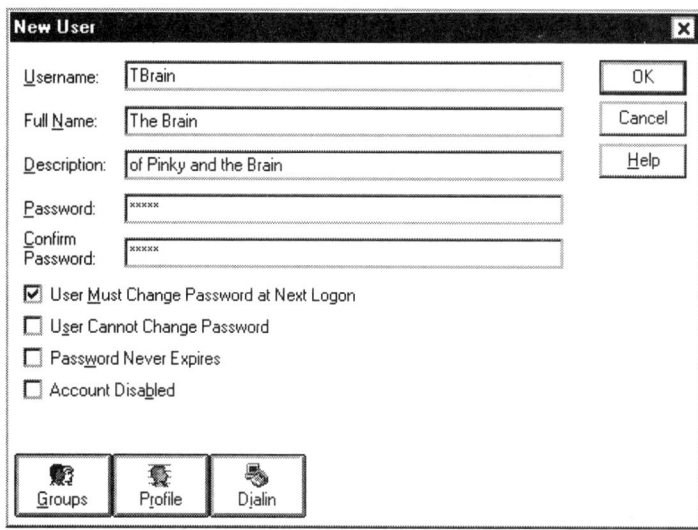

To create a new user, run **New User** from the **User** menu. This displays the **New User** dialog.

Username — Enter a unique username. User names can be up to 20 characters long, containing upper-case letters, lower-case letters, numbers, and special characters except:

" / \ [ ] : ; | + , * ? < >

This is a required field. Windows NT will internally generate an account identifier for the user.

Full Name — This is an optional field. Enter the user's full name. There is no required format for this, but it is suggested to internally develop a standard for full names.

Description — Another optional field, the description is simply a textual description of the user. You can place any information you wish in this field.

Password/Confirm Password
Passwords can be up to fourteen characters long. You have the option of setting a system-wide minimum length for passwords.

NOTE: Passwords are case-sensitive.

You must enter the password twice to verify that it is typed properly. If you leave the fields blank, the user will be created without a password.

Take care when entering a password. Remember that passwords are case-sensitive, so check the **CAPS LOCK** when typing.

User Must Change Password at Next Logon
As a security measure, it is suggested that the user change the password issued to him or her by the Administrator as soon as possible. By checking this box, you can have the system make sure this is done.

User Cannot Change Password
There are only limited cases where you would want to keep a user from changing his or her own password. This might be done to a user who chronically selects bad passwords. Also, if you have any usernames, like Guest, that may be used by more than one person, you might want to prevent the user from changing the password.

Password Never Expires
: You have the option of setting up a maximum password age, causing the password to expire on a regular cycle. This setting overrides the maximum password age parameter.

Account Disabled
: Setting an account as disabled keeps it from being used for logon. There are several situations where you might do this: a valid user who will be gone for an extended period; a template used to copy other accounts but not used for logon; or if an employee has been fired and you have specific reasons for not wanting to remove his or her username.

Account Locked Out
: Not visible when adding a new user, this check box will be visible and checked when an account is locked out. You can clear the check box to unlock an account. If the check box is not checked, you cannot use this option to lock the account. The account may be locked by the operating system based on account policies.

Groups
: The Groups button allows you to assign or remove group membership designations.

Profile
: The Profile button sets the user's profile information. This includes the logon script, if any, and the path to the user's home directory.

Dialin
: The Dialin button allows the user permission to use Dial-Up networking.

After the dialog fields are filled in, click on the **OK** button to create the user account.

If you need to create a number of users with the same settings, you can create one user as a template, then copy the template to create the other users. Since this is something you are more likely to be doing in a domain environment than at a workstation, this process is covered in some detail in the next chapter.

User Environmental Profile

```
┌─ User Environment Profile ──────────────────────────────┐ ✕
│                                                          │
│  User:   TBrain (The Brain)              ┌────────┐     │
│                                          │   OK   │     │
│                                          ├────────┤     │
│                                          │ Cancel │     │
│  ┌─ User Profiles ──────────────────┐    ├────────┤     │
│  │ User Profile Path: \\MAIN\PROFILES\TBRAIN │ Help │   │
│  │ Logon Script Name: [            ]│    └────────┘     │
│  └──────────────────────────────────┘                   │
│  ┌─ Home Directory ─────────────────────────────────┐   │
│  │  ⦿ Local Path: C:\HOME\TBrain                    │   │
│  │  ○ Connect  [▼] To [                           ] │   │
│  └──────────────────────────────────────────────────┘   │
└──────────────────────────────────────────────────────────┘
```

Pressing the **Profile** button will display this dialog. The **User Environmental Profile** sets the values of the user profile path, logon script, and home directory. If values are not specified, default values are used.

The user profile path is used to enable mandatory or roaming user profiles. User profiles are discussed in some detail a little later in the course.

The logon script executes when the user logs onto the workstation. It can be a batch file (with a .BAT or .CMD extension) or an executable (.EXE) file. This allows you to perform any necessary "setup" functions for the user or to launch applications where the order of execution is significant.

The logon script is assumed to be located in the default logon script directory:

```
\SYSTEM\SYSTEM32\REPL\IMPORT\SCRIPTS
```

where *SYSTEM* is the Windows NT directory, normally WINNT. The script must be located in this directory, or its subdirectory. If it is located in a subdirectory, you must specify the remaining relative path. Leave this prompt blank if the account doesn't have a logon script.

For example, if you specified STARTIT.BAT as a user's logon script on a system with Windows NT Workstation installed in the default location, the full path and filename would be:

```
C:\WINNT\SYSTEM32\REPL\IMPORT\SCRIPTS\STARTIT.BAT
```

Enter the filename only if the file is in the SCRIPTS directory, or relative path from the SCRIPTS directory.

The home directory is a private directory assigned to a particular user. Applications that don't have a working directory assigned will default to the home directory for file opens and saves. Command prompts will also default to the home directory. A home directory helps to simplify system management, since the Administrator will know the paths to most, if not all, personal data files.

If no home directory is assigned, a default directory is created. This directory is placed on the same drive as Windows NT as:

```
\SYSTEM\PROFILES\USERNAME\PERSONAL
```

Looking back at the earlier example, the default home directory for a user named DHill would be:

```
C:\WINNT\PROFILES\DHILL\PERSONAL
```

WARNING!
> *If you decide to do a complete reinstall of Windows NT v4.0 into the original directory, the install program will delete the files in your personal directory!*

The "Connect To" field is used to indicate a shared network directory for placement of home directories.

Dialin

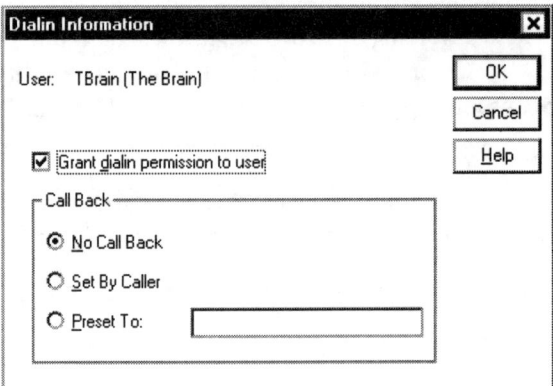

Click on the **Dialin** button to display this dialog. The User Dialin Information is used to enable or disable remote access and set remote access security. You can specify to let a user Dial in, require a call back, and if a call back is required, use a preset number or ask the user for one.

More information on remote access is presented later in the course.

User and Group Account Management

Changing User Definitions

![User Properties dialog showing Username: TBrain, Full Name: The Brain, Description: of Pinky and the Brain, Password and Confirm Password fields, with checkboxes for User Must Change Password at Next Logon (checked), User Cannot Change Password, Password Never Expires, Account Disabled, Account Locked Out, and buttons for Groups, Profile, Dialin, OK, Cancel, Help]

To display the User Properties dialog, double-click on the user's name or select the user and run **Properties** from the **User** menu. This dialog lets you change any information about the user except the Username field.

If a user forgets his or her password, it will be necessary to use this dialog to assign a new password. When changing a user's password through this dialog, it is suggested that you set "User Must Change Password at Next Logon". An Administrator can change the password for any user. Unless otherwise restricted from doing so, a user can change his or her own password only.

This dialog contains an additional entry that does not display on the New User dialog, "Account Locked Out". "Account Locked Out" is set automatically when there is a violation of the account lockout policies. If the account is not locked, the selection is not available. If locked, clear the checkbox to unlock the account.

Changing Multiple Users' Properties

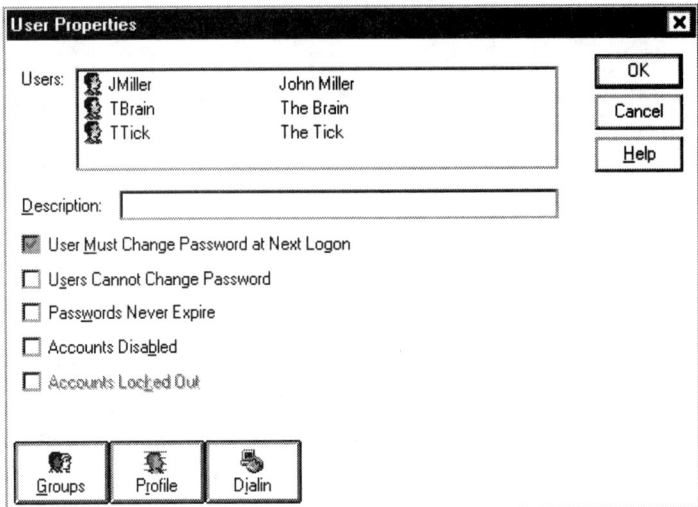

You can also modify multiple users at one time with this dialog. After selecting the users from the User Manager screen, run **Properties** from the **User** menu. With multiple users selected, you can modify:

- Description
- User Must Change Password at Next Logon
- Passwords Never Expire
- Accounts Disabled
- Group Memberships
- Environmental Profiles
- Dialin Information

Exercise 2-1

The purpose of this exercise is to give you practice in defining user accounts. At the beginning of this exercise, your system should be started up in Windows NT and you should be logged on as the Administrator.

1. Open the **Start** menu, move the pointer to **Programs**, then **Administrative Tools**, and then click on **User Manager**. From here forward, a shorter method of indicating a selection will be: **Start/Programs/Administrative Tools/User Manager** menu.

2. Run **New User** from the **User** menu to open the New User dialog.

3. Enter the following user information:

    NOTE: Press **TAB** *to move between fields.*

    ```
    Username:            EMarsh
    Full Name:           Eric Marsh
    Description:         User for SS
    Password:            blank
    Confirm Password:    blank
    ```

    All check boxes should be cleared. Click on **OK** to create the user.

4. Using the procedure described in step 3, open a **New User** dialog.

5. Enter the following user information:

Username:	MSmith
Full Name:	Mary Smith
Description:	Office Manager
Password:	password
Confirm Password:	password

   NOTE: *Remember that passwords are case-sensitive.*

   Verify that the "User Must Change Password at Next Logon" checkbox is checked.

   Click on **OK** to create the user.

6. Select **Exit** from the **User** menu to exit User Manager.
7. Select the Start/Shut Down/Close programs and log on as a different user menu. Click on the **Yes** button.
8. After the Welcome dialog appears, press **CTRL ALT DEL** to logon.
9. Enter MSmith as your username and type your password. Press **ENTER** to logon.
10. You will receive a Logon Message dialog warning you that you are required to change your password. Press **ENTER**.
11. Type your choice of a new password in the "New Password" and "Confirm New Password" fields. Be sure to use a password that you can easily remember.
12. Click on OK. When the dialog appears, stating that the password has been changed, press **ENTER** to continue.
13. Using the procedures described earlier in this exercise, log off the current user. Log back on as Administrator.

Users and Groups

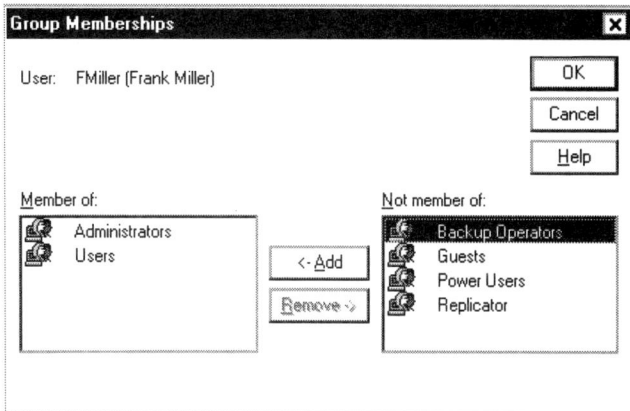

It is often easier to organize users into groups for management purposes. Rights and access privileges assigned to a group are automatically assigned to all of the group members. Security management is more efficient since you can make changes for sets of users, rather than managing each user separately.

You can change group membership by displaying the properties dialog for a user or set of users, then clicking on the **Groups** button. The user can then be added to or removed from any of the local groups defined on the system.

If you are creating, changing, or deleting groups on a workstation, those are workstation local groups. A workstation local group is created any time a new group is defined on a Windows NT workstation.

These groups are used to manage access to local resources and to set local rights policies. Windows NT Server supports additional groups for security management at a domain level. These are discussed in the next chapter.

When you install Windows NT Workstation, only local, built-in groups are created. These are Administrators, Backup Operators, Guests, Users, Power Users, Replicator, and Everyone.

Workstation Local Groups

Windows NT local groups are created through the User Manager utility. A workstation local group can be assigned permissions to local resources, permissions to shared (network) resources, and rights relating to the local machine. Local group members may include:

- Local workstation users.
- Global groups from the local domain.
- Global groups from any trusted domain.

NOTE: Domain groups and domain management are discussed in the following chapter.

A local group cannot become a member of any other group.

Creating Local Groups

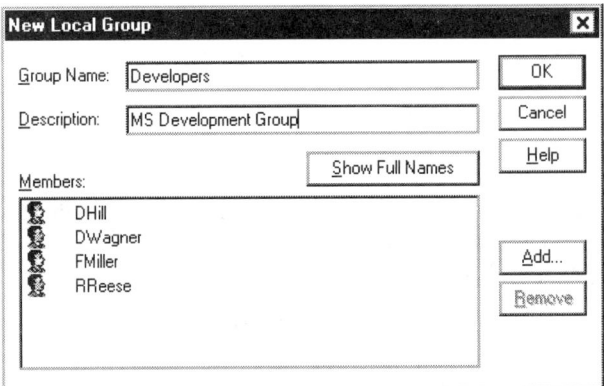

Selecting the **New Local Group** command from the **Users** menu, allows you to create new group definitions.

Group Name	The same restrictions apply to group names as to usernames. Group names can include upper- and lower-case characters, numbers, and limited special characters. You cannot give a group the same name as a user or another group.
Description	This is simply a text description of the group for identification.
Members	This lists the group members. Any user or users selected when you run **New Local Group** will be the initial group members. Click on Add to define additional users or global groups as members. Select account names and click on Remove to revoke membership.

Managing Local Groups

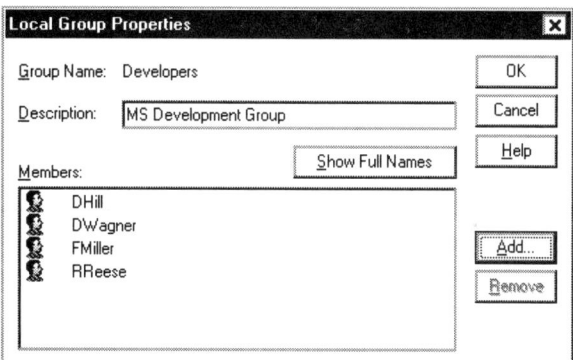

You can double-click on a group name or select a group name and choose **Properties** from the **User** menu to display the Local Group Properties dialog. You can change the description and the group members.

Additional pull-down menu commands let you copy or delete the group. When you copy a group, the group member list is copied.

Adding Group Members

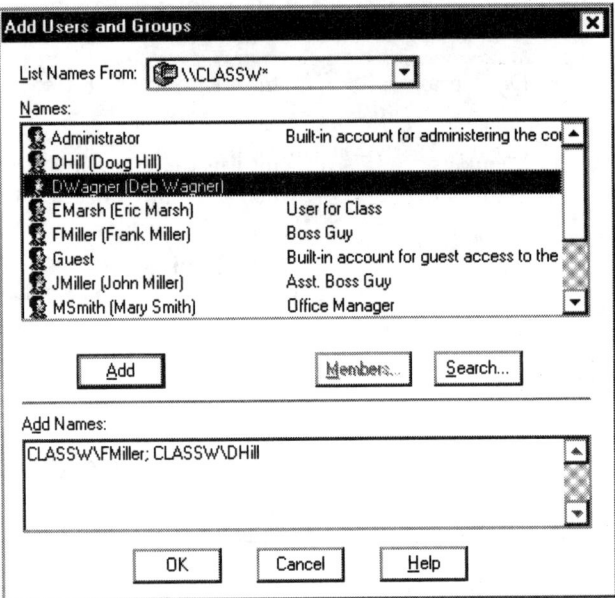

When you click on **Add**, the Add Users and Groups dialog displays. Users defined on the system are listed. Select the users, and click on **Add** below to user list to select users. After making your selections, click on **OK**.

The drop-down list at the top of the dialog, in a domain environment, lets you select a domain from which you can choose domain groups as members.

Default Workstation Groups

Windows NT sets up several default groups during installation. These support many of the system support and administration situations you are likely to encounter.

Administrators

Administrators have full rights to the workstation including the ability to create and manage all accounts, manage resource sharing and permissions, set rights assignments, and install operating system files.

Default rights given to the group are:

- Log on locally
- Access this computer from network
- Take ownership of files or other objects
- Manage auditing and security log
- Change the system time
- Shut down the system
- Force shut down from a remote system
- Back up files and directories
- Restore files and directories
- Load and unload device drivers

Built-in abilities of the group are:

- Create and manage user accounts
- Create and manage group accounts
- Assign user rights
- Lock the workstation or server
- Override workstation or server lock
- Format hard disks
- Create common program groups
- Keep a local profile
- Share and stop sharing directories
- Share and stop sharing printers

Backup Operators

Backup operators are specifically assigned to manage regular server backups and restores. Members of this group can back up all directories and files, whether or not they have permission to access the files.

Default rights given to the group are:

- Log on locally
- Shut down system
- Back up files and directories
- Restore files and directories

Built-in abilities of the group are:

- Keep a local profile

Everyone

All users automatically belong to this account. It is used primarily for management of shared resource permissions. The group name is not listed under User Manager since you cannot change the group's name, properties, or members. It is listed in the group list when defining access permissions.

Default rights given to the group are:

- Log on locally
- Access the system from the network
- Shut down system

Built-in abilities of the group are:

- Lock the workstation or server

Guests

Members of the guest group can access a machine from the network, log on locally, and shut down the system. There are no other default rights or abilities assigned.

Power Users

Power Users provide Windows NT Workstation users with limited administrative abilities.

Default rights given to the group are:

- Log on locally
- Access the system from the network
- Change system time
- Shut down system
- Remote force shut down from another system

Built-in abilities of the group are:

- Create and manage user accounts
- Create and manage group accounts
- Assign user rights
- Lock the workstation or server
- Create common program groups
- Keep a local profile
- Share and stop sharing directories
- Share and stop sharing printers

Replicator

If a system has a member of the Replicator group, it will normally only have one. This user is used for logon when launching the directory replicator service, allowing the system to act as an importer for replication. Other than this, there are no default rights assignments or abilities for replicators.

Users

The users group contains the "average" workstation user. Rights assigned are different for domain members than for workstation users.

Default rights given to the group are:

- Log on locally
- Shut down system

Built-in abilities of the group are:

- Create and manage group accounts

Exercise 2-2

The purpose of this exercise is to provide you with practice in creating groups and assigning group membership. You should be logged on as Administrator at the beginning of this exercise.

1. Select **Start/Programs/Administrative Tools/User Manager**.
2. Double-click on MSmith in the list of users and display the user properties.
3. Click on the **Groups** button.
4. The **Group Memberships** dialog should show MSmith as a member of the group Users.
5. Click on Administrators in the "Not member of" list to select the group.
6. Click on the **Add** button. Administrators should be listed in the "Member of" list.
7. Click on **OK** to save the changes and close the dialog.
8. Click on **OK** to close the User Properties dialog.
9. Double-click on Administrators from the **Groups** box to display the group properties.
10. MSmith should be listed as a member of the group. Click on **OK** to close the Local Group Properties dialog.
11. Click on EMarsh in the Username list to select.
12. Select **New Local Group** from the **User** menu to display the New Local Group dialog.

13. EMarsh should automatically be listed as a member. Enter the following information in the local group definition fields.

    Group Name: SpecApp

    Description: Used for Special Application Definitions

14. Click on the **Add** button to display a list of users.
15. Locate MSmith in the list, click to select, then click on **Add**.
16. Click on **OK** at the bottom of the dialog.
17. Both EMarsh and MSmith should be listed as group members. Click on **OK**.
18. Check the Groups list in the lower window of the User Manager dialog to verify that SpecApp was created.
19. Close the User Manager by selecting **Exit** from the **User** menu.
20. Using the procedures described in earlier exercises, log off and log back on as MSmith.

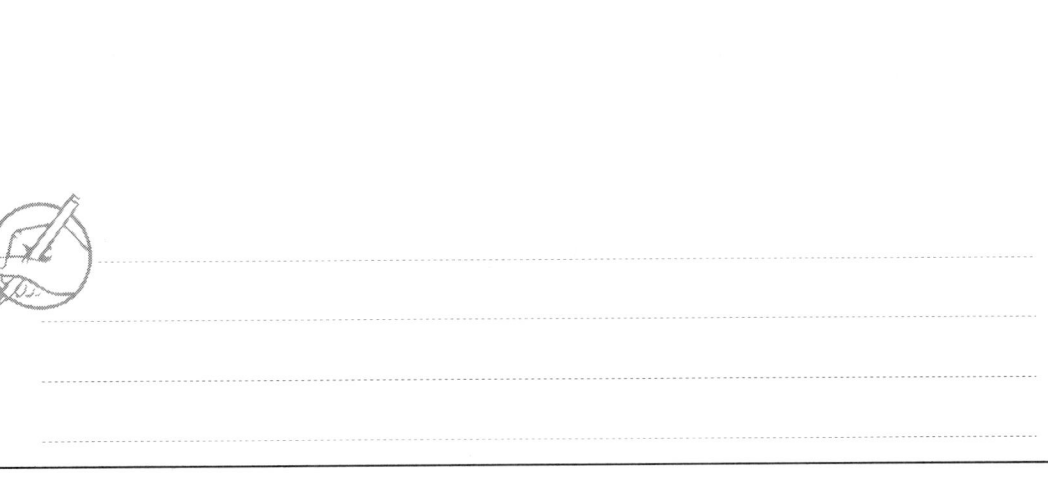

Account Policies

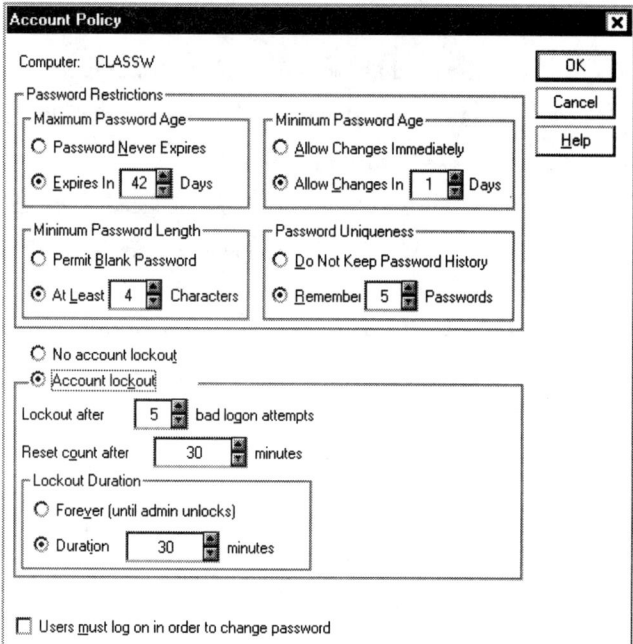

You can set system-wide account policies for your user accounts through User Manager. Select the **Account** command from the **Policies** menu to display the Account Policy dialog. From here, you can set policies regarding passwords and account lockout.

> Maximum Password Age
> : The Maximum Password Age sets the time until the password expires. Any value between 1 and 999 may be entered. The user will be prompted during logon to change the password after it expires.
>
> Minimum Password Age
> : There are some situations where you will want to set a minimum time a user must wait before changing his or her password again. This value may also be set between 1 and 999, and must be smaller than the Maximum Password Age. This helps keep users from getting around Password Uniqueness.

Minimum Password Length
: You can set the Minimum Password Length to any value between 1 and 14. You can also select to not require a password.

Password Uniqueness
: This sets how many "old" passwords the system will remember for the user. It can be set to any value between 1 and 24. The user cannot re-use any of the passwords in the password history.

User Must Log On In Order To Change Password
: This forces users to log on making password changes. In other words, if a password expires, the user will not be given the opportunity to change it while logging on.

These parameters, used together, help to force users to build good habits in setting and changing their passwords.

The Account Lockout settings help you prevent unauthorized access to your system. It works by setting a timer the first time an attempt is made to logon using a valid username but invalid password. If the lockout count is reached before the timer period runs out, the account is locked.

Lockout after
: This is the number of attempts the user will have to "get it right" before the account is locked. This may be set to any value between 1 and 999.

Reset count after
: This is the lockout time period in minutes. This can be set to any value between 1 and 99999 minutes. If the time-out period passes without locking the account, the lockout count is reset to 0.

Lockout duration
: This is the period of time, in minutes, that the account will be locked. This can be set to any value between 1 and 99999, or to lock the account until reset by the Administrator.

User Rights Policy

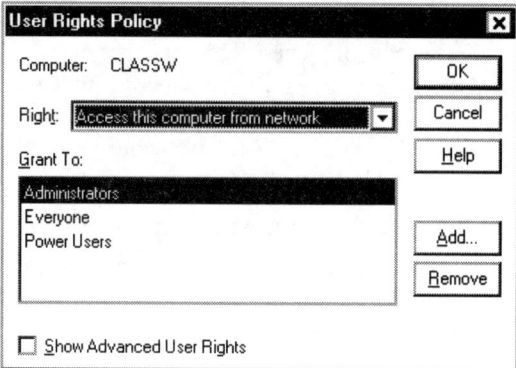

User rights determine actions that users can perform on the system. The "Right" field shows the right for which you are defining access. Click on **Add** to display a list of available users and groups to add to the list. To remove a user or group, highlight the members you wish to remove and click on **Remove**.

A standard set of rights is normally displayed. Clicking on "Show Advanced User Rights" checkbox will include advanced rights in the list. Except in some special cases you should never have to change the Advanced User Rights settings. They are often used by developers to get detailed control over system security.

Standard Rights

The standard rights are given below. 'Grant to' lists the users who are given this right at default during setup.

- Access this computer from network

    Granted to: Administrators, Everyone, Power Users

    This right allows users to connect to the computer over a network.

- Backup files and directories

    Granted to: Administrators, Backup Operators

    Users given this right can back up local files and directories, overriding any access exclusions that may be defined for backup only.

- Change the system time

    Granted to: Administrators, Power Users

    Users with this right can set the time on the internal system clock.

- Force shutdown from a remote system

    Granted to: Administrators, Power Users

    This right is not currently used, but is reserved for future implementations of the operating system.

- Load and unload device drivers

    Granted to: Administrators

    Users with this right can dynamically load and unload device drivers.

- Logon locally

    Granted to: Administrators, Backup Operators, Everyone, Guests, Power Users, Users

    Users with this right can logon to the system.

- Manage auditing and security log

    Granted to: Administrators

    Users with this right can set events to be tracked by system audits and can also view or clear the security log.

- Restore files and directories

    Granted to: Administrators, Backup Operators

    The ability to restore backed up files and directories overrides any access restrictions that have been set.

- Shut down the system

    Granted to: Administrators, Backup Operators, Everyone, Power Users, Users

    Access to the **Shutdown** command in the **Start** menu is controlled by this right.

- Take ownership of files or other objects

    Granted to: Administrators

    Users with this right can take over ownership of system objects, such as files and directories.

These are system-wide, rather than resource-specific access rights. In some cases, an assigned user right may override a specific resource access definition.

SECURITY EVENTS

This section will present information on how to track security related events. Using the Event Viewer, you will be able to see if any security has been violated. The following are topics discussed within this section:

- Audit Trails
- Audit Events
- Viewing Audit Trails
- Event Viewer
- Security Log Entries
- Detail Entries

Administrators can select the events they wish to watch for activity. Events may be tracked by user, system, and application activities.

Audit Trails

While on the subject of system-wide settings, some time should be taken to discuss audit trails. Audit trails can be established for system events, file events, activity events, and printer events.

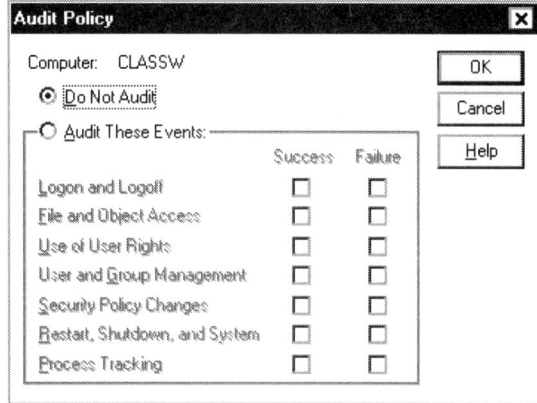

The security log is established through the User Manager by selecting **Audit** from the **Policies** menu. At default settings, auditing is not enabled.

The security log's size is set in the Event Viewer. Since the size is limited, take care to select only those events that you have an interest in auditing.

Audit Events

Audit Policy

Computer: CLASSW

○ Do Not Audit
◉ Audit These Events:

	Success	Failure
Logon and Logoff	☐	☑
File and Object Access	☐	☐
Use of User Rights	☐	☐
User and Group Management	☐	☐
Security Policy Changes	☑	☑
Restart, Shutdown, and System	☑	☑
Process Tracking	☐	☐

[OK] [Cancel] [Help]

You have control over the events to be audited. Your selections are:

Logon and Logoff   Each time a user logs on, logs off, or a network connection is made, an audit entry is created.

File and Object Access This selection enables auditing for the user accessing a file that is set for directory or file auditing, or using a printer that is set for auditing.

Use of User Rights   This selection creates an entry when a user exercises a user right other than logon or logoff. This refers to the user rights set through the user rights policy discussed earlier in this chapter.

User and Group Management
Each time a user or group is created, changed, deleted, renamed, disabled, or enabled, an entry is created in the audit log. This selection also tracks password changes.

Security Policy Changes
If this chapter is set, an audit entry is created each time there is a change made to User Rights Policies or Audit Policies.

Restart, Shutdown, and System
: This selection is used to track each time the system is shut down or restarted. It will also log events affecting system security or the system log. If a system is having spontaneous reset problems, this can be used to record the date/time stamp for each time it restarts.

Process Tracking
: This selection allows for detailed tracking of process-related information, such as activation of a program or exit of a process.

For each, you can select to audit successful or failed events, both, or neither. If you select neither Success nor Failure, no entries will be created for this event type.

Viewing Audit Trails

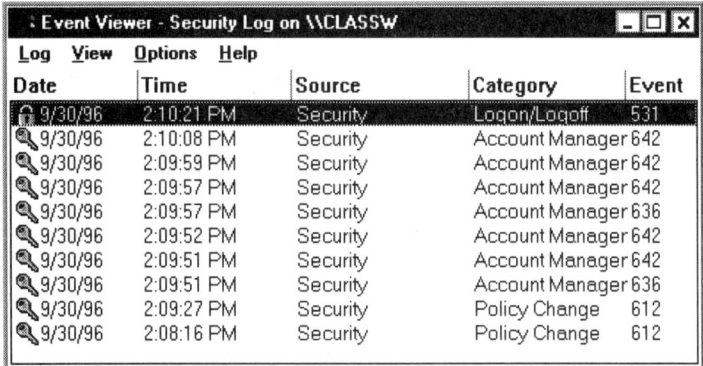

The **Event Viewer** in the **Start/Programs/Administrative Tools** menu is used to view and manage the audit entries, referred to here as the Security Log.

You must be an administrator to view the Security Log. Otherwise, you'll see:

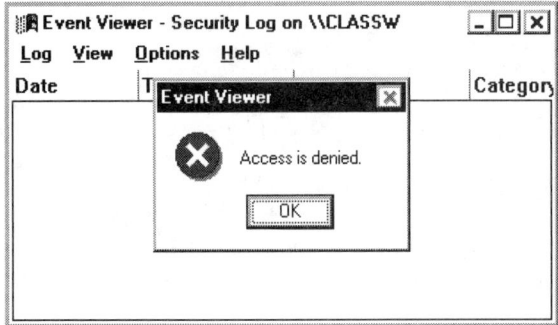

This is one of the specifications of C2 Level security.

Event Viewer

The pull-down menus' control of the Event Viewer lets you manage the logs and control the way they are displayed. The Event Viewer is discussed in more detail later in the course.

The **Log** menu contains the following commands:

System	Displays system events and errors.
Security	Displays audit log events.
Application	Displays application events, primarily errors.
Open	You can select an archived log file for display.
Save as	Log files can be saved to a file or archived for later viewing and analysis.
Clear All Event	This command clears the current log.
Log Settings	Use this command to change the size of the log file and the event wrapping option when the file becomes full. You can select to never overwrite, overwrite events older than a set age, or overwrite the oldest entries, as necessary, to make new entries.

Select Computer   When working on a network configured as either a domain or workgroup, you can select to view logs from a different machine. You must be an administrator to perform this action.

The **View** menu contains the following commands:

All Events   All log events will be displayed.

Filter Events   You can limit the events displayed by date, type, source, category, user, computer, and event ID.

Newest First   This is the default selection, displaying the most recent events at the top of the log.

Oldest First   You can also select to view the oldest events first.

Find   Find searches the log for events matching a user-defined set of search criteria.

Detail   The detail command displays detailed information about a log entry. You can also do this by double-clicking on the entry.

Refresh   Refresh updates the log with current entries.

The **Options** menu contains the following commands:

Low Speed Connection
                      When viewing the log on another computer, select this command if the connection is across a low-speed device, such as a modem.

Save Settings on Exit This tells the Event Viewer to save any settings changes.

Font   This is used to select a different font for viewing the event list.

Security Log Entries

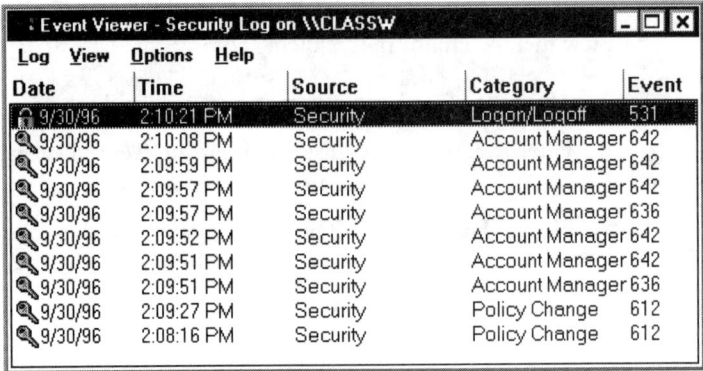

The Security Log dialog gives you a thumbnail sketch of each of the entries.

Date
: The Date records the date on which the event occurred. A key represents the logging of a successful action. A lock represents a failed action.

Time
: The Time field is the system time when the event occurred.

Source
: The Source identifies the software that logged the event, and may include applications, operating system components, and so on. For the security log, the source will normally be "Security."

Category
: This is a classification of the event made by the source logging the event.

Event
: The Event ID is used by Microsoft Product Support representatives for tracking system events.

User
: This field identifies the user responsible for the event. When generated by an operating system action, the user is SYSTEM.

Computer
: On a stand-alone system, this field should always contain the local computer name. It identifies the computer on which the event occurred.

It is important to remember that you must enable logging, and select the events to be tracked, for any entries to appear in this log.

Detail Entries

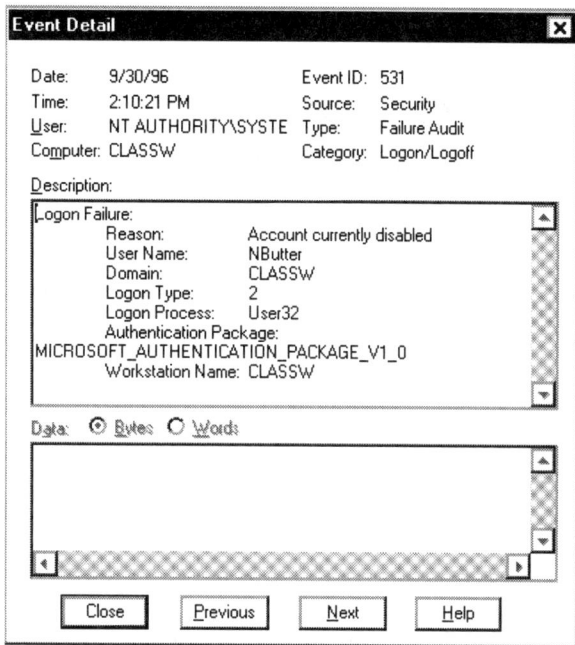

You can display detailed information about a log entry by highlighting the entry and selecting **Detail** from the **View** menu, or by double-clicking on the entry. The Event Detail dialog provides extremely detailed information about the event entry. The specifics of the description field will depend on the type of entry.

User Basics Scenarios

Suggested solutions to each of these scenarios are provided in Appendix A at the end of the manual.

User Basics Scenario One

You are about to finish briefing the person who is going to cover for you while you are on a well-deserved vacation. You end by warning him about Ed.

Ed is an office manager in charge of a group of administrative personnel. Their systems are set up as a workgroup with no rights to the NT Server domain. He has a user who is a member of the Administrators group on each workstation. Unfortunately, Ed is not a very good administrator.

Right before you leave, you get a call from Ed. He's set up a system for a round-the-clock set of temporary personnel. He's created three user accounts, Temp1 through Temp3, and assigned them initial passwords.

He wants you to help with "fine tuning" the users. He wants them all to have the same home directory, shared as \\EdsBrain\TempHome in the workgroup. He also wants to limit each to logging on only during his or her shift.

You have the ability to manage the workstation remotely from your station. What is the quickest way to fill Ed's request?

....

....

User Basics Scenario Two

You've set up a Windows NT Workstation system as part of a workgroup for running some application tests. There are a number of sensitive files on the system. Both of the disk partitions have been formatted as NTFS and you've changed the Administrator account's name.

You suspect that someone has been trying to log onto the machine after hours. How can you determine if someone is trying to log on and when the attempt is being made?

....

....

Exercise 2-3

The purpose of this exercise is to give you practice in setting system policies. You should be logged on as MSmith at the beginning of this exercise.

1. Using the procedures described in earlier exercises, select **Start/Programs/Administrative Tools/User Manager**.
2. Select **Audit** from the **Policies** menu to display the Audit Policy dialog.
3. Click on "Audit These Events". Select both "Success" and "Failure" for the following:

   ```
   Logon and Logoff
   File and Object Access
   Security Policy Changes
   Restart, Shutdown, and System
   ```
4. Click on **OK** to save the changes and close the dialog.
5. Select **Account** from the **Policies** menu to display the Account Policy dialog.

6. Set each of the fields as described below:

`Maximum Password Age`	`Expires in 35 days`
`Minimum Password Age`	`Allows Changes Immediately`
`Minimum Password Length`	`Permits Blank Password`
`Password Uniqueness`	`Remembers 4 Passwords`

7. Click on **OK** to save your changes and close the dialog.
8. If prompted, click on the **Yes** button. Select **Exit** from the **User** menu to exit the User Manager utility.
9. Using the procedure described earlier, log off and log on as Msmith.
10. Select **Start/Programs/Administrative Tools/Event Viewer**.
11. Select **Security** from the **Log** pull-down menu to display the security log.
12. Locate an entry with a Category of Policy Change. It should be near or at the bottom of the log.
13. Double-click on the Policy Change line to display detailed information.
14. Time allowing, view detailed information on other log entries. Exit the Event Viewer when you are finished.

SUMMARY

This chapter continued a discussion of Windows NT system management. This included:

- Default users
- User guidelines
- Password guidelines
- C2 level security
- User Manager
- Creating and managing users
- Creating and managing groups
- Default groups
- System-wide account policies
- System-wide user rights policies
- Event Viewer

In the next chapter, we'll see how Windows NT manages system management and configuration.

POST-TEST QUESTIONS

The answers to these questions are in Appendix A at the end of this manual.

1. To log onto a Windows NT workstation or server, you need a valid _____ and _____.

2. What two user accounts are created during Windows NT installation?

3. How can you make a standard user into an administrator?

4. Without deleting the user account, how can you prevent a user from logging on to an NT Workstation or Server?

5. Members of what group(s) can manage security logs?

CHAPTER 3

Advanced User Management

MAJOR TOPICS

Objectives 120

Pre-Test Questions 120

Introduction 121

Introduction to Domains 121

Security Management 128

Introduction to Profiles and Policies 135

Summary 153

Post-Test Questions 153

Chapter 3—Advanced User Management

OBJECTIVES

At the completion of this chapter, you will be able to:

- Overview key points of single domain management.
- Explain the importance of security IDs.
- List the domain clients supported by NT Server domains.
- Define a roaming profile.
- Describe the significance of user and system policies.
- Define and test user and system policies.

PRE-TEST QUESTIONS

The answers to these questions are in Appendix A at the end of this manual.

1. What utility is used to change workstation workgroup or domain membership?

   ....

   ....

2. What type of group can be made a member of a workstation local group?

   ....

   ....

3. What type of profile would you define to allow a user to see the same desktop no matter what station he or she used to log onto the domain?

   ....

   ....

4. What filename should be used when defining system and user policies for a domain?

   ....

   ....

INTRODUCTION

Now that you understand the basics of user management, it's time to look at some more advanced procedures. The focus in this chapter switches more to a domain environment. The chapter begins by introducing the concept of NT Server domains and the servers that make up a domain. Supported client workstations are listed and described.

Next, the chapter moves into working with users in a domain environment. This includes domain logon concerns and an overview of the additional group types supported in a domain. You will also see how to use user profiles and system and user policies.

INTRODUCTION TO DOMAINS

This section will present some basics about NT Server domains, primary domain controllers (PDCs), and backup domain controllers (BDCs). Since a domain consists of a PDC and typically one or more BDCs, it is important to understand how to intertwine these servers all together. The following are topics discussed within this section:

- Windows NT Network Overview
- About Domains
- Server Roles
- Security IDs
- Domain Clients
- Windows NT Client

As an administrator, you must understand the concept of a domain. By understanding the fundamentals, management of a domain will be easier to comprehend.

Windows NT Network Overview

Up to now, the discussion has centered around NT Workstation and, even though it has not been explicitly described as such, the workgroup environment. That is one of the two primary models supported by Microsoft networking. As an overview:

- Workgroup

    This environment is characterized by user management of resources and lack of centralized security. It is best suited to a small number of workstations with relatively experienced users. This environment is supported by Windows (as a client), Windows for Workgroups, Windows 95, Windows NT Workstation, and Windows NT Server, if installed as a stand-alone server.

- NT Server domain

    This environment is based around a client/server model with one or more NT Server systems acting as domain controllers. It is characterized by centralized user access and resource management and is generally more secure than the workgroup environment. At least one NT Server machine is required as domain controller with support for a wide variety of client stations, including all members of the Windows family.

Most Windows NT networks are based around the NT Server domain model.

About Domains

One server will act as the Primary Domain Controller, providing centralized management of resources, user accounts, group accounts, permissions, and rights. Normally, the domain will also include one or more backup domain controllers to provide additional resources to the domain and assist with logon verification. A backup domain controller can also be promoted to primary domain controller should the primary controller become unavailable.

Domains allow you to support and manage a large number of users and workstations. A single domain can support up to 26,000 users account definitions. User access limits will be set by your Client Access licenses and the physical limitations of your domain controllers.

User accounts, group accounts, resources, and security are all centrally managed. Trust relationships allow you to set up different types of domain models. The flexibility of these models is one of the advantages of using Windows NT Server. Rather than forcing your organization to fit into a specific design dictated by the network operating system, you can design the network to meet your particular needs.

As your organizational needs evolve, you can evolve your domain model to match. While this course focuses on a single domain model for administration and management, you should be aware that multiple domain models are also supported, letting NT Server domains grow to meet your organizational needs.

Server Roles

It is important to understand the roles available to NT Server systems in the domain. A server's role is dependent on that selected during installation.

Primary Domain Controller (PDC)
: The primary domain controller holds the master copy of the domain control database. The primary domain controller must be present and available for you to add any backup domain controllers to the domain.

Backup Domain Controller (BDC)
: Each backup domain controller will have a copy of the domain control database. Primary uses of the BDC is to have additional systems available for logon validation and to take over in case of PDC failure.

Additional server   From a security management standpoint, additional servers are treated like workstations in a domain environment. In fact, an additional server can be part of a workgroup or a domain. Additional servers are used to provide resources to the network without loading the server with the overhead of logon validation. You may also want to set up an additional server when you want its security management to be somewhat isolated from the rest of the domain.

Use care when selecting server roles during installation. Once a server is added to a domain, you can't move it to a different domain without reinstalling Windows NT Server. You must also reinstall if you want to change a server's role from additional server to PDC or BDC.

Security IDs

Windows NT Server tracks account object, users, groups, and servers through security IDs (SID) rather than by the textual name.

The two instances where you are most likely to encounter references to the SID are when working with domain servers and with users are:

- Domain SID

    The domain SID is generated when the domain controller is installed. This ID is then used with the account database for all accounts in the domain, including member systems, additional servers, users, and groups. Even if the domain name is changed, this ID value will not change.

- Account SID

    This is created whenever a user or group account is created on a Windows NT workstation. It is used for tracking access permissions. The domain SID is used in generating each account SID, identifying the domain to which the account belongs.

The use of security IDs, especially the domain SID, helps to determine what you can and cannot do when changing domain definitions.

Domain Clients

Windows NT Workstation and Windows 95 are the suggested clients for Windows NT Server domains. They are not, however, the only clients supported. Windows NT Server domains may include:

- Apple Macintosh

    Services for Macintosh must be installed at the server. Native network communications support is provided.

- MS-DOS

    Client software required. Client software installation disks can be generated from the server.

- OS/2

    Client software required.

- Windows v3.x

    Client software required. Client software installation disks can be generated from the server.

- Windows for Workgroups

    Native support for basic network and resource access is provided with Windows for Workgroups.

- Windows 95

    Native support is provided with the operating system.

- Windows NT Workstation

    Native support is provided with the operating system.

All of these client types can be supported simultaneously on the network.

Windows for Workgroups, Windows 95, and Windows NT Workstation clients can also act as peer servers within the network, providing resources to other network clients.

Support of non-Microsoft client operating systems is beyond the scope of this course. Set up and management of Microsoft clients is covered later in this chapter.

Windows NT Client

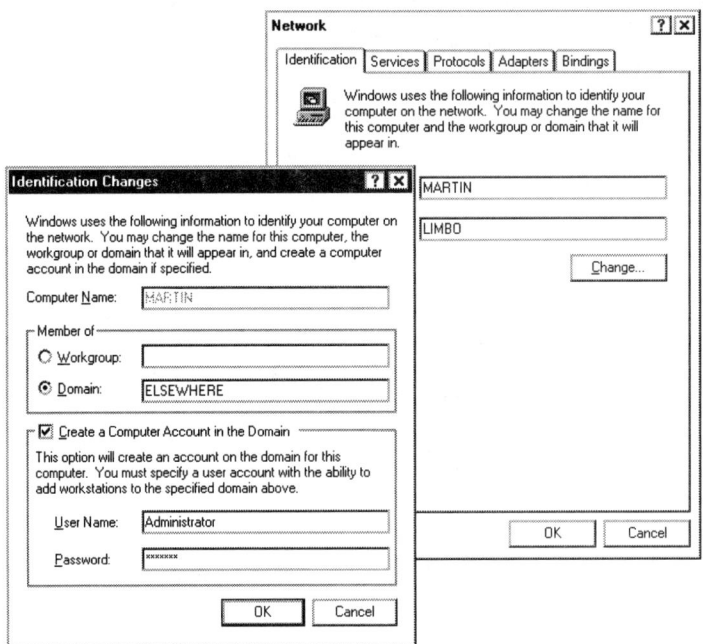

Setting up a Windows NT Workstation system or additional server for use with an NT Server domain is simply a case of verifying that the system is running an appropriate protocol and adding an account for the workstation. Launch the Networks Utility by double-clicking on its icon in the Control Panel and check the Protocols tab to verify that an appropriate protocol is installed.

Click on the Identification tab, then on **Change** to add the workstation to the domain. You will need to click on the Domain option button and type in the domain name. If an account has not been created for the machine, you will need to select to create an account and supply an administrator (or server operator) name and password.

If successful, a confirming dialog will display. When you exit the Network utility, you will be warned that you need to shut down and restart the computer to allow the settings to take effect. You will not be able to act as a domain member until after restarting the system. The same procedure is used for changing domain membership.

Exercise 3-1
Optional Exercise

During this exercise, you will add your workstation to a domain. You will need access to an NT Server domain controller to complete this exercise. Do not attempt this exercise on a corporate or production domain without first checking with your Network Administrator.

You should be logged on locally as an Administrator at the beginning of this exercise. You will need the username and password of a domain Administrator or Server Operator to complete this exercise.

1. Run **Start/Settings/Control Panel**.
2. Double-click on the icon for the Network utility.
3. The Identification tab should be displayed. Click on **Change**.
4. Click on the "Domain" option button and type in your domain name.
5. Click on the "Create a Computer Account in the Domain" checkbox.
6. Type in a domain administrator name and password.
7. Click on **OK**.
8. When the Welcome dialog displays, click on **OK**.
9. Click on **Close**. When prompted to restart your system, click on **Yes**.
10. Press **CTRL ALT DEL**.
11. Click on the Domain drop-down list and select the domain you joined.
12. Enter the username and password you used to add your machine to the domain and click on **OK**.

13. Open the Network Neighbor icon and verify that you can see the domain servers.
14. Close Network Neighborhood.
15. Run **Start/Settings/Control Panel** and launch the Network Utility.
16. Click on **Change**.
17. Click on the "Workgroup" option button and type in your original workgroup name.
18. Click on **OK**.
19. When warned about losing access, click on **Yes**.
20. Press **ENTER** when the "Welcome" dialog appears.
21. Click on **Close**. When prompted to restart system, click on **Yes**.
22. After the system restarts, log on as a local administrator.

SECURITY MANAGEMENT

This section will present the differences between working in the workgroup environment and in the domain environment. The following are topics discussed within this section:

- User Management Overview
- Group Accounts
- About Trust Relationships
- Workstation Local Group
- Domain Local Group
- Domain Global Group

In a given work environment, groups are created to identify departments within a company on the network. As new employees enter the company, it is necessary to add them to the appropriate group.

Security Management

Security is an important part of Windows NT Server. You were introduced to the security model in the previous chapter. This chapter demonstrates the differences between working in the workgroup environment and in the domain environment. Areas of special interest include:

- User management
- Group management
- Profiles
- Policies

User Management Overview

The user management procedures in a domain environment are similar to those already discussed during this course. Major differences include:

- Domain logon

    Unless otherwise restricted, usernames can be used for logon from any domain workstation and any type of domain client.

- Server logon

    Local logon at the server is more restricted than logon at the workstation. Only a limited number of users are allowed to log onto a server.

- Logon validation

    Logon validation is performed by a domain controller, either PDC or BDC, rather than the local machines. Local client still supports local logon, but are then restricted from access network resources.

- Group definitions

    Two new group types are supported, domain local groups and domain global groups. These can be used to set up access security to both server-based and peer server (workstation) shared resources.

User management is performed through User Manager for Domains. This utility is similar to the User Manager utility, but with additional features reflecting the domain environment.

Group Accounts

Group account definitions are primarily used to manage access permissions and user rights. Any rights and permissions granted to a group are granted to the group members. Security management is more efficient since you can make changes for sets of users, rather than managing each user separately.

You will likely encounter three types of groups in a Windows NT Server domain environment:

- Workstation local group

    A local group is created any time a new group is defined on a Windows NT workstation. These groups are used to manage access to local resources and to set local rights policies.

- Domain local group

    Domain local groups can be created through User Manager for Domains only. These groups apply to the local domain, including the domain controller and all additional servers. They are used to set domain access permissions and rights policies. Local groups may be created on domain controllers or additional servers.

- Domain global group

    Domain global groups can be created through User Manager for Domains only. They are used to group users for assigning rights and permissions to resources located on NT workstations or in other domains. Global groups cannot be created on Windows NT Workstations or on additional servers.

Each of these group types plays an important role in domain management.

Typically, permissions are assigned to local groups. When a domain global group is made a member of a local group, any rights and permissions pass to the domain global group, and through the global group to its members.

About Trust Relationships

You are going to see the term "trusted domain" mentioned occasionally. Trust relationships are only significant in a multiple domain environment, which is beyond the scope of this course. However, a quick overview might make some of the discussion easier to follow.

A trust relationship is a one-way logical relationship established between two NT Server domains. Once established, the domains are referred to as the trusted domain and the trusting domain. The trusted domain can be assigned rights and permissions in the trusting domain. Think of it as the trusting domain saying, "I trust you to access my resources."

The trusted domain does not automatically receive rights or permissions in the trusting domain. These must be explicitly assigned. The trust relationship makes it possible for these assignments to be made.

You can also have two-way trust relationships, a mutual trust between domains. This is established as two one-way trusts, one in each direction.

Workstation Local Group

Windows NT local groups are created through the User Manager utility. A workstation local group can be assigned permissions to local resources and rights relating to the local machine.

Local group members may include:

- Local workstation users
- Global groups from the local domain
- Global groups from any trusted domain

A local group cannot become a member of any other group.

A common use of local groups is to give domain users the permission to access and use local workstation resources. To do this:

- Create a local group on the local machine with the resource you wish to share to the network.
- Assign access permissions as appropriate to the local group.
- Create a global group made up of users who need access to the resource.
- Assign the global group as a member of the local group you created.

Use workstation local groups any time you want to give domain users access permissions to workstation resources.

Some assignments of this type are made automatically. For example, when a Windows NT Workstation joins a domain, the Domain Admins global group is automatically assigned membership in the workstation's local Administrators group. This is so that the domain administrators can manage member workstations.

Domain Local Group

Domain local groups are created through the User Manager for domains. A domain local group can be assigned permissions to resources on any domain controller in the local domain.

Domain local group members may include:

- Local domain users
- Trusted domain users
- Local global groups
- Trusted domain global groups

A domain local group cannot become a member of any other group.

One use of local groups is assigning domain users access to resources on a member additional server. For example:

- Create a local group which will be granted access permissions to the resources on the additional server.
- Create a global group on the domain controller.
- Assign users requiring access to the resources membership in a global group.
- Assign the global groups membership in the local group.

This way, resource access can be assigned to a server even though it is not a domain controller.

Domain Global Group

Domain global groups are created through User Manager for Domains. They are provided as a way of organizing users and making access permission assignments by way of local groups.

Domain global groups may contain:

- Local domain users

When a global group becomes a member of a domain, server, or workstation local group, permissions assigned to the local group are passed through to the global group's members. A global group can be made a member of:

- Workstation or additional server local groups that are members of the same domain.
- Workstation or additional server local groups in trusting domains.
- Domain local groups in the same domain.
- Domain local groups in trusting domains.

Domain global groups cannot be defined on an additional server. They are a domain object and supported on domain controllers only.

When a Windows NT Workstation system joins a domain:

- Domain Admins is added as a member to the local Administrators group.
- Domain Users is added as a member to the local users group.

This is done to allow valid network users and administrators access to the workstation without any special management overhead requirements.

Quick Example

Let's look at a practical example in a domain setting. You're setting up a domain with one domain controller, two additional servers, and several workstations. From a security management standpoint, the additional servers are treated the same as workstations. Both of the additional servers have printers attached that are shared to the network. In addition, two Windows NT workstations have printers you want to make available to domain users. How can you give a selected set of users access to all of these printers? You want to keep administrative overhead to a minimum and make it easy to add or remove users from the authorized list.

To do this, you would need both global and local groups.

First, let's take care of the users. Determine which users need access to the printers. Create a global group and make all of the users members of that group. Should you need to add or remove users at a later date, you can do so by assigning or removing group membership.

You have the users grouped, but they still can't access the printers. Create a domain local printer group and assign it permission to use the printers located on the servers. Then, create a local workstation group at *each* workstation with a printer. Give each group permission to use the printer at that workstation. With the permissions in place, you can assign the domain global group of users that you've already created membership to *each* of the printer groups. The permission is automatically passed on to the global group users.

Security Management Scenario

You are currently using a Windows NT Workstation system to archive selected records. The workstation is part of your corporate NT Server domain. Your network is configured as a single domain.

You have stored the records on an NTFS partition and are not allowing local access to the directory in which they are stored. Instead, you shared the directory to the network. You want EMarsh, JJones, and MWorth to be able to reference the records for reporting, but not be able to make any changes. You want JSmith and WKemp to have responsibility for record management and need full access to the directories.

You've created two local groups on the workstation. RecRead has read only access to the directory. RecAll has full access to the directory. What else must you do to finish configuring user access?

....

....

A possible solution to this scenario is provided in Appendix A at the end of the manual.

INTRODUCTION TO PROFILES AND POLICIES

This section will present the use of profiles and policies. Profiles and policies allow for certain aspects of the system to remain consistent or relative when users log on at other workstations. They also provide easy management for selected configuration parameters. The following are topics discussed within this section:

- Profiles and Policies
- About Profiles
- Profile Locations
- Defining Profile Location
- During Logon
- Managing Profiles
- System Policies
- System Policy Editor
- Using Registry Mode
- Using Policy File Mode
- System Policies

- User Policies
- About Policy Settings
- Making It Work

By setting profiles and policies, certain aspects of users and systems can remain consistent. As you will see, Administrators can use system policies to override prior Registry entries.

Profiles and Policies

There are two more areas relating to user and system management that should be discussed before leaving this chapter. They are:

- Profiles

    Each time a user logs on at a Windows NT station, the user's environment and desktop appearance is determined by a profile. It may be one defined specifically for that user, or a default profile that is used if the user's profile is not defined or not available.

- Policies

    Policies are also used to set configuration parameters by user or by system. Changes are written directly to the current station's registry.

A common problem in working with these is that they tend to be easily confused. They have similar names and perform similar functions.

About Profiles

You will need to know a few new terms before you can start working with profiles.

Default profile	Each system has a default profile. The default profile is used when a user's profile is not available.
Local profile	A local profile is a machine-specific profile created when a user logs on at a Windows NT station. A local profile can only be used or modified while the user is logged on at that station.
Roaming profile	A roaming profile is normally stored on a network server is available to the user when logging on at different NT stations on the network.

Mandatory profile   This is a user profile definition that the user is not allowed to change. Any changes made during the user session are not stored with the profile.

Personal profile   This is a user profile to which a user is allowed to make permanent changes. Any changes are written to the profile when the user logs off.

System default profile
   Only used when there is no user logged on at a station, this defines the background color, screen saver, and wallpaper while a system is waiting for a user to log on.

Profile management under Windows NT v4.0 is quite a bit different than it was under Windows NT v3.5(1). The User Profile editor no longer exists. Restrictions that were previously defined through user profiles are now defined through user and system policies.

Profile Locations

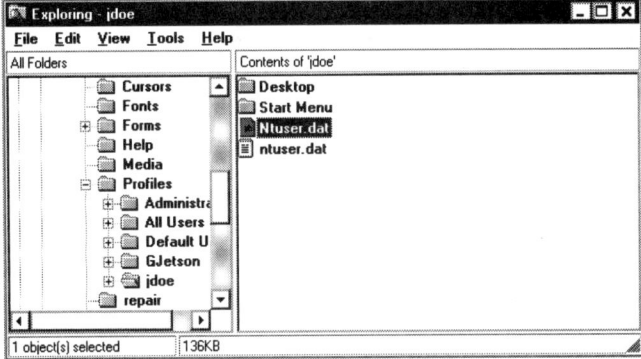

The default profile location and filename is:

   system\profiles*username*\NTUser.dat

System is the local Windows NT directory. The *username* directory is created the first time the user logs on at that station. When created in this fashion, the profile is treated as a local profile only. Changes made to the desktop at this machine will not be reflected on other machines. The default user profile is identified by a directory name of Default User.

You can copy one user's desktop settings to another user by simply copying the user profile. If you copy the entire contents of the user's directory, you will also be replacing desktop contents, start menu settings, and possibly even personal data files.

Defining Profile Location

```
User Environment Profile

User:  AWood (Arnie Wood)                    OK
                                             Cancel
  User Profiles                              Help
  User Profile Path:  \\stimpy\profiles\%USERNAME%
  Logon Script Name:  standard.bat

  Home Directory
    ⊙ Local Path:
    ○ Connect  [  ▼ ] To
```

You can also define the profile location through User Manager, or in a domain environment, User Manager for Domains. The path, with the exception of the username, must exist.

When the user logs on and back off, a profile will be created automatically at this location. Subsequently, each time the user logs off, the profile will be updated, unless it is a mandatory profile. If you already have a profile defined that you would like to assign to the user, it can be copied to the location and will take effect the next time the user logs on.

To make this into a mandatory profile, so that the user will not be allowed to change desktop settings, change the name of NTUser.dat to NTUser.man.

During Logon

What happens during logon depends on how the profile is defined. If a profile has not been defined for the user, a directory is created in the default location and the default user profile written into that directory. That becomes the user's profile. This will only be available as a local profile.

If a profile has been defined for the user, the system will attempt to load that profile during logon. If the *username* directory does not exist, the system assumes that this is the first time the user has logged on. The *username* directory will be created:

- In the specified profile directory.
- In the local station's default profile directory.

On subsequent logons, the stored copy of the profile will be used.

Whenever you define a user's profile location as a network location, Windows NT assumes that this is to be used as a roaming profile. As long as the server with the profile directory is available, so is the profile. Optionally, you can configure the system so that the cached copy is used when connecting over a slow link.

Should the profile directory not be available at logon, a warning dialog is displayed. This user is informed that the roaming profile is not available and that the local copy will be used.

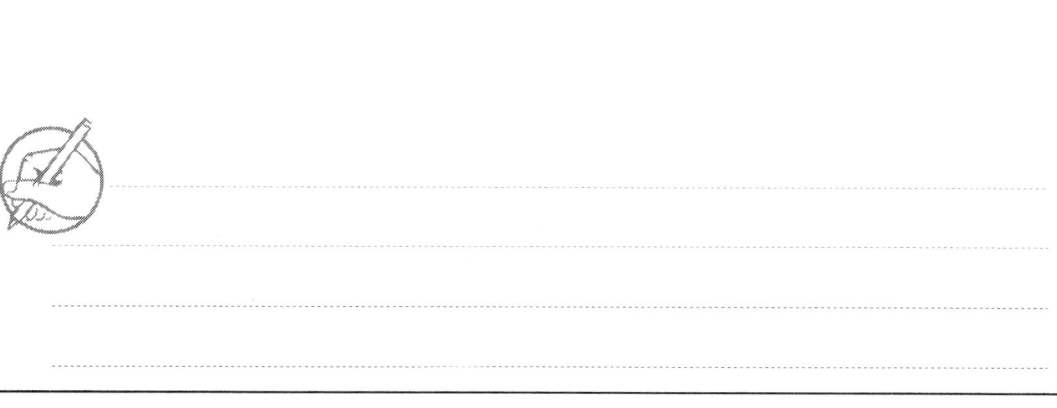

Managing Profiles

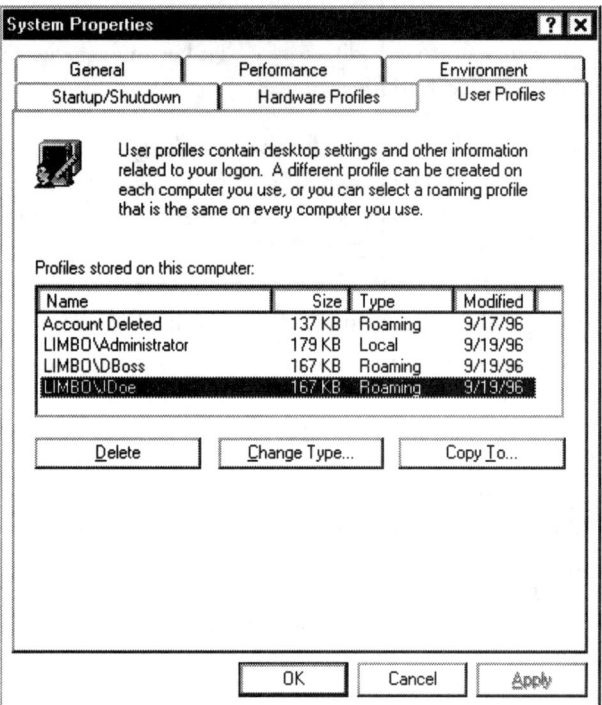

The Control Panel System utility is used to manage profiles. Launch the Control Panel and double-click on the System utility icon. When the system utility displays, click on the User Profiles tab.

All profiles stored on that computer will be listed. To select between a local and roaming profile, click to select the profile then click on the **Change Type** button. This will display the Change Type dialog, letting you set the profile type and whether a roaming profile should be downloaded when logging on over a slow link.

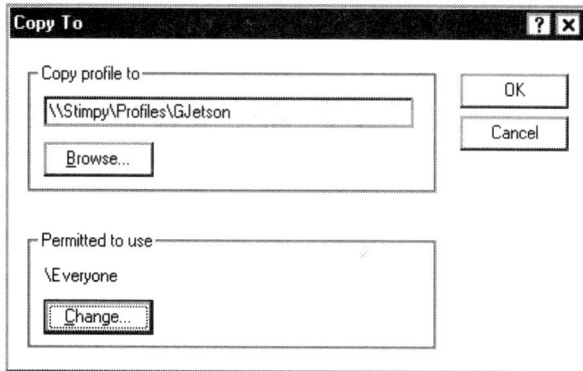

The **Copy To** button lets you copy a profile definition of another user. When you click on the **Copy To** button, you will be prompted for a destination directory. Enter or browse to locate the directory. The **Change** button lets you determine who can use the profile. Click on **OK** to copy the profile after completing the prompts.

System Policies

System policies allow an administrator to override local Registry values for user or computer settings. Policies are defined in a policy (.POL) file defaulting to NTCONFIG.POL. When a user logs on, the system checks the NETLOGON shared directory for a policy file on the validating server. If one is located, any registry changes are applied to the system at which the user is logging on.

Some of the benefits of using policies include:

- Customization of desktop configuration by restricting what users are allowed to do from the desktop.
- Configuration of network settings, such as the network client configuration and the ability to install or configure File and Printer Sharing services.

- The Administrator can easily change important Registry settings through the use of the system policy file.
- The Administrator can restrict access to options contained within the Control Panel.
- Group policies can be used to define a specific set of policies to be applied based on the membership of groups already defined on a Windows NT or NetWare network.
- The Administrator can allow only approved applications to be accessed.

The system policy file changes the registry by modifying the HKEY_CURRENT_USER key for desktop settings, and the HKEY_LOCAL_MACHINE key for network access settings.

> NOTE: Registry structure is discussed later in this course.

System Policy Editor

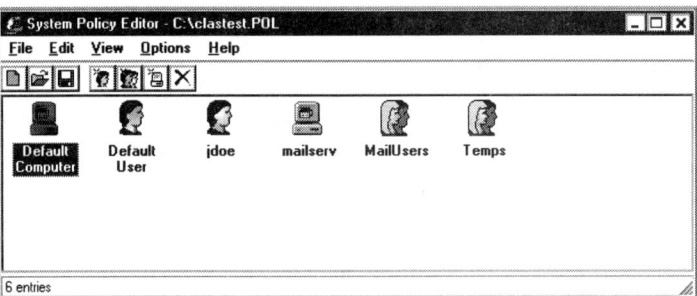

Policies are set through the System Policy Editor. The System Policy Editor has two different modes:

Registry	In the registry mode, changes are being made directly to the registry. By default, changes are made to the local registry. Optionally, you can connect to a different system and then enter the registry mode, editing that machine's registry.
Policy File	In the policy file mode, you are creating or modifying a registry policy file. This file will be processed when users log on. Policies can be defined for all systems, all users, individual systems, individual users, and groups.

If you define policies for more than one group, you will need to set the group priority. When a user logs on, the system checks for group memberships. If the user belongs to more than one group with a defined policy, the policy from the group having the highest priority is used.

By default, the System Policy Editor installs on NT Server only.

Using Registry Mode

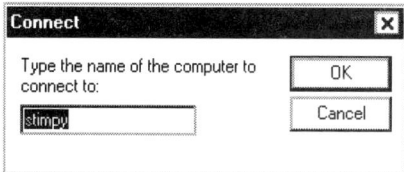

First, you need to decide if you want to edit the local machine or a different domain member. To connect to a different system, run **Connect** from the **File** menu, type in the machine name, and click on **OK**. You will be prompted with any accounts on the machine, so you can select the user registry entries to modify.

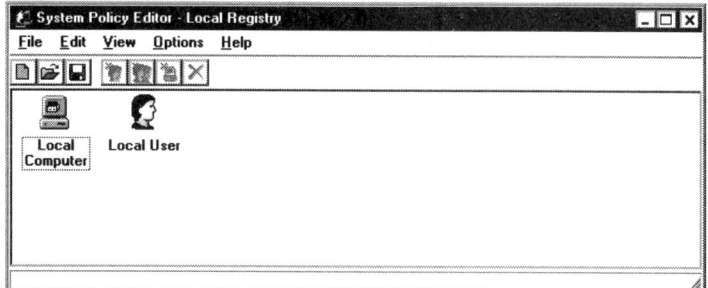

Run **Open Registry** from the **File Menu**. Even if modifying another machine, the icons will read "Local Computer" and "Local User", but the changes will be made to the machine to which you are connected.

Using Policy File Mode

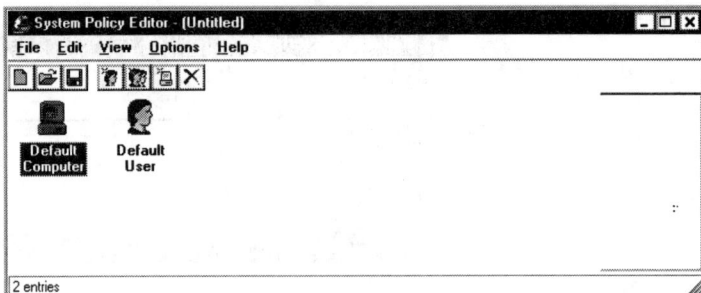

Under the policy file mode, you can create a new policy file or modify an existing policy file. Run **New Policy** from the **File** menu to create a new policy. Run **Open Policy** to modify an existing policy file, which will open a dialog through which you can locate and select the policy file.

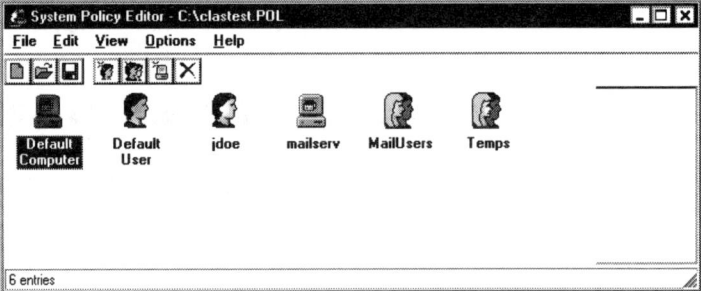

Initially, a policy file will contain entries for Default Computer and Default User only.

You can define additional users, groups, and systems through the **Add User**, **Add Group**, and **Add Computer** commands in the **Edit** menu. To modify properties for a system, user, or group, click to select its icon and run **Policies** from the **Edit** menu, or double-click on the selected icon.

System Policies

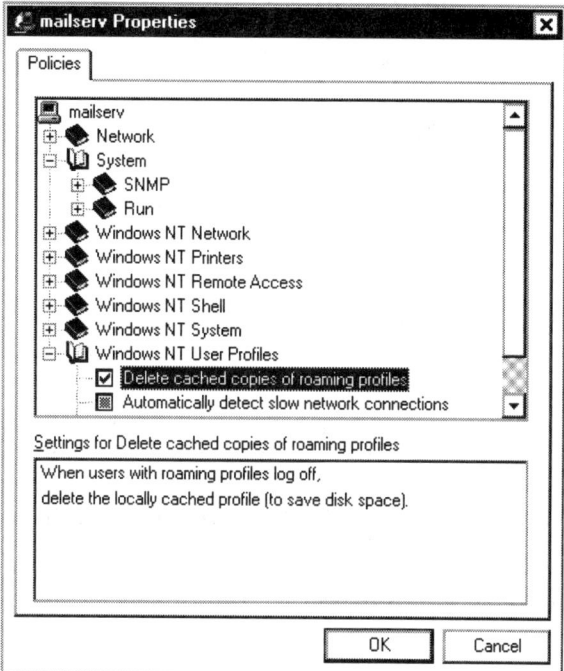

The following general areas are available for the Default Computer and any specific computers:

  Network   You can specify a file for remote policy updates.

  System   This allows you to set Simple Network Management Protocol (SNMP) options and set items to run at system startup.

Windows NT Network
: This selection lets you create hidden **workstation or server** drive shares.

Windows NT Printers
: You can set browse and spooler priority options.

Windows NT Remote Access
: This heading gives you access to remote access services configuration parameters.

Windows NT Shell
: This lets you define custom shared program folders and desktop icons.

Windows NT System
: You can set logon and file system options through this set of parameters.

Windows NT User Profiles
: This includes parameters relating to how slow network connections are handled and whether or not cached copies of roaming profiles should be automatically deleted when the user logs off.

System and user properties are stored in the same file. Make all of your policy changes, then save the file.

User Policies

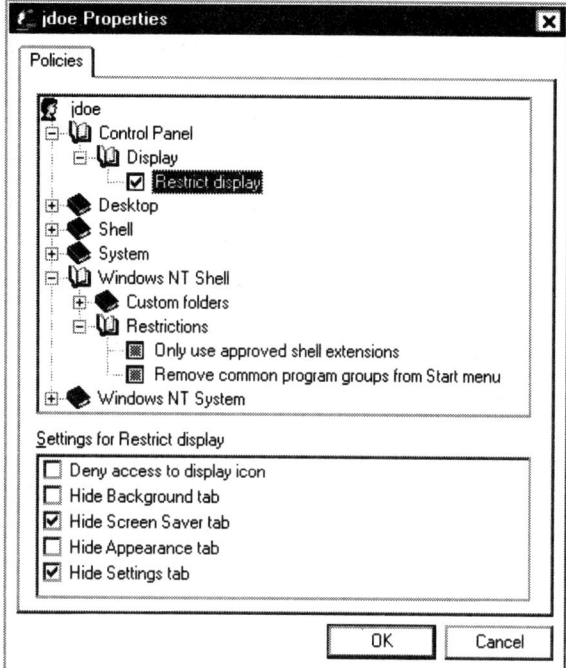

The same policy selections are available for the Default User, specified users, or groups. These are:

Control Panel	This allows you to display access to selected Display property sheet tabs.
Desktop	You can define the wallpaper and color scheme to be applied for the user or group.

Shell	This is where you set restrictions, similar to the User Profile Editor in Windows NT v3.5(1). You can hide items normally available on the Start menu or desktop, such as the Run command, the Network Neighborhood icon, and so forth.
System	You can set two restrictions through the System parameters. You can disable registry editing and limit the system to running Windows applications only.
Windows NT Shell	You can define custom settings for program folders and remove common program groups through these selections.
Windows NT System	This determines how AUTOEXEC.BAT and logon scripts are treated when the user logs on.

Run **Save** or **Save As** from the **File** menu after making your changes.

About Policy Settings

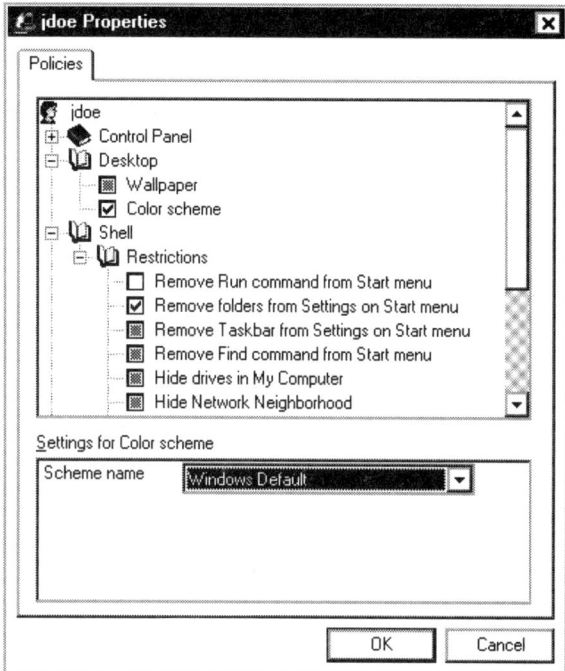

Policy options are set through check boxes. Each checkbox will be at one of three states:

Checked	Set this parameter in the system registry. For example, this would be used to set restrictions.
Cleared	Reset this parameter in the system registry. You could use this to remove restrictions set earlier.
Grayed	No change is made to the local registry.

Some parameters, when checked, will also prompt for additional information.

Making It Work

For a policy file to be applied, it must be located in the shared NETLOGON directory on the server validating the logon attempt, and must be saved as NTconfig.pol. Each domain controller will have a NETLOGON share. Physically, the location and filename will be:

    \system\system32\repl\import\scripts\NTconfig.pol

System is the Windows NT installation directory. This is the same location as is used for system logon scripts.

You can have this information copied automatically through replication. Replication is covered later in the course, but briefly, it is a way of automatically copying changed files from one machine to other machines. You can use one server as the export source, holding the master copy of the policy file. That server will then update the NETLOGON share directory on all other domain controllers.

User Management Scenarios

Proposed solutions to these scenarios are provided in Appendix A at the end of the manual.

User Management Scenario One

You have a relatively small NT Server domain. You have the PDC and one BDC. There are currently 20 workstations, all Windows NT Workstation v4.0, configured as domain members.

Your organization is relatively informal. Rather than having assigned desks, or even work areas, users tend to sit down and log onto the network at whatever workstation is currently most convenient. You want to make sure each user sees his or her own custom desktop settings at logon. Describe how you would configure the network.

....

....

User Management Scenario Two

You have an NT Server domain with one BDC in addition to the PDC. You've recently started using machine and group profiles. You created the profiles and saved the file to the directory shared as NETLOGON on the PDC. The default directory is shared as NETLOGON.

The problem is that profiles are being applied inconsistently. There doesn't seem to be any pattern as to when or if the profile will be applied to a particular system or user.

What is most likely wrong and how would you correct the situation?

....

....

Exercise 3-2

During this exercise, you will set and test user profiles. You should be logged on as an administrator at the beginning of this exercise.

1. Run **Start/Programs/Command Prompt**.
2. Run **Start/Programs/Administrative Tools/User Manager**.
3. Using the procedures described in earlier exercises, create the following users:

Username:	JWalton
Full Name:	blank
Description:	blank
Password:	password
Confirm Password:	password

   Remove the "User Must Change Password at Next Logon" check.

```
Username:        RSmith
Full Name:       blank
Description:     blank
Password:        blank
Confirm
Password:        blank
```
Remove the "User Must Change Password at Next Logon" check.

4. Click to select JWalton. Hold the **CTRL** key and click to select RSmith.
5. Press **ENTER** to display the User Properties dialog.
6. Click on **Profile**.
7. Type the following in the "User Profile Path", then click on **OK**.

    `C:\PROFILES\%USERNAME%`

8. Click on **OK**, then exit User Manager.
9. Log off and log on as JWalton.
10. Run **Start/Programs/Windows NT Explorer**. Click to expand the profiles folder.
    You will see a subdirectory for JWalton.
11. Click on JWalton. There is nothing listed underneath.
12. Run **Start/Settings/Control Panel** and double-click on the Display icon.
13. Click on the Appearance tab.
14. Click on the "Scheme" drop-down list and select Eggplant.
15. Click on **OK**.
16. Log off and log back on as JWalton.
17. Windows NT Explorer should be open on your desktop. Click on the folder for JWalton.

    There are several directories listed under JWalton.
18. Close Windows NT Explorer.
19. Log off and log on an Administrator.

SUMMARY

During this chapter, you were introduced to the following:

- Domains
- Windows family clients
- Domain users
- Domain local groups
- Domain global groups
- Built-in groupsLogon restrictions
- Local and roaming profiles
- Policies
- System Policy Editor

The next chapter introduces system configuration.

POST-TEST QUESTIONS

The answers to these questions are in Appendix A at the end of this manual.

1. You want to give Wanda, Jorge, and Al access to a color printer connected to Windows NT Workstation. The system is a domain member. These are the only domain users who should have access to the printer. What should you do?

....

....

2. You want to make sure you see the same desktop no matter where you log on. How can you do this?

   ....

   ....

3. Your domain is a single domain controller. Windows NT is installed on drive C: at the default directory for a new installation. You want to start using system and user policies. In order to be effective, to what path and filename must the system policy file be saved?

   ....

   ....

4. What will be the state of a policy option if you don't want that option changed in the system registry?

   ....

   ....

5. You want to add your workstation to a domain. A machine account for your Windows NT Workstation has not been defined on the domain controller. What do you need to know before you can have the account created while you are joining the domain?

   ....

   ....

CHAPTER 4

Peripheral Management

MAJOR TOPICS

Objectives 156

Pre-Test Questions 156

Introduction 157

Control Panel Utilities 158

Using the Event Viewer 179

Introduction to Printers 182

Summary 202

Post-Test Questions 203

OBJECTIVES

At the completion of this chapter, you will be able to:

- Describe the procedures for changing the following:
    - Mouse device driver
    - Keyboard device driver
    - Display appearance and configuration
    - SCSI adapter device drivers
    - Tape device drivers
    - UPS
- Describe the procedures for adding or removing Windows NT components.
- Use the Event Viewer to display detail event information.
- Install a local printer.

PRE-TEST QUESTIONS

The answers to these questions are in Appendix A at the end of this manual.

1. Which Mouse properties tab lets you change the installed mouse driver?

   ....

   ....

2. Which utility lets you view and change installed SCSI device drivers?

   ....

   ....

3. If a filename is specified in the "Execute command file" prompt, it should be able to finish execution in _____ seconds or less. Otherwise, it may interfere with proper shut down.

   ....

   ....

4. You are installing a new printer. You will be sharing the printer to the network. You want Windows 95 clients' device drivers to be updated when they attach to the printer. How can you do this?

....

....

INTRODUCTION

User and group management are only part of the Windows NT management requirements. You must also be concerned about peripheral management requirements. During this chapter, we'll look at some basic peripherals and available management tools.

This chapter could also be named the "Control Panel" chapter. This is the area for managing almost everything about your Windows NT computer. The Control Panel allows you to manage the keyboard, mouse, SCSI adapter device drivers, tape drive device drivers, other devices and services.

During this chapter, an effort is made to not only look at the "what", but the "why" of management as well. Examples are provided as to why you will want or need to configure some of the devices listed.

A couple of equally important areas are also discussed in this chapter. You will have a chance to take a closer look at the Event Viewer during the chapter. You will also see how to properly configure printers, including some suggestions on setting up printer pools.

CONTROL PANEL UTILITIES

This section will present a selection of utilities available in the Control Panel. These utilities are used for peripheral configuration. The following are topics discussed within this section:

- Control Panel
- Windows NT Setup
- Install/Uninstall
- Mouse Properties
- Keyboard Properties
- SCSI Properties
- Tape Drives
- UPS
- UPS Settings
- Display Settings

Peripheral management utilities let you configure devices on your system. It is important to understand how each device is used in order to optimize performance. As these utilities are discussed in detail for you. It is still important to monitor any configuration changes made as problems may occur.

Control Panel

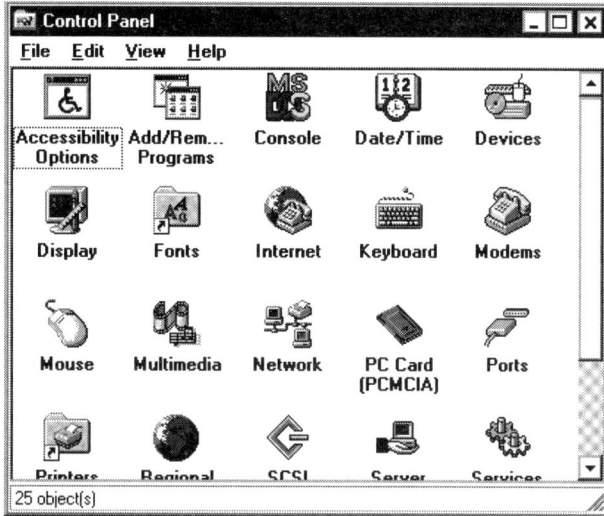

Any discussion of Windows NT configuration utilities has to start with the Control Panel. You have several options for launching the Control Panel, including:

- Run **Start/Settings/Control Panel**.
- Open **My Computer** and double-click on the Control Panel icon.
- Launch Windows NT Explorer, scroll down, and click on the **Control Panel**.

The first two methods open the Control Panel as a window on the desktop. The third method displays the Control Panel utilities in the Explorer Contents window.

Once the Control Panel is open, you will see available configuration utilities. The utilities shown in the sample graphic are typical. The utilities available on your system will depend on optional components installed during configuration and additional software support installed.

Control Panel utilities work by directly modifying the Windows NT registry which contains the operating system configuration files. While it is possible to edit the registry directly, you should use Control Panel utilities for this purpose whenever possible. The registry was discussed in the previous chapter.

Care must be taken when changing system configurations, even when using Control Panel utilities. It is possible to introduce problems through improper device configuration settings. These can range from performance problems to being unable to start Windows NT.

Windows NT Setup

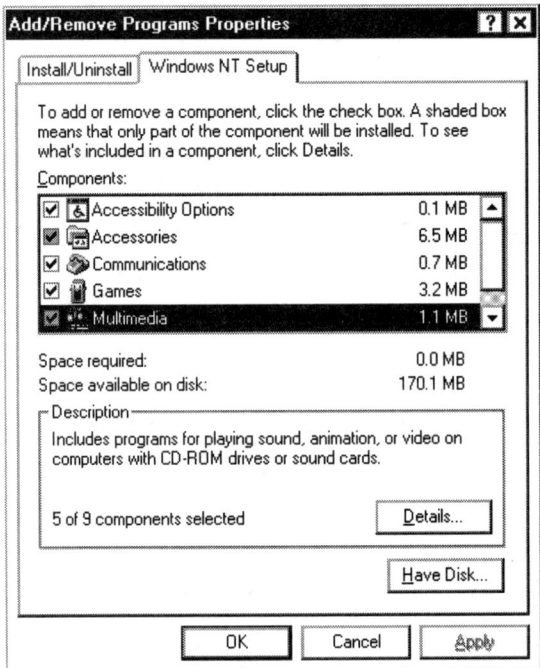

The Windows NT Setup tab is located on the Add/Remove Programs properties in the Control Panel. The Control Panel can be found under the **Start/Settings** menu. This is the sheet you use to add or remove Windows NT components. The utility is also used to install new applications and uninstall previously installed applications. Use the check box in front of each component to add or remove the component. A box that is checked and shaded means that only part of the component is, or will be installed.

Control Panel Utilities

To see what is included in a component, click on the **Details** button. The following components of Windows NT may be removed or added:

Accessibility Options
: You can change keyboard, display, sound, and mouse behavior for people who are visually, hearing, or mobility challenged.

Accessories
: These are enhancements and accessories such as Calculator, Character Map, Clipboard Viewer, Clock, Wallpaper, Document Templates, Imaging, Mouse Pointers, Object Packager, Paint, Quick View, Screen Savers, and WordPad.

Communications
: These are accessories that allow you to connect to other computers and online services. These include Chat, Hyper Terminal, and Phone Dialer.

Games
: Windows NT ships with Freecell, Minesweeper, Pinball, and Solitaire.

Multimedia
: These are programs for animation, playing sound, and video on computers with sound cards and/or CD-ROM drives. Included in this set are the CD Player, Sound Schemes, Media Player, Sound Recorder, Sample Sounds, and Volume Control.

Windows Messaging
: These are messaging and electronic mail utilities, including Internet Mail, Microsoft Mail, and Windows Messaging. If you install Internet Mail, you must also install Windows Messaging.

Install/Uninstall

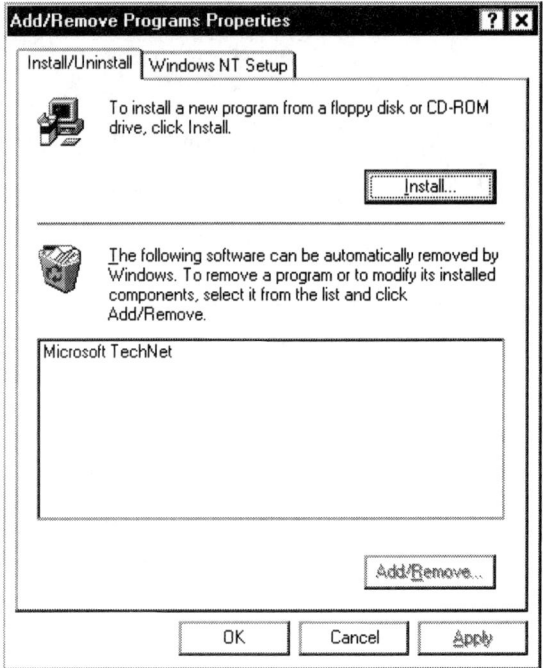

The Windows NT Install/Uninstall tab is located on the Add/Remove Programs properties in the Control Panel. This is the sheet you use to add or remove application programs from your computer. To install a new application program, select the **Install** button.

To change or remove an application, highlight the application and select the **Add/Remove** button.

Mouse Properties

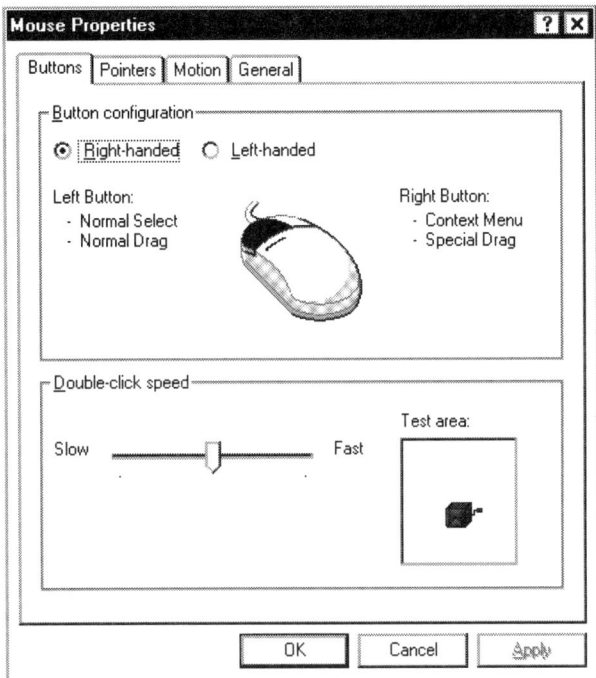

Mouse configuration is managed through the Mouse properties dialog in the Control Panel. This is where you can configure your mouse buttons, pointers, motion, and change your mouse driver. Available tabs are:

    Buttons Tab   This tab is used to configure your mouse for right- or left-handed, and the double-click speed.

Chapter 4 — Peripheral Management

Pointers Tab — If you did not install Accessories/Mouse pointers, your selection of available schemes will be minimal. Otherwise you can experiment with the 11 schemes provided to see which you like best. The "Magnified" scheme is best for computers that will be connected to projectors.

Motion Tab — You can adjust the speed at which your pointer moves. If you check the box "Snap mouse to the default" button then whenever a dialog box appears the mouse will already be placed over the default button.

General Tab — This tab is used to display the current mouse device or devices being used on this computer. Use the **Change** button to install new devices.

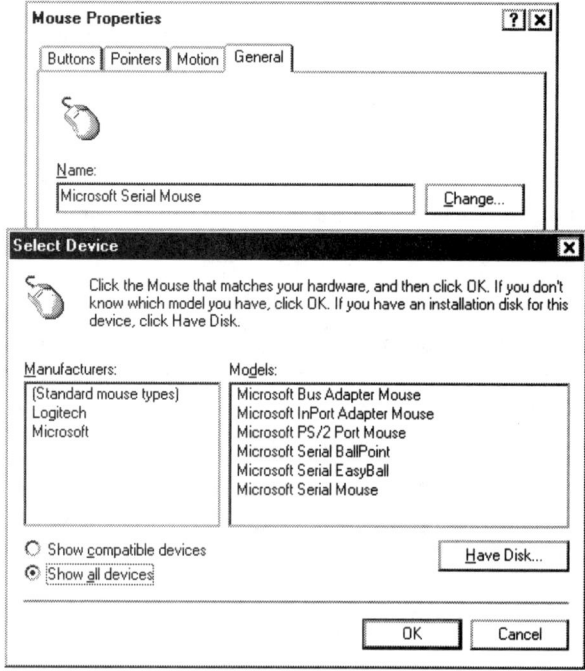

If you cannot find your mouse device listed, you can click on the **Have Disk** button. This selection requires a driver supplied by the mouse manufacturer. After copying the driver files, you are prompted to restart your system. Windows NT will not load the new driver files until system restart.

Keyboard Properties

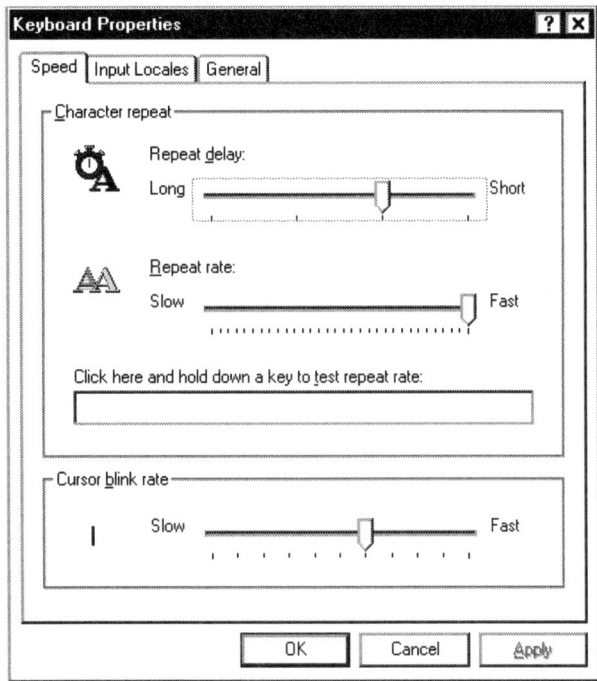

Keyboard configuration is managed through the Keyboard properties dialog in the Control Panel. This sheet is where you can configure your keyboard speed, input locales, and change your keyboard driver.

Available tabs are:

Speed Tab	This tab allows you to customize your character repeat delay and rate. When you hold down a key, the delay is the time before it begins repeating. The rate sets the repeat rate when you're holding down a key. You can also adjust the cursor blink rate.
Input Locales Tab	Here you can select different keyboard languages and layouts. The installed locales are displayed. This tab is also located in the Regional Settings dialog.
General Tab	The General tab allows you to change your keyboard and install the appropriate drivers for the new keyboard.

If you cannot find your keyboard device listed, you can click on the **Have Disk** button. This selection requires a driver supplied by the keyboard manufacturer. After copying the driver files, you are prompted to restart your system. Windows NT will not load the new driver files until system restart.

SCSI Properties

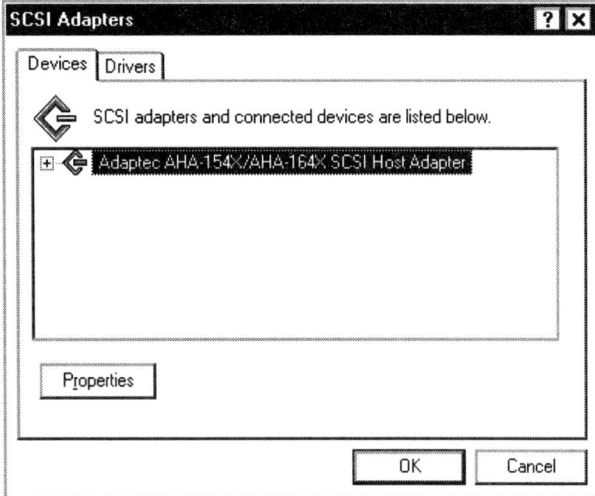

Small Computer System Interface (SCSI) is a standard high speed parallel interface used for connecting computers to peripheral devices. It is most often used for large hard disks and CD-ROM devices. One SCSI controller can control up to seven peripheral devices-daisy chained together.

Multiple SCSI hard disks can be combined to provide fault tolerance such as mirrored disks or striped sets with parity. On boot up NT will automatically search for SCSI tape backup devices.

SCSI configuration is managed through the SCSI properties dialog in the Control Panel. This is where you can view your SCSI devices and drivers. When you first make this selection, currently installed SCSI adapters are displayed. You can choose to remove existing drivers or add new drivers to the list.

Available tabs are:

> Devices Tab
>
> This tab displays the installed SCSI adapters in this computer. During boot up, NT looks for SCSI adapters and tape backup devices automatically. Selecting the Properties button will display the following information about this SCSI device:
>
> Drivers Tab
>
> The installed drivers are listed. You can add new drivers, remove current drivers, click on **OK** and save your changes, or click on **Cancel** to abort any changes.

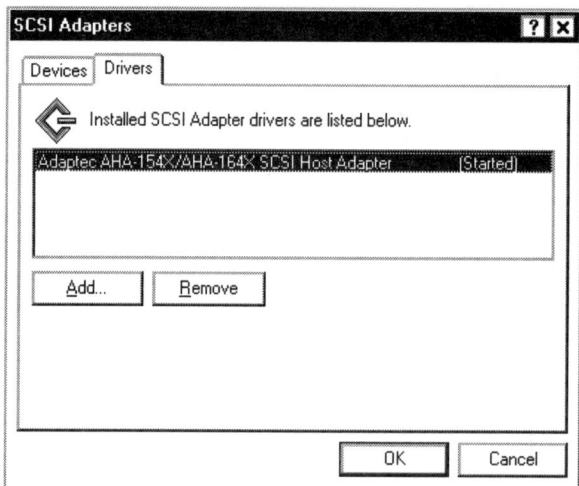

When adding a SCSI driver, if you cannot find your SCSI device listed, you can click on the **Have Disk** button. This selection requires a driver supplied by the SCSI device manufacturer. After copying the driver files, you are prompted to restart your system. Windows NT will not load the new driver files until system restart. A SCSI device driver is required for SCSI device support.

Use care when adding or removing SCSI device drivers. Adding a device driver for SCSI controller that is not installed may keep your system from booting properly. Removing a driver that you need can keep you from accessing system resources.

Tape Drives

Windows NT includes tape backup and restore software. You can use this software and a supported tape device to back up your computer's hard disks, both FAT and NTFS. A tape device has to be defined before it can be used as a backup device. Backup and restore procedures are discussed in some detail in the following chapter.

Tape device configuration is managed through the Tape Devices properties dialog in the Control Panel. This is where you can view your tape devices and drivers. When you first make this selection, currently installed tape devices are displayed. You can choose to remove existing drivers or add new drivers to the list.

This tab displays the installed tape devices in this computer. During boot up, NT looks for SCSI adapters and tape backup devices automatically. If you select the **Detect** button, NT will attempt to find tape devices.

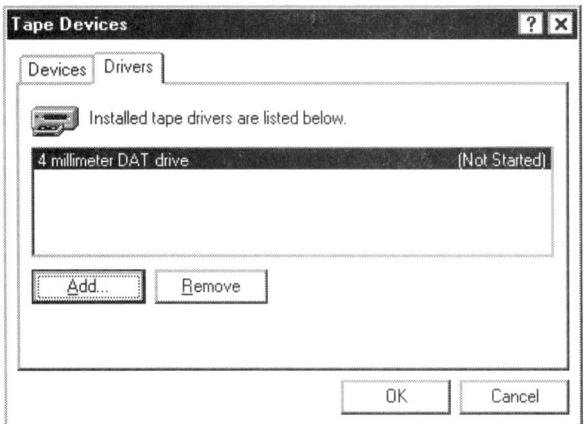

The drivers tab shows the installed drivers. You can add new drivers, remove current drivers, click on **OK** to save your changes, or click on **Cancel** to abort any changes.

When adding a tape driver, if you cannot find your tape device listed, you can click on the **Have Disk** button. This selection requires a driver supplied by the tape device manufacturer. After copying the driver files, you are prompted to restart your system. Windows NT will not load the new driver files until system restart.

A supported tape drive is required to use the Backup/Restore utility in the **Start/Programs/Administrative Tools** menu.

UPS

Uninterruptible power supply configuration is managed through the UPS properties dialog in the Control Panel. This is an important accessory for a Windows NT system. It keeps your system from going down unexpectedly due to line power loss.

- Continued operations

    Depending on the time provided by the UPS batteries, you can continue working. This gives you a chance to complete critical applications.

- Data security

    Since a UPS gives you time to gracefully shut down your system, you can exit applications and save your open files. It also keeps you from losing any files that are buffered in memory.

- Network support

    Since it's possible that other users may be accessing files on your system, this gives you time to warn them that your system will be shutting down.

- Hardware protection

    A quality UPS provides protection against power events such as surges and spikes.

The UPS utility in the Control Panel allows you to configure UPS support for your system.

UPS Settings

![UPS dialog box screenshot]

Windows NT supports a UPS connected to COM1, COM2, COM3, or COM4. The UPS utility in the Control Panel lets you configure support for your UPS.

UPS Configuration lets you specify what signals are supplied by your UPS for monitoring and whether a positive or negative voltage interface is used.

- Power failure signal

    This identifies that the UPS will send a message if line power is lost. The CTS (Clear to Send) line is used for this purpose.

- Low battery signal at least two minutes before shutdown

    If the UPS will send a signal as the battery gets low, this should be checked. This signal uses the DCD (Data Carrier Detect) line.

- Remote UPS Shutdown

    Check this selection to enable remote UPS shutdown which allows the UPS to shut down your system in case of line power loss. This uses the DTR (Data Terminal Ready) signal line.

    WARNING!

    Some UPS devices will not work as intended if the voltage active signal is configured incorrectly. If the voltages are reversed, they may force your system to shut down on power loss, even if remote shutdown has not been enabled.

"Execute Command File" contains the name of a file to be executed if there is a power interruption. The file is executed immediately before shutdown. Make sure that the file you specify can complete execution in no more than 30 seconds. If not, there is a chance that it will interfere with proper system shutdown.

Set the UPS characteristics to reflect the expected battery life, the amount of time you have before the battery drops too low to run the system, and the recharge time per minute of run time. These selections are only available if Power failure signal under the UPS Configuration is checked. If Low battery signal at least two minutes before shutdown is also checked, these selections are unavailable.

The UPS Service parameters set the time between the power failure and the first warning message. They also set the delay before sending warning messages. Use care when configuring UPS support. Selecting the wrong signals can cause a number of problems, such as automatic and immediate shut down of either the UPS or the server when power is lost.

Always test your configuration in advance of an actual power failure. Once everything is set up properly, simulate line power loss by unplugging the UPS.

This will let you see if UPS monitoring is set up properly and if the UPS is able to keep the server running.

Display Settings

Display configuration is managed through the Display properties dialog in the Control Panel. This utility gives you an easy-to-use means of setting and testing display controller configurations. You can also right-click (click with mouse button 2) on your desktop, and run **Properties/Settings**.

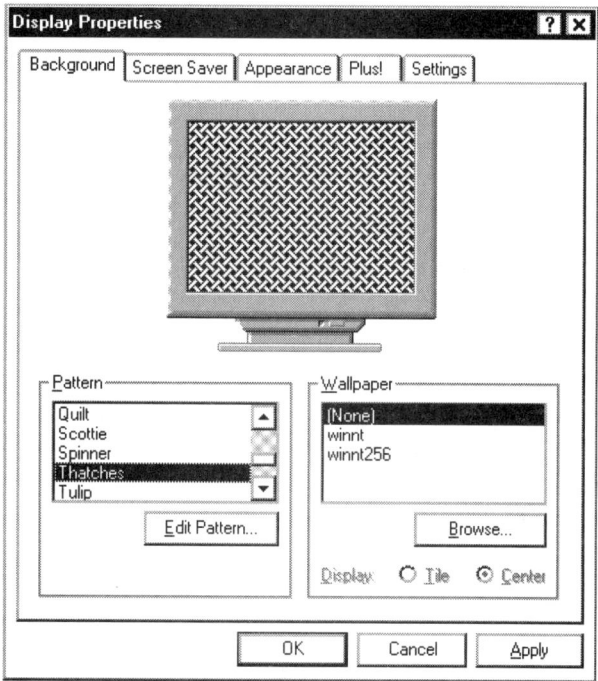

The Background tab is used to select the background pattern and wallpaper to display on your desktop.

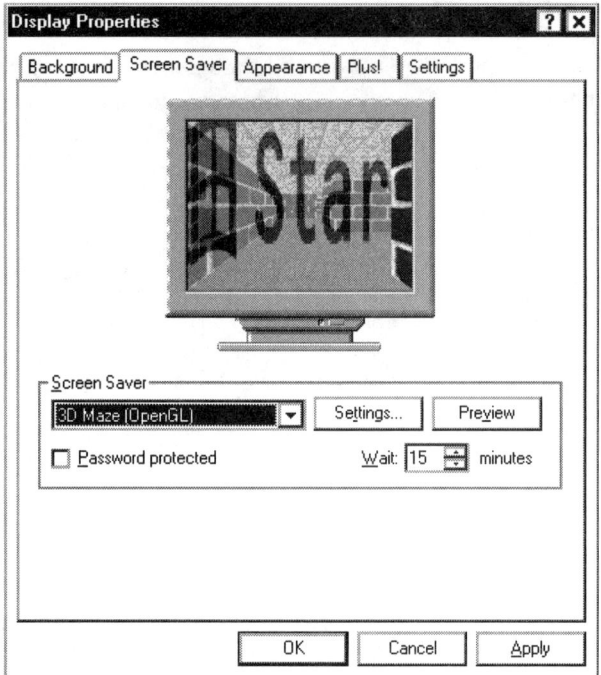

The Screen Saver tab is used to enable and choose a screen saver to be used on this workstation. Some of the choices allow you to enter text to be displayed.

Use caution when enabling the screen saver. You should test its compatibility with applications you run on a regular basis. This is especially true if you run any Win16 or MS-DOS applications. In some cases, the applications may fail in the background when the screen saver starts.

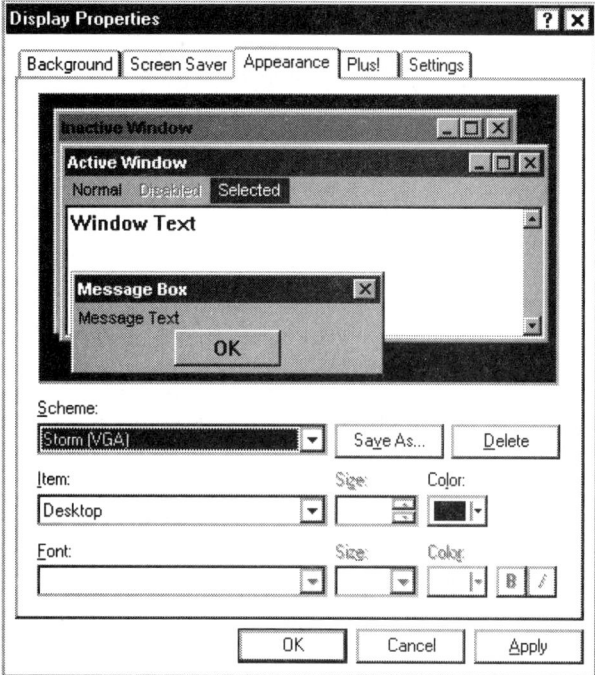

The Appearance tab allows you to select a predefined color scheme for your display. You can also select individual windows items and change their color, font type, and size.

Chapter 4—Peripheral Management

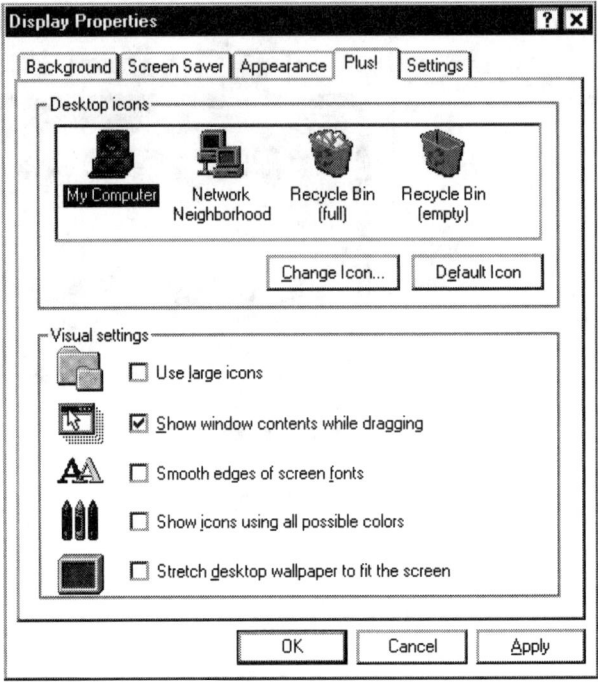

The Plus! Tab is used to change the icons that are used for the items on your desktop. There are five check boxes to tailor the visual settings.

Control Panel Utilities   177

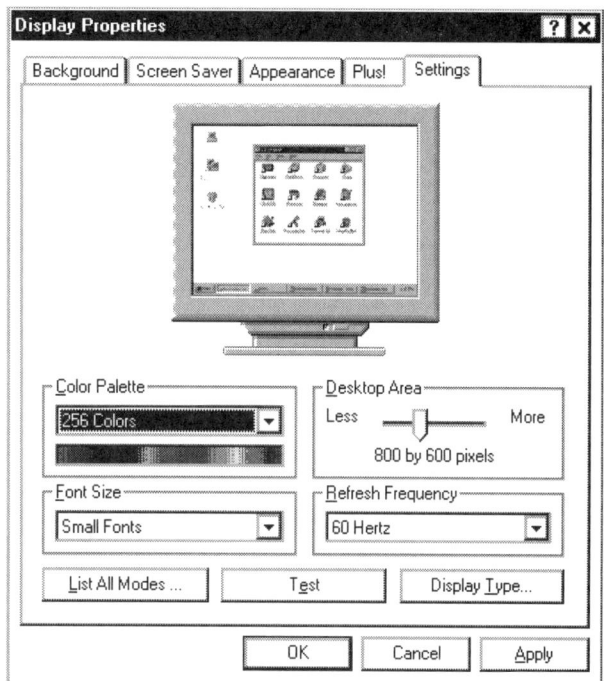

The Settings tab displays your current settings, as well as configuration selections:

Color Palette	This is the number of colors you want to display.
Desktop Area	This sets the number of pixels used to define your desktop. Care must be taken in that, even though a mode might be supported by your display controller, it may be beyond the resolution limits of your monitor.
Font Size	This selection lets you set the font size.
Refresh Frequency	This sets the adapter refresh rate. Higher refresh rates may not be supported by some adapters.

The **List All Modes** button will list all display modes supported by your adapter. The **Change Display Type** button lets you override the detected adapter type. It also displays adapter and driver information.

After making any changes, you must test the new configuration. If the configuration works as desired, you are prompted to reset your system. Adapter configuration changes do not take effect until after the system is reset.

If you make changes that prevent your display from working properly, you can reboot the system and select "Windows NT Workstation Version 4.00 [VGA Mode]".

Exercise 4-1

During this exercise, you will work with configuration utilities. You should be logged on as an administrator at the beginning of this exercise.

1. Run **Start/Settings/Control Panel**.
2. Double-click on Add/Remove programs.
3. Click on the Windows NT Setup tab.
4. Click on Accessories in the "Components" window, then on **Details**.
5. Click to place a check beside Desktop Wallpaper.
6. Scroll down and click to place a check beside Mouse Pointers.
7. Click on **OK**, then on **OK** again.

   NOTE: *If your installation CD is no longer in the CD-ROM drive, you will be prompted to replace the CD or provide a path to the installation files. Replace the CD and press* **ENTER** *.*

8. Double-click on the Mouse utility, then click on the Pointers tab.
9. Click on the "Scheme" drop-down list and click on Variations. Observe the sample pointer.
10. Click on the "Scheme" drop-down list and select **Windows default**.

    NOTE: *You may select a different pointer scheme if you wish.*

11. Click on **OK**.
12. Double-click on **Display**.

Take a few minutes to try the different Background, Screen Saver, and Appearance selections on your display. Click on **OK** to save your changes or **Cancel** to cancel all changes when you are finished.

USING THE EVENT VIEWER

This section will present an administrative tool that may be used to monitor peripheral management. You will see the extent of errors provided within the Event Viewer. The following are topics discussed within this section:

- Event Viewer
- Detail Event Information
- Device/Service Errors

From an administrative standpoint, the Event Viewer serves as a troubleshooting tool. Any system, device, or application errors will be displayed here. By understanding the details provided on any given errors, you will be able to locate the cause of the problem and provide a solution.

Event Viewer

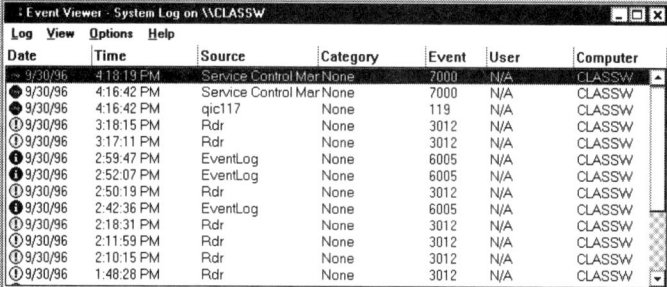

The Event Viewer displays information about your system, system errors, application errors, and hardware problems. Your computer has many components that can cause a failure. Common causes include disk problems, network interface card problems, application program problems, users changing the configuration and causing a problem, and sharing problems with other workstations and servers.

When you suspect you're having a problem, use the Event Viewer to check the logs and find the problem. The **Event Viewer** is located in the **Start/Programs/Administrative Tools** menu.

You've already used the Event Viewer to look at the contents of the security log. It also lets you view the contents of the system and application logs. The event logging service is started automatically when you boot Windows NT. You can stop event logging through the Services dialog in Control Panel.

Status messages from NT system devices and services are recorded in the System log. If you had a hardware failure and the associated device driver failed to load, a message would be placed in the System log.

Status messages from application errors and Windows initialization file migration are recorded in the Application log. An application, such as a spreadsheet or database, might record file or link errors in the Application log.

Status messages from NT security events are recorded in the Security log. The security log is used to track security system changes and identify possible breaches of security. Only an administrator can view the Security log.

You can view the different logs by using the **Log** menu and selecting either **System**, **Security**, or **Application**.

Both the System and Application logs support the same fields for event entries:

Date	The Date field contains the date when the entry was generated. It will also contain an icon identifying the entry. Warnings have an exclamation on a yellow background. Errors have the word "Stop" written across a red background. Informational items have a white letter "i" on a blue background.
Time	This is the time when the event was logged.
Source	The Source will identify the device driver or application that logged the event.
Category	The category field will normally have the entry "none" for system and application files.
Event	The Event field contains a code which identifies the error.
User	This field will have the name of the user that was logged on when the error occurred.

Computer   This field will have the computer name on which the event occurred.

The size of the log files can be changed by running **Log Settings** from the **Log** menu. The size of each log can be set independently. The larger the Maximum Log Size, the more disk space it potentially uses.

Detail Event Information

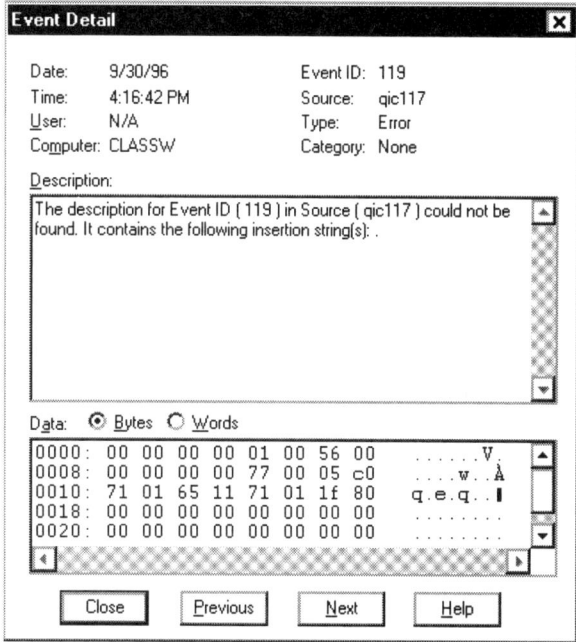

You can view detail information for any entry by double-clicking on the entry. The Event Detail dialog displays information about your system and some basic error information. It also contains a textual description of the error.

Device/Service Errors

You will have several devices and services that are configured to load each time you launch Windows NT. If one should fail, you'll receive an error dialog.

You can often locate the failing device or service in the Event Viewer. Look for services with a red stop sign attached. Double-clicking on a line in the log will display the details of the message.

It is not uncommon to see multiple errors in the Event Viewer after a failure occurs. A service will often be dependent on another service or device driver loading. If a device or service fails to initialize properly, all of its dependent services will also fail.

INTRODUCTION TO PRINTERS

This section will introduce the installation of printers. We will also take a look at managing a printer as a network resource and setting up printer pools. The following are topics discussed within this section:

- Printers
- General
- Ports
- Scheduling
- Sharing
- Security
- Device Settings
- Implementing Printers
- Client Support
- Client Connectivity
- Special Configuration
- Multiple Definitions
- Pooling
- Spooler

When a printer is set up as a network resource, multiple individuals may access the same resource, but one at a time. Priorities of course may be set along with scheduled times for printing large reports and so on.

Printers

There are several methods for getting to the Printers properties dialog. You can run **Start/Settings/Printers**. You can open the Printers folder from either Windows NT Explorer or the My Computer icon. You can also double-click on the Control Panel Printers utility.

The Printers properties dialog is used for installing and configuring local printers and attaching to network (shared) printers. The first icon you see is the Add Printer icon. Double-click on this icon to define a new printer to your system.

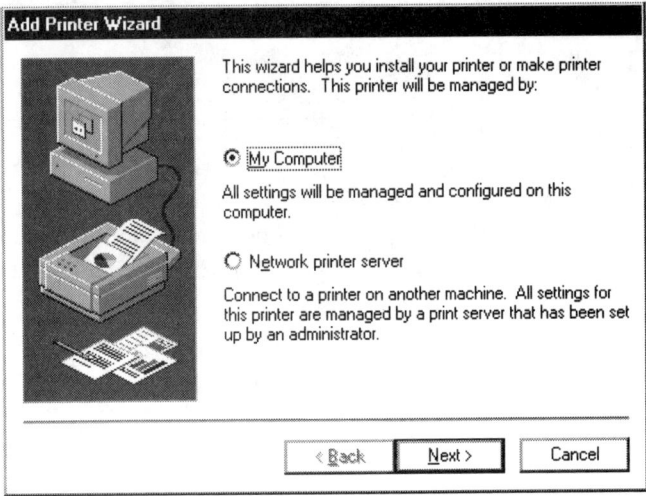

This dialog lets you indicate where the printer is connected. Select "Network Printer Server" if the printer is physically located on another server. Another server could be a Windows NT Server, a Windows NT Workstation, a Windows 95 station, a Novell NetWare server, or a dedicated print server connection.

Select "My Computer" if the printer is attached to the local computer by a parallel or serial port.

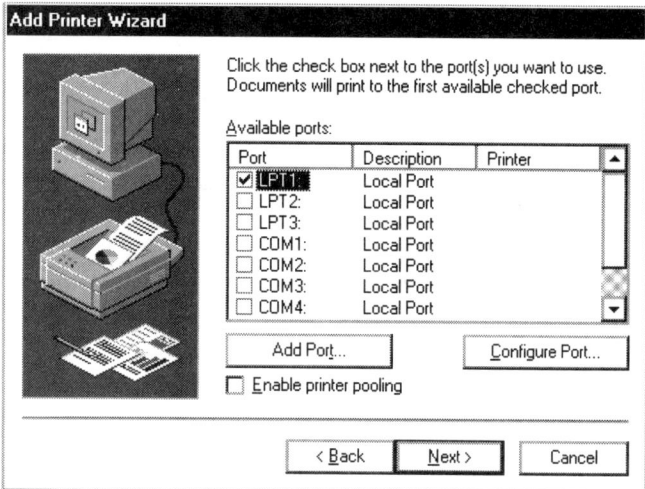

This is the property sheet you will see if you are attaching the printer to this computer. Select the port that the computer will use to communicate with the printer. If you are attaching to a network printer, Windows NT would scan the network and display the list of available printers. You would then select the printer for which drivers will be installed. Working with shared resources is discussed in more detail later in the course.

If you enable printer pooling you are going to connect two or more identical printers and show them as one printer to this computer and the network. Printer pooling is used to let Windows NT service a print queue using multiple printers.

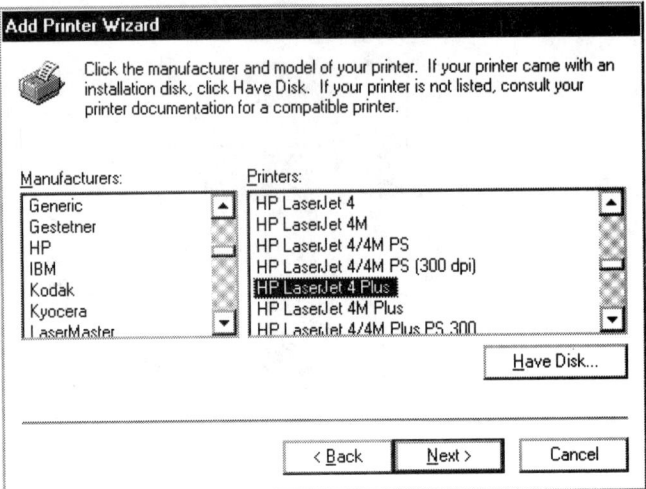

Find the printer manufacturer on the left side of the window and click to select. Find the printer model on the right side of the window and click to select. If your printer is not listed, click on the **Have Disk** button and select the drivers off of the diskette supplied to you by the printer manufacturer. Make sure that the printer drivers are compatible with Windows NT v4.0.

If the driver already exists on your hard disk, you will be prompted to either keep or replace the driver.

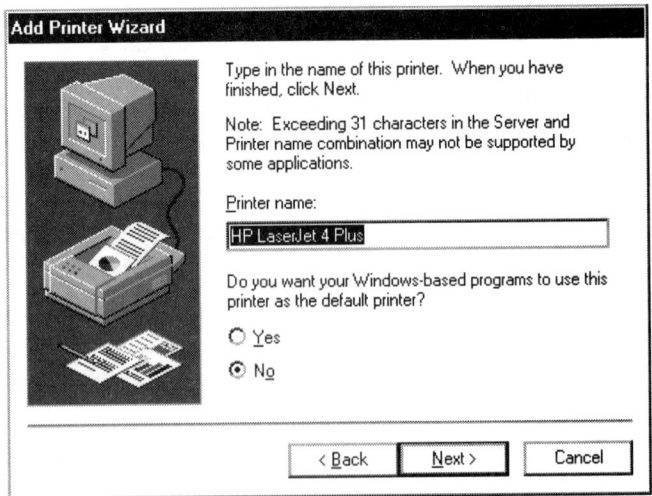

Type in the name of the printer. This is the name that will be displayed whenever you are prompted to select a printer. You will need to select whether you want to use this as your default printer.

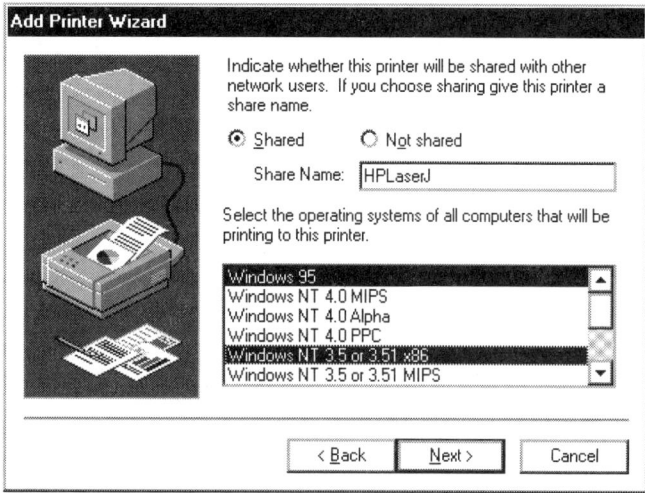

Select whether you are going to allow others to use this printer. If you are going to share the printer, you need to enter a share name. It will default to the printer name you entered previously.

You can also select additional printer drivers for other operating systems. Other computers using Microsoft Windows family operating systems can use this printer without having to install the printer drivers locally. For Windows 95 stations, if you have the proper drivers available on the server, they will download automatically when you set up an attachment to the printer.

It can be a little more difficult when supporting older operating systems as clients.

You will need to install the appropriate printer drivers on any MS-DOS, Windows, or Windows for Workgroups clients that will be attaching to the printer.

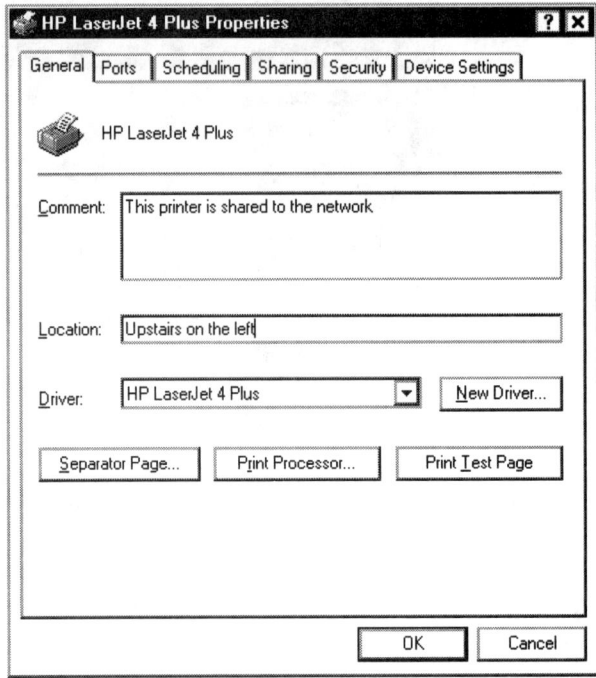

You should have an icon in the Printers folder for each printer you have defined. You can right-click on the icon and run **Properties** or double-click on the icon and run **Properties** from the **Printer** menu to modify the printer's configuration settings.

From the tabs available through this dialog you can:

- Select a different print driver.
- Print a test page.
- Select a different port or network printer.
- Enable/disable print pooling.
- Schedule when the printer is available.
- Configure sharing and alternate drivers.
- Assign printer control permissions.
- Configure printer device settings.

General

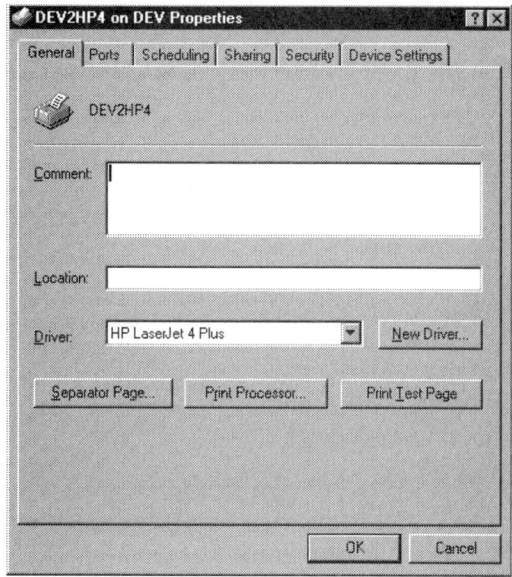

The General tab lets you add comment and location text for the printer. The current driver is displayed. Click on **New Driver** to select a different driver for the printer.

The remaining buttons are used as follows:

Separator Page	This lets you select the separate page to print between print jobs. The default is to not use a separator page.
Print Processor	You can select the print processor and default datatype through this selection.
Print Test Page	A text page will be printed, letting you run a quick test of the selected driver.

Ports

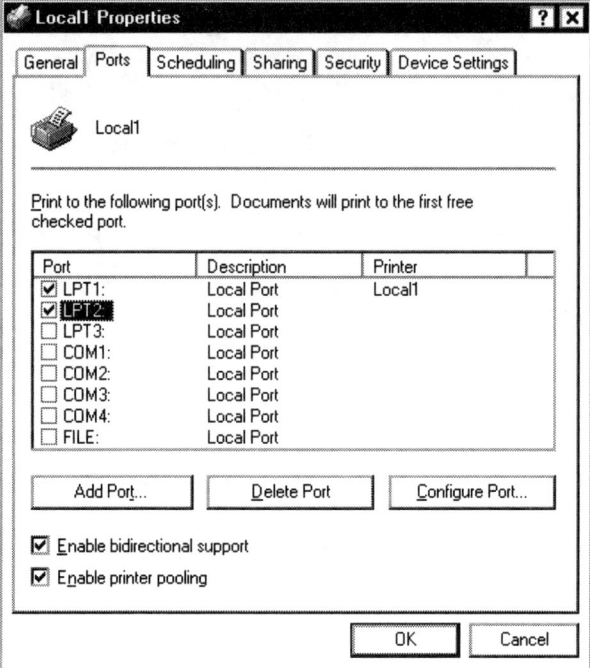

The Ports tab lets you define the output port for the printer, or ports if setting up printer pooling. Printer pooling is discussed in some detail later in this chapter.

Scheduling

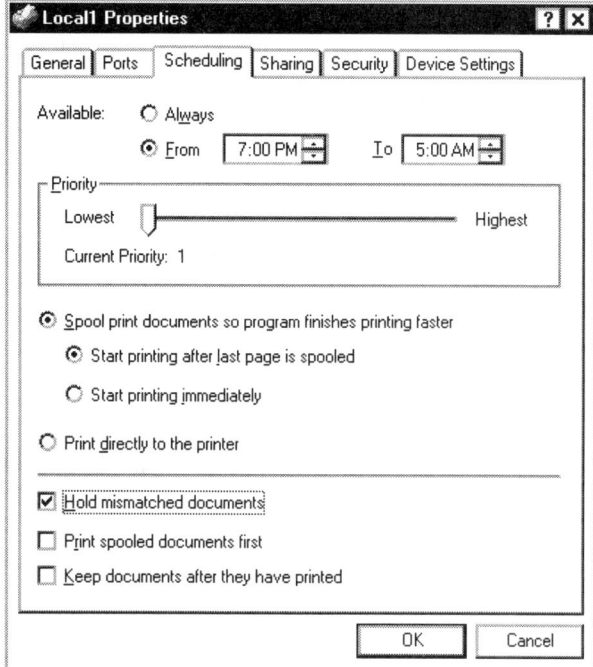

Several printing parameters are set through the Scheduling tab. The "Available" settings let you restrict use of this printer to specified times. The printer will accept and spool print jobs, then print them during the available times.

Priority settings are used when multiple printer definitions print to the same physical printer. Print jobs with the highest priority are printed first.

You will normally want to spool documents. You have the choice of waiting until a document is finished spooling before printing starts, or to start as soon as the first page is spooled. If you have programs that take a long time to complete documents or have significant pauses between pages, you will most likely want to defer printing until the entire document is spooled. Select "Print directly to the printer" to bypass spooling. This can correct some printer problems and allow you to print if you have limited space for spooling, but may lead to conflicts when printing from multiple applications.

The remaining check boxes are defined as follows:

> Hold mismatched documents
> > Printer and document setup are compared before printing. If they don't match, the document is held in the queue to be printed later.
>
> Print spooled documents first
> > This is typically the most efficient way to print. Completely spooled documents are given precedence over documents that are still spooling. If not checked, print job priorities are used to determine which document should print next.
>
> Keep documents after they have printed
> > Normally, print jobs are deleted after printing. This selection forces the documents to be held in the spooler. This gives you the option of selecting and reprinting documents. You will need to manually delete documents that are no longer needed to preserve disk space.

Set the Scheduling options as appropriate to your printing requirements.

Sharing

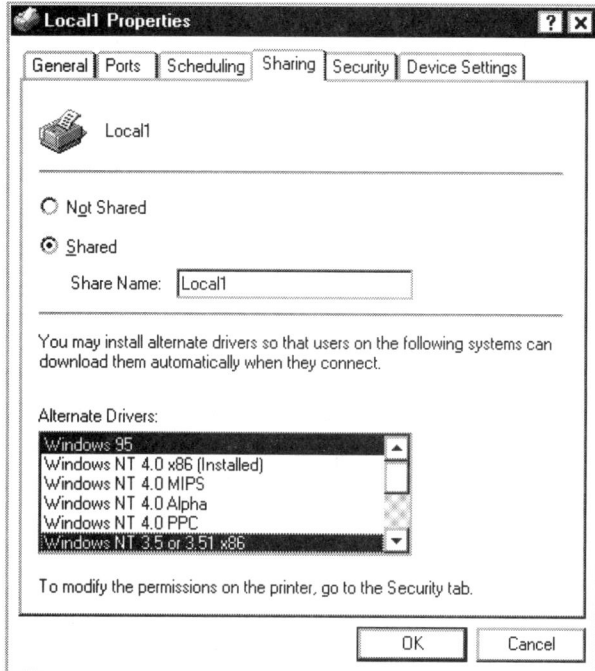

The Sharing tab lets you share the printer to the network. Share permissions are defined under the Security tab.

This is also the dialog used to install additional device drivers. Supported clients will be able to use these drivers, rather than you having to manually install the driver on each system.

Security

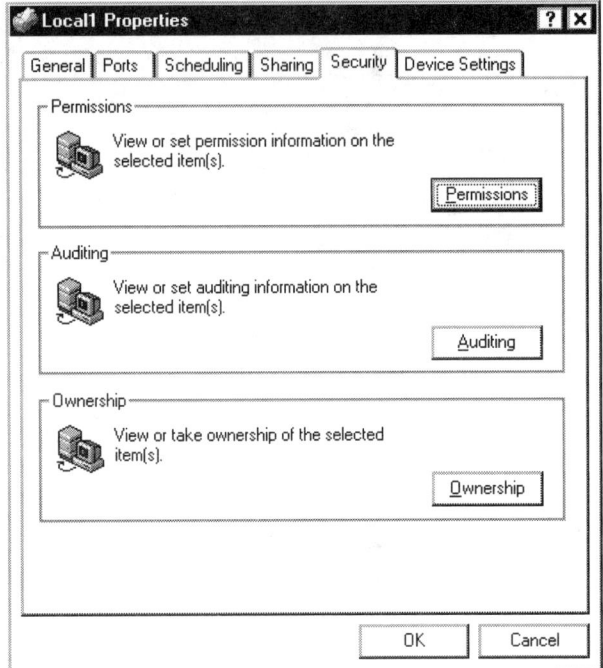

The Security tab has three selections. These are:

Permissions	Use this selection to set printer access permissions. Permissions can be set as No Access, Print, Manage Documents, and Full Control.
Auditing	Click on auditing to determine the printer events to be audited. You must first enable file and object access auditing before you can audit printer events.
Ownership	This selection lets you take over ownership of the printer.

Device Settings

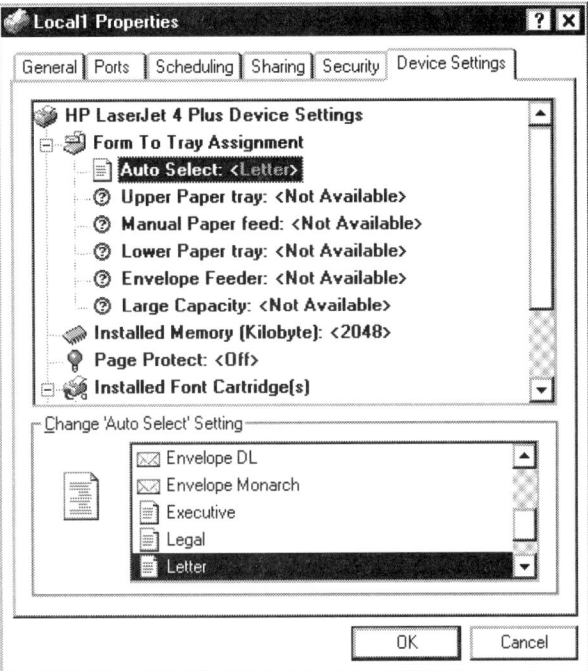

The device settings page is somewhat printer specific. The options shown in the example are typical.

Implementing Printers

Well-planned and well-executed configurations are key to printer implementation and support. Set up properly, your biggest concern will typically be making sure that consumable supplies, such as paper and toner, are available. However, a poorly planned implementation can lead to constant end-user complaints and a support nightmare.

Part of the problem is that different users will have different and sometimes conflicting requirements.

It would be impossible to discuss every possible printer configuration you might encounter. Instead, this discussion is going to look at a two key areas:

- Client support
- Special configurations

The spooler will also be discussed in a little more detail, as well as some pointers on printer optimization.

Client Support

First, you need to know understand what types of clients you will be supporting. In addition to the local workstation, which is seen by the printer monitor as a printer client, Windows NT Workstation supports an assortment of network clients:

- Windows NT
- Windows 95
- Windows v3.1/Windows for Workgroups v3.11
- MS-DOS
- UNIX

Windows NT and Windows 95 clients are relatively easy to support. You can copy the drivers locally for Windows NT v3.5, v3.51, and v4.0, as well as for Windows 95. The clients will be able to download these driver files automatically. It is important to remember that you not only need to match the operating system, but the hardware platform as well.

It will be necessary to install appropriate printer drivers locally on MS-DOS and 16-bit Windows clients. They will also need the appropriate network client software.

Remote UNIX host (LPR client) support requires TCP/IP and installation of TCP/IP Printer Services at the workstation. Windows NT Workstation does not provide support for Macintosh clients or Novell NetWare clients.

Client Connectivity

There are a number of limitations when using Windows NT Workstation as a peer print server. It has already been mentioned that support for Macintosh and NetWare clients is not provided. In addition:

- There may be no more than 10 concurrent connections.
- All connections must be within the same LAN.

Windows NT Server is usually going to be a more appropriate choice in situations where additional support is needed. Also, printing is given a higher priority on Windows NT Server. It should, therefore, provide better performance.

Special Configurations

There are a number of special situations and configuration requirements you may encounter when supporting network printers. These include:

- Multiple definitions

    You can define multiple devices for the same physical printer. While all will have the same print device driver, you can set other configuration parameters and access permissions as necessary for each.

- Printer pooling

    Printer pooling was mentioned earlier in this chapter. By combining printers into a pool, you can often improve overall throughput as well as make a temporarily unavailable printer less critical.

Let's take a look at these along with some examples of how they might be used.

Multiple Definitions

To create multiple definitions for a printer, create a new print device and select an existing device's output port. This would give you the ability to have a printer configured as a single device and part of a printer queue. Some other situations where you might want to set up multiple definitions include:

- Priorities

    Each of the printer definitions can be given a different priority. The priority is passed along to the print job. When there are multiple print jobs queued and waiting for the printer, those with the highest priority that have been waiting the longest are printed first.

- Printer scheduling

    You can set up a printer scheduled to print after-hours only. This could be used to print long, time-consuming jobs when there is less need for the printer. Other print devices could be set up for the printer with no schedule limits so that it could be used during the day for "standard" print jobs.

Both scheduling and priority are defined on the Scheduling tab of the properties dialog.

While you can set up as many definitions as you need, keep in mind these do add to your management overhead.

Pooling

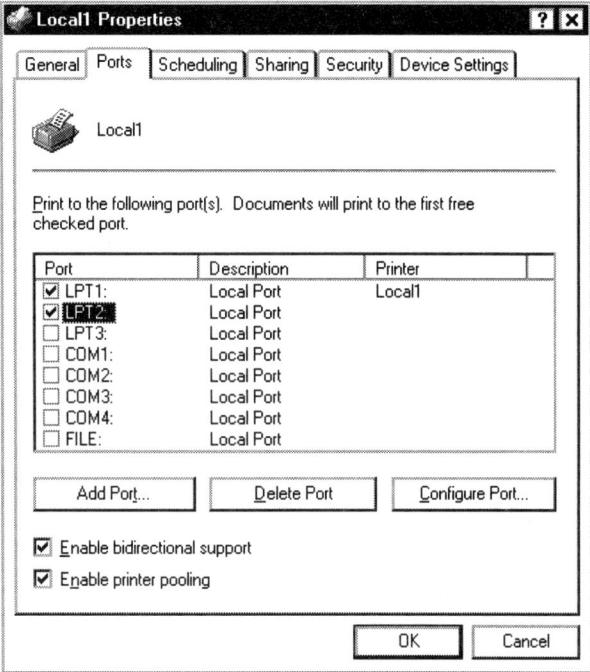

Printer pools were discussed earlier, but are deserving of some special mention. In a printer pool, you have multiple physical printers supporting the same print queue as a group. If one printer is busy, the print job is sent to the next available printer. If all of the printers are busy, the job is spooled and will be sent to the next available printer.

When setting up a printer pool:

- Both local and network (shared) printers may be included.
- All printers must use the same printer driver.
- All printers will be supported using the same configuration parameters.

It is likely that you would want to set up a printer pool on Windows NT Server rather than Windows NT Workstation. This configuration would support additional connections and typically provide better overall performance.

Printers taking part in a printer pool can also be supported as a single printer, or even as part of another printer pool.

Spooler

The local print provider component on the Windows NT print server will spool, or queue, both local print jobs and print jobs coming from remote clients. Remote clients may also spool jobs locally before passing them to the print server.

The default spooler location is:

```
\system\system32\spool\printers
```

System represents the Windows NT installation directory. You must edit the registry to change the spooler file location.

The default location, if printer-specific locations are not defined, is specified in the SpoolDirectory key under:

```
HKEY_LOCAL_MACHINE\SYSTEM\CurrentControlSet
    \Control\Print\Printers
```

To set the spool location for any specific printer, locate the key:

```
HKEY_LOCAL_MACHINE\SYSTEM\CurrentControlSet
    \Control\Print\printer_name
```

Replace *printer_name* with the name assigned the printer when it was created. Add a new SpoolDirectory value to specify the spool location. If you attempt to set the spool to the root of a drive, the value will revert to the default location.

Spooler components are Windows NT Services. You can start and stop the spooler from the Control Panel Services utility or from the command line. To stop the spooler, run:

```
net stop spooler
```

To start the spooler, run:

```
net start spooler
```

You will be unable to print while the spooler is stopped.

Printer Implementation Scenario

You have four printers installed and shared to the network. Because much of what your workgroup does is very document intensive, you've decided to set them up as a printer pool. Overall, it's worked out rather well, but there have been a few minor problems.

Some of the documents you need to print are very lengthy. They are not time-critical, but tie up the printer and delay time-critical documents during the day. Also, your boss wants to make sure that anything he prints comes out on the printer nearest his office, and he says he's tired of waiting all day for his stuff to print.

Other than these complaints, everyone seems to be relatively happy. What should you do?

Exercise 4-2

The purpose of this exercise is to give you practice working with configuration utilities. You will need access to the Windows NT Workstation installation file set to complete this exercise. You do not need a printer to complete this exercise.

1. Log on as MSmith.
2. Select **Start/Settings/Printers**.
3. Launch the Add Printer utility.

4. If not already selected, click on the **My Computer** check box, then the **Next** button.
5. Select the port **LPT1** and then the **Next** button.
6. Scroll down the list of manufacturers and select **HP**.
7. Scroll down the list of printers and select **HP LaserJet 4** then the **Next** button.

   NOTE: If you have a printer attached to your system, load the appropriate printer driver rather than the option presented here.

8. Give your printer a name. Click on the **Next** button.
9. Click on the **Shared** check box and then the **Next** button.
10. Select no, you do not want to print a test page, then select the **Finish** button.
11. NT will now attempt to find the drivers for this printer. If it cannot find them you will be prompted for the location. Provide the path to the installation files, such as, the path to the installation CD.
12. You have now installed a printer. There should be an icon for it in your **Start/Settings/Printers** window.

SUMMARY

During this chapter, you were introduced to the following:

- Add/Remove Programs utility
- Mouse properties
- Keyboard properties
- SCSI device driver setup and removal
- Tape Drive device driver management
- UPS configuration
- Display configuration
- Event View and Event Viewer logs
- Printer installation
- Printer configuration

The next chapter moves into more advanced hardware configuration issues.

POST-TEST QUESTIONS

The answers to these questions are in Appendix A at the end of the manual.

1. What aspect of Windows NT is managed through Windows NT Setup of Add/Remove programs utility?

   ....

   ....

2. When will the command file, if any, identified in the Control Panel UPS utility execute?

   ....

   ....

3. A user reports a device failure. How can you tell if the failure has occurred recently on the system?

   ....

   ....

4. What is the significance of installing additional drivers when you set up a shared printer?

   ....

   ....

5. What groups can view the security log?

   ....

   ....

6. What problem may arise from using a screen saver if you are running 16-bit applications?

   ....

   ....

CHAPTER 5

Configuration Management

MAJOR TOPICS

Objectives 206

Pre-Test Questions 206

Introduction 207

System Management 208

Additional Control Panel Utilities 218

Introduction to the Registry 234

Summary 250

Post-Test Questions 250

OBJECTIVES

At the completion of this chapter, you will be able to:

- Control Panel utilities

    Server

    System

    Date/Time

    Ports

    Multimedia

    Sounds

    Devices

    Services

    Regional Settings

    Telephony

- Configure multiple hardware profiles.
- List and explain the startup types supported for devices and services.
- Describe the purpose and use of the Windows NT registry.
- Describe the procedures to back up and restore the registry.

PRE-TEST QUESTIONS

The answers to these questions are in Appendix A at the end of this manual.

1. Under the Performance tab of the Control Panel System utility, what is the default performance boost for Windows NT Workstation?

    ....

    ....

2. You want to install the driver for a sound card. Which Control Panel utility will let you do this?

   ....

   ....

3. Critical devices that must start before any others when booting windows NT will have what as a start type under the Control Panel Devices utility?

   ....

   ....

4. What utility or utilities will let you directly edit the registry?

   ....

   ....

5. Under which registry hive would you find the current control set?

   ....

   ....

INTRODUCTION

This chapter continues looking at Control Panel and other utilities, focusing primarily on working at the system level. One of the areas where Windows NT shines is system management and configuration. Rather than using cryptic commands or configuration files with difficult to remember syntax requirements, Windows NT provides a wide array of graphical utilities which let you view and set system configuration parameters. The majority of these are located in the Control Panel, supplemented with specialized utilities such as the Disk Administrator.

This chapter focuses on some key areas relating to devices and services, including some of the operating system's core requirements. International settings receive a brief overview, so that you know where to make these configuration changes.

Configuration settings are stored in the system registry. With this in mind, the chapter takes a brief look at the registry, how it is organized, and ways to back up and protect the registry.

SYSTEM MANAGEMENT

This section will present the properties within the Control Panel System utility. You can view and modify configuration information regarding hardware and user profiles, startup/shutdown, performance, and environment here. The following are topics discussed within this section:

- Server
- System
- Performance Settings
- Environment
- Startup/Shutdown
- Recovery
- Hardware Profiles
- User Profiles

Many times, it is necessary to consider current system settings and alter configurations accordingly. As an administrator, it is especially important to understand the functions of each of these properties.

Server

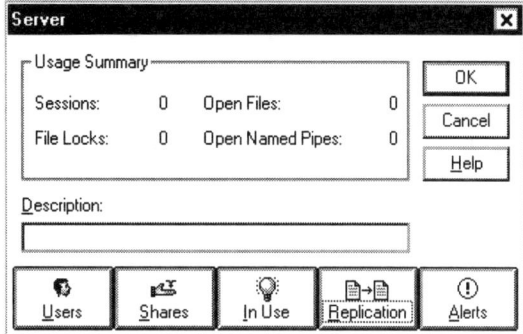

The Server icon takes you to the Server properties. Through this dialog, you can view and manage attached users, resource shares, resource usage, replication, and alerts for your station.

System

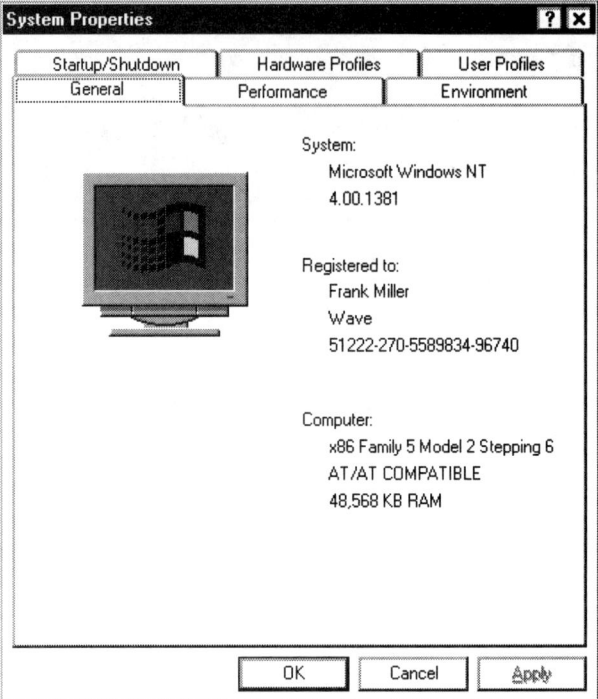

The System utility opens with the General tab displayed, which displays some summary system information. There are no parameters that can be modified on this property sheet.

Performance Settings

![System Properties Performance tab dialog showing Application Performance boost slider set to Maximum and Virtual Memory total paging file size of 48 MB]

The Performance tab lets you give foreground applications a boost in relation to background applications. The default is shown, which is the most appropriate setting for most workstations and many servers. Reducing the performance boost gives any background processes a higher relative priority. For domain controllers, as well as additional servers supporting resource intensive network-based applications, you may improve performance by reducing this value.

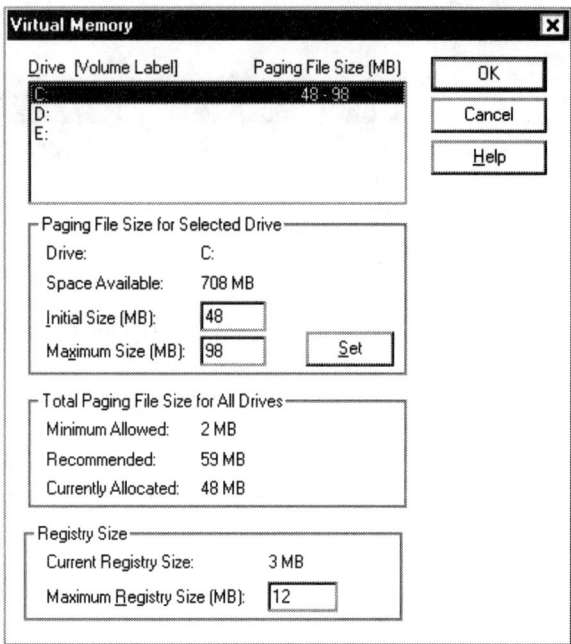

Click on **Change** to modify the virtual memory swap file settings. You can set the initial size, maximum size, and drive locations. This dialog also lets you set the maximum size of the registry.

Windows NT uses virtual memory, a combination of physical RAM and emulated memory that is physically located on one or more hard disks.

Windows NT is regularly moving pages of memory into and out of the swap file. There is a potential of this becoming a performance bottleneck. Some points to keep in mind when setting swap file locations include:

- System drive

    Even though it will be placed there initially by Setup, it is generally suggested that you not put the swap file on the same physical hard disk as the system files. This drive already tends to be somewhat active.

- Multiple files

    You can improve performance by spreading the swap file across multiple physical drives.

- Initial file size

    Monitor swap file size over a period of time. If you can determine a typical swap file size, use this as your guideline for modifying the file size.

Optimizing the swap file is often an easy and inexpensive way of tuning system performance.

Environment

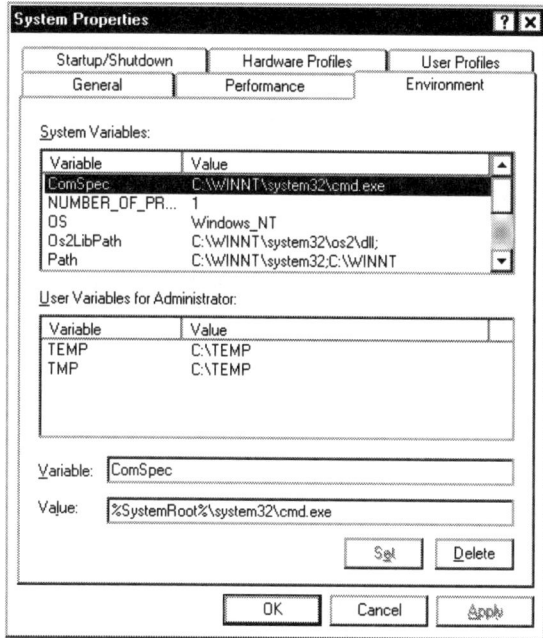

The Environment tab lets you view and modify system and user environmental variables. The upper window contains the system variables, with the user variables in the lower window.

To remove an environmental variable, click on the variable entry, then on **Delete**. To modify a variable:

- Click to select the variable.
- Edit the Variable or Value field.
- Click on **Set**.

To add an environmental variable:

- Click in the system or user window.
- Edit the Variable and Value fields.
- Click on **Set**.

The new environmental variable will be added to the list.

Startup/Shutdown

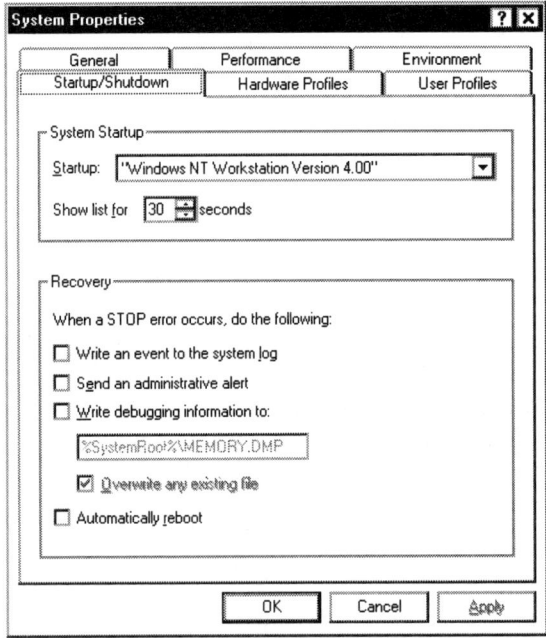

The upper portion of the Startup/Shutdown properties sheet lets you modify the default operating and set how long the selection menu is displayed before launching the default option.

If you want the operating system to boot directly into the selected operating system without prompting the user with a select menu, set the "Show list for" value to 0.

Changing these parameters will directly edit the BOOT.INI file. You can also manually edit BOOT.INI, but this is the preferred method for making changes.

The lower portion of the properties sheet lets you set the system's response to STOP errors. The server default settings are shown in the sample graphic. For a workstation, the default is for none of the recovery options to be selected.

Recovery

The System Properties Startup/Shutdown tab lets you set how the system will react to STOP errors. Your available selections are:

- Write an event to the system log.
- Send an administrative alert.
- Write debugging information to a file.
- Automatically reboot.

Windows NT will attempt to complete each of the recovery options configured for the system. You should only select those options that are significant to your system and the applications you are running.

Hardware Profiles

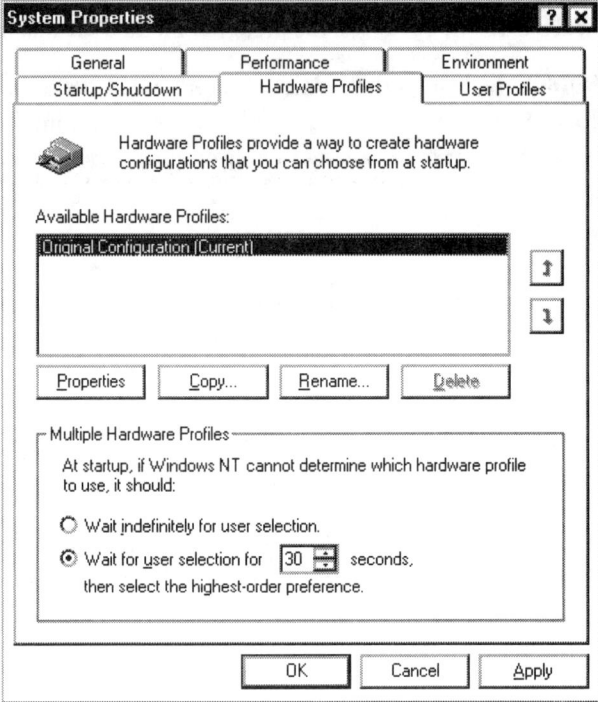

The Hardware Profiles tab lets you add, view, or modify hardware profiles.

This allows you to quickly reconfigure a system to meet changing situations. For example, you could set up hardware profiles for a portable system to act as a:

- Stand-alone system.
- Stand-alone connected to a docking station.
- Networked system connected to a docking station.

You have the option of having the system wait for the user to select a hardware profile, or have the system wait a specified time out period, then start up using the default profile. You will be prompted with your configuration options at startup. Select the configuration you want and press **ENTER**. Otherwise, the default will be selected automatically.

The system will complete startup using the selected hardware profile. After specifying multiple hardware profiles, configuration changes are made to the current profile only. This gives you a convenient back door when trying out different hardware configuration settings.

User Profiles

You've already seen the User Profiles tab. This lets you view, modify the type settings for, and delete user profiles. Profiles are identified as either local or roaming. Click to select a profile, then on **Change Type** to toggle this setting. To copy a profile to another user, select the profile, click on **Copy To**, and type in the destination username.

Profiles for users who have been deleted will still be listed, but identified as "Account Deleted" rather than the account name. To remove any profile (including deleted users), click to select the profile, then click on **Delete**. You can also define a system policy to have local copies of profiles deleted automatically when the user logs off.

ADDITIONAL CONTROL PANEL UTILITIES

This section will present additional utilities provided through the Control Panel. Some of these utilities may be used based to modify user preferences while others may be used to change system and device configurations. The following are topics discussed within this section:

- Date/Time
- Ports
- Multimedia
- Sounds
- Devices
- Working With Drivers
- Services
- Service Configuration
- Selected Service Overview
- Regional Settings
- Telephony

As changes made within some of these utilities may affect system performance, it is important to understand the features and functions of each of the utilities.

Date/Time

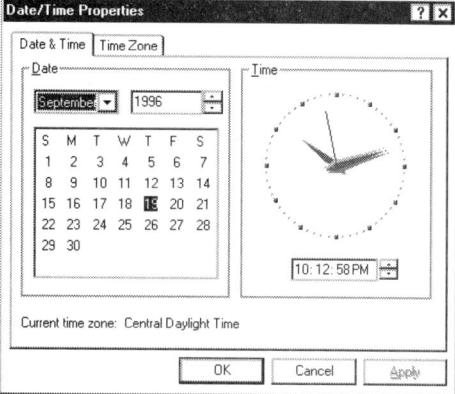

Launch the Date/Time utility to set system date, time, and time zone information.

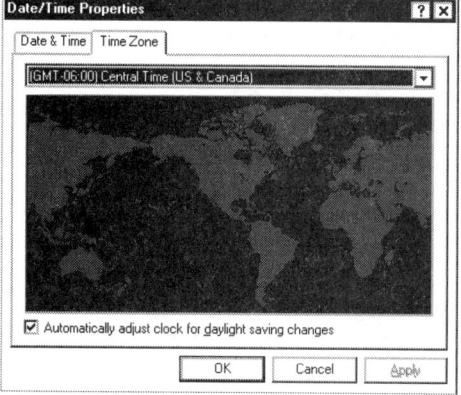

Click on the drop-down list to choose the appropriate time zone for your system. You can also set whether or not Windows NT automatically adjusts for daylight savings time.

Ports

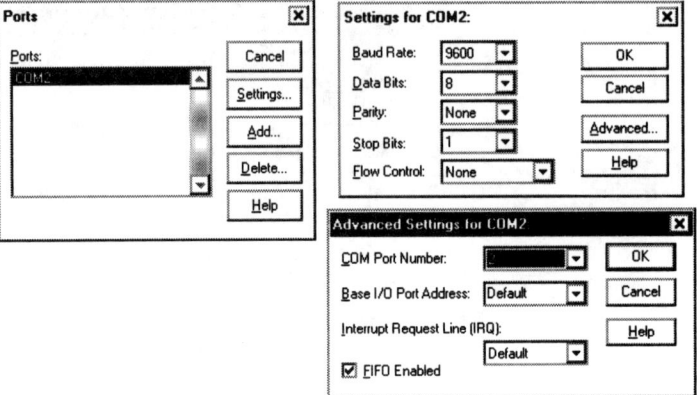

The Ports utility has not changed from earlier NT releases. It lets you view and modify COM (serial) port settings. Communications settings can be overridden through software. The Advanced Settings dialog lets you configure NT to support nonstandard COM port configuration settings.

Multimedia

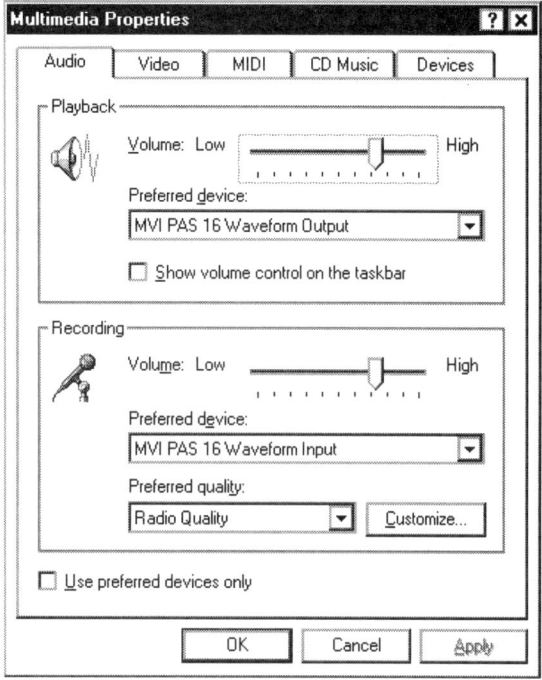

Like Windows 95, Windows NT Server is designed to support a rich multimedia environment. Unlike Windows 95, Setup will not automatically detect your sound card. You will need to install and configure the appropriate driver after installation.

The Multimedia properties dialog lets you set configuration options for:

- Audio playback and recording.
- Video playback.
- MIDI configuration.
- Audio CD playback.
- Device drivers.

Once only found in entertainment software, many commercial applications are now taking advantage of multimedia.

Sounds

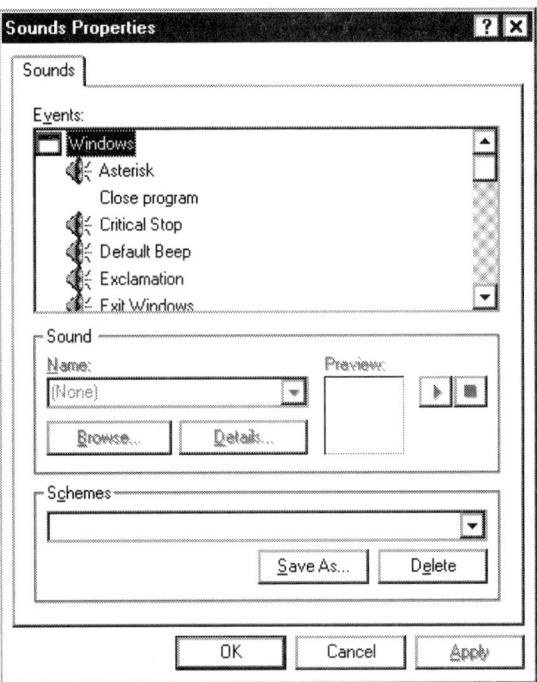

Somewhat related is the Sounds utility. The sounds utility lets you select a sounds scheme for your system, as well as test individual sounds within the scheme and change the sounds assigned to system events.

Devices

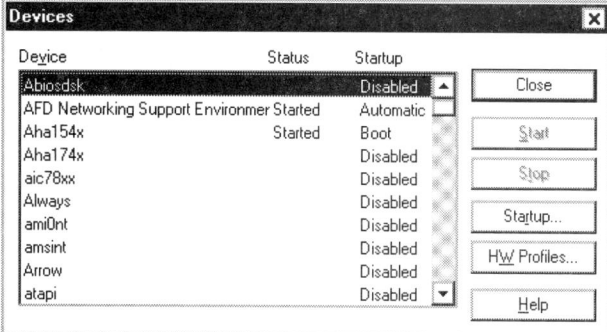

The Devices dialog lists all the device drivers supported by Windows NT. The dialog includes the driver name, current status, and startup settings. From this dialog, you can manually start device drivers, stop drivers, and set startup options.

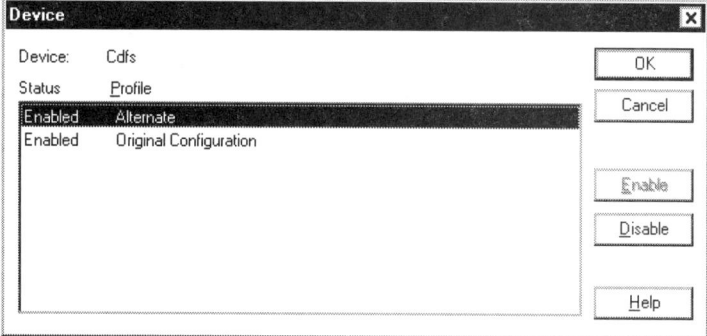

This utility also lets you customize your hardware profile. Configuration is managed by device. Select the device you want to configure and click on **HW Profiles**. All defined hardware configurations are listed. Click to choose a configuration, then on **Enable** or **Disable**.

Working With Drivers

Five startup configuration options are supported. These are:

Boot	Devices configured as boot devices will start before any others. This setting is used for devices critical to system operation, such as disk devices.
System	Systems devices are also essential to system operation, but are either less critical than or dependent on the boot devices. Devices such as network adapters fall in this category.
Automatic	Devices configured for automatic startup will start after boot and system devices. Devices such as I/O ports and network protocols fall under this category.
Manual	These devices launch on an as needed basis, either by user interaction or when called by a dependent device. Devices such as modems fall under this category.
Disabled	Disabled devices will not launch during startup and cannot be launched through user interaction. The system can launch disabled devices.

In most cases, you will not have any cause to change the startup configuration for a device. Sometimes this can result in serious problems. For example, enabling some disabled devices for which there are no driver files installed can cause Windows NT to crash during startup.

Another potential problem is that devices are often there to support one or more services. If the device doesn't start at the right time, it can keep those services from loading properly. For example, if you disabled a network adapter, any network protocols bound to that adapter would also fail during startup.

Services

[Services dialog image]

The Services dialog gives you the ability to manage and control installed services. As with drivers, you can start, stop, enable, and disable services. In addition, many services will let you pause, then later continue the service. You can customize a hardware profile by enabling or disabling services. For example, for a stand-alone hardware profile, you may want to disable network related services.

As with devices, you can set the startup type for the service. In addition, many services support option switches that control how the service launches. This is often true of applications, such as Microsoft's SQL Server, that install as a service.

Service Configuration

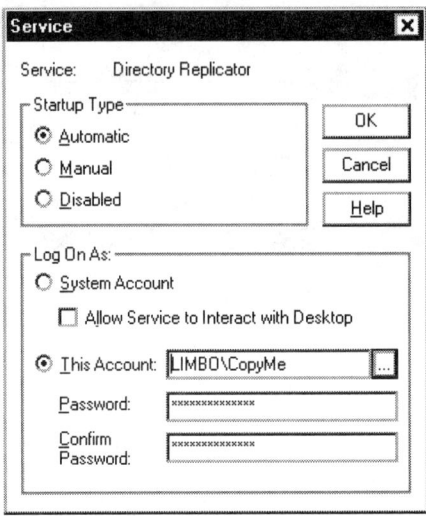

Three startup types are supported for Services. These are:

- Automatic

    Services set to automatic startup will launch when the system starts. Automatic services will not attempt to start on systems with less than 12 MB of physical RAM. These include core and other important services.

- Manual

    Manual services can be started through user interaction or by a dependent service. Services such as Telephony, Network DDE, and the ClipBook server fall under this category.

- Disabled

    If marked as disabled, the service cannot be started by a user or dependent service. For example, you would disable the Alerter service if you didn't want to receive administrative alerts at your system.

You can configure more than just the startup type for service. Many services let you specify an account to use for logon, defaulting to the local system. This sets the security focus under which the service runs. Most services log on as the system account. This setting is not appropriate for some network applications, however. In that case, you will want to have the service log on using a username. The user must have the "Log on as a service" right assigned.

Selected Service Overview

Sometimes, system problems can be traced back to a service that didn't start or has been configured improperly. Some of the services in this category include:

Alerter
: The Alerter service is used by the Server, and can be used by other services to notify specified users or machines of administrative alerts. This service is dependent on the Messenger service, that is, Messenger must be running. Disable this service to avoid receiving administrative alerts.

Computer Browser
: The Computer Browser service must be running for you to receive an up-to-date list of network computers and shared resources. If Windows NT utilities or network-aware applications do not show any other systems when a browse dialog is called, it could be that this service failed to start or was disabled.

Directory Replicator
: You've already had a brief introduction to the concept of replication. If you decide to implement replication, you will need to set this service to Automatic startup and have it log on with a username prepared for this purpose.

License Logging Service
: The License Logging Service monitors and reports on client connections.

Messenger
: The Messenger service is used to pass messages. The same service both sends and receives messages.

Net Logon
: For a domain controller to be able to validate logon attempts or to keep the domain directory database synchronized, Net Logon must be running.

Remote Procedure Call (RPC) Locater

This is used with distributed applications. A server application will register its availability with the RPC locater, where it is written into the RPC name database. Client applications will query this database to locate compatible server applications.

Remote Procedure Call (RPC) Service

This service is required if you want to support remote procedure calls (RPCs). Based on a message-passing model, it allows an application to call server applications running on other machines. One common use of RPC is remote administration.

Schedule	This service supports the AT command. The AT command lets you schedule programs to run at a specified time and date. Recurring activities, those that run on a regular schedule, are also supported.
Server	The Server service is required for a machine to provide resources and services across the network to other systems. RPC is also dependent on this service. While the name might imply that this is a server-only service, it is also supported on NT Workstations.
Spooler	Unless printing directly to a locally connected part, the Spooler manages "traffic control" on spooled documents.
Workstation	The Workstation service must be running before a machine can access shared resources.

This is one of the areas to check when encountering hard to isolate system problems.

Exercise 5-1

During this exercise, you will work with selected Control Panel utilities. You should be logged on as an administrator at the beginning of this exercise.

Use caution and follow the steps in this exercise exactly as given. Failure to do so may result in system corruption, requiring you to reinstall Windows NT Workstation.

1. Run **Start/Settings/Control Panel**.
2. Double-click on the System utility.
3. Click on the Hardware Profiles tab.
4. "Original Configuration (Current)" should be selected. Click on **Copy**.

5. Type the following as the hardware profile name and click on **OK**:

    Alternate

6. Click on **OK** to close the System properties dialog.
7. Double-click on the Services utility.
8. Locate and select the Workstation service, then click on **HW Profiles**.
9. If not highlighted, click on Alternate, then on **Disable**.
10. Click on **OK**, then on **Close** to close the Services dialog. Close the Control Panel.
11. Shut down and restart your system. Select to start Windows NT when prompted.
12. When prompted with the Hardware Profile/Configuration Recovery Menu, press ↓ to highlight Alternate, then press **ENTER**.
13. Log onto the workstation as Administrator. With the Workstation service disabled, there may be a long delay before your desktop displays.
14. You will receive a message that at least one service or driver failed to start. Click on **OK**.
15. Double-click on the Network Neighborhood icon.
16. Double-click on **Entire Network**, then on **Microsoft Windows Network**. You will receive a message that the system is unable to browse the network because it is not started.

    You cannot browse the network or access network resources because the Workstation service didn't start.

17. Close all open windows, shut down, and restart your system. Using the procedures described earlier, select to start your Original Configuration and log on as Administrator.
18. Launch the Control Panel and open the Services utility.
19. Locate the Workstation service, click to select, and click on **HW Profiles**.
20. If not highlighted, click on **Alternate**, then on **Enable**.
21. Click on **OK**, then on **Close**.
22. Double-click on the Devices utility.

23. Locate and select the Disk device, then click on **HW Profiles**.
24. If not highlighted, click on **Alternate**, then on **Disable**.
25. Click on **OK**, then on **Close**, and close the Control Panel.
26. Shut down and restart your system using the Alternate hardware configuration.
27. You will get a "blue screen" error during startup, with the error code telling you that it was due to an inaccessible boot device.
28. Turn your system off and back on, and start up using the Original Configuration. The system should start up normally.
29. Delete your alternate configuration.

Regional Settings

The Regional Settings properties lets you configure for use in countries other than the United States. Many applications will query Windows NT for its regional settings and configure themselves appropriately. You can also set:

- The format to display numbers, decimals, and positive and negative values.
- Currency symbols and formats.
- Time and date format.
- Input locale and default keyboard layout.

The ability to change these settings quickly and easily is especially useful when testing applications for international distribution.

Telephony

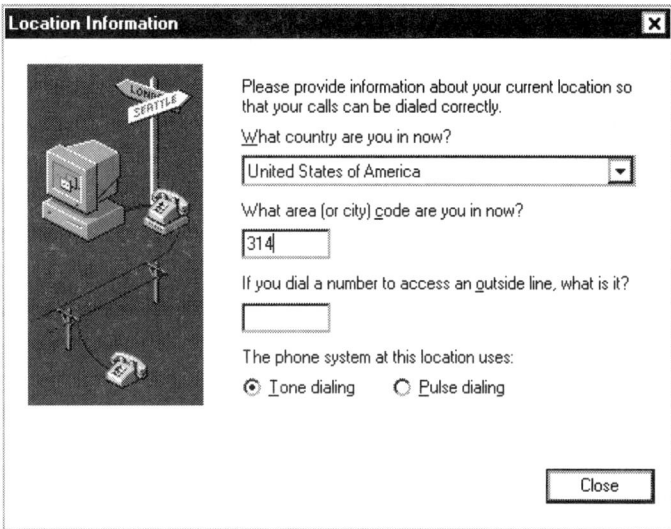

The Telephony utility lets you configure the system so that the Telephony API (TAPI) is supported for applications such as the phone dialer and remote access services (RAS) dial out. The first time you launch the utility, you are taken through a configuration wizard. You are prompted for your location, area code, code for an outside line, and whether to use pulse or tone dial.

You can configure your system to support multiple locations. While not significant for most servers or desktop workstations, it can save a lot of time and headache on portable machines. The dialog prompts you for information on how dialing should be handled from the location. The "I am dialing from" drop-down list lets you select from your defined locations. Click on **New** to create a new definition, or on **Remove** to delete the currently displayed definition.

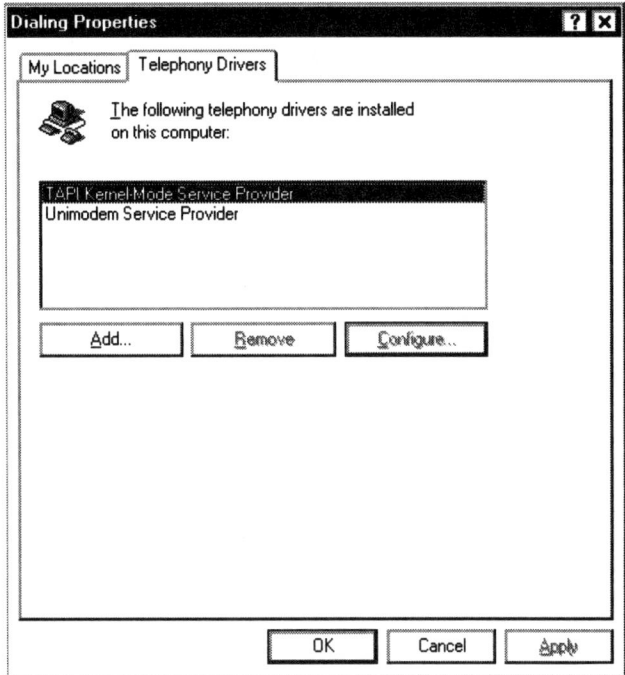

The Telephony Drivers provided with Windows NT are shown in the sample graphic. You must define your modem before you can set configuration options for the Unimodem Service Provider. To install a manufacturer-provided driver, click on **Add**, then on **Have Disk** at the Add Driver dialog.

Modem setup and configuration is discussed later in the course.

Configuration Scenario

A proposed solution to this scenario is available in Appendix A at the end of the manual.

You have Windows NT Workstation installed on a laptop computer. When you boot the system while at work, you want to have it configured as a local client. That is how the system is currently configured.

When working at home, you want the system to be configured as a RAS client, dialing in to the network for access. You want all local area network devices disabled while working at home.

How would you set up your system to meet these specifications?

....

....

INTRODUCTION TO THE REGISTRY

This section will introduce the basics of the Registry. The structure of the Registry will be discussed to better understand the interface and use of this utility. The following are topics discussed within this section:

- Registry
- System Components and the Registry
- Registry Local Organization
- Registry Keys and Values
- Value Entries
- Registry Key
- Control Sets
- Modifying the Registry
- Registry Editors
- REGEDIT
- REGEDT32

- Registry and .INI Files
- Registry Backup
- Registry Recovery

As we have been discussing system and device configurations, it is important to note that during that same time, appropriate registry entries are also created. The Registry is a very important informative tool available to you.

Registry

Windows NT has to keep up with a great deal of information. It has to track system hardware information, device drivers, system-wide configuration, user specific configurations, startup information, even the startup order for devices and services. This is done through a special database known as the registry.

The Windows NT registry is somewhat similar to the initialization files (.INI files) used with DOS Windows.

In fact, if you install Windows NT in an existing Windows directory, existing .INI file information can be migrated automatically to the registry. This is user specific, with the user prompted to decide whether or not .INI file information should be migrated the first time he or she logs on at a station.

There are, however, several differences between DOS Windows initialization files and the registry. The registry holds a great deal more detailed information with hundreds of available parameters. It is also formatted differently. A special utility is required for editing the registry, and registry entries must follow a precise format.

Most registry entries are managed indirectly. Each time you make device configuration changes through the Control Panel, corresponding registry entries are made to a user's environment. These changes are reflected in the registry.

System Components and the Registry

The registry interacts with various components in the Windows NT operating system. Some provide information to the registry; others use the registry as an information source, while still others do both.

Setup
: Running Windows NT Setup, Windows NT application installations, or hardware setup routines adds appropriate configuration information to the registry database.

Kernel
: Each time you start Windows NT, the kernel (NTOSKRNL.EXE) passes kernel information to the registry, such as the kernel version. The kernel reads configuration information from the registry relating to startup, such as device drivers, and the order in which they should be loaded.

Hardware Recognizer
: During startup, Windows NT builds a list of the hardware installed in your system. This information is then loaded into the registry database. On x86 systems, this data is gathered by NTDETECT.COM and the Windows NT kernel. The configuration is extracted from the ARC firmware on RISC-based systems.

Hardware Device Drivers
: Each device driver reports system resources that it uses, such as IRQ, DMA, and so forth, to be recorded in the registry database. They also send initial load parameters and other configuration data to the registry. This information is read on each successive load, the data acting like DEVICE= statements in a DOS environment. Applications and device drivers can also read this information as a reference for installation and configuration programs.

Administrative Tools
: Windows NT provides administrative tools for modifying the registry database, such as those in the Administrative Tools submenu and the utilities in the Control Panel. The Registry Editor (covered later in this chapter) is used to view or make detailed edits to the registry.

Registry Logical Organization

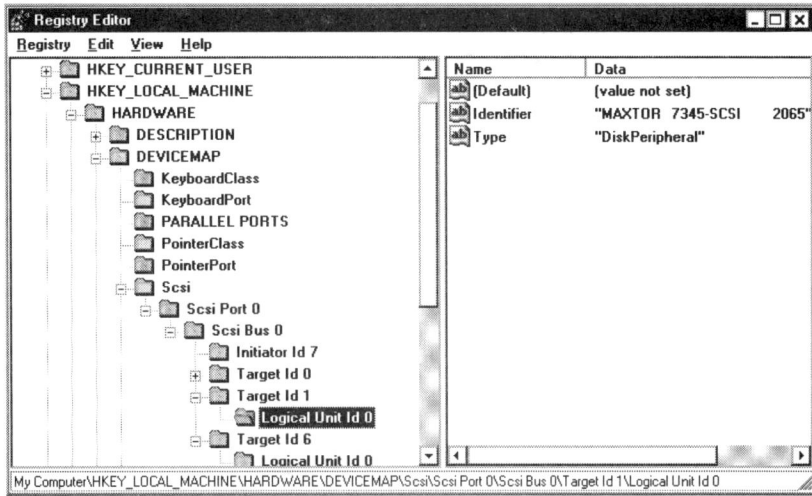

The registry is based on a hierarchical structure. First, there are the registry sub-trees that contain user- and computer-unique configuration data. Beneath each of these, you have keys and subkeys, which form a logical organization for the configuration data. Finally, you have the key values, defining the registry parameters. There are hundreds of key entries available for the registry.

For physical storage, the registry is organized into hives which contain the keys, subkeys, and values making up the registry. Each hive has a data file and a .LOG file. The hives are stored under:

   system\SYSTEM32\CONFIG

System represents the Windows NT system directory.

Registry Keys and Values

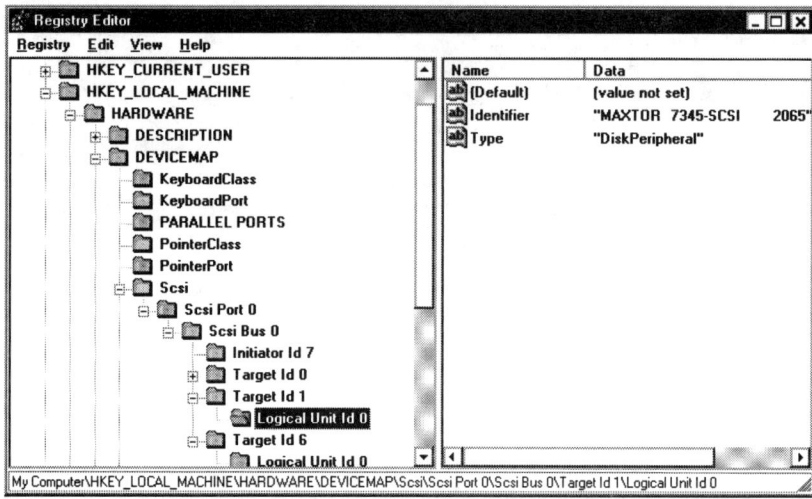

Data in each of the registry subtrees is organized in a hierarchical structure of keys and subkeys. As you can see in our example, some keys contain subkeys, and others contain key values.

Each registry value entry is listed as a string consisting of three parts. The general syntax for this string is:

```
Name: Data_type: Value
```

For example, the value entry defining the default username for logon could appear as:

```
DefaultUserName: REG_SZ: Fmiller
```

Value Entries

The value entries must exactly match the syntax format. The possible contents of each component is also defined.

The Name value will be a Unicode character string of up to 16,000 characters and can contain backslash (\) characters. The name can be a null string, displayed as <No name>.

The Registry Editor supports five specific data types, REG_BINARY, REG_DWORD, REG_EXPAND_SZ, REG_MULTI_SZ, and REG_SZ. Programs may define other data types.

The value can contain data in any format, including arbitrary strings and raw binary data. The value size can be up to 1 MB (except for REG_DWORD). If the value size is larger than 2048 bytes, it is suggested that the data be stored in a file and the file name be stored as the registry value.

Case is preserved as you type value entry information, but is not always used. Name entries are not case sensitive.

Value entries may be case sensitive, depending upon what they define and how the program using the entry treats the data.

Registry Key

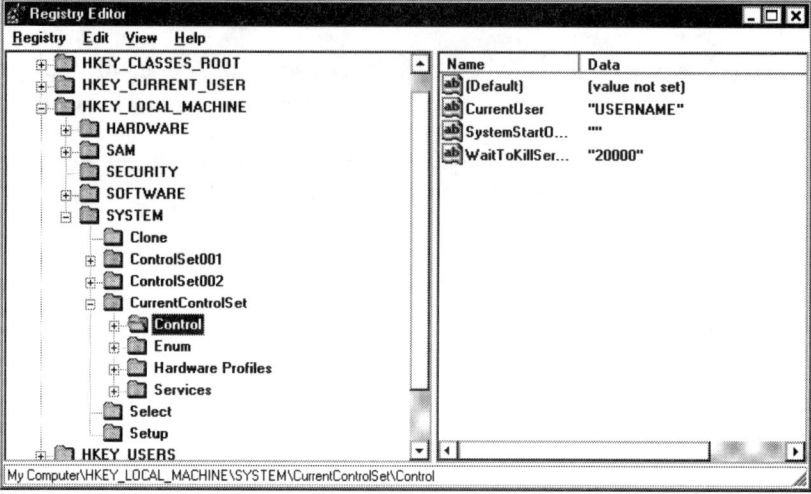

Let's take a look at an example of key values, specifically the control sets controlling system startup. These control sets contain values for control sets used to launch the current session, the set to be used the next time Windows NT launches, the last known good configuration, and the failing configuration if LastKnownGood was used to launch the system.

Each control set contains the following subkeys:

Control	This subkey contains data used to control the system.
Enum	This subkey tracks detailed device information and legacy error information.
Hardware Profiles	Each configured hardware profile is represented under this subkey
Services	This subkey contains driver, file system, service programs, and virtual hardware key information.

The control set keys are identified as follows:

Clone	This is a clean copy of the control set that was used to start the system.
ControlSetnnn	The system will store up to four control sets, identified by replacing nnn with the values 001 through 004. In these, Windows NT stores the current control set, the default control set, LastKnownGood, and a failed set, if any.
CurrentControlSet	This is actually a symbolic link to the control set identified under the Select subkey as the current control set.
Select	This works with the ControlSetnnn subkeys to identify the control set. Each is identified by its control set number value.

Control Sets

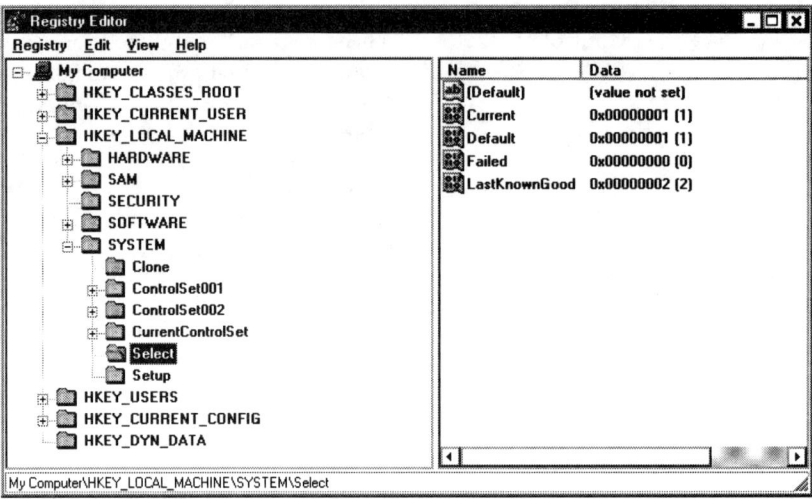

Click on the Select key to view its contents and see how the control sets are defined. You will typically see entries for:

Current	This is the control set that was most recently used to start the operating system.
Default	This is the control set that will be used the next time you start the operating system. Unless you have recently made configuration changes, the Current and Default values will be the same.
Failed	This is the control set that most recently resulted in a failed startup, if any.
LastKnownGood	This is the control set that will be invoked if you use the Last Known Good selection the next time you start up your system.

Modifying the Registry

There are two basic ways of modifying the registry. These are:

- Indirect

    This is accomplished through configuration utilities, such as the Control Panel utilities, or through defined policies.

- Direct

    This is accomplished through use of one of the registry editors.

Whenever possible, it is generally preferred that you modify the registry through indirect editing. There will be some situations, however, where you will need to manipulate the registry directly.

> *WARNING!*
> *Use extreme caution when directly editing the registry.*

You can also modify the registry through the registry mode of the system policy editor. This falls in sort of a gray area in that you are directly changing the registry, but only selected keys and only to supported values.

Registry Editors

As mentioned earlier Windows NT ships with two registry editors:

- REGEDIT.EXE

    This editor uses a user interface similar to the explorer with all hives and keys listed in the same window.

- REGEDT32.EXE

    This editor opens a separate window for each hive.

These can be launched the same as any other application. It is strongly suggested, however, that you not create a program item or desktop icon for either.

Either editor can be used to view or modify the registry contents. Either can be used to edit local or remote registries. There are some differences, however, in what the editors can do. Each deserves a special look.

REGEDIT

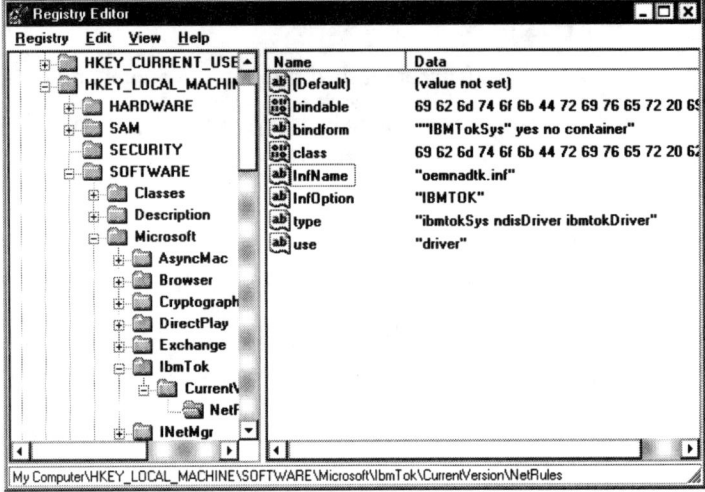

Regedit displays the entire registry as a single tree structure. Keys are listed in the left pane and key values are listed in the right. This editor has enhanced search capabilities when compared to Regedt32, letting you search key values for text strings.

If you export a key using Regedit, it is exported as a text file. This file can be stored as a backup to the registry values, or you can edit the file then import it back into the registry.

The **Connect Network Registry** command in the **Registry** menu lets you connect to a remote computer. The registries for all connected computers will be displayed.

REGEDT32

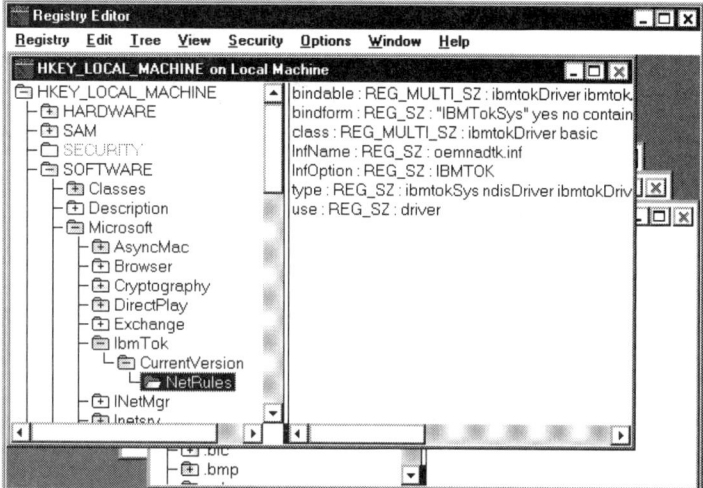

Regedt32 saves key values as compressed files, similar to their native format on disk. It can also only retrieve files in that format. Its search capabilities are somewhat limited, only letting you search for keys, not values.

An area where Regedt32 has greater functionality than Regedit is security. You can set permissions on keys, audit keys and subkeys, and change ownership. You can also set Regedt32 in a Read-only mode, letting you view values without accidentally making changes.

The **Select Computer** command in the **Registry** menu lets you connect to and modify the registry for a remote computer. You can only view or modify one computer's registry at a time.

Registry and .INI Files

Mapping Keys

If you installed Windows NT into an existing Windows directory, you have the option of importing .INI file information into the registry. The registry contains a mapping of each of the areas represented in the registry, and by what key. This information is located in HKEY_LOCAL_MACHINE, at:

```
\System\Microsoft\Windows NT\CurrentVersion\IniFileMapping
```

Subkeys below this key represent .INI files. The value entries for each of these locate where settings under the file headers were written into the registry.

Applications that use the Profile API to generate .INI information when installed under Windows NT will automatically generate registry entries.

The data portion of each of the value entries under the IniFileMapping key starts with a mapping key value. This describes how the entry is managed and helps to locate the key entry described.

!	This symbol forces all writes to both the registry and the original .INI file.
#	This symbol causes the registry value to be set to the DOS Windows .INI file value each time a new user logs into the system.
@	This is used to prevent reads from going to an existing .INI file if the data requested is not in the registry.
USR	This value identifies the key as being located in HKEY_CURRENT_USER.
SYS	This value identifies the key as being located in HKEY_LOCAL_MACHINE\System.

Registry Backup

Since Windows NT depends so heavily upon the registry, it is important that this data be backed up on a regular basis. You have several methods available for doing this:

- Windows NT Backup

    The Windows NT Backup utility has a selection to back up the local registry files. This is the suggested method for backing up registry files. NT Backup requires a supported SCSI tape drive.

    NOTE: If you back up registry files through Windows NT Backup, you must be able to boot Windows NT to restore the registry.

- Emergency Repair Diskette

    If you update the Emergency Repair diskette, either through the **Disk Administrator** or with **RDISK**, critical registry information is copied to the diskette.

- From a different operating system

    You cannot copy registry hive files from Windows NT since the files are open while NT is running. You can, however, start up from a different operating system and copy the files to a different directory or diskette. The operating system used for startup must support the file system for the partition on which the registry is stored.

- Export Registry File

    The **Export Registry File** selection in the Registry Editor's **Registry** menu. This will copy a selected registry branch, or all registry branches, to a specified disk location.

Registry Recovery

Backup copies of registry files can be used to restore the registry in case of damage, corruption, or improper edits. Depending on the situation, it may be necessary to reinstall Windows NT before you can launch Windows NT.

The recovery method used depends on how the files were backed up to external media.

- From tape

    The Windows NT Backup utility can be used to restore registry files backed up to tape. This method requires that you be able to boot Windows NT.

- From the Emergency Repair diskette

    One of the repair options is to recover the registry files. Keep in mind that the registry files reflect those present on the system the last time the Emergency Repair diskette was updated. It may be necessary to manually reenter any recent configuration changes.

- From files

    If you backed up the registry by starting up from an alternate operating system, the same method can be used to restore the files. Start up from the alternate operating system and copy the files to the \SYSTEM\SYSTEM32\CONFIG directory.

- From import Registry File

    Run **Import Registry File** from the **Registry** menu to import a copy of the registry file. The file will be imported and applied to the registry currently being edited.

Exercise 5-2

During this exercise, you will work with the Registry Editor to make changes to your system's registry. You will need to be logged on as an administrator at the beginning of this exercise.

1. Select **Start/Run**.
2. Type the following in the Open: prompt and click on **OK**:

    ```
    regedit
    ```

3. Click to expand HKEY_LOCAL_MACHINE.
4. Click to expand SYSTEM.

5. Click on Select. Record the current control set below:
6. Expand the current control set, then the Control subkey.
7. Expand ComputerName and click on ActiveComputerName. Your system's name should be listed.
8. Collapse the ComputerName subkey.
9. Scroll down, locate, and click on the Windows subkey.

   This will display directory and error mode information.
10. Collapse the Control subkey and expand the Services subkey.
11. Record the Start value below:

    If this value has never been modified on your system, there may be no current value.
12. Launch the Control Panel and open the Services utility.
13. Locate and select the Directory Replicator service and click on **Startup**.
14. Click on the Startup Type option button for "Automatic".
15. Click on **OK**, then on **Close**, and close the Control Panel.
16. Bring the Registry Editor into the foreground and press   to refresh the display.
17. Record the \Replicator\Start value below:

    Compare this value with the one recorded in step 11.
18. Click on Start in the right-hand window and run **Modify** from the **Edit** menu. Change the value to 3 and click on **OK**. Close the Registry.
19. Shut down and restart your system.
20. Log on as Administrator.
21. Open the Control Panel and launch the Services utility. Verify that Directory Replicator is set for Manual startup.
22. Close the Control Panel.

SUMMARY

During this chapter, you were introduced to the following:

- Control Panel
- Server Utility
- System Utility
- Performance settings
- Swap files
- Environmental settings
- Startup and Shutdown
- Hardware profiles
- User profiles
- Date/Time settings
- Multimedia
- Devices
- Services
- Registry

POST-TEST QUESTIONS

The answers to these questions are in Appendix A at the end of this manual.

1. What is the significance of the control set identified as LastKnownGood?

   ....

   ....

2. Which Control Panel utility lets you modify the virtual memory swap file size?

   ....

   ....

3. In general terms, how can you easily manage configurations for a laptop system that is sometimes used as a stand-alone system and the rest of the time is mounted in a docking station that is connected to the network?

....

....

4. What is required if you want to use the Windows NT Backup utility to back up the registry?

....

....

5. To what value should the BOOT.INI delay ("Show list") value be set if you want to boot directly into the default selection?

....

....

6. What startup settings are supported for services?

....

....

CHAPTER 6

Disk and File Management

MAJOR TOPICS

Objectives 254

Pre-Test Questions 254

Introduction 255

Using Disk Administrator 256

Resource Management 264

Introduction to Windows NT Explorer and Access
Security 268

Summary 285

Post-Test Questions 286

OBJECTIVES

At the completion of this chapter, you will be able to:

- List the tasks that can be performed with the Disk Administrator.
- Compare and contrast FAT and NTFS file systems.
- Format a disk partition as NTFS.
- Explain the affect file copy and file move have on access permissions in an NTFS partition.
- Establish and test local access permissions.

PRE-TEST QUESTIONS

The answers to these questions are in Appendix A at the end of this manual.

1. You installed a new disk drive. You want to create one partition on the drive through Disk Administrator, identifying the entire drive as a primary partition. What Disk Administrator command do you run?

   ....

   ....

2. A stripe set without parity requires at least _____ physical drives.

   ....

   ....

3. What is the command line command to format drive E: as NTFS?

   ....

   ....

4. Which file system or file systems support local access security?

   ....

   ....

5. You move a file from one directory to another on the same disk partition. Will the directory's permission settings reflect those of the source or destination directory?

....

....

INTRODUCTION

One of the primary areas of resource management is that of disk and file management. Because of this, we are taking time to place a special emphasis on these management areas.

The primary tool for working with disks and disk partitions is the Disk Administrator. This graphic tool replaces the MS-DOS FDISK program. In fact, more than just replacing FDISK, Disk Administrator is a much more powerful and flexible tool. Not only can it establish and delete disk partitions and logical drives, it allows you to manage custom disk volumes and disk fault tolerance features. You can even format your hard disks from within the Disk Administrator.

The primary tools for file and directory management is the Windows NT Explorer and My Computer. Both let you perform common file maintenance functions, manage shared directories, manage network directories, and manage local or attached printer resources.

During this chapter, you will have a chance to see the capabilities of both of these utilities and to get some hands-on experience using them.

USING DISK ADMINISTRATOR

This section will introduce the menu options available in the Disk Administrator tool. Disk Administrator is one of the available administrative tools installed with Windows NT. This tool allows you to work with disks and disk partitions. The following are topics discussed within this section:

- Disk Administrator
- Disk Administrator Menus
- Standard File Systems
- Volume Sets
- FORMAT Command

Disk partitions may be created and formatted in Disk Administrator. Preventative measures against disk failures may also be taken here. As you will see, an Administrator may have full control over all disk configurations.

Disk Administrator

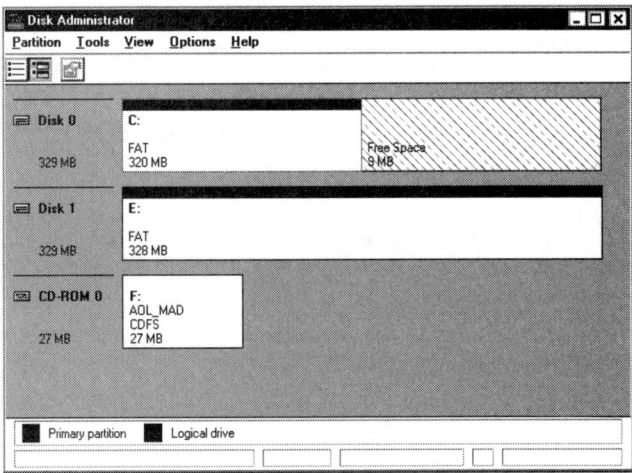

Disk Administrator gives you complete control over disk drive configurations. You can create or delete disk partitions and logical drives. You can assign drive IDs to meet your particular needs or preferences. You can create logical disk volumes and stripe sets. Windows NT Server also supports mirrored pairs and stripe sets with parity.

Under Windows NT, any partition may be formatted using either of the supported file systems: FAT, or NTFS. File systems are covered in detail later in this chapter.

Disk Administrator Menu

The **Partition** menu contains basic partition and volume management commands:

Create	This command will create a primary disk partition from selected free space.
Create Extended	This command will create an extended disk partition from selected free space.
Delete	This command will delete a selected partition, volume, or logical drive. If you delete a partition or volume, all information in the partition or volume is lost.
Create Volume Set	Use this selection to create a disk volume from selected free space.
Extend Volume Set	This command lets you add additional free space to an existing volume, increasing its size.
Create Stripe Set	The Create Stripe Set command creates a stripe set, but does not include RAID 5 parity stripes. Creating a stripe set requires at least 2 drives. Do not confuse this command with the Fault Tolerance menu's "Create Stripe Set with Parity" command.
Mark Active	This command identifies a selected partition on an x86-based system as the active, or bootable partition.
Configuration	This command lets you save the current configuration, restore backed up configuration information, or search for a different configuration. You can use this selection to update your Emergency Repair diskette.

Commit Changes Now	
	This command lets you commit changes you have made to disk configurations without having to exit Disk Administrator.
Exit	This command exits Disk Administrator. If you have made any changes, your system will restart automatically.

The **Fault Tolerance** menu lets you define and manage fault tolerance features. **Fault Tolerance** menu selections are only available when using Disk Administrator to manage disk storage on a Windows NT Server system. Fault tolerance features are supported on both domain controllers and servers installed as additional servers.

> NOTE: *Fault Tolerance selections are only supported on Windows NT Server.*

Establish Mirror	This command will create a mirrored pair from a selected disk partition, copying its data to a selected area of free space.
Break Mirror	Use this command to end the mirroring between drives. After breaking the mirror, each can be used as a separate partition.
Create Stripe Set with Parity	
	This command will create a stripe set with parity from selected free space. At least three drives must be selected for this command to be available.
Regenerate	Use this command, after repairing a failing stripe set, to tell Windows NT Server to regenerate the data on the repaired or replaced drive.

The **Tools** menu contains format and labeling commands.

Format	This command will format the selected partition using the file system you select, either FAT or NTFS.
Assign Drive Letter	This command lets you assign a drive letter you select to a partition, logical drive, or CD-ROM.
Eject	This command lets you eject a CD-ROM from the drive.
Properties	This command lets you display properties sheet for the selected partition.

The **View** menu lets you switch between volumes view and disk Configuration view.

The **Options** menu lets you determine if the status bar, tool bar, and legend are displayed. You can also set the identifying colors and patterns, how region displays are sized, and customize the tool bar.

Standard File Systems

The computer's role, costs, and company policies all influence system configuration. A critical database server would be a good candidate for fault tolerance. On the other hand, a backup domain controller whose only purpose is helping with logon validation probably would not need fault tolerance.

Disk partitions are created through the Disk Administrator. When you launch Disk Administrator, you will see available disk devices, including current partition settings and any available free space. Hard disks that have been configured through Disk Administrator but have failed or are unavailable will typically be represented, but labeled as Unavailable.

> NOTE: *The first time you run Disk Administrator after adding a drive, you may be prompted to write a signature on the disk. This does not affect the usability of the disk under other operating systems.*

To define a disk partition, click to select an area of free space and run **Create** or **Create Extended** from the **File** menu. The **Create** command will create a primary partition, **Create Extended** will create an extended partition. Disk Administrator will prompt for the partition size, defaulting to the total selected space. Accept the size as prompted or type in a smaller size and click on **OK**. If you create an extended partition, you will need to run **Create** from the **File** menu to create a logical drive.

Run **Commit Change Now** from the **Partition** menu. Otherwise, you will have to shut down and restart the system before you can format the partition. Select the new partition, which will be labeled as Unknown and run **Format** from the **Disk** menu. When the Format dialog appears, select either FAT or NTFS and click on **Start**. The "Quick Format" check box disables scanning for bad sectors during the format. When the Done Formatting dialog appears, the partition is ready for use.

Volume Sets

Volume sets allow you to combine file space from different hard disks, or even different areas on the same hard disk, into one large logical drive. This is treated as any other drive. The volume can be formatted with any of the supported file systems. File blocks are assigned normally, filling the first disk area, then working across to the next.

You can extend an existing volume without data loss. If any part of the volume becomes damaged or unavailable, you will be unable to access any of the volume.

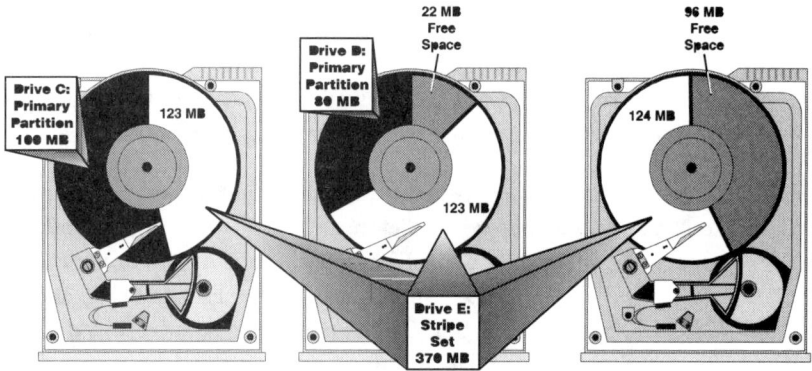

As with a volume set, a stripe set allows you to combine disk space from multiple drives into one large logical partition. Between 2 and 32 drives can be placed in one stripe set. Each segment of the set must, however, be about the same size, due to how a stripe set is organized. The segment on each drive will be based on the smallest segment selected. Once defined, the stripe set can be formatted as FAT or NTFS.

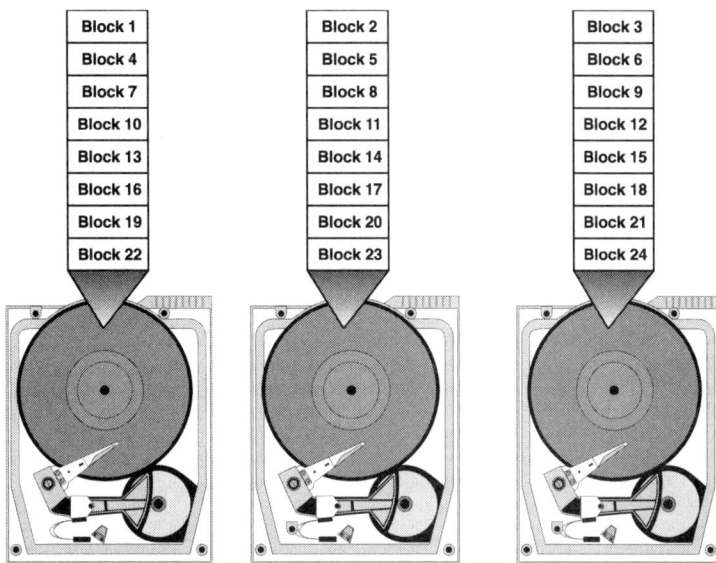

Stripe sets are based on the same idea as RAID disk configurations, without the parity that allows for error detection and recovery. In a stripe set, data blocks are set up so they are spread across all the drives in the stripe set. This provides better performance, since most disk read and write operations are split across multiple drives rather than having to manage the entire file on one drive.

FORMAT Command

After you create a logical partition, volume, or stripe set, you must format the partition before it can be used. Drives may be formatted through the Disk Administrator or with the FORMAT command.

You must use the FORMAT command to format drives, volume sets, or stripe sets after definition.

```
FORMAT d: [options]
```

Replace *d:* with the drive ID of the disk you wish to format.

> *NOTE: Floppy disks can also be formatted through the NT Explorer and My Computer utilities.*

Format is controlled through option switches:

/FS: *type*	The /FS switch is used to specify the file system as FAT or NTFS. The default system is FAT.
/A:unitsize	This option sets the allocation unit size (block size) for an NTFS file system. Unit size is specified in bytes, either 512 (default if disk <512 MB), 1024 (default if disk is 512 MB - 1 GB), 2048 (default if drive is 1 GB - 2 GB), or 4096 (default if drive is over 2 GB).
/V:label	The /V: switch lets you specify the volume label. If you do not specify a label, you will be prompted to enter one when FORMAT completes.
/Q	You should only use the Quick Format option on previously formatted disks of known good quality. The file table and root directory are deleted, but the media surface is neither formatted nor verified.
/T:n	The /T switch lets you specify the number of tracks for formatting the disk.
/N:n	Use /N to specify the number of sectors per track.
/F:size	The /F switch is used to specify floppy disk size and density to insure a proper format. Valid sizes are: 160, 180, 320, 360, 720, 1.2, 1.44, 2.88, or 20.8.
/1	Use the /1 switch, if necessary, to format a diskette as one-sided.

/4	The /4 is an alternate option to format a 360 KB diskette in a high density diskette drive.
/8	This forces the diskette into the original IBM format of 8 sectors per track instead of 9. This is also done if you enter 160 or 320 after a /F: switch.

Floppy diskettes will always formatted as FAT. NTFS is only supported on mass storage.

Exercise 6-1

The purpose of this exercise is to give you practice working with the disk administrator. You will need your Emergency Repair diskette to complete this exercise.

Your system should currently be configured with an area of free space on the hard disk.

1. Log on as Administrator.
2. Run **Start/Programs/Administrative Tools/Disk Administrator**.
3. If prompted that this is the first time you've run Disk Administrator, click on **OK** to continue.
4. Locate and select the disk area identified as Free Space.
5. Run **Create Extended** from the **Partition** menu.
6. Leave the drive size at default and click on **OK**.
7. Run **Commit Changes Now** from the **Partition** menu.
8. When prompted to verify that you want to save the changes, click on **Yes**.
9. You receive a recommendation to update your Emergency Repair diskette. Press `ENTER`.
10. The area is still labeled as Free Space. Select the same area and run **Create** from the **Partition** menu. When prompted to verify drive space, click on **OK**.

    Before, you created an extended partition. You are now creating a logical drive in that partition.

11. Click on the **Tools** menu and verify that none of the selections are available.

    You will have to commit the changes to the partition before you can format. Using the procedures you practiced earlier, commit the changes to the partition.

12. Select the disk partition you created.
13. Run **Format** from the **Tools** menu.
14. Select the File System as NTFS. Type the following in the Label field:

    ```
    New NTFS
    ```

    Leave the other settings at default and click on **Start**.

15. You are prompted to confirm the operation. Click on **OK**.
16. When prompted with the Format Complete dialog, press **ENTER**. Click on **Close** to close the format dialog.
17. Run **Exit** from the **Partition** menu.

The following steps are optional and should only be attempted if you have an Emergency Repair diskette available for your system.

18. Select the **Start/Run**.
19. Type the following in the command line prompt and click on **OK**:

    ```
    RDISK
    ```

20. Place your Emergency Repair diskette in drive A: and click on **Update Repair Info**.
21. When prompted to verify this action, click on **Yes**.
22. When prompted with the Repair Disk Utility dialog, click on **No**.
23. Click on **Exit**.

RESOURCE MANAGEMENT

This section will discuss issues relating to resource management. These include filenames, permissions available to users or groups within a domain, and file system types. The following are topics discussed within this section:

- File Management
- File Allocation Table (FAT)
- New Technology File System (NTFS)
- File System Conversion
- File and Directory Names

As you will see, there is much to think about when it comes to resource management. Once key issue is the decision of which type of file system is most beneficial for performance on your system and will also meet your security needs.

File Management

Windows NT excels not only in the area of disk management, but in file management as well. One of the decisions you need to make when setting up your systems is what file system, or file systems, you need to use.

	FAT	NTFS
File names	255	255
File size	4 GB	1 EB (16 billion GB)
Partition size	4 GB	1 EB
Extended attributes	No	Yes
Directory sort	None	B-tree
File Allocation	Clusters	Clusters

The FAT file system is the simplest in its design and compatible with DOS, OS/2, and Windows NT. It's also the most limited. While NTFS supports the largest partition and file sizes, it is only compatible with Windows NT.

File Allocation Table (FAT)

The FAT file system is the most commonly used desktop file system in the world.

- Operating system compatibility

    FAT partitions are fully accessible under Windows NT. An advantage over other file systems is that they are also accessible if you start your system up under DOS.

- Widely accepted

    The FAT file system is well known and, despite its shortcomings, widely accepted.

- Available utilities

    There are a number of disk utilities available for management and recovery of FAT partitions and files, for disk optimization, and so forth.

- Filename format

    Long file names are supported for FAT partitions under Windows NT v4.0. A DOS style filename, in the 8.3 format, is automatically created for each file with a long filename.

    NOTE: Support for long filenames can be configured by setting System policies.

- Limited security

    You cannot set access restrictions under Windows NT for local FAT partitions. You do have a limited set of file attributes available to protect files.

Under Windows NT, all diskettes are formatted under a FAT file system.

New Technology File System (NTFS)

The NTFS file system was designed for Windows NT. It provides speed, reliability, and support for very large disk volumes and data files.

- Operating system compatibility

    NTFS partitions can only be accessed while running Windows NT. The partitions are not available to DOS.

- Filename formats

    File names of up to 255 characters are supported. When you create a long file name under NTFS, the operating system automatically creates a DOS/Windows compatible file name.

- Fully recoverable

    NTFS is designed to have a fully recoverable directory structure. A log is kept of disk activities to "roll back" the disk in case of system failure. Windows NT also provides the AUTOCHK and CHKDSK utilities to repair a corrupted disk or in case automatic recovery fails.

- Secure

    With an NTFS partition, you can make full use of the Windows NT security system, including rights assignments and auditing.

NTFS provides performance improvements over FAT file systems when working with large drives and data files. The physical organization of NTFS uses data bands to provide larger contiguous blocks.

File System Conversion

Windows NT provides a command line utility, CONVERT, that lets you convert an existing FAT partition to NTFS. The format for this command is:

```
CONVERT d: /FS:NTFS
```

The Convert command cannot directly convert the current drive. Instead, the drive is flagged for conversion. The next time you restart the system, the drive will be converted.

When you convert a partition to NTFS:

- All files and directories are given default permissions.
- The owner for all files and directories is set to Administrators.

This is a one-way operation. You can't convert the volume back to FAT. The only way to go back is to reformat the volume as FAT and recover from backups.

File and Directory Names

Windows NT v4.0 supports long filenames on both FAT and NTFS partitions. In our usage, a long filename refers to any name that is not a legal filename under MS-DOS. Features of long filenames include:

- Filenames may include up to 255 characters, including extensions.
- The following characters are not allowed:

    ? " \ / < > * | :

- Case is preserved, but filenames are not case sensitive.

Windows NT will automatically create an MS-DOS style filename for each long filename. To do this:

- All spaces are removed.
- All periods, except the last period in the filename, are removed.
- Any of the following characters in the filename are changed to underscore (_):

    + , ; = [ ]

The MS-DOS filename will include:

- The first six characters, unless the first period is encountered.
- A tilde (~) and number, starting at 1.
- A period and the first three characters of the extension.

After the first four files, only the first two characters are used, followed by four system-generated characters, then a tilde and a number.

INTRODUCTION TO WINDOWS NT EXPLORER AND ACCESS SECURITY

This section will begin with an introduction to Windows NT Explorer. Explorer provides you with the ability to manage files in different directories, drives, and even network drives. Next, we will discuss how to set file and directory security permissions. The following are topics discussed within this section:

- Windows NT Explorer
- Windows NT Explorer Menus
- Using Windows NT Explorer

- File Access Security
- Security Properties
- Directory Permissions
- File Permissions
- Types of Access
- File and Directory Permissions
- File Move and Copy
- Directory/File Auditing
- Selecting Events to Audit
- Security Guidelines
- Access Failures

Explorer's primary function is to provide an easy to understand method of managing your resources. As an administrator, it is important to be familiar with the types of access available through file, directory, and share permissions. Often times, users or groups will need to share critical files with others in their organization.

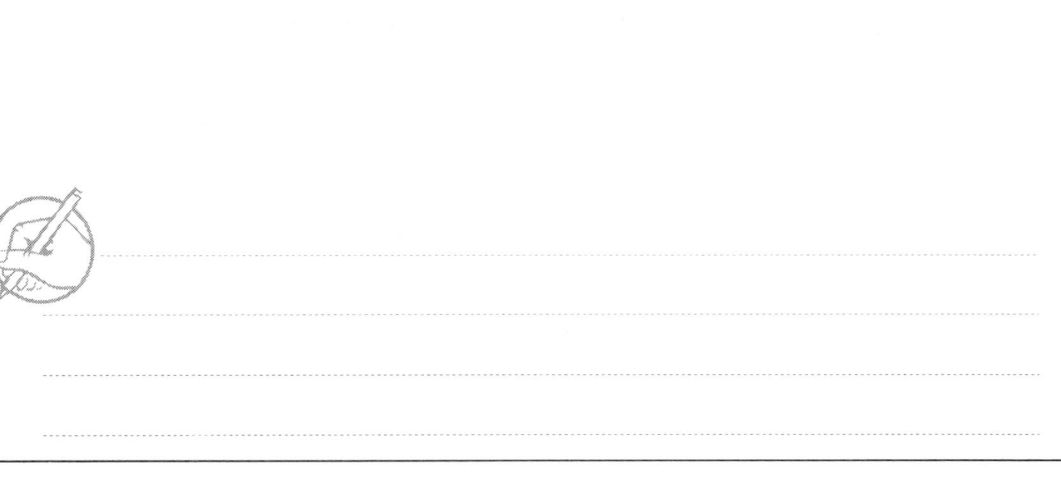

Windows NT Explorer

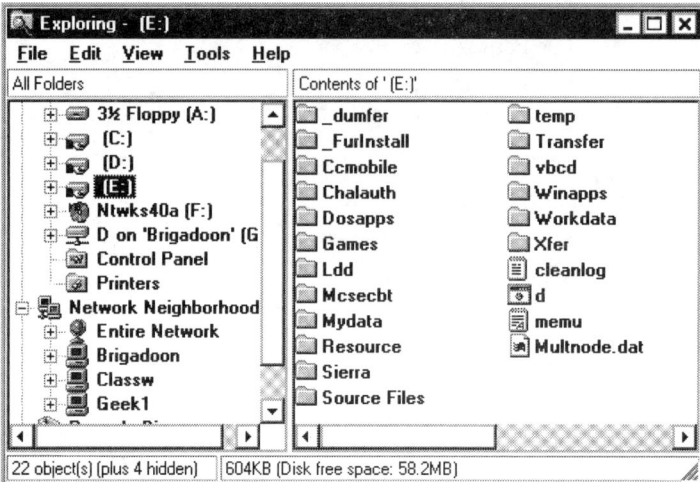

The Windows NT Explorer and My Computer are the primary tools for general file management in Windows NT. Windows 95 users will find it to be almost identical to the Windows Explorer. Windows and Windows for Workgroups users will find some difference, but will find it to be more flexible and more powerful than File Manager.

The All Folders window displays the resources available to this computer. Double clicking on a resource in this window, changes the "Contents" window appropriately. There are toolbar buttons for mapping network drives, disconnecting a mapped drive, pasting, cutting, undoing, deleting, and changing how the contents are displayed.

Your local drives, network drives, Control Panel, printers, and Network Neighborhood are all visible in the "All Folders" window.

Windows NT Explorer Menus

The Windows NT Explorer menus give you access to Windows NT Explorer commands. The commands are grouped into related sets.

File	The File menu contains file and directory management commands.
Edit	The Edit menu includes commands for cutting, pasting, selecting, and undoing file deletions.

View	The View menu sets what is to be displayed in the drive window and how files are to be sorted.
Tools	The Tools menu contains general Windows NT Explorer file and folder commands.
Help	The Help menu calls the on-line help system.

NOTE: Press at any point to display context sensitive help.

Using Windows NT Explorer

What types of procedures are supported under Windows NT Explorer? A few examples include:

- File management procedures

    Windows NT Explorer lets you move, copy, delete, and rename files. You can also rename, create, and delete directories. This includes recursive delete, deletion of a directory and all of its subdirectories.

- Floppy disk management

    You can use Windows NT Explorer to format and copy diskettes.

- Application launch

    You can launch applications by either double-clicking (or selecting and opening) the first executable or a data file with an associated application. You can also specify associations between applications and file extensions.

- Network drive management

    Windows NT Explorer lets you share directories to the network and set the share permissions. It is also used for connecting to shared directories.

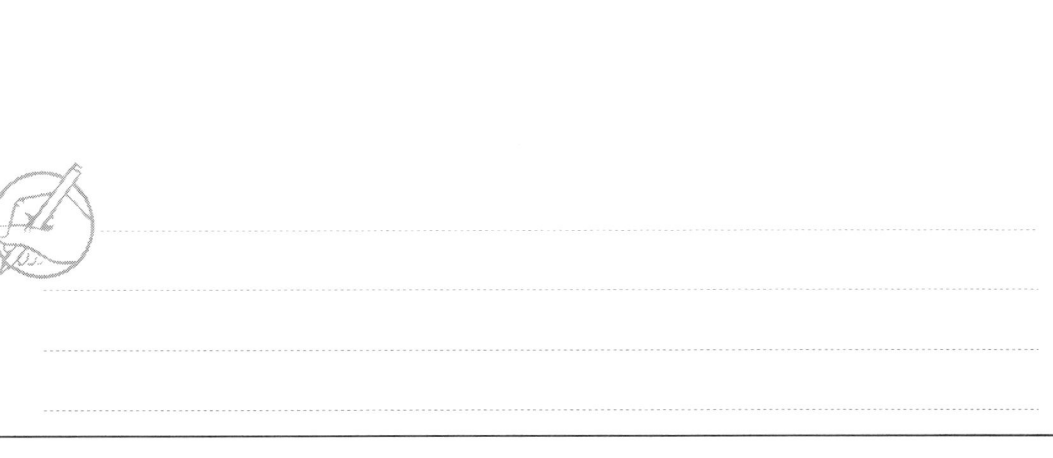

- Security management

    Windows NT Explorer lets you set local access security for files and directories in NTFS partitions. It is also used to set object ownership and to specify auditing options.

Let's take a closer look at some of these options.

File Access Security

The Windows NT Explorer or My Computer may be used for managing directory and file access security. Local access limits can only be set on disk partitions formatted with the NTFS file system.

Security selections are accessed by highlighting the file or directory and selecting **Properties** from the **File** menu, then clicking on the Security tab. You right-click on the directory or file and click on **Properties** to display the Properties dialog. There are selections available to set file permissions, define auditing parameters, and set ownership of files and directories.

When the selected drive has a FAT file system, the Security tab is not available.

Security Properties

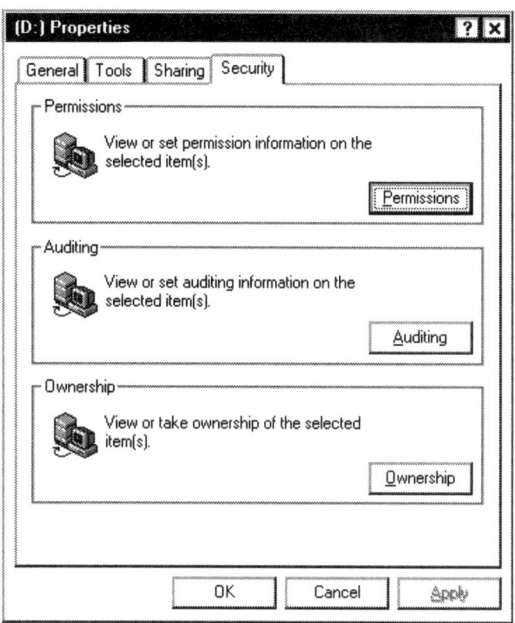

The Security tab has three security areas. These are:

Permissions   Click on Permissions to display the file or directory permissions dialog. This is used for setting local access security.

Auditing   Click on Auditing to set file and directory auditing.

Ownership   Click on Ownership to view the object (file or directory) owner. An administrator can take over ownership of a file or directory.

These selections are only available for NTFS partitions.

Directory Permissions

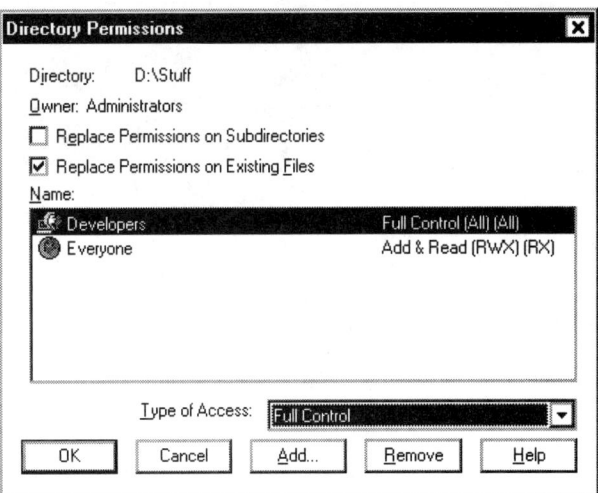

To set directory permissions, highlight the directory and select **Properties** from the **File** menu, then click on the Security tab, and click on the **Permissions** button. If you want to change permissions on multiple directories, select them in the Contents window using your CTRL key while selecting.

Directory	The Directory field displays the full directory path. This field cannot be modified.

Owner	The Owner field displays the name of the directory's owner. This field cannot be modified from this dialog.

Replace Permissions on Subdirectories
Normally set to Off, permissions are changed on the current directory and its contents, but not subdirectories. If you check this selection, permissions will be changed on subdirectories and their files as well.

WARNING!
This overwrites permissions on files and subdirectories and their files.

Replace Permissions on Existing Files
Normally set to On, this specifies that any rights definitions should be copied to all of the files in the directory.

Name   The Name box lists all of the users and groups for whom rights assignments have been made. Click on the Add button to include additional names. The rights listed in parentheses next to each name are the directory, then the file, permissions.

Type of Access   The Type of Access sets the access permission for the selected name.

Click on **OK** after making any access changes.

File Permissions

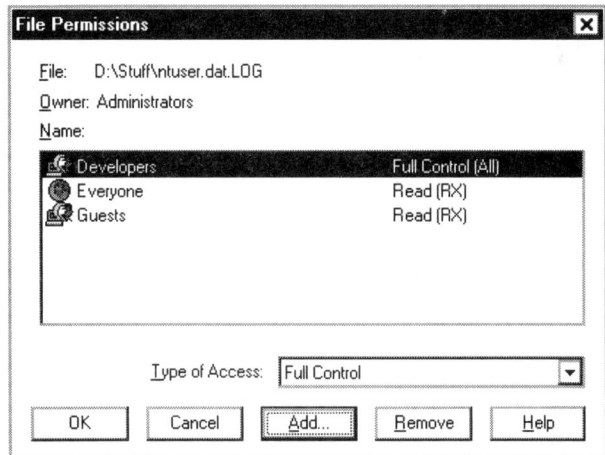

The dialog for file permissions is nearly the same as for directories. Highlight the file or files and select **Properties** from the **File** menu, click on the Security tab, then click on the **Permissions** button.

> *NOTE: If you want to change permissions on multiple files, select them while holding down your* **CTRL** *key or* **SHIFT** *key.*

File	The File field lists the full path and filename of the selected file.
Owner	The owner field identifies the file's owner.
Name	The Name box lists all of the users and groups for whom rights assignments have been made. Click on the Add button to include additional names. The rights listed in parentheses next to each name are the directory, then the file, permissions.
Type of Access	The Type of Access sets the access permission for the selected name.

Click on **OK** after making any access changes.

Types of Access

The selections under Types of Access allow you to choose a predefined permission level.

No Access	Permissions assigned: None
	When No Access is selected, any rights are removed from the directory and its files. This overrides any other rights assignments for a user or for group members.
List (Directory only)	Permissions assigned: Read and eXecute
	This selection assigns directory rights, but does not make any file rights assignments. It allows you to view the contents of a directory.
Read	Permissions assigned: Read and eXecute
	The read and execute rights are assigned to the directory and its files. The user cannot modify or delete files.
Add (Directory only)	Permissions assigned: Write and eXecute
	Directory rights are assigned, but no changes are made to existing file permissions. The user can create new files and subdirectories.

Add and Read (Directory only)
: Permissions assigned: Read, Write, and eXecute

  In addition to read, write, and execute assignments at the directory level, read and execute are assigned to existing files.

Change
: Permissions assigned: Read, Write, eXecute, and Delete

  This is normally used for directories containing standard application data files. This setting allows users to perform most file management activities.

Full Control
: Permissions assigned: All

  With Full Control, all rights are assigned at the directory and to all existing files. This is the default assignment.

Special Directory Access... (Directory only)
: Permissions assigned: Custom

  This selection allows you to choose the particular rights assigned to the directory. This has no affect on file rights.

Special File Access...
: Permissions assigned: Custom

  This selection allows you to choose the rights assigned to a file or group of files. Directory rights are not changed.

File and Directory Permissions

If you select **Special Directory Access** or **Special File Access**, the following permissions are available:

R
: The Read right allows users to open the file and view file contents.

W
: The Write right allows users to modify the data in a file.

X	The eXecute right gives users the ability to execute program files.
D	The Delete right allows users to delete files or directories.
P	When change Permissions is assigned, a user can modify the access permissions for that file or directory.
O	The take Ownership right allows users to take over ownership of a file.

The same set of rights are supported for making both file and directory permission assignments.

File Move and Copy

It's likely you don't often give much thought to file moves and copies. Usually, there's no need. Under NTFS partitions, however, you need to be aware of how moving or copying files between directories and drives affects access permission settings.

- File Copy

    When you copy files between directories or drives, the files inherit the permissions in the destination directory. These will overwrite any original file permissions.

- File Move (same volume)

    When you move files between directories on the same disk volume, the files retain their original file access permissions. The destination directory permissions are ignored.

- File Move (different volume)

    When files are moved between disk volumes, the files inherit the destination directory access permissions. Any original access permissions are overwritten.

An easy way to remember this is to think what is happening to the file. When you move a file to a different directory on the same partition, the file doesn't physically move. You're just changing the directory pointers to the file. When you copy a file or move a file to a different partition, a new copy of the file is physically created. A file inherits the new directory permissions when it is created.

Exercise 6-2

The purpose of this exercise is to give you practice working with Windows NT Explorer and file access permissions. This exercise assumes that you have a DOS directory with a full set of MS-DOS files.

1. Log on as Administrator.
2. Launch Windows NT Explorer from the **Start/Programs** menu.
3. Launch a second instance of the Windows NT Explorer from the **Start/Programs** menu.
4. Right-click on the desktop taskbar and run **Tile Windows Horizontally.**
5. Select the top window and click on the root of drive C: in the All Folders window.
6. Select the bottom window and click on the root of the drive you created in the previous exercise.
7. Select **New,** then **Folder** from the **File** menu.
8. Type the following in the Name field and press **ENTER**:

    This is a test

9. On drive C: in the top window, select the DOS directory with a right mouse-click and hold to drag..
10. Drag the DOS directory to the New NTFS drive you created (bottom window).
11. Release the mouse button to complete your drag-and-drop copy.
12. When prompted, select **Copy Here.**
13. After copy has completed, select your new copy of the DOS directory and run **Rename** from the **File** pull-down menu.
14. When prompted, type the following and press **ENTER**:

    A copy of MS-DOS v6.x

15. Select "A copy of MS-DOS v6.x" and run **Properties** from the **File** menu. Select the Security tab, then the **Permissions** button.

16. With the group Everyone selected, click on the drop arrow next to the "Type of Access" field. Note that Everyone has Full Control for the directory as a default.
17. Click on **OK**.
18. Click on **OK** to close **Properties**.
19. Locate and select the file APPEND (bottom window) in the directory A copy of MS-DOS v6.x..
20. Hold the Shift key and select DEFRAG and all files in between.
21. Select **Properties** from the **File** menu. Select the Security tab, then the **Permissions** button..
22. Click on **ADD**.
23. Click on **Show Users**.
24. Select EMarsh and click on **Add**. Record the user name.
25. Click on the drop arrow next to "Type of Access" and select **Read**.
26. Click on **OK** to close Add Users and Groups.
27. Click on **OK** to close File Permissions and also to close **Properties**..
28. Select the directory "This is a test" and select **Properties** from the File pull-down menu. Select the Security tab, then the **Permissions** button..
29. With the group everyone selected, click on the drop arrow next to "Type of Access" and select **Add & Read**.
30. Click on **OK** to close Directory Permissions and also This is a test Properties.
31. Select "A copy of MS-DOS v6.x".
32. Right mouse-click to select APPEND.EXE, then drag and drop the file into "This is a test". When prompted select "Move Here".
33. Click to select "This is a test", then click to select APPEND.EXE.
34. Select **Properties** from the **File** menu. Select the Security tab, then click on the **Permissions** button.

    The permissions did not change when the file was moved within the same volume. Everyone has Full permissions and JDoe still has read.
35. Click on **OK** twice to close the screens.
36. Select the directory "A copy of MS-DOS v6.x".
37. Right mouse select the file DEFRAG, drag and drop the file into "This is a test." When prompted, select "Copy Here."
38. Click to select "This is a test", then click to select DEFRAG.

39. Select Properties from the **File** menu. Select the Security tab, then click on the **Permissions** button. EMarsh is not listed.

    The permissions changed when the file was copied.

40. Exit Windows NT Explorer (both copies).

Directory/File Auditing

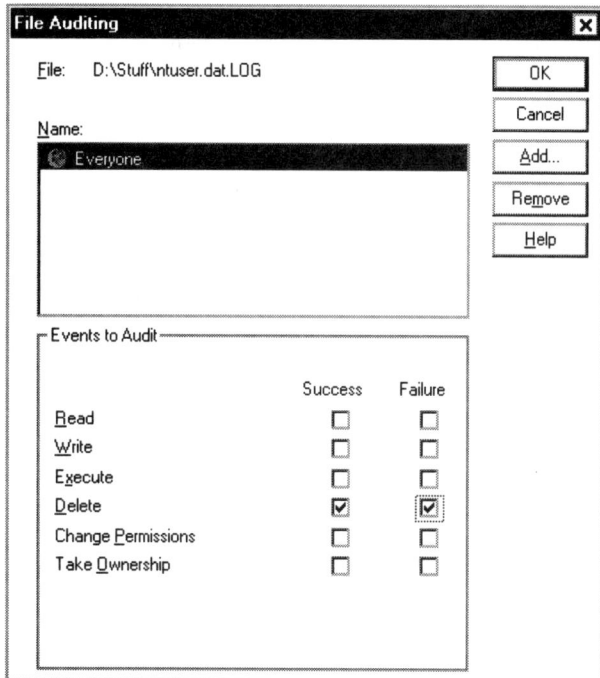

Use the Auditing button under the Windows NT Explorer Security tab, under the properties of a file or directory, to set up directory and file auditing.

Directory/File   This field displays the pathname to the directory or file for which you are specifying audit information. For file auditing, this path will end with a filename.

Replace Auditing on Subdirectories
                      This selection is only available for directory auditing. When it is set on, your auditing specifications are copied to this directory's subdirectories. This selection defaults to off.

Replace Auditing on Existing Files
                      This selection is only available for directory auditing. It defaults to on, copying auditing specifications to the directory's files.

Name   The name box contains users and groups that are being audited. Initially, this field is blank.

Events to Audit   The selections under events to audit can be used with security auditing and may assist troubleshooting efforts in some situations.

You must enable auditing of file and object access through **Audting** in the User Manager (or User Manager for Domains) **Policies** menu before you can set up file and directory auditing.

Selecting Events to Audit

Since the Audit log is limited in size, choose the events you audit carefully. A few suggested uses are given below:

Read   You may want to audit reads on confidential files. A successful audit will tell you which users are accessing the files. A failed audit may indicate users attempting unauthorized copies of the files.

Write   One use of write auditing is to track users posting to a critical database. This will tell who is accessing the database and when.

Execute   Auditing of secure applications, such as payroll or accounting, can help you find users attempting unauthorized access of these applications.

Delete   Auditing deletes is especially helpful when users complain of files "disappearing" from a system. The audit log will tell you who deleted the files, and when.

Change Permissions	One common situation where you may audit permission changes is when you suspect a user is "playing" on the system. This will help you find users attempting actions for which the user has neither the authorization nor the experience to perform.
Take Ownership	Tracking ownership changes may indicate a possible security breach, or a user who has no idea what he or she is doing on the system.

These are, of course, only suggestions. There are many other situations where auditing would also be appropriate.

Security Guidelines

Access security is a critical issue. Careful planning is vital to proper implementation for both local access and shared access security. When in doubt, err on the side of caution. Users will let you know if don't give them sufficient access permission. You may not find out until serious problems have occurred if you give them too much.

Some points to keep in mind include:

- Use NTFS whenever possible and limit local access to sensitive files.
- Use groups to assign access rather than individual users.
- Only share those directories to which other users need access, not the root of the drive.
- Implement auditing on an as needed basis to avoid filling the security log with unnecessary entries.

As your shared resource requirements grow, you will likely reach a point when it will be worth implementing a client/server network, such as NT Server domains, to allow centralized security management.

Access Failures

When access problems occur, start with the obvious with the most obvious causes:

- Network errors

    For shared resources, start by checking that there are no network failures. Verify that both the source and requesting stations are visible on the network.

- Access not configured properly

    If the user has never accessed the resource before, the most likely cause is in how access has been set up.

- Access permissions

    Check the user's access permissions, keeping in mind that "No Access" assigned to the user or a group overrides all other permissions. Log on at the users workstation as an Administrator and see if you can access the resource.

- Visible share

    For shared resources, verify that the share is visible from other stations.

Any access errors can be traced back to user errors rather than system errors or improper security settings. It may be necessary to watch the user duplicate the error to determine what he or she is doing. If the error cannot be duplicated, the error may have been due to a transient system or network condition.

SUMMARY

During this chapter, you were introduced to the following:

- Disk Administrator
- Volume sets
- Disk striping without parity
- FAT vs. NTFS
- FORMAT
- CONVERT
- Local access security
- File and directory auditing

In the next chapter, we take a look at application management basics.

POST-TEST QUESTIONS

The answers to these questions are in Appendix A at the end of this manual.

1. You select the following drives for a stripe set without parity: 200 MB, 300 MB, 300 MB, 250 MB. If you leave all prompts at default, what will be the storage capacity of the new stripe set?

   ....

   ....

2. Which file systems support long filenames and automatically generate an MS-DOS type filename?

   ....

   ....

3. Local access security can be defined for partitions with what file system(s)?

   ....

   ....

4. What is the default local security for any directory?

   ....

   ....

5. What command is used to covert a partition from FAT to NTFS?

   ....

   ....

6. What access permission setting overrides any other access definitions?

   ....

   ....

CHAPTER 7

Application Management

MAJOR TOPICS

Objectives 288

Pre-Test Questions 288

Introduction 289

Introduction to the Windows NT Application
Environment 290

Applications Supported By Windows NT 308

Properties of MS-DOS Applications 320

Managing Data Transfers 333

Introduction to DCOM 339

Summary 349

Post-Test Questions 350

Chapter 7 — Application Management

OBJECTIVES

At the end of this chapter, you will be able to:

- List the applications supported by Windows NT v4.0.
- Compare and contrast preemptive and cooperative multitasking.
- Set multitasking priorities to meet specified requirements.
- List the options for launching programs under Windows NT.
- Describe the purpose and use of the Windows NT Task Manager.
- Describe the features of the Windows NT command prompt.
- List the restrictions for running 16-bit Windows applications.
- Set program properties for an MS-DOS application.
- Describe the purpose of the CONFIG.NT and AUTOEXEC.NT files
- Compare and contrast the data exchange methods supported under Windows NT.

PRE-TEST QUESTIONS

The answers to these questions are in Appendix A at the end of this manual.

1. At default, 16-bit Windows systems use _____ multitasking within a Windows on Windows application session.

   ....

   ....

2. What is the key combination to call the Task Manager?

   ....

   ....

3. What is the significance of having a 16-bit application run in separate memory space?

   ....

   ....

4. How can you access memory configuration settings for an MS-DOS application?

   ....

   ....

5. What do you run to configure DCOM applications?

   ....

   ....

INTRODUCTION

This chapter looks at issues relating to application support under Windows NT. Windows NT Workstation and Server are designed to support most of your existing applications. In fact, they support a wide variety of applications, including MS-DOS, 16-bit Windows, OS/2, POSIX, and native 32-bit applications.

The chapter opens with a look at the Windows NT application environment. A number of fundamental terms relating to applications and applications management are introduced, as well as a block diagram of the Windows NT application environment.

Some time is spent discussing the Windows NT command prompt. Its similarity to an MS-DOS prompt can sometimes be confusing, and it is important that you understand the differences.

The chapter then moves into a look at the different application types supported, including some specific concerns. You will also see how data transfers are managed under Windows NT.

The chapter ends with a short discussion of the Distributed Component Object Model. This model is fundamental to most of Microsoft's current applications.

INTRODUCTION TO THE WINDOWS NT APPLICATION ENVIRONMENT

This section will introduce some terms related to the Windows NT environment. The following are topics discussed within this section:

- Protected Subsystems
- Multitasking Applications
- Multitasking
- Multitasking Priority
- START Command
- Multithreading
- Multiprocessing
- Launching Programs
- Program Items on the Start Menu
- Switching Between Applications
- The Windows NT Task Manager
- Command Prompt
- Command Symbols

It is important to be familiar with the basics of the Windows NT interface. In some cases, a work environment may be changing from a Windows product prior to Windows 95 to the Windows NT environment. Therefore, these end users may not be familiar with how to work with the new interface.

Protected Subsystems

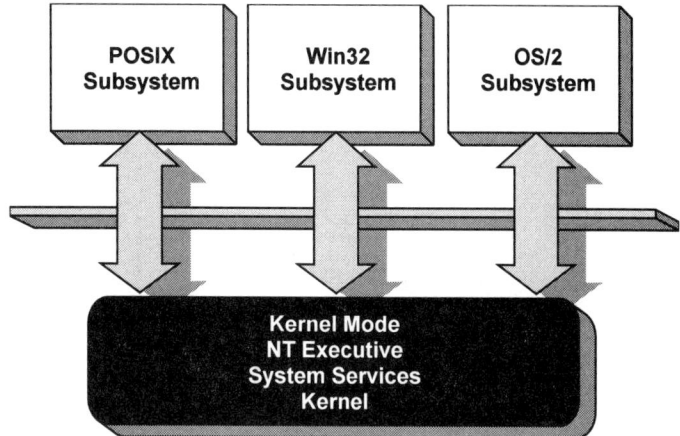

Windows NT carries the client/server model internally, which has led to the modular design of the operating system. This makes it more flexible, and potentially more stable.

Application support is provided through protected subsystems, also called environmental subsystems, since they provide the environment for your applications. Each of the subsystems tracks its own client applications. There is no one system in overall control. The subsystems make requests of the environment subsystem in charge of that particular area of the system. The subsystems provide API routines to the applications, then make calls for the applications to the NT executive services, also referred to as NT native services.

The environmental subsystems are commonly referred to as server objects in the operating system, the applications as client objects.

Multitasking Applications

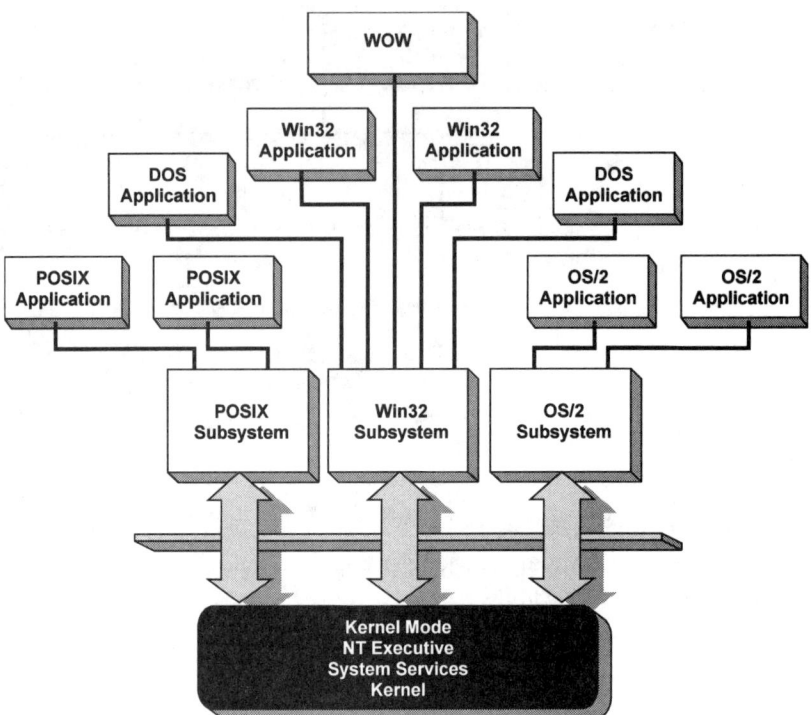

Windows NT uses preemptive multitasking to manage client applications and internal operating system processes. Windows NT uses variable priorities and supports 32 levels of priority.

An exception to this is Win16-based applications that run in the WOW (Windows On Windows) session. Those applications share the session cooperatively.

On a multiprocessor system, Windows NT uses symmetric multiprocessor support to schedule threads to get maximum performance out of the processors. Multithreading is supported for applications that have been written to take advantage of this feature.

Multitasking

In order to understand the support provided by Windows NT to applications, a brief discussion about multitasking is necessary. Two important terms are:

- Preemptive Multitasking: Operating System in Control

    In preemptive multitasking, processor time is divided into time slices. The operating system assigns these to applications, actually to threads, according to their relative priority. Control is never released completely to the applications. This method gives the best performance and provides the most stable application environment.

- Cooperative Multitasking: Applications in Control

    In cooperative multitasking, each application must release the processor before control can be passed to the next application. This method depends on well-written, well-behaved applications. In this method of multitasking, it is possible for one application to tie up all of the processor's time.

Windows NT uses preemptive multitasking to divide processor time between applications sessions. 16-bit Windows applications use cooperative multitasking to share the time allotted to a single WOW session, unless you specify that the application should run in separate address space. You will see how to configure a Win16 application to run in a separate address space later in this chapter.

Multitasking Priority

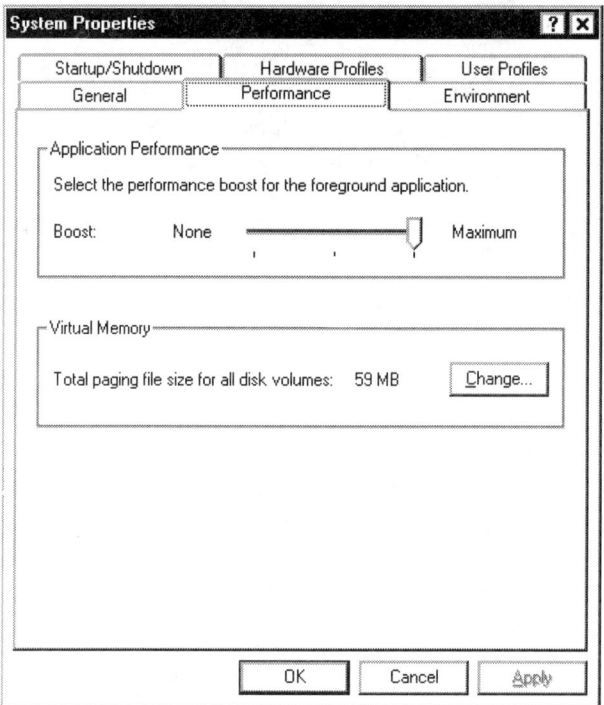

Time allotted to each application session depends on the application's priority, activity, and whether it is in the foreground or background. By default, Windows NT gives priority to the foreground application, so it receives more processor time than programs in the background.

Open the System utility in the Control Panel and click on the Performance tab. Use the "Boost" slider control to boost the relative percentage of resources provided to the foreground application. The default is operating system dependent, set to Maximum for NT Workstation and None for NT Server.

If a system is primarily providing services or files to other systems, you may want to set the performance boost to None. If you adjust this parameter, you will be prompted to restart your system when you exit the utility.

START Command

The START command gives you control over application priority and environment when launching an application from a command prompt or batch file. The syntax for START is:

```
START ["title"] [/dpath] [/i] [/min] [/max] [/separate]
    [/low] [/normal] [/high] [/realtime] [/wait] [/b]
    [filename] [parameters]
```

Supported parameters include:

none	Used without parameters, START opens a second command prompt window.
"title"	Title to display in window title bar.
/dpath	This identifies the startup directory.
/i	Passes CMD.EXE startup environment to the new window.
/min	Starts window minimized.
/max	Starts window maximized.
/separate	Starts 16-bit Windows programs in separate memory space.
/low	Starts application in the idle priority class.
/normal	Starts application in the normal priority class.
/high	Starts application in the high priority class.
/realtime	Starts application in the realtime priority class.
/wait	Starts application and waits for it to terminate.

/b	Do not create a new window. `CTRL`+`C` handling is ignored unless the application enables `CTRL`+`C` processing. Use `CTRL`+`BREAK` to interrupt the application.
filename	Specifies the command or program to start.
parameters	Specifies parameters to pass to the command or program.

Multithreading

Windows NT is also able to improve application performance through a process called multithreading. In DOS and DOS Windows, applications can only perform one operation at a time. With multithreading, several operations can be occurring at the same time. This helps to improve application performance and cuts the time users spend waiting for operations to finish.

While Windows NT supports multithreading, applications must be written specifically to take advantage of this feature.

Multiprocessing

Windows NT shows significant performance increases when run on multiprocessor systems. There are two common methods of multiprocessor support:

- Asymmetric Multiprocessing (ASMP)

    This is the most commonly used method, since it is easy to build out from a single-processor operating system. One processor is dedicated to system processes. Application threads are sent to the other processor. With additional processors, specific applications are assigned to specific processors. It is often difficult to port an ASMP operating system between different platforms.

- Symmetric Multiprocessing (SMP)

    In an SMP operating system, the operating system can run on any processor, or share tasks between several processors. User and applications threads can also be shared between processors, making best use of processor time and reducing bottlenecks. This method gives greater extensibility in the system.

Windows NT is an SMP operating system. This helps to give better performance on multiprocessor platforms and helps to make the operating system more portable. The SMP implementation on Windows NT v4.0 provides an 10-15% increase in performance over NT v3.51 according to Microsoft benchmark testing. Standard copies of Windows NT Workstation can support two processors. Standard copies of Windows NT Server can support up to four processors. Some OEM versions of the operating system, provided by manufacturers with their systems, can support up to 32 processors.

Launching Programs

Windows NT gives you several options for launching programs. These include:

- Run Command

    Click the **Start** button and select **Run** from the choices displayed. This can be used to launch any executable file.

- Windows NT Explorer

    You can launch a program by either double-clicking on its file icon, by opening it from the **File** menu, or by right-clicking on its icon and selecting **Open**. If you open a data file that is associated with an application, the application launches automatically. Applications can be launched in the same manner from the My Computer window.

- Start Menu

    A quick way to launch often-used programs is to place them on the Start menu. Click and drag the desired object, either executable file or associated data file, to the **Start** button then drop. The item will be added to the top level of the Start menu.

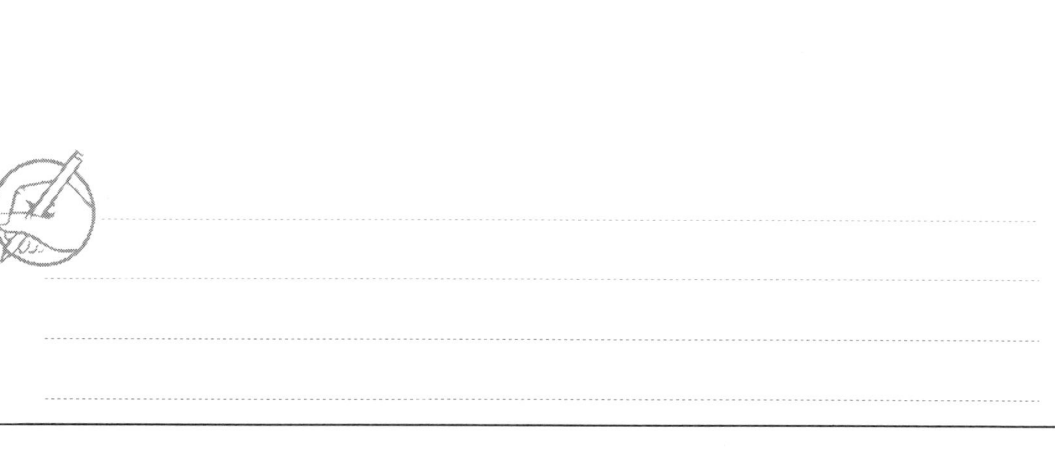

- Shortcut

    A Shortcut is a link to a data file, an application, or any other object. Shortcuts appear as normal objects, but can be identified by the small "right-turn" arrow on the bottom left of the icon. You can place shortcuts in a folder, on the Start menu, or on the desktop. To create a shortcut, right-click within the window that you wish it to appear and select **New** then **Shortcut**. A wizard appears to help you with the process. An alternate way to create a shortcut is to right-click and drag the object for which you want to create a shortcut and release where you wish the shortcut to appear. Select **Paste Shortcut** from the pop-up menu.

- Command Prompt

    You may find it convenient to run certain programs from a command prompt. When you run an executable from the Windows NT command prompt, it determines the program type and launches an appropriate application environmental session.

Program Items On the Start Menu

One way to place a new shortcut onto your Start menu is to right-click on an empty area of the taskbar and select **Properties**. Select the Start menu Programs tab and click on **Add**. A wizard walks you through the steps necessary to add a new shortcut to the Start menu.

An alternate way to accomplish this task is to click on the **Advanced** button on the Start menu Programs tab.

This will open a Windows NT Explorer window that displays all items on the Start menu. You can arrange folders and shortcuts through dragging and dropping.

To create a new shortcut, select the folder in which you wish to place the shortcut by clicking on it in the left pane of the Explorer window. Right-click in an empty spot in the right pane, move the mouse pointer to **New**, then click on **Shortcut**. A wizard appears to assist you.

After you create your shortcut, you may wish to change some of its advanced properties, such as whether it runs in a separate memory space. To accomplish this, right-click on shortcut and select **Properties**, then click on the Shortcut tab.

Exercise 7-1
Configuring The Start Menu

The purpose of this exercise is to give you practice in setting up a shortcut for use on the Start menu by All Users. Log on to the workstation as an administrator before the start of the exercise.

At the beginning of this exercise, you should be running Windows NT and should be logged in with the appropriate user account.

1. Right-click on the **Start** button.
2. From the options displayed, choose **Explore All Users**. A Windows NT Explorer window opens.
3. In the right pane of the Explorer window, right-click on Programs and select **Properties**.
4. From the General page of the Programs property sheet, you can determine the location of this folder. Record the location below:
5. Close the property sheet.
6. Right-click on an empty area in the right pane of the Explorer window.
7. Select **New**, then **Folder**.
8. Name the new folder **Public**. Click in the empty area in the right pane.
9. Double-click on Public to open your new Public folder.
10. Right-click in the right pane of the Explorer window.
11. Select **New**, then **Shortcut**. The Create Shortcut wizard appears.
12. At the command line for the shortcut, type the following:

    ```
    C:\WINNT\system32\mspaint.exe
    ```

    This assumes that Windows NT was installed as C:\WINNT. If not, adjust your path accordingly.
13. Click on **Next**.

14. Name the Shortcut MS Paint.
15. Click on **Finish**. A new shortcut appears in the Public folder.
16. Click on the **Start** button. The new Public folder appears as a submenu at the top of the Start menu.
17. Return to the Windows NT Explorer.
18. In the left pane, open the following folder:

    \WINNT\PROFILES

19. View the contents of the folders present.

    These are local user profiles.

20. Locate the following directory in the left pane of the Windows NT Explorer:

    \WINNT\SYSTEM32

21. Locate the file named **CALC.EXE** in the right pane of the Explorer window.
22. Right-click on CALC.EXE and select **Copy**.
23. Locate the following directory:

    \WINNT\Profiles\All users\Start menu\Public

24. Explorer's right pane should be displaying the contents of the Public folder. Right-click in the right pane of your Explorer window.
25. Select **Paste Shortcut** from the pop-up menu.
26. Click on the **Start** button, and move to the Public item at the top of the menu. List the displayed items below:

Switching Between Applications

Thanks to the Windows 95 user interface and other enhancements, Windows NT v4.0 makes it easy to switch between applications. There are several ways to bring an application into the foreground, including:

- Click on the exposed window.

    If the program is running in a window, click on any exposed portion to bring it into the foreground.

- Click on the taskbar button.

    You can click on the desired button on the Taskbar to call the program to the foreground.

- Use a shortcut key.

    When you create a shortcut on the Start menu, you have the option of defining a shortcut key. Once a shortcut key is defined, any time the program is running you can bring it into the foreground by pressing the shortcut key combination.

- Use the Cool Switch.

    Use **ALT TAB** to switch between applications. Called the "Cool switch", it has been enhanced in Windows NT v4.0 to allow you to see all active applications.

- Use the Task Manager.

    Pressing **CTRL ALT DEL** displays the Task Manager.

Users familiar with other Windows products may be a little surprised by the features built into the Task Manager, when compared to the earlier Task List.

The Windows NT Task Manager

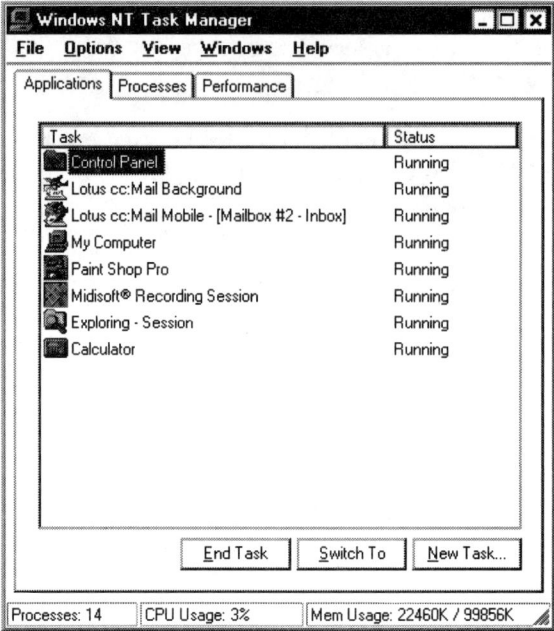

The Task Manager Applications tab displays all currently active applications. You can use the buttons at the bottom of this screen to end a task, switch to a task, or run a new task.

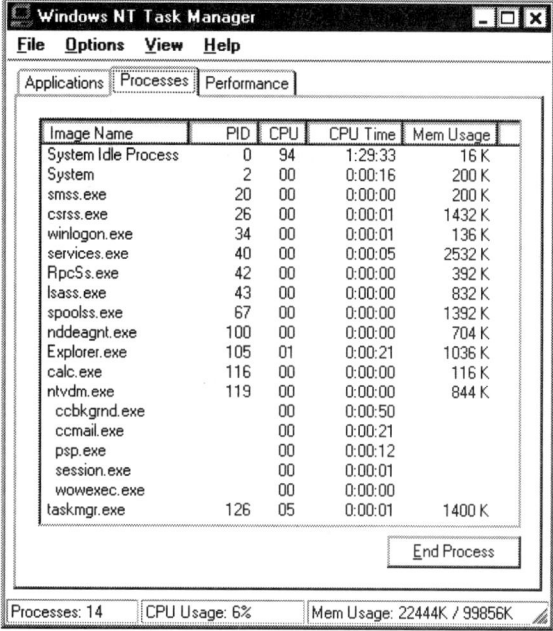

The Processes tab displays all active processes. You can sort processes by Image Name, PID (Process ID), CPU, CPU Time, or Memory Usage. If you right-click on a process, you can end the process or set the process priority.

Chapter 7 — Application Management

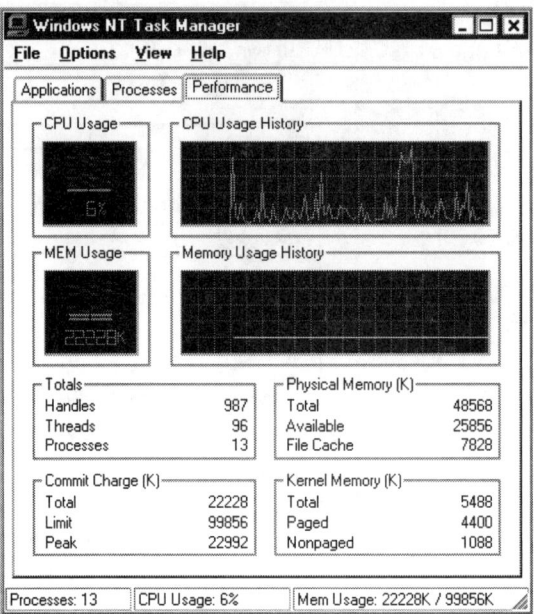

The Performance tab provides a graphic display of CPU and memory usage. Additional resource details are listed at the bottom of this screen.

When the Task Manager is active, an object displaying current processor utilization is added to the Systray on the right side of the taskbar.

Exercise 7-2
Using the Windows NT Task Manager

The purpose of this exercise is to give you practice in using the Windows NT Task Manager.

At the beginning of this exercise, you should be running Windows NT and should be logged in with an appropriate user account.

1. Click on the **Start** button and select **Run**.
2. Type the following in the **Open** field:

    TASKMGR

3. Click on **OK**. This will display the Windows NT Task Manager.
4. Click on the Applications tab. List the current applications below:
5. Click on the **New Task** button.
6. Type the following in the **Open** field:

    MSPAINT

7. Click on **OK**. MS Paint opens.
8. On the Applications tab of the Task Manager, right-click Paint, click on **End Task**, and observe the results.
9. Click on the Processes tab. Determine which current process is taking the most CPU time. You can sort by this parameter by clicking on the **CPU Time** header.
10. On the Processes tab, right-click the System process.
11. Click on **End Process** and observe the results.
12. Click on **No** at the Task Manager Warning dialog.
13. Click on the Performance tab.

14. Click and drag the Task Manager window from left to right several times rapidly. Observe the results on the CPU usage graph.
15. Look at the lower right of the taskbar. Point at the green box next to the time in the Systray area and observe the results.

Command Prompt

Despite the advent of graphical environments for personal computing, it is difficult to completely abandon the command prompt. It's often required when supporting other operating environments and when running commands that have carried over from MS-DOS.

Start\Programs\Command Prompt launches the Windows NT command prompt. While it may look like a standard MS-DOS command prompt, it uses a different command processor than MS-DOS and Windows 95.

If you run an executable file from the Windows NT command prompt, the operating system determines the type of application. The appropriate type of application session will be launched for the command.

In addition, Windows NT supports a number of character-based commands, many based on earlier MS-DOS commands. Command operators and batch files are supported, with a wider range of support and more flexibility than the MS-DOS prompt.

Command Symbols

Command symbols, sometimes called command operators, let you modify the execution of a command. Windows NT supports the following command symbols:

> The output redirection symbol sends the output of a command to a destination other than the display screen. This lets you capture the output in a text file or send the output to a printer. If the name of an existing file is used, the original contents are overwritten.

```
dir > list.txt
```

\>\> The append symbol is also used to redirect output to a file. The difference between this and the > symbol is that the output is appended to the file contents.

```
chkdsk d: >> 0122chk.txt
```

< The input redirection symbol is used to tell the command to use a source other than default (typically the keyboard) for input. This is commonly used to specify a file as the input source for a command.

```
sort < list.txt
```

| The pipe symbol uses the output of one command as the input of the next command.

```
dir | sort | more
```

|| This is a conditional symbol. The command following this symbol will only run if the command preceding the symbol fails or encounters an error.

```
cd temp_dir || md temp_dir
```

&	This symbol is used to string commands together on a line. Each command executes regardless of the completion status of the prior command. `md temp & copy \windows\*.ini \temp`
&&	This symbol is also for conditional execution. The command following the symbol will only run if the command preceding the symbol completes without error. `md \testdir && copy \util\runtest \testdir`
(*cmd_string*)	You can group commands by placing parentheses around them. `(cd fst||md fst&cd fst)&copy \devtest`
^	This is the escape character. It allows you to use command symbols as text. `cd \a^&l`
; or ,	These are separator symbols. They are used to separate command parameters. `del *.tmp;*.bak;*.tbk`

APPLICATIONS SUPPORTED BY WINDOWS NT

This section will discuss the application types are supported under a Windows NT environment. You will also learn which applications are supported, and how. The following are topics discussed within this section:

- Windows NT Applications
- OS/2 Application Support
- OS/2 Supported Features
- POSIX Applications
- 16-Bit Windows Applications
- Separate Address Space

- 16-Bit Windows Application Restrictions
- 16-Bit Windows Support
- WOW Errors
- Windows 95 Applications
- DOS Applications
- VDM Support
- MS-DOS Restrictions
- MS-DOS Support

Even though a work environment may be upgrading or installing Windows NT systems, there is a possibility that applications used will be of various different types.

Windows NT Applications

Windows NT applications are supported through the Win32 subsystem. Windows NT applications are written to the Win32 API, a 32-bit API set. You can have multiple Win32 client applications running, effectively limited only by system resources, of which memory is often the primary limiting factor.

The Win32 subsystem also provides other services to your system such as supporting the graphic interface, and controlling the keyboard, mouse, and display.

OS/2 Application Support

OS/2 applications are only supported on Intel x86-based platforms, with one exception. OS/2 real-mode applications, sometimes called bound or family applications, are supported on RISC platforms. These are OS/2 applications that can run in an MS-DOS environment.

Windows NT ships with support for OS/2 v1.x character-based applications only. There is a Windows NT add-on subsystem that provides OS/2 v1.x Presentation Manager support. The following are not supported:

- Presentation Manager applications, unless the Presentation Manager add-on is installed.
- AVIO (Advanced Video I/O) applications, unless the Presentation Manager add-on is installed.
- OS/2 v2.x or above
- Applications attempting to address I/O ports or system hardware at ring 2 or below.
- Applications that require custom device drivers.

You can sometimes get a bound application to run on a RISC platform by forcing it to run in the MS-DOS subsystem. This is done with the FORCEDOS command, using the syntax:

```
forcedos [/D directory]filename[optional_parameters]
```

You must include the *filename* of the command you want to run, as well as any *optional_parameters* that may be required. The /D option switch sets the current directory for the application as the *directory* value.

OS/2 Supported Features

Most OS/2 features are supported, either directly through the subsystem or through emulation performed by Windows NT services.

- Multitasking

    OS/2 application threads are managed by the kernel the same as any other process thread. OS/2 priorities are mapped to Windows NT priorities.

- Dynamic Linking

    The OS/2 subsystem supports a full OS/2 loader. This provides support for dynamic linking (Dynamic Data Exchange, or DDE) and can load DLLs, executables, and resources.

- Memory

    Windows NT provides protected address space for the OS/2 subsystem and applications. Protection between applications is provided by the subsystem. Virtual memory is provided through Windows NT paging.

- Interprocess Communications (IPC)

    All of the OS/2 IPCs are implemented for OS/2 applications. OS/2 named pipes run on top of the Windows NT named pipes system. Anonymous pipes are supported as part of the OS/2 file handle space. OS/2 semaphores are implemented by combining a Windows NT semaphore object and Windows NT event object. OS/2 signals are fully supported through the OS/2 subsystem.

- I/O and disk support

    Standard device driver calls are supported, but by Windows NT device drivers. The device calls are translated by the OS/2 subsystem and passed to the I/O Manager in the Windows NT Executive Services. Printer support for OS/2 applications is fully transparent. NTFS volumes are translated by the OS/2 subsystem to appear to be HPFS volumes. Note that Windows NT v4.0 no longer supports the HPFS file system.

- Network Connectivity

    The OS/2 subsystem provides access to redirected drives and printers. Connection must be made through Windows NT redirectors.

OS/2 applications are subject to all security restrictions imposed by Windows NT. Security validation for OS/2 processes is under the same user and security token as Win32 applications.

POSIX Applications

Since the mid-1980s, POSIX has been used as a standard for government computing contracts. POSIX is an acronym for Portable Operating System Interface based on UNIX. The IEEE 1003.1 standard for POSIX was released in 1988. POSIX is designed to provide application source level portability between platforms. To run on a Windows NT platform, the POSIX application must be compiled using Windows NT.

POSIX and POSIX compliance is primarily limited to government contract compliance requirements. Windows NT meets all requirements of the POSIX specification. Some of the features built into the NTFS files system, such as hard links (alternate filenames) and case-sensitive naming, are there for POSIX support.

There are several limitations inherent in POSIX support. These are due to limitations of the specification restriction access to the Win32 subsystem. POSIX applications have no access to mapped files, networking, graphics, or Dynamic Data Exchange. They do, however, have transparent access to redirected drives.

16-Bit Windows Applications

Windows v3.1x and Windows for Workgroups v3.1x, sometimes called DOS Windows or 16-bit Windows, run applications based on the Win16 API set. These are supported through the Win32 subsystem. By default, a VDM is created for and shared by all the Windows v3.1x applications. You also have the option of running any or all Windows v3.1 applications each in its own separate address space.

Win16 support is often referred to as WOW, for Windows on Windows. The support process is transparent to the end-user.

> NOTE: VDM support is described later in this section.

Separate Address Space

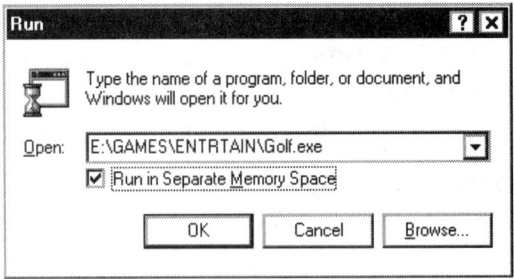

You can launch a Win16 application and have it run in a separate memory through the **Start/Run**. When a Win16 application is selected, the "Run in Separate Memory Space" checkbox becomes available.

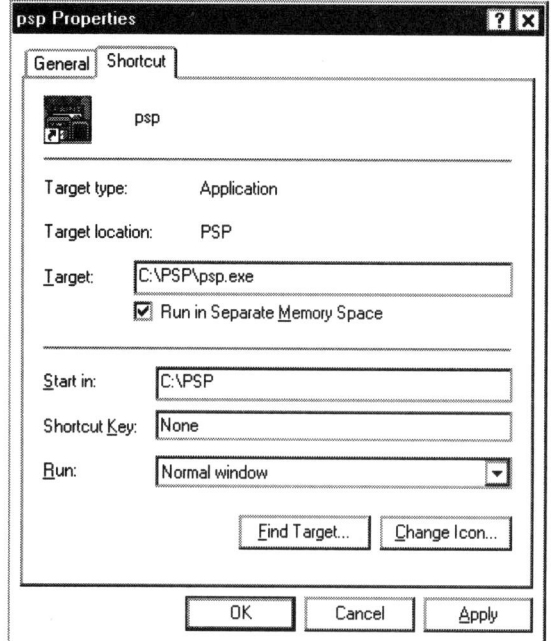

If you use an application regularly, you may wish to create a shortcut to the item on the Start menu, the desktop, or in another folder.

After creating the shortcut:

- Right-click on the shortcut icon.
- Run Properties.
- Click on the Shortcut tab.
- Mark the checkbox for "Run in Separate Memory Space".

NOTE: *You can also run a Win16 application in a separate memory space using the START command, as discussed earlier.*

Reasons for running a Win16 application in a separate memory space include:

- Security

    A higher level of security protection is provided.

- Protecting other applications

    If an application in the shared memory space crashes, it can crash all other applications running in that memory space. If a misbehaving application is isolated, it can't harm other active applications.

This is not without a potential drawback. Running a Win16 application in a separate memory space increases processor and memory requirements for application support. In general, a Win16 application running in its own memory space will require an additional 1 MB of RAM and 2 MB of paging file space. In addition, the Win16 application may not work if the application is designed to share memory addresses with other applications.

16-bit Windows Application Restrictions

You may encounter some applications that will not run correctly under Windows NT.

- Direct Hardware Access

    Windows NT does not allow applications to directly access system hardware. This is done for security and system integrity reasons.

- DOS device drivers

    If a Windows application requires a specific DOS device driver, you will have to update the application or find a Windows NT equivalent driver in order to use the application.

- Emulated components

    Windows NT does not use the Windows GDI, User, or kernel components. This may keep you from running some applications that require special device drivers or particular API calls.

- Virtual drivers

    The Windows v3.x virtual device drivers (VXDs) are not supported. Enhanced mode applications requiring VXDs cannot be run under Windows NT.

- Multimedia applications

    Many early 16-bit multimedia applications directly accessed the multimedia hardware. Because of this, they cannot be used under Windows NT.

Applications that utilize "real" Windows internal data structures will not work under Windows NT emulation, since these are not available.

With earlier versions of Windows NT, Windows applications were limited to the Standard mode of operation when running on RISC platforms. Windows NT v4.0 supports enhanced mode applications on RISC platforms.

16-Bit Windows Support

Windows NT will run most current Windows v3.1-based (Win16) applications without any problems.

Issues relating to the use of Win16 applications include:

- Windows environment migration

    If you install Windows NT in an existing Windows 3.x directory, you can select to migrate application and environmental information from your WIN.INI, SYSTEM.INI, and REG.DAT files.

- Application initialization files

    As long as an application follows Microsoft's development guidelines, initialization file information is stored in the Registry. This is an improvement over individual application INI files, keeping all configuration information in a central location.

- Virtual memory

    Virtual memory is provided for Windows on all platforms.

    NOTE: *Earlier versions of Windows NT supportted Windows virtual memory on x86-based systems only.*

- File system support

    Since system calls are through the Win32 subsystem, you have complete access to NTFS file system files. NTFS longname files are accessed using a shortname associated with the file at creation. This shortname complies with the 8.3 filename convention.

- Full data exchange

    A full range of static and dynamic data exchange services are supported, including Object Linking and Embedding (OLE) and Distributed Object Component Model (DCOM, formally Network OLE).

It may be desirable to upgrade to Win32 (NT or Windows 95) versions of your existing applications, as they become available. Newer versions of many applications take better advantage of the 32-bit environment and are often mail (and even Internet) aware.

WOW Errors

WOW does a very good job of approximating the Windows v3.x environment. In fact, many of the same errors that may occur when running an application on Windows v3.x can potentially show up under Windows NT. Even though Windows NT provides a stable environment, unreliable applications and damaged data files can still cause problems.

- GPF (General Protection Fault)

    GPFs occur when an application attempts to address a protected area of memory. Under Windows NT, this will be part of the protected memory dedicated to WOW.

- Application Errors

    Application errors can result from problems with the application or from bad data files.

- "Hung" applications

    Windows NT uses a non-serial input queue. A serial queue is used, however, in the WOW session for full Windows compatibility. It is possible for one application to block the queue, hanging your Win16 application session.

An advantage is that (in theory) you don't have to shut down your entire system to clear these errors. In most cases, it will be necessary to end the WOW session. However, it won't affect your other applications and can be restarted at any time.

If the error will not clear, logoff and then log back on. This will reload configuration information and let you restart your application sessions.

Windows 95 Applications

Windows 95 runs applications based on the Win32 API for Windows 95 and the Win32c API sets. You can run a Windows 95 application on Windows NT 4.0 provided that it is written to the Win32c API.

> *NOTE: Win32c is the common API to Windows 95 and Windows NT.*

Any Windows 95 application that is written specifically to the Windows 95 Win32 API may not run on Windows NT. However, the majority of Windows 95 applications on the market are written to the Win32c API set.

Windows 95 applications are supported through the Win32 subsystem. You can have multiple Win 32 Windows 95 applications running, the limit depending upon available system resources.

DOS Applications

MS-DOS application support is provided through the Win32 subsystem. MS-DOS applications are supported through DOS emulation. The emulation used is based on the DOS 5.0 API resources.

Each DOS session runs in its own Virtual DOS Machine, or VDM. A VDM acts like a "computer within a computer". The memory assigned to the VDM emulates the first megabyte of system memory, and from inside the DOS session, it looks like the only thing running on the system. This also helps to protect Windows NT from DOS applications.

Windows NT v4.0 running on RISC-based platforms provides 80486 emulation. This is an improvement over earlier versions which provided 80286 emulation only.

VDM Support

A VDM is a Win32 application that creates a complete virtual x86 machine in memory. The Intel x86 processors have a Virtual mode of operation available which provides direct support for most instructions a DOS application would call. When running on a RISC-based system, a virtual environment is built through software emulation.

The DOS emulation module provides ROM BIOS interrupt services and DOS Interrupt 21 services. The Instruction Execution Unit supports processing of x86 instructions. Access to system hardware is provided through VDDs (Virtual Device Drivers). To the application, VDDs look like standard DOS devices, but actually are communicating with the Windows NT device drivers.

MS-DOS Restrictions

While Windows NT will support most of your DOS applications, it may not run all of them. There are also restrictions on the way some applications are supported:

- Direct hardware access

    To ensure adherence to security restrictions and avoid compromising the integrity of the operating system, direct access of system hardware is not supported. This means that many disk utilities and system diagnostics will not run under Windows NT.

- Special device drivers

    Under Windows NT, all device drivers must be written to a 32-bit specification. This means that DOS device drivers are not supported. If you have an application that requires a special driver, you will need to obtain a Windows NT version of the driver or exit Windows NT and run the application under DOS.

- Graphics mode support

    On an Intel x86 system, graphics programs are supported in full screen only. If a program running in a window switches into the graphics mode, the application automatically goes to full screen. If you switch a graphics program from full screen to a window, program execution is suspended.

- Multimedia support

    Many DOS applications that use multimedia work by directly accessing the multimedia hardware. These are not supported under Windows NT, but may run without their multimedia components.

Since Windows NT uses DOS emulation, applications depending on version-specific features or other DOS internals may not run properly.

MS-DOS Support

Windows NT supports the majority of DOS applications without any problems. In many ways, it provides a more stable environment for DOS applications than DOS.

- Launch options

    You can run DOS programs from a Windows NT command prompt, through **Start/Run**, from a Windows NT Explorer icon, or by setting up a shortcut.

- Custom environments

    When you launch your DOS applications, Windows NT runs CONFIG.NT and AUTOEXEC.NT files to configure your DOS environment. There are the equivalent to the CONFIG.SYS and AUTOEXEC.BAT files on a DOS-based system.

- Memory Management

    Each VDM has approximately 635 KB of conventional memory available. Windows NT provides both extended (XMS) and emulated expanded (EMS) memory on an as-needed basis to those applications requiring them.

- Drive access

    DOS applications have access to all of your disk partitions, including redirected drives. NTFS files with long filenames are accessed through the short 8.3 filename created for the file.

- Data Exchange

    You can transfer text data between DOS sessions and any other application sessions. You can also transfer graphics from DOS into a Windows or Windows NT session. Data transfers are static, that is, simple cut (or copy) and paste.

Because of the protected memory management and reliability of Windows NT, it provides a more stable environment for most DOS applications than running them under DOS.

PROPERTIES OF MS-DOS APPLICATIONS

This section looks in detail at issues relating to MS-DOS application support. The following are topics discussed within this section:

- DOS Program Properties
- Customizing DOS Program Properties
- General Settings
- Program Settings
- Windows NT Settings
- Font Settings
- Memory Settings
- Screen Settings
- Miscellaneous Settings
- Custom Configuration Files
- CONFIG.NT
- AUTOEXEC.NT

To ensure that the MS-DOS application will run efficiently in an NT environment, the proper settings must be made in the appropriate properties sheets. Otherwise, system resources will be utilized to full capacity.

DOS Program Properties

When you launch a DOS program, Windows NT recognizes it as such and starts a virtual DOS machine session in memory. The DOS session is nearly isolated from the rest of the system, reducing the changes of an unruly application causing problems in other sessions.

The DOS environment is determined by the application's properties. These properties are the equivalent of PIF files in previous versions of NT. As part of that legacy, the PIF file extension is still used to store property information.

The _DEFAULT.PIF file contained in the Windows NT system directory is the template used for all default DOS program properties. The default properties will allow most DOS applications to run, but it is defined for a worst case scenario. This means that you may not get optimum performance from an application unless you modify its properties.

To view the properties for an MS-DOS application, right-click on the program's icon in the Windows NT Explorer or through the My Computer windows and run **Properties**.

Customizing DOS Program Properties

DOS programs are written for a single-user, single-tasking environment. Because of this legacy, a DOS program often tries to claim and use all available system resources. To keep this from happening, Windows NT must have information on how to handle such programs. Property sheets provide this information to Windows NT, allowing Windows NT to provide the resources the application needs to run, but limit it from "hogging" available resources.

The properties sheet for a DOS application has six tabs:

- General

    This displays information such as type, location, size, MS-DOS name, and attributes.

- Program

    You can set the command line, working directory, and window type information through this dialog. Advanced program settings, including Windows NT CONFIG.NT and AUTOEXEC.NT parameters, are also available.

- Font

    This sets the font that the application uses to display information.

- Memory

    Through this dialog, settings controlling conventional, expanded, extended, and MS-DOS protected-mode (DPMI) memory usage can be modified.

- Screen

    This sets window usage, settings, and performance values.

- Misc

    Windows NT shortcut keys, mouse environment, and termination settings can be viewed and modified through this dialog.

Anytime that you edit a DOS application's default properties or make a shortcut to a DOS program, a PIF file is created.

General Settings

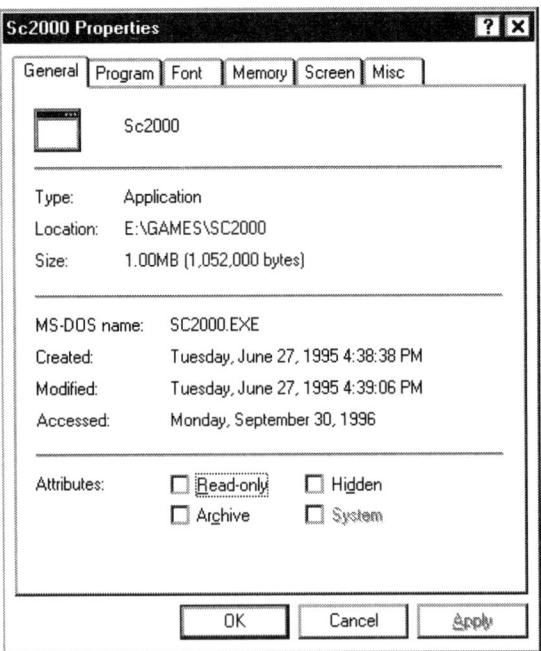

Open the property sheet for a DOS application and click on the General tab to display general information pertaining to the application. This includes the MS-DOS name, size, location, and file attributes. To change file attributes, check the appropriate box.

Program Settings

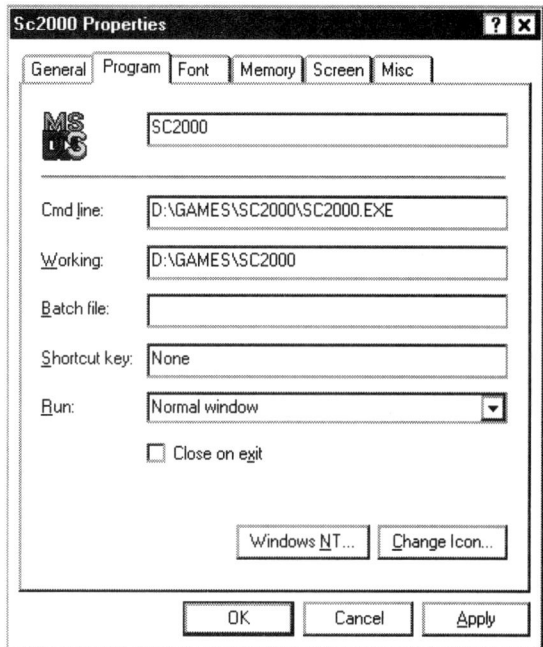

The Program settings tab identifies the application and lets you configure much of the application environment.

You can specify a batch file and have it run before the program launches. You might use this, for example, to make environmental changes such as defining additional environmental variables. The two buttons at the bottom of this page allow you to change the icon for the program and to access Windows NT-specific settings.

Windows NT Settings

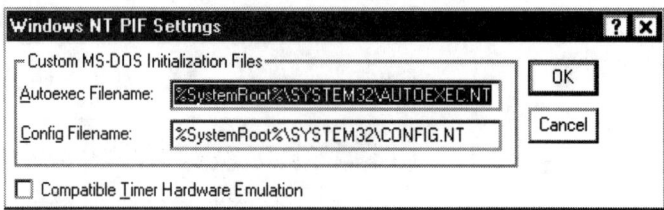

Click on the **Windows NT** button to display the Windows NT PIF Settings dialog. This specifies the location and filename for the AUTOEXEC and CONFIG files to be run when the application launches. The example above shows the default selections. Edit the path and filename to select a different file. This gives you the option of multiple configuration files meeting the particular needs of your applications.

The "Compatible Time Hardware Emulation" selection is usually not checked. DOS applications specify the timing signal rate to Windows NT. Some applications are especially sensitive to the time rate being set too high. Checking the "Compatible Timer Hardware Emulation" box will force the timing signals to be sent at a slower rate. They may correct the problem of some programs that launch normally, but lock up shortly afterward.

Font Settings

Set font information through the Font tab. Windows NT provides a preview of the window and font settings selected. Note that both TrueType and Bitmap fonts are available.

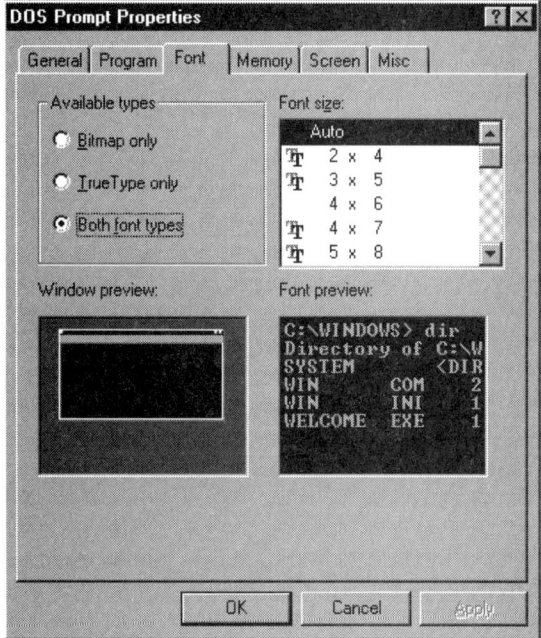

Memory Settings

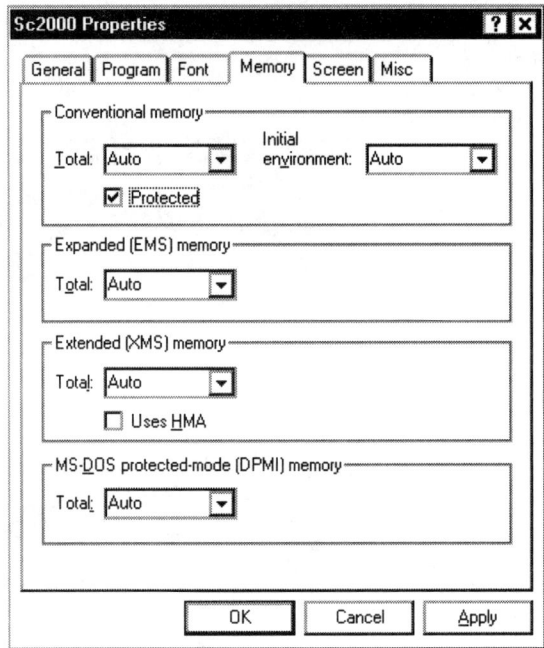

As the name implies, memory settings can be viewed and modified through the Memory tab. Conventional, expanded, extended, and MS-DOS protected-mode memory (DPMI) values allow the user to specify the memory allocated to the application.

Windows NT provides DPMI memory to applications that require that memory standard.

Screen Settings

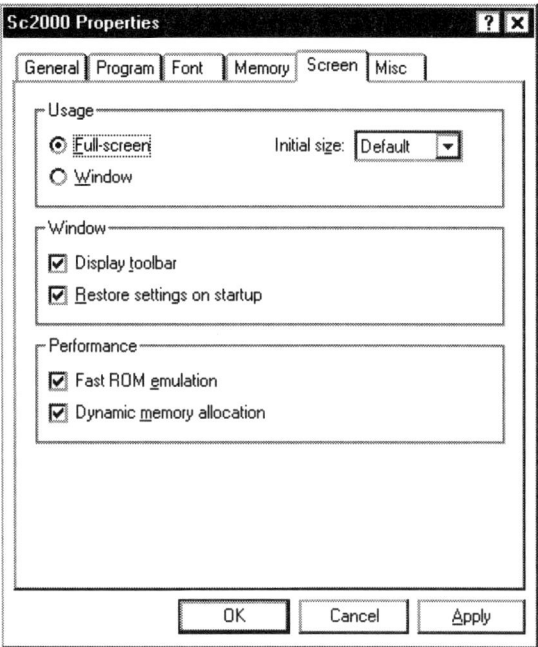

Click on the Screen tab to view and modify information about how the application will display. "Dynamic Memory Allocation" uses the Windows NT video ROM-handling capacity. "Fast ROM Emulation" enables virtual device driver emulation of video ROM services to improve the speed of video operations.

Miscellaneous Settings

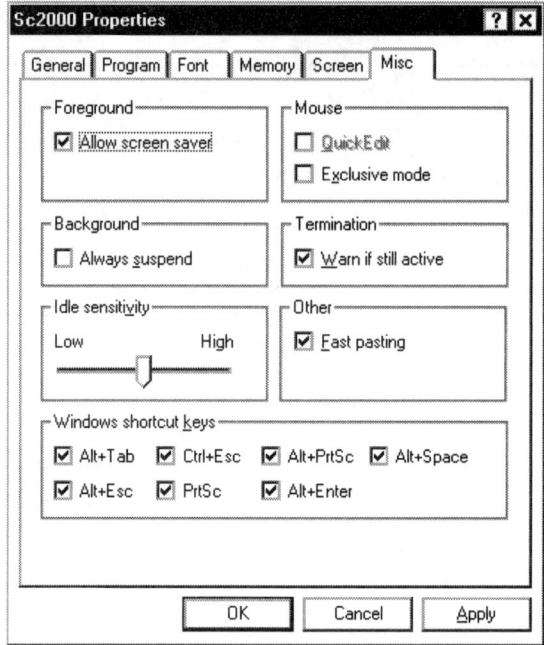

Remaining settings are grouped under the Misc tab. It sets foreground and background parameters, whether to warn the user when terminating the application, and shortcut keys.

Idle sensitivity deserves special mention. This determines how long, after the program has gone idle, before the system reduces CPU resources given to the program. The higher the setting, the sooner CPU resources are reduced, leaving the resources for other applications. If the program appears to not be getting the resources it needs while running in the background, reduce this value.

Custom Configuration Files

The CONFIG.NT and AUTOEXEC.NT files are normally used to configure your DOS application environment. These perform the same function as the DOS CONFIG.SYS and AUTOEXEC.BAT files. They set up environmental variables, load memory resident programs, and so on.

It normally is not suggested that you edit the CONFIG.NT or AUTOEXEC.NT files, unless it is a change that needs to be made for all DOS applications. If you need custom configuration files, you should create new ones, or copy CONFIG.NT and AUTOEXEC.NT to different filenames and then edit the new files.

One advantage is that you can quickly check your configuration changes. After modifying your configuration files, run the application. If the changes do not do what you want, exit, re-edit, and try again. In a DOS environment, you would have to restart the system each time you want to test.

CONFIG.NT

The commands on this page are supported by Windows NT for use in a configuration file. If any other commands are included in your configuration file, they are ignored.

country xxx [,yyy] [filename] — The COUNTRY command lets you set up your DOS application sessions for support of international time, currency, and number formats. Replace xxx with the country code. The yyy and filename parameters are options code path and country information file parameters.

DEVICE=filename [parameters] — The DEVICE command is used to load device drivers. You must include the full path and filename, including extension. DOS device drivers are not supported, but selected device drivers are provided in the \winnt\system32 directory.

DOS=[high|low][,][umb|noumb]	The DOS command determines how DOS is loaded and if DOS has a link with upper memory. Specifying DOS=high loads DOS into upper memory. The default is DOS=low, keeping DOS in conventional memory. The umb parameter provides a link between conventional and upper memory. The noumb, the default, disconnects this link.
DOSONLY	The DOSONLY command doesn't have any optional parameters. When specified, it prevents any applications other than DOS applications from starting at the COMMAND.COM prompt.
ECHOCONFIG	The ECHOCONFIG command does not support any additional parameters. When added to your CONFIG.NT file, messages will be displayed as CONFIG.NT and AUTOEXEC.NT commands are processed.
FCBS=n	Replace n with the number of file control blocks, or FCBs, that DOS can simultaneously support. The valid range is between 1 and 255. Most newer programs do not use FCBs to manage open files, but this parameter may be required to support some older DOS applications.
FILES=n	Replace n with the number of files that DOS can simultaneously access (hold open). The valid range is between 8 and 255. The default value is 8. A typical setting is in the 20 to 40 range, depending upon the particular application.
INSTALL filename [parameters]	The INSTALL command is used to load a memory resident program into memory. You must provide the full path and filename, including extension, and any command parameters required by the file.

LOADHIGH filename [parameters]
LH filename [parameters] The LOADHIGH (LH) command loads a program into upper memory, leaving more conventional memory available for your applications. Enter the path, if necessary, and filename along with any command parameters required by the program.

NTCMDPROMPT The NTCMDPROMPT command runs without additional parameters. This specifies that the Windows NT command interpreter, CMD.EXE, should be loaded instead of COMMAND.COM.

REM text The REM command is used at the beginning of a line to identify it as a remark, or non-executed line.

SHELL filename [parameters] The SHELL command identifies the command processor to be used by Windows NT. By default, Windows NT uses a special version of COMMAND.COM that is designed to work with the other application subsystems. While you can specify a different 16-bit command interpreter, it is not recommended.

STACKS n,s The STACKS command is used to set the data stacks available for hardware interrupts. Replace n with the number of stacks and s with the stack size. The default is 9,128. You can configure 0 or between 8 and 64 stacks, at 0 or 32 through 512 bytes in size.

AUTOEXEC.NT does not have a special commands list. It supports standard batch file commands and MS-DOS AUTOEXEC.BAT commands.

The CONFIG.NT file can be found in the \WINNT\SYSTEM32 directory. It contains additional notes regarding use.

AUTOEXEC.NT

The AUTOEXEC.NT file acts like the DOS AUTOEXEC.BAT file. You can place any executable statements that need to run before launching the application in the AUTOEXEC.NT file.

```
@echo off
REM AUTOEXEC.BAT is not used to initialize the MS-DOS
    environment.
REM AUTOEXEC.NT is used to initialize the MS-DOS environment
    unless a REM different startup file is specified in an
    application's PIF.
REM Install CD ROM extensions
    lh %SystemRoot%\system32\mscdexnt.exe
REM Install network redirector (load before dosx.exe)
    lh %SystemRoot%\system32\redir
REM Install DPMI support
    lh %SystemRoot%\system32\dosx
```

Rather than changing AUTOEXEC.NT, it is probably best to create additional AUTOEXEC files on an as-needed basis.

The AUTOEXEC.NT file can be found in the \WINNT\SYSTEM32 directory. It contains additional notes regarding use.

MANAGING DATA TRANSFERS

This section looks at the options for "cut-and-paste" data exchange in the Windows NT environment. Both static and dynamic exchange are discussed. The following are topics discussed within this section:

- Data Exchange
- Static Versus Dynamic Exchange
- Data Exchange Basics
- Clipboard
- ClipBook Viewer

One of the main comparisons presented in this section is between the Clipboard and the ClipBook Viewer. Each has its own benefits or reason to use one over the other.

Data Exchange

Windows NT lets you exchange data between applications, even between different application subsystems.

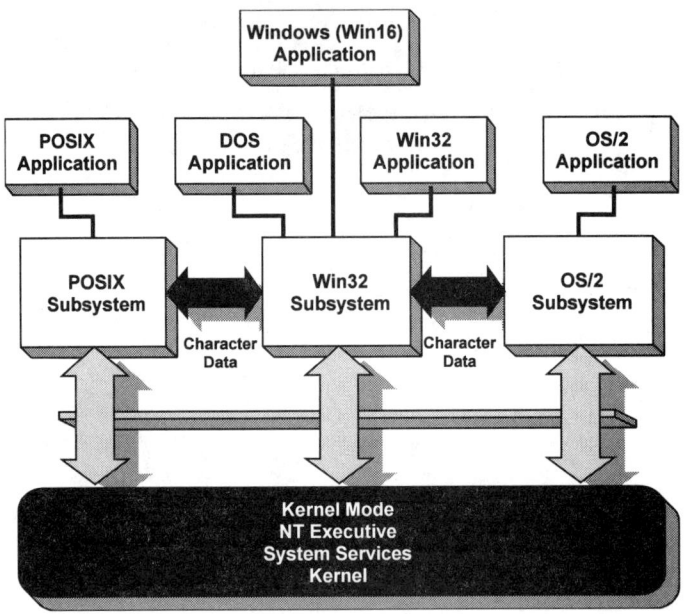

Windows users are already familiar with exchanging data between Windows applications, as well as between Windows and DOS. Windows NT also lets you exchange character data with POSIX and OS/2 applications.

Static Versus Dynamic Exchange

Three categories of data exchange are supported:

- Static Data Exchange

    This is the traditional cut-and-paste through the Clipboard, familiar to users of other operating environments. Data is copied (or copied and deleted) from one application and dropped into another. The destination copy of the data is independent of the source copy. All application types are supported: Windows, Windows NT, DOS, POSIX, and OS/2.

- Object Linking

    In earlier releases of Windows products, object linking was simply referred to as Dynamic Data Exchange, or DDE. Object linking adds an additional feature to cut-and-paste, the automatic update of linked data between multiple documents and applications. When the source document is updated, all related documents and applications are informed and updated. Only Windows and Windows NT applications are supported under DDE.

- Object Embedding

    Object embedding was introduced with Object Linking and Embedding (OLE). You can take an entire document, or any part of that document, and embed this into another document as an object. This object becomes part of the document. Windows keeps a database of server applications, associating data types with their applications. Object embedding is supported for Windows and Windows NT applications only.

Each of these works toward the same general aim, to reduce the work required to generate data and improve end user productivity.

Data Exchange Basics

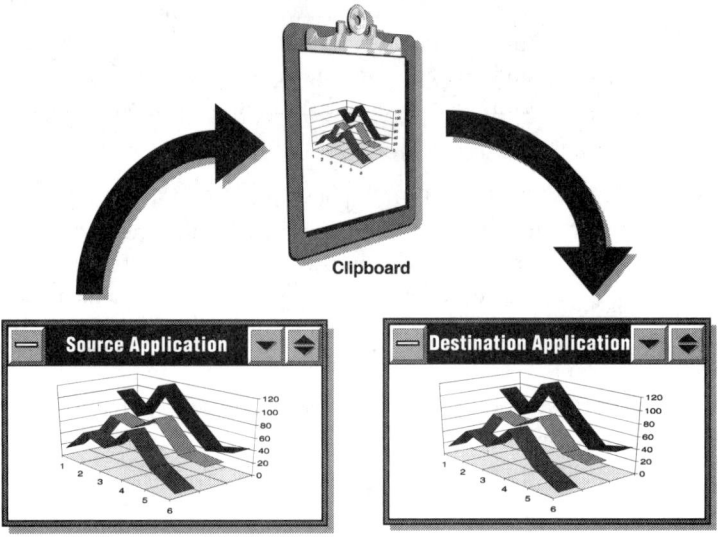

Whether you are transferring static data, setting up a data link, or embedding a data object into a destination object, the basic steps are the same.

- Copy data to clipboard.

    Mark the data to be copied and select **Copy** or **Cut** from the **Edit** menu. **Copy** leaves the source data in place. **Cut** removes the source data. For text-based applications, you have to choose **Mark** from the **Edit** selection in the **System** menu, mark the data, then choose **Copy** from the **Edit** selection in the **System** menu.

- Paste data to destination document.

    The type of exchange is determined by your paste selection. **Paste** is a static exchange. **Paste link** creates a DDE link. **Paste object** inserts an OLE object. Both the source and destination applications must support DDE or OLE.

If the process looks simple, that's because it is. In most cases, the most confusing things about DDE and OLE are the explanations.

Clipboard

The Clipboard is basic to all data exchange operations. It is a dedicated area of memory used for temporary storage of data for transfer.

Whenever you copy or cut data from a source document, it goes into the Clipboard. The data will be kept in the Clipboard in multiple formats, depending upon the formats supported by the source application. For example, text from a Microsoft Word document would be available as ASCII text, Rich Text Format (RTF) text, and in its native Microsoft Word format.

Clipboard data isn't limited to traditional data definitions, such as text and graphics. It can also include multimedia data, such as digital audio or digital video.

When you paste the data into the destination document, the most appropriate format is selected from those available. In some cases, where the source and destination are vastly different application types, there will not be a mutually compatible format.

ClipBook Viewer

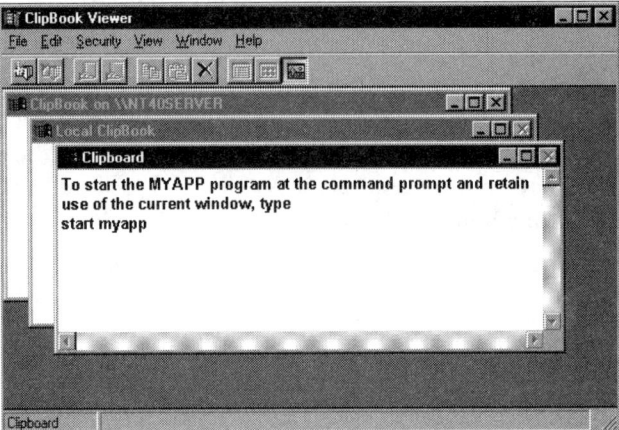

One of the problems with the Clipboard is its temporary nature. It is also limited in that you can only have one set of data in the Clipboard at any time. The ClipBook, first introduced with Windows for Workgroups, gives you a way around these restrictions.

Any data that can be stored in the Clipboard can be placed into permanent storage in the ClipBook. The ClipBook Viewer, launched as **Start/Program/Accessories/Clipboard**, lets you view the contents of the Clipboard as well as view and manage your local ClipBook.

The ClipBook Viewer also allows you to connect to another computer and view the contents of its Clipboard and ClipBook.

INTRODUCTION TO DCOM

This section will introduce the new technology known as Distributed Component Object Module otherwise known as DCOM. The following are topics discussed within this section:

- DCOM
- DCOM Configuration Properties
- Applications Settings
- Default Properties Settings
- Default Security Settings

This application is useful for establishing communication between two systems. As you will see, it is necessary to set properties for the application before actually launching the DCOM utility.

DCOM

Distributed Component Object Module (DCOM) is a new technology that extends Microsoft's COM technology. The Component Object Model, Microsoft's architecture for component software and the basis for OLE Automation, is often used to integrate end-user features between applications. While COM allows software components to be shared on a single computer, DCOM provides the extension for connecting the objects on two systems, and maintaining uniform communication between the objects.

Through DCOM, you can integrate distributed applications in a network. A distributed application consists of multiple processes that cooperate to accomplish a single task.

Why does this matter? This is the model around which Microsoft products, including the Microsoft BackOffice products, are built. It is blurring the lines between what we traditionally consider client and server systems. It becomes especially significant when building custom applications. One application could conceivably communicate with and pull information from any number of other applications, all running on different systems.

The DCOM Configuration tool can be used to configure 32-bit COM and DCOM applications. To run this tool, launch **Start/Run**, then type **DCOMCNFG**.

DCOM Configuration Properties

Before you can use an application with DCOM, you must use the DCOM Configuration tool to set properties, such as security and location, for the application. On the computer running the client application, you must specify the location of the server application that will be accessed or started. For the server application, you must specify the user account that will have permission access (and start, if necessary) the application, and the user accounts that will be used to run the application.

The Distributed COM Configuration has the following tabs:

- Applications

    This page allows you to view currently available DCOM applications and their properties, including location, security, and identify properties.

- Default Properties

    This sets the default properties, including enabling of DCOM, default authentication levels, and default impersonation levels.

- Default Security

    This page allows you to edit default access permissions and default launch permissions.

Applications Settings

When DCOMCNFG is launched, the Applications tab is displayed first. At this level, you can define default settings for all DCOM applications.

You can view and modify properties for any listed application.

Highlight the desired application and click on **Properties**. Configuration information specific to that application is displayed. The General tab is displayed first. This page has information about the DCOM application, including the local path to the executable.

The Location tab contains settings allowing DCOM to locate the computer on which the server application is located. DCOM will use the first applicable setting that is checked. Client applications may override selections set on this page.

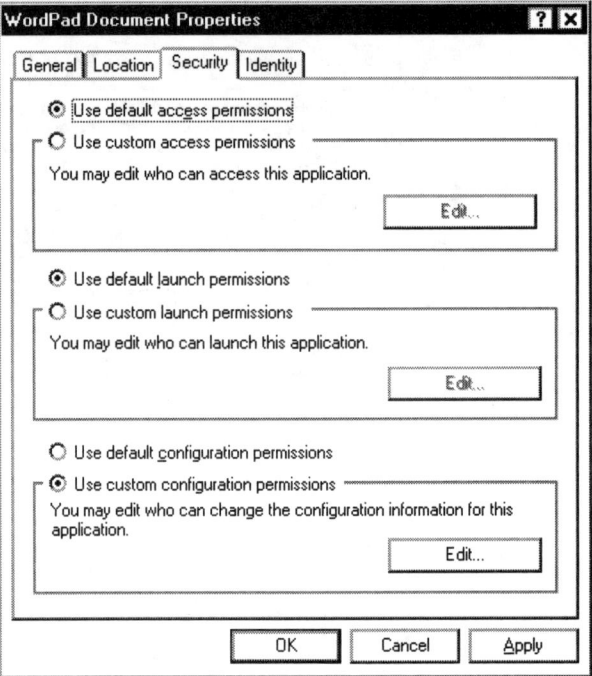

Access permissions for the application are set by the Security tab. You can modify who has access and launch permissions to the application by clicking on the appropriate **Edit** button to access the **Permissions** dialog. For each, you have the option of using the default permissions or defining custom permissions.

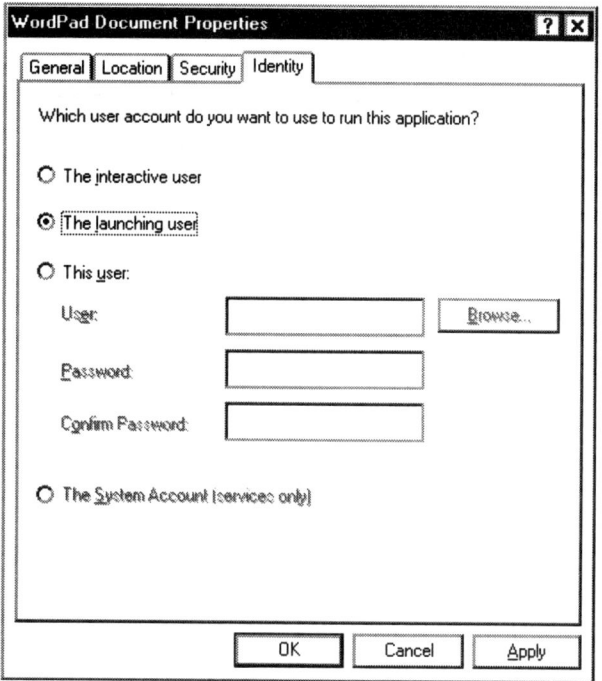

The Identify tab allows you to specify which user account acting as security focus when the application is launched. Click on the **Browse** button to see a list of domain users and groups from which you can make your selection. If the DCOM application is configured as an NT service, the System Account option is available.

Default Properties Settings

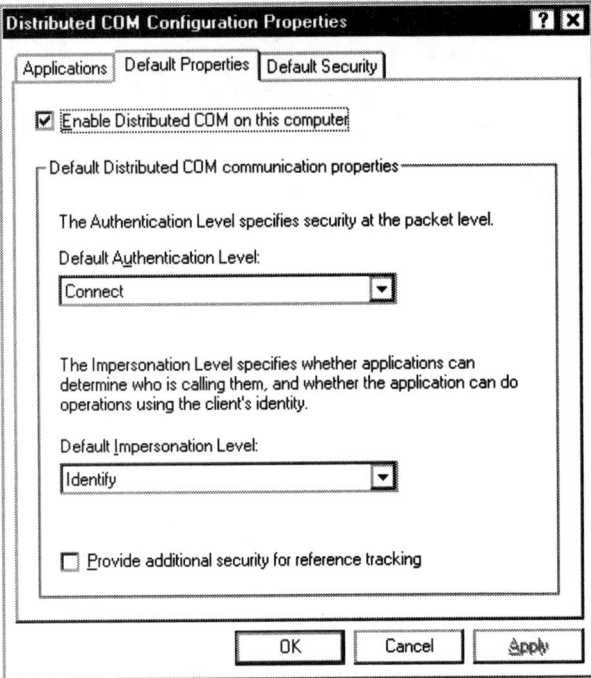

The Default Properties tab on the DCOM Configuration property sheet allows you to set the options affecting all DCOM applications, unless overridden by individual settings.

DCOM applications can be enabled on local computer by checking the appropriate checkbox. The "Default Authentication Level" has 7 possible values:

- None
- Call
- Connect
- Default
- Packet
- Packet Integrity
- Packet Privacy

The "Default Impersonation Level" has three possible values:

- Delegate
- Identity
- Impersonate

Default Security Settings

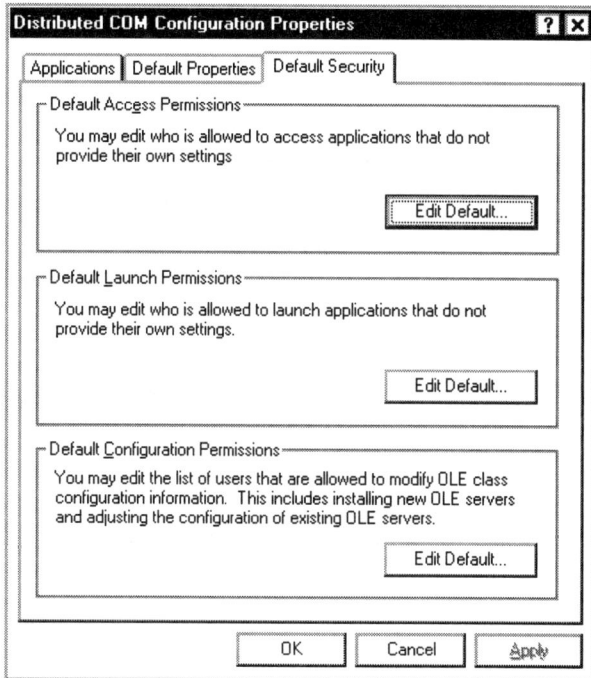

Security settings are managed through the Default Security tab. This dialog takes you to the access and launch permission settings.

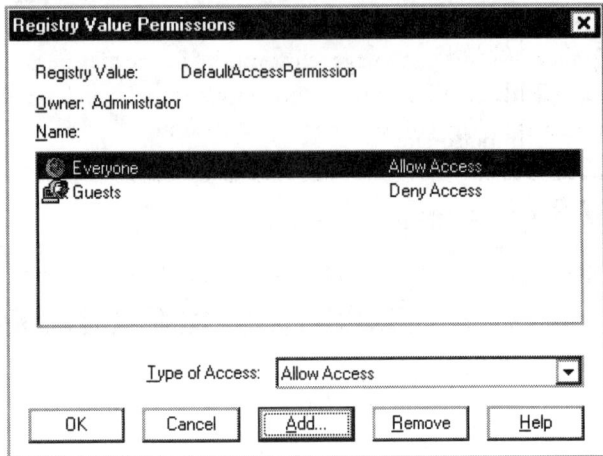

Click on **Edit Default** in the "Default Access Permissions" chapter of the Default Security tab to display the permissions dialog. The sample shows default settings. You may add local or domain users to have permission to access this application by clicking on the **Add** button.

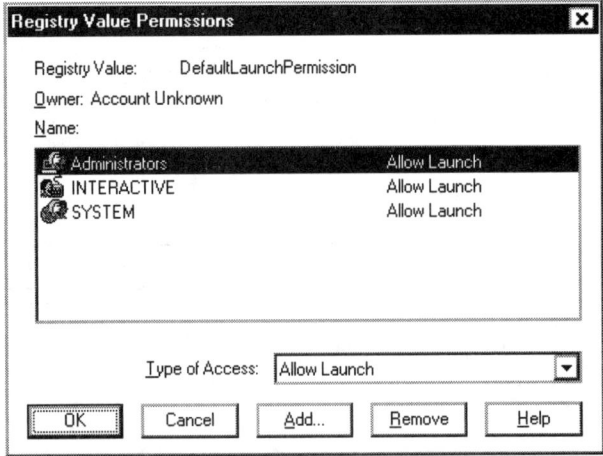

Click on **Edit Default** in the "Default Launch Permissions" section of the Default Security tab to view or modify launch permissions. By default, the Interactive user has permission to launch DCOM applications. The Interactive user represents any user logged on locally to the system.

You can disable DCOM for a specific application by denying access or launch permissions to the built-in Network user account. To do this, select the application in the Applications property page, click on the **Properties** button, select the Security tab, and then click on "Use custom access permissions". Click on **Add** to add Network as the user, and set the "Type of Access" as DenyAccess.

SUMMARY

This chapter introduced application support under Windows NT. This included:

- Application support through protected subsystems
- The Windows NT application environment
- Multitasking, multithreading, and multiprocessing support
- Using the Windows NT command prompt
- DOS applications and VDMs
- DOS application properties
- The Windows NT Task Manager
- Win16 applications, Win32 applications, and WOW
- Distributed COM basics

The next chapter discusses network management, including network components, configuration, protocols, and file sharing.

POST-TEST QUESTIONS

The answers to these review questions are in Appendix A at the end of this manual.

1. Which protected subsystem provides support for VDM sessions?

   ....

   ....

2. Do applications running in a WOW session multitask using preemptive or cooperative multitasking?

   ....

   ....

3. What is the filename of the Windows NT command processor?

   ....

   ....

4. What is the command symbol to append the output of a command to an existing file?

   ....

   ....

5. What API set must a Windows 95 application be written to in order to function under Windows NT v4.0?

   ....

   ....

CHAPTER 8

Network Management

MAJOR TOPICS

Objectives 352

Pre-Test Questions 352

Introduction 353

Network Configuration 354

Examining Network Services 378

Resource Sharing and Access 385

Summary 400

Post-Test Questions 401

OBJECTIVES

At the completion of this chapter, you will be able to:

- Describe the components of the Windows NT networking model.
- Describe the procedures for installing a network adapter.
- Compare and contrast NetBEUI, DLC, NWLink, and TCP/IP.
- Given networking requirements, select the most appropriate transport protocol.
- Configure selected NWLink properties.
- Configure selected TCP/IP properties.
- Describe situations where you would use DHCP.
- Briefly describe using LMHOSTS and WINS for NetBIOS name resolution.
- Share selected directories to the network.
- Share a defined printer to the network.
- Access shared network resources.

PRE-TEST QUESTIONS

The answers to these questions are in Appendix A at the end of this manual.

1. You are setting up a workstation on a TCP/IP LAN with no routers. At minimum, what addressing information is required?

   ....

   ....

2. What protocol is required if you want to support Client Service for NetWare?

   ....

   ....

3. What are two terms used to refer to a device that connects two TCP/IP subnetworks?

   ....

   ....

4. What would you install on a client if you wanted it to have an IP address assigned automatically?

....

....

INTRODUCTION

Throughout most of the course, you have been working in a network environment. In fact, Windows NT was designed to fill the client and server roles in a network. While they can be used as stand-alone products, you would be missing out on many of the product benefits.

Up to now your network involvement has been somewhat passive. In this chapter you take a more active role in network design and implementation. The chapter opens with a look at basic network configuration. You will see how to configure network adapter drivers and transport protocols. Due to increasing interest, much of it fueled by the Internet, this chapter has a special focus on TCP/IP implementation.

The remainder of the chapter focuses on resource sharing and access. Procedures for both directory and printer sharing are explained, as well as the steps for attaching to a shared resource. There is also a discussion about how Windows NT manages access permissions.

Stop now and view the following video presentation on the Interactive Learning CD-ROM:

Windows NT v4.0 Workstation Administration Resource Sharing

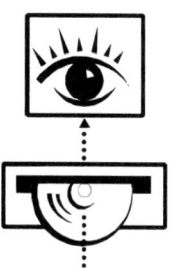

NETWORK CONFIGURATION

This section will present information on the types of adapters and protocols that are supported by Windows NT. The steps to install each of these items will be covered as they appear in the Network control panel. The concept of TCP/IP and IP addresses is also introduced here. The following are topics discussed within this section:

- Networking Model
- NDIS Interface
- Network Properties
- Adapter Installation
- Adapter Configuration
- Transport Protocols
- Picking the Right Protocol
- Protocol Installation
- NWLink IPX/SPX Properties
- About TCP/IP
- Internetworks
- About IP Addresses
- TCP/IP Properties Sheet
- IP Address
- Using DHCP
- Name Resolution
- LMHOSTS
- WINS
- About WINS

If systems do not have a common protocol installed, they will not be able to communicate.

Networking Model

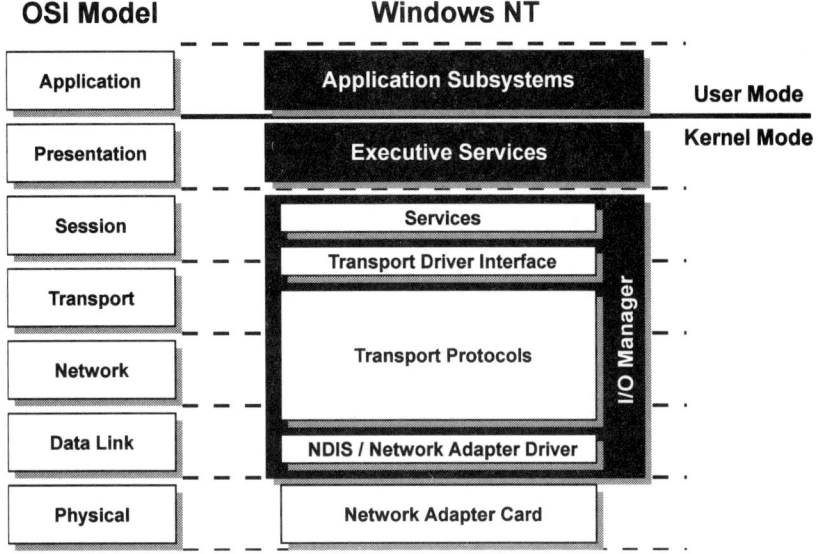

Windows NT uses a layered network architecture, modeled after the ISO/OSI seven layer model. This layered design provides a platform that is readily expandable, giving third party providers a base upon which to build.

It provides a common interface between the layers and also creates discrete divisions. Changes can be made within a layer without having to change the entire model.

- NDIS Interface/Network Adapter Card Driver

    The Network Driver Interface Specification (NDIS) was developed jointly by Microsoft and 3Com in 1989. This standard provides a standard means for device drivers at the Media Access Control (MAC) level to communicate with higher level protocol drivers. This standard makes it easier for a vendor to support multiple network operating system environments, as long as the network operating system (NOS) adheres to the NDIS standard. All network adapter card device drivers in Windows NT are NDIS-compliant.

- Transport Protocols

    The transport protocol manages network communications. It determines how data, moving up and down through the communications model, should be presented to the next layer. This course's coverage is limited to NetBEUI, NWLink (IPX/SPX compatible), DLC, and TCP/IP.

- Transport Driver Interface (TDI)

    The TDI is a protocol specification that defines how the upper level of transport protocol drivers are written. It provides a common interface between upper level services and the transport protocol drivers. This provides a standard platform for the development of distributed applications.

- Network Services

    Windows NT provides a number of services allowing the system and its applications to work in a network environment. These services allow the system to share resources and access shared resources on the network. They provide Interprocess Communication (IPC) services and standard interfaces for the support of distributed applications.

NDIS Interface

The NDIS specification was created to provide a more flexible network design environment. Network operating systems used to be designed where each required a proprietary network adapter driver which also bundled the network protocol in the same file. Since this meant providing a different driver for each implementation, it was difficult for vendors to supply a broad base of support.

With the NDIS specification, the driver is written so that all of the protocols see a standard NDIS interface. Any NDIS-compliant protocol can communicate with any NDIS-compliant adapter card. Initial communications between the protocol driver and adapter driver is established through a process called binding. Another advantage of NDIS is that it allows a single adapter card to support multiple transport protocols. This makes it much easier to implement Windows NT in mixed network environment.

NDIS is implemented in a slightly different manner under Windows NT than in many other NDIS-compliant network products. The standard method has been to use a protocol manager module, called PROTMAN in the LAN Manager environment, to link each layer's components. Windows NT does this through an NDIS wrapper program that establishes necessary links using information stored in the registry.

Network Properties

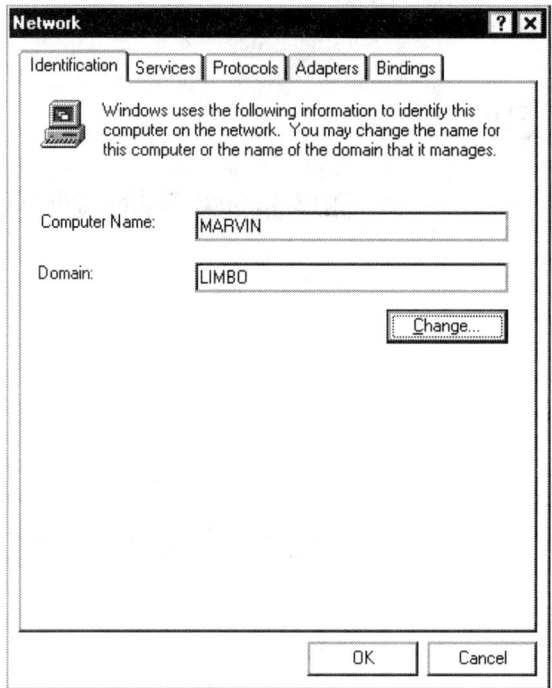

The Control Panel Network utility is your primary tool for network configuration. It has five property sheet tabs:

- Identification

    The Identification tab is used to set the machine name and workgroup or domain membership.

- Services

    This tab lets you manage network services. You can add services, managing installed services, or delete services through this property sheet.

- Protocols

    The Protocols tab is used for transport protocol installation and management.

- Adapters

    You can add, remove, or modify configuration properties through this tab.

- Binding

    This tab lets you view and manage the transport protocols bound to network adapters and the upper level services bound to transport protocols.

The course materials will refer back to this utility at various times.

Adapter Installation

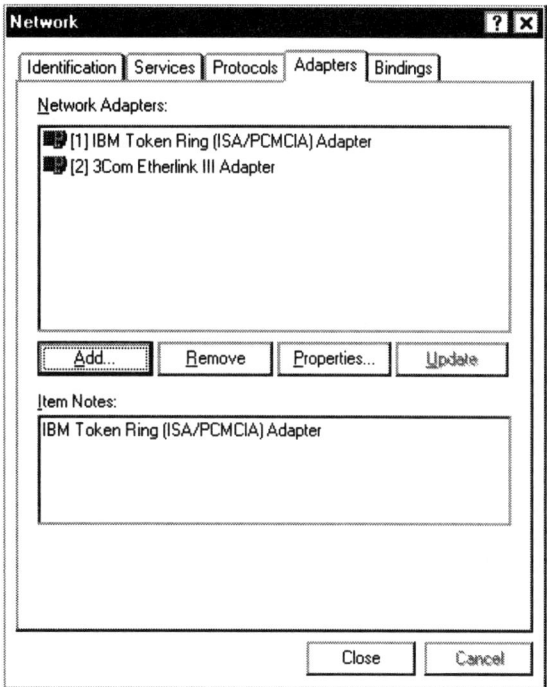

The Adapters tab of the Control Panel Network utility lets you add, remove, and configure network adapter drivers.

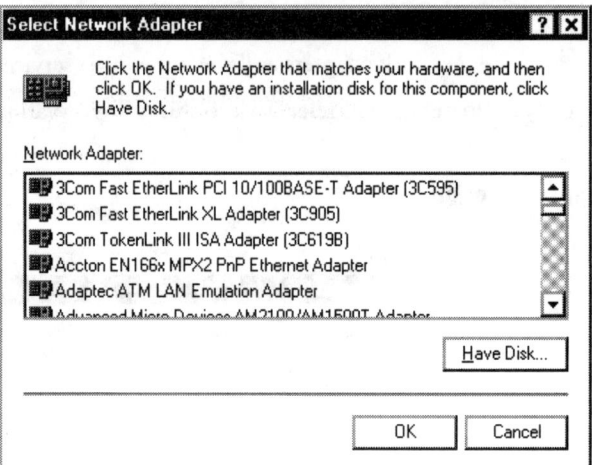

Click on **Add** to open the Select Network Adapter dialog. This displays a list of supported adapters. Click to select an adapter from the list or click on **Have Disk** to install an adapter driver from a manufacturer's diskette. If installing a supported adapter, you will be prompted for the path to the installation source files. You may enter a drive or universal naming convention (UNC) path. The general syntax for UNC is:

`\\server\sharename\directory_path`

The *server* is the machine name of the machine providing the resource. The *sharename* is the name used to share the resource. The *directory_path* is optional and should only be included if necessary.

Adapter Configuration

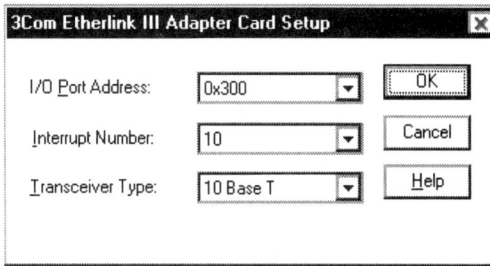

During adapter installation, you will be prompted for configuration parameters. You can also display configuration parameters by selecting an adapter from those installed and clicking on the **Properties** button. The configuration dialog will be somewhat adapter specific, but typical settings include the adapter's IRQ (interrupt) and I/O address. Other information may also be requested, depending on the adapter type.

Transport Protocols

Along with the network adapter, you need to install one or more transport protocols. You can bind up to four transport protocols to an adapter.

During this course, the discussion is limited to:

- NetBEUI

    NetBEUI is a small program providing a relatively fast response, but is not routable. NetBEUI is the default protocol for LAN Manager and compatible network operating systems.

- Microsoft Data Link Control (DLC)

    DLC provides access to printers directly attached to the network (not attached to a machine acting as a print server) and to mainframe systems.

- NWLink

    NWLink is an NDIS-compatible version of Novell NetWare's IPX/SPX protocol. It is primarily used in conjunction with the NetWare Client for Windows NT to provide access to NetWare file servers.

- TCP/IP

    Well suited to wide area networks, TCP/IP is a fully routable protocol. Of late, TCP/IP has become the de facto standard in networks with routing requirements. Another factor driving TCP/IP's recent popularity is that it is required for Internet access.

Windows NT Workstation defaults to installing TCP/IP. Windows NT Server defaults to installing TCP/IP and NWLink. Each network adapter card can support multiple protocols. You have the option of installing multiple adapters in both NT Workstation and NT Server systems. The Control Panel Network utility lets you install, remove, and configure network adapters, transport protocols, and network services.

Picking the Right Protocol

The best protocol selection for your networking environment will depend on your routing requirements, existing protocols, and connectivity requirements. It's important to remember that you aren't limited to picking one best protocol. Windows NT is able to bind multiple protocols to the same network adapter.

- NetBEUI

    NetBEUI was originally introduced by IBM in 1985. It is written to the NetBIOS interface. It was designed to be an efficient protocol requiring minimal overhead and optimized for use on small LANs. There is minimal configuration or management overhead. NetBEUI is a broadcast protocol. Instead of using routable addresses, NetBEUI uses only the NetBIOS names. Because of this, NetBEUI is not routable and therefore it does not do well in a wide area network (WAN) environment.

    Use NetBEUI on small LANs with no routing requirements and in environments where NetBEUI is already in use, such as Microsoft LAN Manager networks.

- DLC

    Data Link Control is not used for general LAN communications, but is required for communications with other systems running the DLC protocol stack. Currently, there are two applications where you are likely to see it used.

    One is IBM Mainframe connectivity. Windows provides all the tools you need for 3270 connectivity. As long as you have the DLC transport protocol loaded, you can select 3270 emulation in the Terminal applet in the Accessories program group to connect to IBM mainframes.

    The other is network printer connections. DLC is used to connect with HP (and compatible) printers directly attached to the network. When you create the printer in the Print Manager, select Hewlett-Packard Network Port as the printer port.

    If you aren't supporting either of these applications, there is no reason to install DLC transport protocol support.

- NWLink

    NWLink is a fully routable protocol that provides Windows NT connectivity with Novell NetWare networks using the IPX/SPX transport protocol. NWLink lets your system talk with NetWare servers, other NT systems running NWLink, and other workstations running IPX/SPX. NWLink also supports transfer of Novell NetBIOS communications packets across IPX/SPX.

    NWLink support is a default selection on Windows NT Servers, and on NT Workstation if installing Client . If you do not have the need for NWLink, it can be removed to save on system resources. NWLink is a fully routable protocol.

    The most common reason for using NWLink is that you have an environment where IPX/SPX is already in use, such as Novell NetWare network. You will need to install IPX/SPX support if you want to provide resources to or support client/server applications with NetWare clients.

- TCP/IP

    TCP/IP is a term used in the industry to refer to the Internet family of protocols. It is the default protocol for UNIX and has become a de facto standard for wide area networking. It is fully routable and is available on most system platforms. It provides utilities to facilitate communications and information sharing between dissimilar hardware platforms.

    Windows NT provides tools that help to make TCP/IP an excellent platform for client/server applications. In addition, a wide variety of management utilities and tools are available for supporting, testing, and troubleshooting TCP/IP networks.

    There are several situations where you should use TCP/IP, such as when your network has significant routing requirements or you think that TCP/IP utilities could aid you in network management. You should strongly consider using TCP/IP is it is already in use on your network. You will need to use TCP/IP if you want connectivity with UNIX systems, want to connect to the Internet, or are planning to set up a corporate intranet.

Select the most appropriate protocol for your networking needs. Keep in mind that, should it be required, you can install multiple protocols.

Quick Checks

For each of the following, determine the appropriate protocol selection or selections. Suggested solutions are provided in Appendix A at the end of the manual.

1. You recently changed over from a Novell NetWare network to NT Server domains. Originally, the plan had been to minimize the changes on client stations. Now the plan is to install some UNIX machines as specialized servers. You need to be able to connect to these directly across the network. You've also been told that the new standard is that all stations will be running only one transport protocol.

2. You are preparing to replace your existing LAN Manager network with an NT Server domain. The new servers have not been delivered, but the five machines that are to be set up as Windows NT Workstation systems have arrived. You want to set the systems up to test network communications and to verify that the machine can connect to an IBM mainframe using the Terminal applet. You want to keep the impact on the existing stations to a minimum.

3. You are setting up a small workgroup on its own network. Eventually, you will be installing a Novell NetWare server running a custom application. All of the stations will need to access this server.

4. Your organization has been experiencing rapid growth and it has become obvious that your current network configuration is not going to support your long range computing needs. You currently have several small LANs using NetBEUI as a transport protocol. You want to connect these into an internetwork configuration. You need to design the network to support additional growth. You don't know how much larger it is going to grow, but it is likely to be by a significant amount. You also want to have as many network management tools as possible readily available.

Protocol Installation

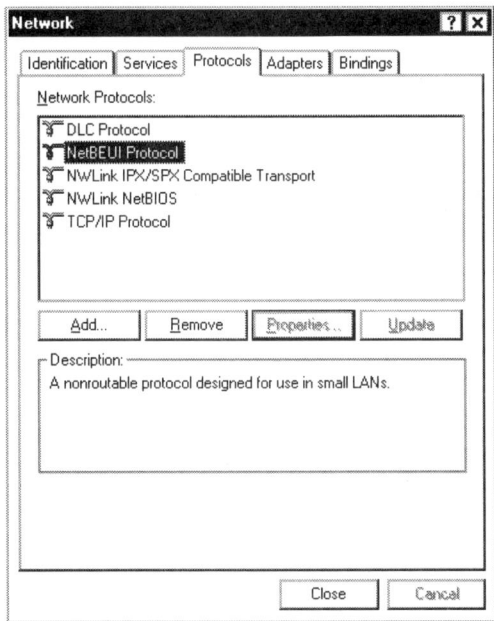

The Protocols tab of the Control Panel Network utility lets you add, remove, or configure transport protocols.

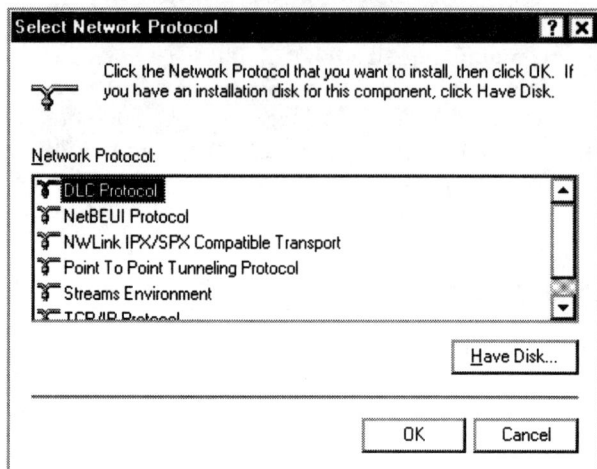

Click on **Add** to install an additional protocol. A list of supported protocols will be displayed. Click to select a protocol or click on **Have Disk** to install from a manufacturer's diskette. You will be prompted for a path to the installation files if installing a supported protocol.

DLC and NetBEUI do not have any configurable properties. NWLink and TCP/IP, on the other hand, need special attention.

NWLink IPX/SPX Properties

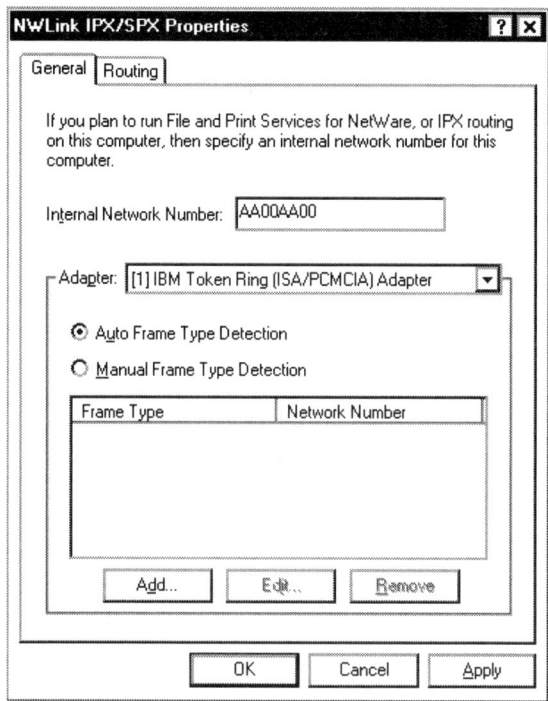

You will need to install and configure NWLink, Microsoft's IPX/SPX compatible protocol if you want to access resources from a NetWare server, if your server will be providing file and print services to NetWare clients, or if you want this machine to support IPX routing. Click to select NWLink, then on **Properties**.

The following configurable parameters are configured through the General tab:

- Internal Network Number

    Enter an 8 digit hexadecimal number in order to run services such as File and Print services for NetWare, IPX routing, SQL Server, or SNA Server. An internal network number makes it easy for a NetWare file server running on a multinet host to be identified by being assigned a logical network for the NetWare Server.

- Adapter

    All installed adapters will be available through this drop-down list. This makes it relatively easy for you to configure all of your adapters.

- Auto Frame Type Detection

    This allows automatic detection of the frame type for your network.

- Manual Frame Type Detection

    Manual Frame Type Detection allows the administrator manually set one or more frame types per adapter.

If you know the frame type being used on your network, it can be entered manually. If more than one frame type is in use, enter all frame types.

If you need to support NetBIOS communications over IPX, you will have to install NWLink NetBIOS.

About TCP/IP

Before discussing TCP/IP configuration in any detail, it may be helpful to introduce a few terms and concepts relating to the protocol. Core protocols, utilities, and services associated with the TCP/IP suite include:

- IP (Internet Protocol)

    IP provides connectionless (non-acknowledged) delivery between computer systems. Since this is a connectionless protocol, there is no guarantee of proper sequencing or even arrival at the destination.

- TCP (Transmission Control Protocol)

    TCP provides acknowledged, connection oriented communications. It includes fields for packet sequencing and acknowledgment as well as source and destination socket identifiers to allow communications with higher level protocols.

- ICMP (Internet Control Message Protocol)

    ICMP is used to control and manage information transmitted using TCP/IP. It allows nodes to share status and error information. This information can be passed to higher-level protocols. It also helps to re-route messages when a route is busy or has failed.

- ARP/RARP (Address Resolution Protocol/Reverse Address Resolution Protocol)

    ARP and RARP are maintenance protocols. They are used on Local Area Networks to enable hosts to translate IP addresses to the low level MAC (network adapter) addresses.

    ARP is used to request a station's MAC address when only its IP address is known. RARP is used when the MAC address is known, but not the IP address.

- UDP (User Datagram Protocol)

    UDP is designed for connectionless, unacknowledged communications. UDP also supports optional checksums for verifying header and data integrity.

- TELNET

    TELNET would be more accurately described as a connectivity utility. It is a simple remote terminal emulation application, allowing one host to connect to and run a session on another.

- FTP (File Transfer Protocol)

    FTP supports file transport between dissimilar systems. Assuming sufficient rights are in place, directory searches and file operations are supported.

- SMTP (Simple Mail Transfer Protocol)

    SMTP provides a mechanism for the exchange of mail information between systems. SMTP is the most widely used service on the Internet.

- SNMP (Simple Network Management Protocol)

    SNMP uses UDP to send control and management information between TCP/IP hosts.

- DNS (Domain Name System)

    Through DNS, a common naming convention is provided throughout the Internet. It is implemented as a distributed database supporting a hierarchical naming system. DNS requires a static name-to-IP address mapping.

- NFS (Network File Services)

    NFS is the industry standard for UNIX environment distributed file systems. It provides a common, transparent environment in which users can share files, regardless of their hardware platform.

A detailed discussion of TCP/IP implementation is beyond the scope of this course.

Manufacturers, including Microsoft, have developed products and procedures to help work around these problems and simplify TCP/IP management.

Internetworks

TCP/IP is the de facto standard for internetworking, dividing your network into subnets for traffic management. TCP/IP is also popular in single network environments because of wide variety of platforms supported and its management and troubleshooting utilities.

Some key points about internetworks include:

- Made up of two or more subnetworks connected by routers (called gateways).
- Each subnetwork is uniquely identified by a network address.
- Each host (individual system) is uniquely identified by a host address.
- A subnet mask identifies the network and host portions of the host address.
- Subnetworks may be connected by high or low speed links.
- Hosts may connect to the network through high or low speed links.
- Hosts may be identified by IP address or host name.

There is no set correlation between NT Server domains and subnetworks. A single domain can spread across multiple subnetworks, and multiple domains can be defined on a single subnetwork. It helps to keep in mind that an NT Server domain is a logical grouping of systems, not a physical definition according to location. A system's subnetwork, however, is determined by its location.

Windows NT supports the TCP/IP protocol suite, name resolution methods, and common utilities. This course will overview some critical points about setup and configuration, but does not include a complete discussion of all facets of TCP/IP management.

About IP Addresses

Each node in an IP network will have a 32-bit IP address. This address is divided into four bytes, or a *w.x.y.z* format, as shown in the example below:

    206.11.125.1

This actually contains two addresses, the network ID and host ID. The network ID identifies your network as unique on the Internet and the host ID identifies your station as unique on the network.

Addresses are divided into IP address classes. The class definitions are:

Class	w values	Subnet mask	Network ID	Host ID
A	1-126	255.0.0.0	w.	x.y.z
B	128-191	255.255.0.0	w.x.	y.z
C	192-223	255.255.255.0	w.x.y.	z

Network address 127 is not a valid IP address. It is used for loopback testing and interprocess communications at the local system.

The subnet masks shown are the default subnet mask. Further masking can be used to subdivide the class address. When you assign a host address, you must supply both the IP address and the subnet mask.

    NOTE: *Subnet masking is beyond the scope of this course.*

A network connecting to the public Internet must obtain an official ID from the Defense Data Network-Network Information Center (DDN-NIC) to guarantee that it has a unique network ID. This is not required for private networks. However, with a valid network ID from DDN-NIC, the network can connect to the Internet at a later date without having to change assigned network addresses.

Realistically, if you are connecting to the Internet, you will most likely get your class address by renting or leasing it from your Internet Service Provider.

TCP/IP Properties Sheet

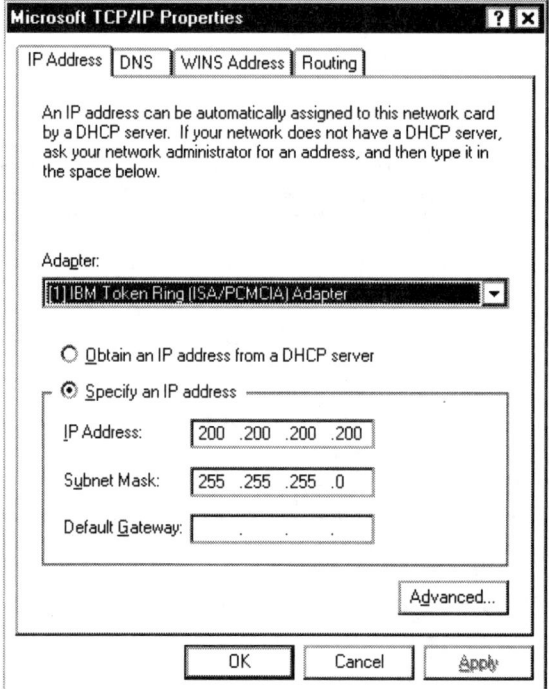

The TCP/IP Properties sheet has tabs that allow you to configure not only TCP/IP itself, but installed utilities as well. This is available through the Control Panel Network utility Protocols tab. Click to select TCP/IP Protocol, then click on **Properties**.

The following property tabs are available:

- IP Address

    This tab allows you to assign an IP address, subnet mask, and default gateway to a particular adapter card. If the station is configured as a DHCP client, this information will be configured automatically.

    NOTE: It is only necessary to define a default gateway if your network is supporting multiple subnets.

- DNS

    This tab allows you to configure the Domain Name System (DNS) to which the server subscribes. This is one of the host name to IP address resolution systems supported under TCP/IP.

- WINS

    This tab allows you to configure the Windows Internet Names Service (WINS) to which the server subscribes. WINS automates the process to resolving NetBIOS (machine) names and IP addresses.

- Routing

    This tab allows you to enable IP forwarding. This allows a multi-homed system, one supporting multiple IP addresses, to act as an IP router.

This course will be looking at selected configuration information only.

IP Address

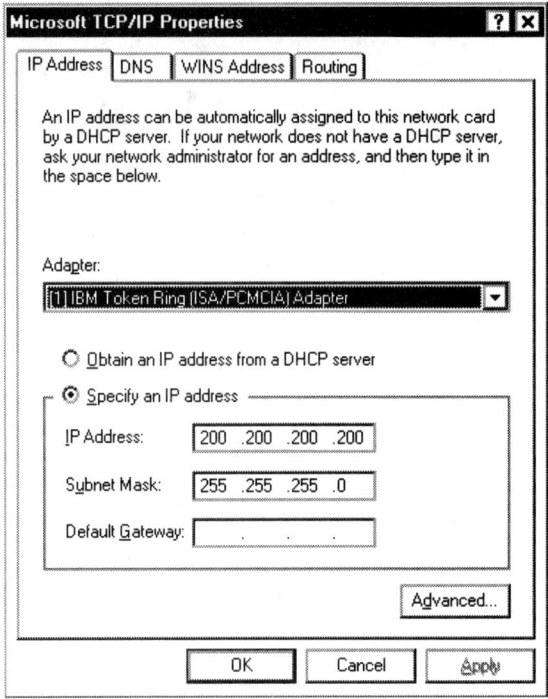

The IP Address tab allows you to configure an adapter either by identifying the system as a DHCP client or by entering a specific IP address. If the system has multiple adapters, each is configured separately.

> NOTE: To obtain a specific IP Address you should see your network administrator.

Configuration parameters include:

- Adapter

    Select the adapter to which you would like the IP Address assigned. Click on the drop-down arrow to view a list of available adapters.

- Obtain an IP address from a DHCP server

    Check this box to allow the DHCP server to assign an address to you. The system will automatically be assigned an IP address, subnet mask, and if appropriate, default gateway.

- Specify an IP address

    When this option is selected, you can manually enter IP address information.

    Enter a specific IP Address in the IP Address field.

- Subnet Mask

    The subnet mask is a filter that separates the address into network and host addresses.

    NOTE: *You will need to obtain a subnet address from your network administrator. Designing internetwork environments and determining appropriate subnet masks is beyond the scope of this course.*

- Default Gateway

    This identifies the address of the default gateway used to route packets to other networks or subnets. This is only required if your station is part of an internetwork.

The **Advanced** button lets you set more advanced TCP/IP options such as defining multiple IP addresses for an adapter, defining multiple gateways, and setting port and protocol security options.

Using DHCP

Dynamic Host Configuration Protocol is a means by which you can automate IP address assignment and management. Any NT Server system, as long as it is not defined as a DHCP client, can be set up as a DHCP server and installing and configuring the DHCP server service.

   NOTE: *DHCP server setup and configuration are beyond the scope of this course.*

When a DHCP client comes on line:

- The client broadcasts a request for an IP address.
- The DHCP server responds with an IP address offer.
- The client accepts the offer and configures itself with the IP address and subnet mask.

The DHCP server can be configured to provide the DHCP client with other information, such as default gateway address and WINS server address. The server will have a set pool of addresses, known as its address scope.

The client is given the address for a specified period of time, known as a lease period. The client will attempt to renew the address before the lease period runs out, and if unable, will attempt to bid for a new address after the lease expires.

Name Resolution

Another critical issue is name resolution, especially in a Microsoft networking environment. Microsoft's implementation of TCP/IP supports:

- HOSTS file

    This method uses a text file to associate a host name to an IP address. This method does not support NetBIOS-based applications.

- DNS

    The domain naming system supports fully qualified host names including an IP domain, subdomain, and host name.

- NetBIOS broadcasts

    This method resolves NetBIOS names and IP addresses through broadcasts. This method is severely limited in that the broadcasts are not propagated past the local subnetwork.

- LMHOSTS file

    Similar to the HOSTS file method, this method specifically supports NetBIOS names. Name resolution is through a text file located on the local machine or accessed through network shares.

- WINS

    This is an automated NetBIOS name resolution method. WINS clients automatically register themselves with the WINS server, which can then be queried for name resolutions. NetBIOS names can also be manually entered into the database.

Each of these methods will have its place in a mixed network environment. For the purpose of this course, the discussion will be limited to NetBIOS name resolution methods. As discussed earlier, Microsoft networking is a NetBIOS-based application and NetBIOS name resolution is required for proper support for browsing, attachment to shared resources, and other services.

LMHOSTS

LMHOSTS lookup is enabled through the WINS Address of the Control Panel Network utility. Each machine using LMHOSTS for name resolution must have an LMHOSTS file on that machine. You can also have the LMHOSTS file reference files located on other machines. Click on the **Import LMHOSTS** to import a prepared file.

This method is best suited to situations where there are only limited name resolution requirements that cannot be handled through NetBIOS broadcasts. Potential drawbacks of this method include:

- Performance

    Each time a NetBIOS name cannot be resolved from a local cache of names or NetBIOS broadcasts, the system will read through the LMHOSTS file and referenced files. This can result in a performance hit at the station.

- Updates

    If there are any changes, the LMHOSTS files must be updated manually. This can be somewhat eased by the use of referenced files, though their use could significantly increase background traffic on the network.

- Volatile addressing

    It would be almost impossible to manage address resolution for DHCP clients through this method. Only static address should be included in the LMHOSTS file.

In many cases, you will find WINS to be a more appropriate solution.

WINS

WINS automates NetBIOS name resolution. As a WINS client comes on line, it registers itself with its WINS server. The client's name and IP address are written into the WINS database.

If a WINS client is unable to resolve a name locally, it will query its primary or secondary WINS Server. This method is much easier to manage in an active network environment, since dynamic address changes are automatically reflected in the database.

About WINS

Implementation of WINS requires you to set up at least one WINS server, though you may need multiple servers to support a large network. There are no significant requirements except that the machine must be running Windows NT Server. Many times, you may find it convenient to have a system perform double duties as both a WINS and DHCP server.

In most cases, you are likely to find WINS a better solution than using LMHOSTS in an internetwork environment. In situations where there are minimal requirements for name resolution outside of the local subnetwork, there may be no need for WINS.

EXAMINING NETWORK SERVICES

This section will present some of the additional services available through the Network control panel. The following are topics discussed within this section:

- Network Services
- Browsing
- Bindings
- Bindings and Performance

Service selections are made according to user, system, and network needs. Installing unnecessary services adds to system overhead.

Network Services

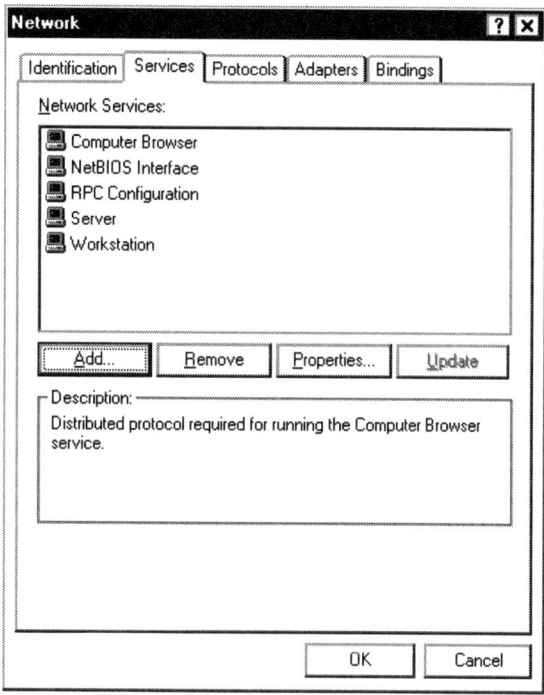

The Network utility's Services tab displays the installed network services. The services shown are typical for a "plain" installation. Your list of services will depend on your installation choices.

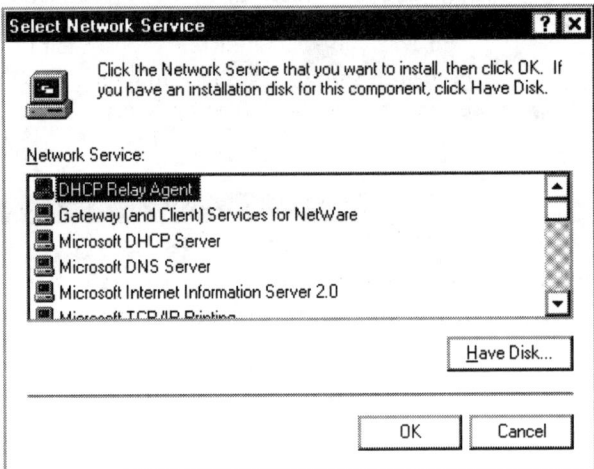

Click on **Add** to install additional network services. These include a number of selections already mentioned, such as DHCP and WINS server services. If necessary, you will be prompted for a path to the installation files to complete service setup. Configuration prompts will be service specific.

Browsing

Browsing is quickly becoming a term that can lead to some confusion. In a Microsoft networking environment, it refers to viewing available network resources. However, tools for browsing through the Internet, such as Internet Explorer, use the same term. As Internet support becomes more prevalent and more tightly integrated to the operating system, the confusion may get worse before it gets better.

For the current purpose of this course, the former usage is assumed.

Rather than have systems constantly querying each other for a list of shared resources, Windows NT will have one machine hold this information for the domain or workgroup.

- Master browser (browse master)

    The master browser carries the master list for the domain. It will supply client browse requests and periodically update any backup browsers.

- Backup browser

    A backup browser acts as the supplement the master browser. When the domain is spread across multiple subnetworks, each will have its own backup browser which will provide for local browse requests.

- Clients

    All other machines are browse clients. They will request the master browser for available resources as needed to support application requests.

A machine must be running the Computer Browser service to act as a master or backup browser. Normally, the first domain member active on a domain will become the master browser.

Bindings

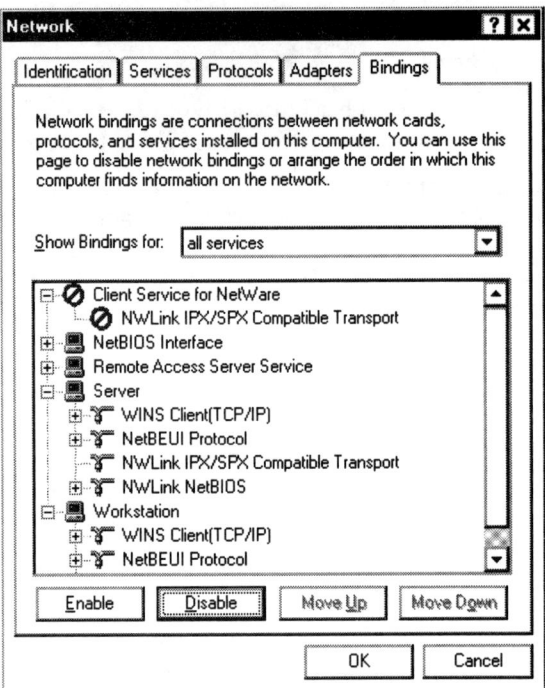

Bindings are connections established between network adapters, protocols, and services. The relationship can be thought of as:

- One or more protocols will be bound to each network adapter.
- Each protocol may be bound to one or more services.

The Bindings tab on the Control panel Network utility displays bindings by service, by protocol, and by adapter. This utility also lets you enable or disable services, protocols, or adapters. Disabling is a way in which you can make the selection inactive without having to uninstall, and possibly reinstall, the selection. Many times, this can be helpful in troubleshooting system and network problems. For example, if you think an error is related to the Client Service for NetWave, you can disable the service as shown in the example graphic.

Bindings and Performance

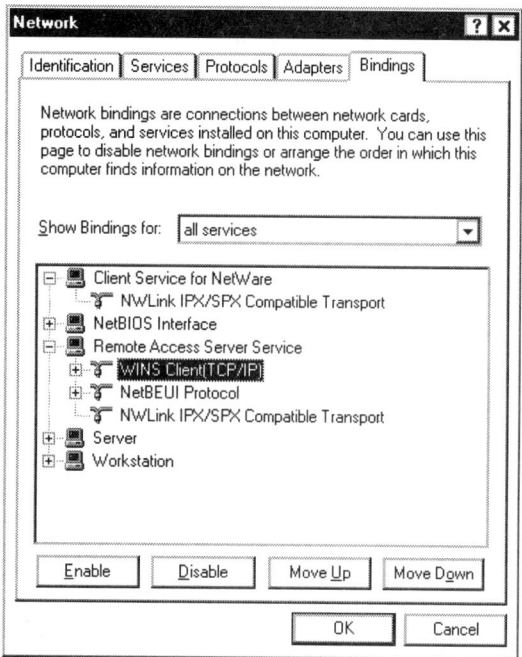

You can sometimes improve performance on a very active system by changing protocol priorities. The protocol listed at the top of the list has the highest priority. To change a protocol's relative priority:

- Click to select the protocol.
- Click on **Move Up** or **Move Down**.

Move the protocol responsible for the greatest percentage of the machine's network traffic to the top of the protocol list. You must change the relative priorities for each service separately.

Exercise 8-1

During this exercise you will reconfigure network support on your system. This exercise assumes that you installed network support using the parameters supplied in Exercise 1-1.

This exercise assumes that you are connected to a training network or an isolated network segment. If you are connected to an operational network, you will need to contact your network administrator before completing this exercise. Your network administrator can provide you with IP address and subnet mask information.

1. Open a command prompt, type the following, and press **ENTER**:

    ipconfig

    Record the results below:

2. Close the command prompt and launch the Control Panel Network utility.
3. Click on the Protocol tab.
4. Click to select TCP/IP, then click on **Properties**.
5. Click on the "Obtain an IP address from a DHCP server" option button.
6. When prompted to verify your action, click on **Yes**.
7. Click on **OK**, then on **OK** to exit the Network utility.
8. Shut down and restart your system.
9. Log on as an administrator.
10. Open a command prompt, type the following, and press **ENTER**:

    ipconfig

    Compare the results to those you received in step 1.
11. If your network does not have a DHCP server, you will see both the IP address and subnet masks set to all zeros. If there is a DHCP server available, you will see values other than those originally set for the system.
12. Launch the Control Panel Network utility and click on the Protocol tab.
13. Select TCP/IP and click on **Properties**.

14. Click on the "Specify IP address" option button and enter the values you recorded in step 1 for the IP address and subnet mask.

15. Click on **OK**, then on **OK** again.

16. Return to your command prompt window and run ipconfig. The IP address and subnet mask should have reverted to their original values.

RESOURCE SHARING AND ACCESS

This section will discuss sharing resources and providing access to these resources. The process by which sharing can be established will also be displayed. The following are topics discussed within this section:

- System Logon
- Resource Access
- Directory Sharing
- Share Parameters
- Share Permissions
- Connecting to Shared Directories
- Sharing Printers
- Attaching to Shared Printers
- Printer Management

Sometimes, it is necessary to access a resource that is normally not available to a user. Therefore, to grant permission to the user to utilize the requested resource, permissions must be granted.

System Logon

Before talking about resource sharing, let's quickly review the logon process. Logon and validation is an important part of managing resource access.

- The user presses `CTRL` `ALT` `DEL` to display the logon dialog.

    The default domain, initially the local domain, is displayed in the From field. The user may also select a trusted domain or the local workstation. A valid user account name and password must be entered.

- The local Security Authority attempts validation.

    If a local account is used for logon, the user account and password are checked against the local account database.

- If not authenticated locally, pass-through validation occurs.

    User accounts residing in trusted domains are passed to the appropriate domain for validation against its user database. If validated, the user's SID and group memberships are passed back. If the user cannot be validated by either the local or trusted domain, logon is not allowed.

- An access token is created for valid users.

    If validated, the Logon Process creates an access token for the user. This includes the user's SID, group SIDs, and user rights.

- A process is created and the token is attached to the process.

    The Win32 subsystem is called to create the process and attach the token. For an interactive logon, Win32 launches the Program Manager.

Resource Access

Resource (object) access is determined by comparing security information in the user's access token to security information in the object's security descriptor. An access mask is generated reflecting the level of access requested by the user. This mask is compared against object permissions.

- Access Token

    The access token is generated during the logon process. It contains the user's SID, the SID for any group to which the user belongs, and user rights information.

- Security Descriptor

    This contains security information directly relating to the object. User and group SIDs with no access (AccessDenied) are listed first, blocking access to the object.

The process is the same whether validating local or network resource access. Users in trusted domains must be given permission in trusting domains before they can access resources.

Directory Sharing

The easiest way to share directories for either Windows NT Workstation or Windows NT Server is through the graphical management tools. You can set up directory sharing through:

- My Computer.

    Locate the directory that you wish to share. Right-click (click with mouse button 2) on the directory and run **Sharing**, or run **Sharing** from the **File** menu. The same procedure is used to modify share information for the directory.

- Windows NT Explorer.

    Locate the directory that you wish to share. Right-click on the directory and run **Sharing**. The same procedure is used to modify share information for the directory.

You will be able to recognize a shared directory through its icon. It will look like a file folder with a hand holding it out as available.

Share Parameters

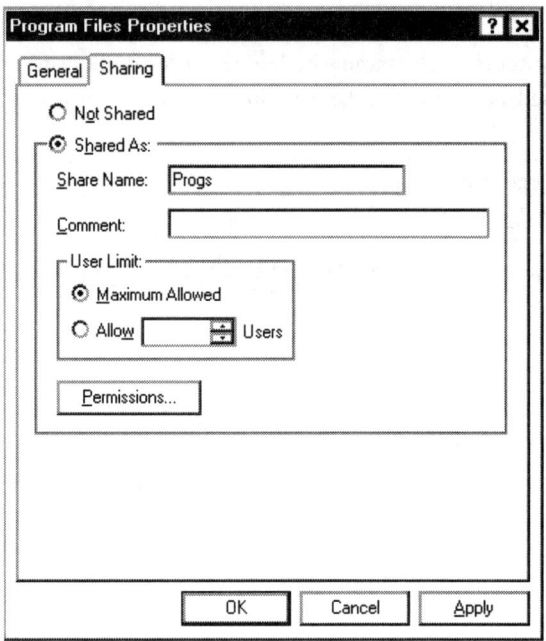

You will see the same dialog when initiating a share from either My Computer or Windows NT Explorer.

Share Name — This defaults to the directory name, or a name based on the directory. You may overwrite this with a different name. If you have MS-DOS or DOS Windows stations, use names that are MS-DOS compatible.

Comment — You have the option of including a text comment to be displayed with the share name when users browse through available directories.

User Limit — You can specify a limit for the number of concurrent user shares, or leave this as unlimited.

If you follow the share name with a dollar sign ($), it becomes a system share. This also referred to as an administrative or hidden share. Resources shared in this fashion will not display in a browse list. However, you can still connect to the resource by typing its name in explicitly.

Click on the **Permissions** button to set or modify share permissions. Click on **OK** after filling in all necessary information.

Share Permissions

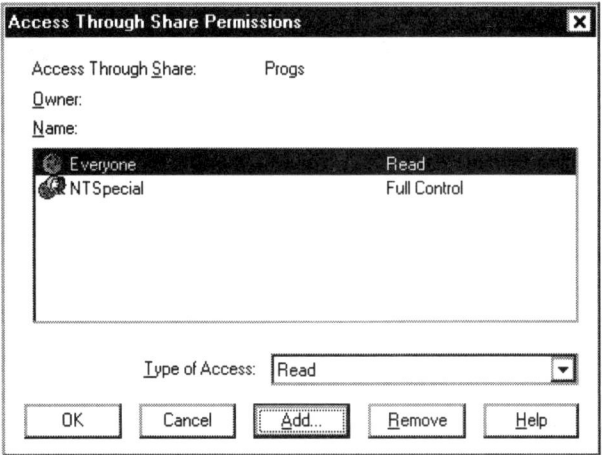

When you share a directory, the default is to give the group Everyone Full Control over the directory. You can change the permission settings, adding or removing users or groups as necessary.

To remove access permissions for a user or group, select the user or group and click on **Remove**.

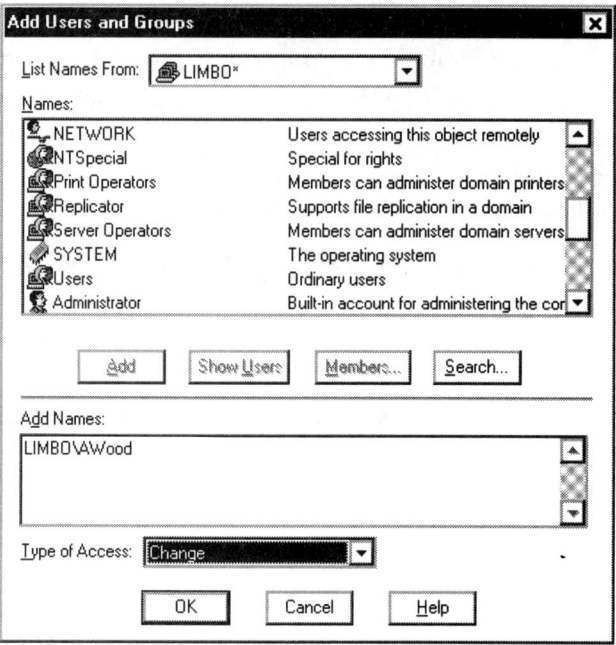

Click on **Add** to define permissions for additional users and groups. Initially, only available groups will display. Click on the **Show Users** to display user accounts. Click to select, then click on **Add**. This moves the user or group to the "Add Names" window.

From here, you can select the user or group and click on the "Type of Access" drop-down arrow to select the access permission assigned. Click on **OK** after making your changes.

The following permission levels are supported:

No Access	All access to the directory, its files, and any subdirectories is prevented.
Read	The user can view file and subdirectory names, change to subdirectories, view data files, and run executable files.

Change   The change permission grants all the rights
                                    of the read permission. In addition, users
                                    can add files to the directory, add
                                    subdirectories, change data in files, and
                                    delete files and subdirectories.

Full Control   Full control grants all the rights of the
                                    change permission. In addition, users can
                                    change permissions and take ownership.

As mentioned earlier, a permission assignment of "No Access" to either the user or to any group to which the user belongs blocks all access to the resource.

In a domain environment, you will normally assign permissions to a workstation local group, then users to a domain global group to pass the permissions to domain user.

Connecting to Shared Directories

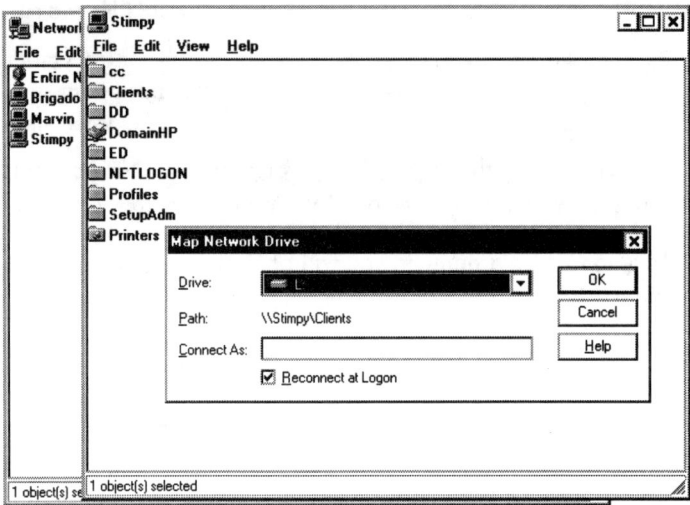

The procedures for connecting to a network drive are somewhat different between using Network Neighborhood and Windows NT Explorer. Under Network Neighborhood:

- Locate the share to which you want to map a drive.
- Right-click on the share and run **Map Network Drive**, or run **Map Network Drive** from the **File** menu.
- Select the local drive ID and, optionally, the user name to use for the connection.
- Click on **OK**.

You cannot change the resource path through this dialog. By default, the system will attempt to reconnect to the resource each time the user logs on. Resource connections are user specific.

You will get this same dialog if you right-click on a share name under Windows NT Explorer and run **Map Network Drive**.

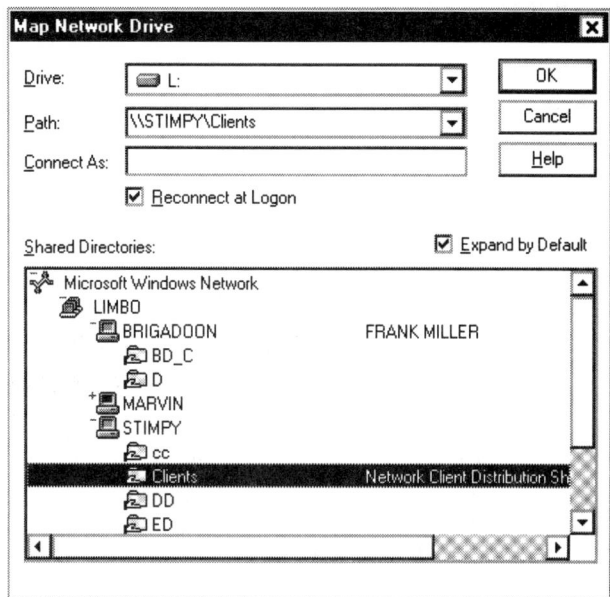

Run **Map Network Drive** from the Windows NT Explorer **Tools** menu to see a slightly different dialog for attaching to shared directories. You can either type in the path to the resource, which means you can use this to attach to a system (hidden) share, or locate and select the resource in the "Shared Directories" window. Click on **OK** after making your selection.

As before, you can use the "Connect As" field to connect as a different user. At default, the system will attempt to reconnect to the resource each time the user logs on.

Access Scenario

This scenario presents you with a shared resource access problem. You need to determine the best solution. List all necessary procedures to meet the criteria, but you do not need to provide detailed procedural steps. A sample solution is provided in Appendix A at the end of the manual.

You've added a hard disk to a Windows NT Workstation that is part of an NT Server domain. You are in a change-over process on your network and some of your applications.

For now, you are going to keep all of the accounting data files, including archived files, on this drive. The plan is to later move the files to a stand-alone Windows NT Server.

You want local access to be strictly controlled. Only administrators will be allowed direct access to the files. All other users will access the files through network shares.

Domain users will need access to three sets of data files. Members of the domain Acct group will need read and write access to a Reports directory, while all other users will be allowed read access only. Only members of the Acct group should have any access to the Current directory, limited to read and write only. All users will have access to the Archive directory, but only for look-up purposes.

Since this is a new system, you also want to do some security spot checks. You want to know if anyone tries to delete any files from the Current directory or if anyone tries to delete or modify files in the Archive directory.

How would you configure system security?

Sharing Printers

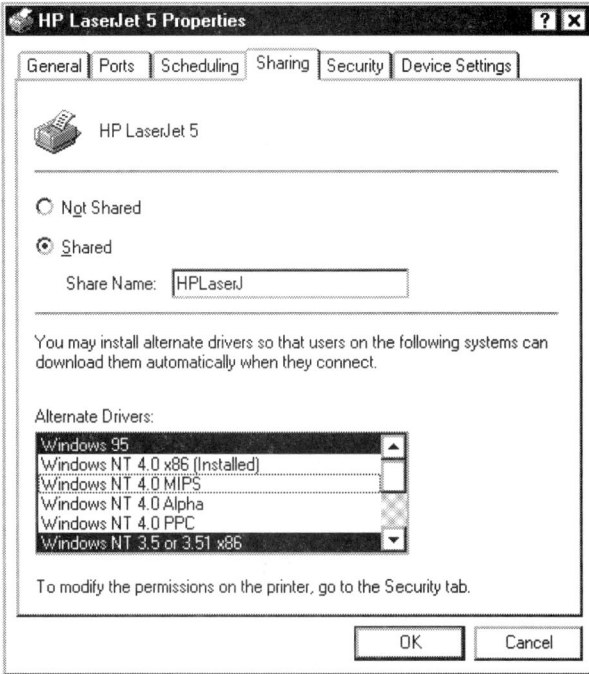

You can share a printer to the network while you are setting up the printer initially or after installation. Select the printer from the Printers folder and either right-click and run **Sharing**, or run **Sharing** from the File menu. This displays the Sharing tab of the Printer properties. You can also display the printer properties and click on the Sharing tab to get to this dialog.

You have the option to install alternate drivers. By installing the drivers locally when you share the printer, you don't have to install the drivers locally on those clients. They will automatically use the shared driver. You will be prompted for a path to the appropriate driver files for each of the selected clients.

It will still be necessary to install drivers locally on MS-DOS, Windows, or Windows for Workgroups clients that attach to the printer.

Attaching to Shared Printers

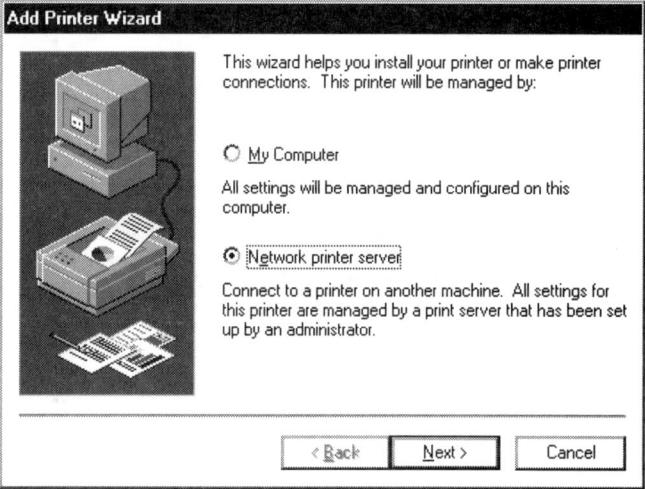

One way to attach to a network printer is to double-click on the Add Printer icon in the Printers folder to launch the Add Printer Wizard. Click on the "Network printer server" option button, then on **Next**.

Resource Sharing and Access

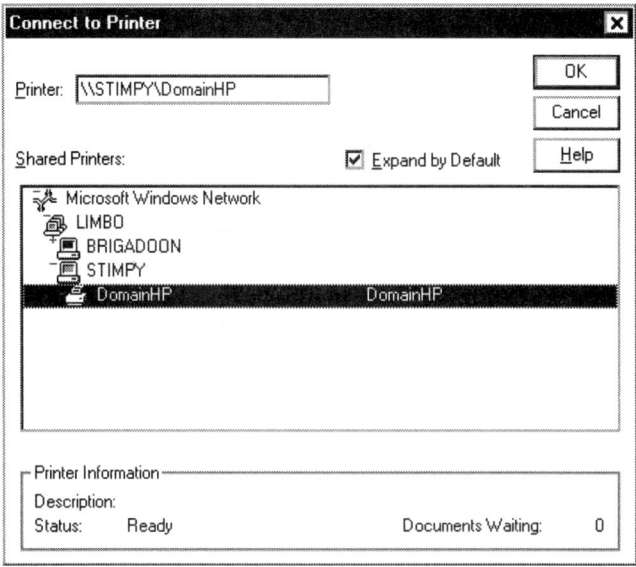

Locate and select the printer from the "Shared Printers" window or type the path to the printer in the "Printer" prompt. Click on **OK** after making your selection.

You will be prompted to specify whether or not the printer will be used as a destination for MS-DOS programs, then receive a message that the printer has been added.

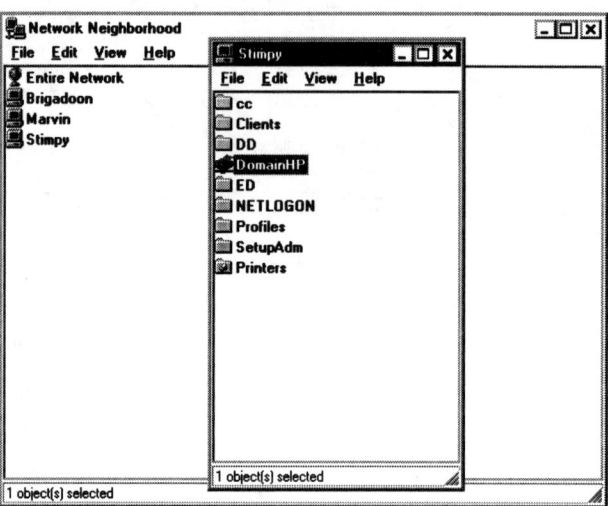

As long as the necessary drivers are present on the printer server, the process is somewhat easier through the Network Neighborhood. Browse through to locate and select the printer. Right-click and run **Install**, or run **Install** from the **File** menu. The printer will be added to your printers folder.

Printer Management

Assuming that you have at least Manage Documents as your access permission, printer and spooler management is the same for remote printers as for local printers. You can pause or resume printing, pause or resume individual print jobs, and view and modify print job properties.

Exercise 8-2

During this exercise, you will set up and test a network share. You can share a resource from a system then connect to the same resource for network rather than local access.

1. Launch Windows Explorer and select the NTFS drive you created earlier in the course.
2. Right-click (click with mouse button 2) in the Contents window, move the pointer to New, then click on Folder.
3. Type the following as the folder name and press **ENTER**:
   ReadMe
4. Repeat the above procedure to create a folder with the following name:
   WriteMe
5. Right-click on **ReadMe** and run Sharing.
6. Click on the "Shared As" option button. Leave the share name at default.
7. Click on **Permissions**.
8. Click on the Type of access drop-down list and select Read.
9. Click on **OK**, then on **OK** to finish creating the share.
10. Repeat steps 5 through 9 for WriteMe, leaving the access permission for Everyone at default (Full Control).
11. Using procedures described earlier in the course, copy a selection of files to each of the directories.

    NOTE: *Be careful to copy, not move, the files to the directories.*

12. Locate and expand the Network Neighborhood in the All Folders window.
13. Right-click on **ReadMe** and run Map Network Drive.
14. Select drive U: from the Drive drop-down list.
15. Click to remove the check from the "Reconnect at Logon" check box.

16. Click on **OK**.
17. Repeat steps 13 through 16 to map WriteMe as drive W:.
18. Locate and select drive W. It will also be identified by its share name.
19. Click on a file in the directory and press `DEL`. Press `ENTER` to verify your action. The file is deleted.
20. Locate and select drive U:
21. Click on a file in the directory and press `DEL`. Press `ENTER` to verify your action. You receive a message that access is denied. Click on **OK**.
22. Select the ReadMe directory (not the network map share, but the physical directory), select, and attempt to delete the same file. You can now delete the file.

You can set different access permissions for local and shared access to a directory. The user's access will depend on whether the directory is being accessed as a local resource or a shared resource.

SUMMARY

During this chapter, you were introduced to:

- NDIS interface
- Adapter installation and configuration
- Transport protocol selections
- NetBIOS overview
- Protocol installation
- NWLink properties
- TCP/IP properties
- IP Address overview
- DHCP
- LMHOSTS file
- WINS
- Browsing
- Access validation

- Shared directories
- Shared printers
- Using shared resources

The next chapter continues with network related subjects, looking at NetWare integration.

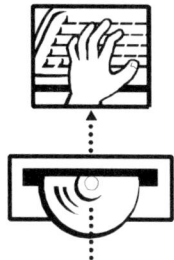

Stop now and complete the Chapter 8 NEXTSim simulation exercises on the Interactive Learning CD-ROM.

POST-TEST QUESTIONS

The answers to these questions are in Appendix A at the end of this manual.

1. You want to share a directory, but you don't want it to appear on the workgroup browse lists. Is there any way to do this?

   ....
   ....

2. You are installing a workstation on a network consisting of a single subnetwork. The network uses TCP/IP. What addressing information must you provide for the client?

   DHCP is not being used on the network.

   ....

   ....

3. You've tried everything to give EWood access to a shared directory, including making him a member of two groups with access permissions and even explicitly assigning permissions to the user. The user is still not allowed to access the directory. What is most likely wrong?

   ....

   ....

4. You are setting up a large network with several subnetworks. A number of the network members will be laptops that are connected intermittently to the LAN. You are going to use DHCP for IP address assignment. What method should you use for NetBIOS name resolution?

   ....

   ....

5. What protocol is required for attaching to a printer directly connected to the LAN?

   ....

   ....

CHAPTER 9

Advanced Networking

MAJOR TOPICS

Objectives 404

Pre-Test Questions 404

Introduction 405

NetWare Services for Windows NT 405

Introduction to Remote Access Service 412

Introduction to the Internet 427

Summary 445

Post-Test Questions 445

OBJECTIVES

At the completion of this chapter, you will be able to:

- Install Client Service for NetWare.
- List the connection types supported by RAS.
- List the protocols supported by RAS.
- Install the RAS client service.
- Describe the purpose and use of Microsoft Internet Explorer.

PRE-TEST QUESTIONS

The answers to these questions are in Appendix A at the end of this manual.

1. You have a number of sales persons who need to call in from different locations every day. What type of connection device are you most likely to use to give them access to a RAS server?

   ....

   ....

2. You have the same user name and password on an NT Server domain and on a NetWare file server. You installed Client Service for NetWare on your system and connected to a NetWare print queue. What must you do to have a banner printed for each print job you send to that printer?

   ....

   ....

3. What utility is used to install the RAS client?

   ....

   ....

4. What Windows NT v4.0 utility lets you view information published on a corporate Intranet?

....

....

INTRODUCTION

This chapter continues the networking discussion with a look at some additional network and network related services. Client Service for NetWare, the first one discussed, gives your workstation direct access to NetWare servers. Installation and configuration procedures are discussed, along with an overview of the procedures for connecting to NetWare resources.

From there, the discussion moves to Remote Access Service. You'll see how to install and configure the RAS client for access to remote networks. This includes a look at the procedures for installing and configuring a modem

The chapter ends with a brief look at Internet and Intranet issues, including an introduction to Microsoft's Internet Explorer.

NETWARE SERVICES FOR WINDOWS NT

This section will explain how a system set up with Windows NT Workstation can communicate with a NetWare system. The procedure for installing this service will also be presented. The following are topics discussed within this section:

- Client Service for NetWare (CSNW)
- CSNW Configuration
- Choosing a NetWare Option
- Resource Access

As departments and companies merge these days, so do systems and network resources. Often, one department will use a NetWare network, and the other a Windows NT network. An even more common scenario is the integration of NT into an existing NetWare environment. For the two networks to communicate, a gateway service must be installed on the NT system.

Client Service for NetWare (CSNW)

The Client Service for NetWare ships with Windows NT Workstation. It gives you access to file and printer resources physically located on NetWare or accessed through NetWare file servers.

Client Service for NetWare is installed and configured through the Control Panel Network utility.

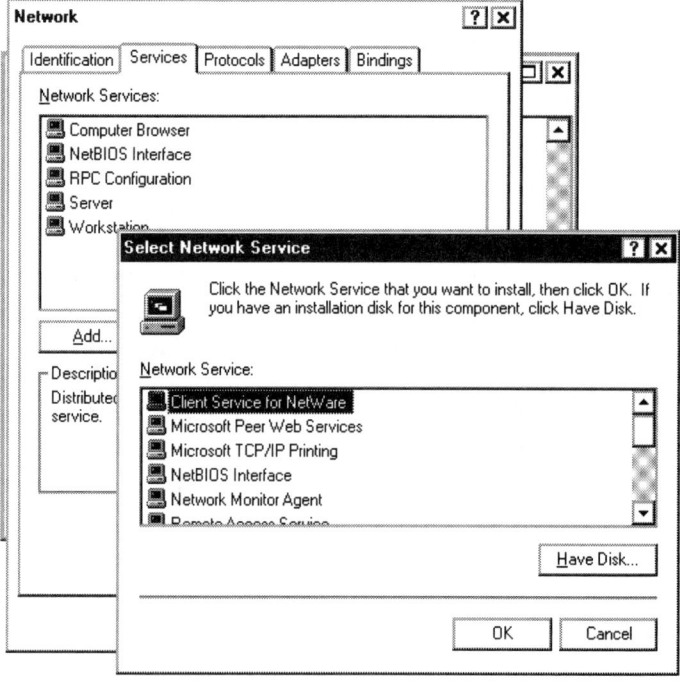

Click on the Services tab, then on **Add**. Click on **Client Service for NetWare**. You will be prompted to provide a path to the installation files.

NOTE: *You must have NWLink installed to install CSNW.*

After installation, click on **Close** to exit the utility. You will be prompted to restart your system.

The first time you log on, you will be prompted to enter a Preferred Server, if your network doesn't support NetWare Directory Services (NDS), or Default Tree and Context if your network does support NDS. You can also select whether or not your system should run the NetWare login script. You cannot change your user name from this dialog. Your current user will be assumed as your NetWare security focus.

CSNW Configuration

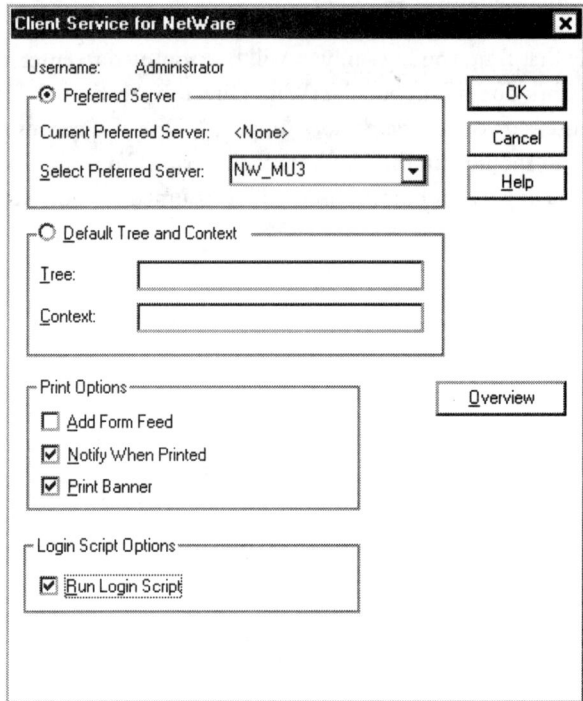

Run CSNW from the Control Panel to configure Client Service for NetWare. The options are nearly the same as for initial logon. You can select the preferred server or default tree and context. You can select whether or not to run NetWare login scripts.

There are also a set of printer options, letting you set how print jobs are managed.

- Add Form Feed

    A form feed will be appended to the end of your print job. For most applications, this will not be necessary.

- Notify When Printed

    The user will be sent a notification message after his or her document prints.

- Print Banner

    This causes a banner to be printed before the print job.

"Notify When Printed" and "Print Banner" are default selections.

Choosing a NetWare Option

Depending on your network configuration, you may have options for how you support NetWare connectivity. In addition to client services for NetWare, Windows NT Server supports Gateway Service for NetWare. With Gateway Service for NetWare, the server connects to NetWare resources, then shares them as NT Server resources to the domain.

- Use Gateway Service for NetWare

    This option typically has less administrative overhead. It is most appropriate when the majority of your users need access to the same resources. A major drawback is that Windows NT Server is required.

- Use Client Service for NetWare

    This option will be required if you don't have a Windows NT Server available. While it may require more administrative overhead, it allows for greater flexibility at the client. Each client can easily access a different set of NetWare server resources.

The decision of which to use will depend on your configuration and your requirements.

Resource Access

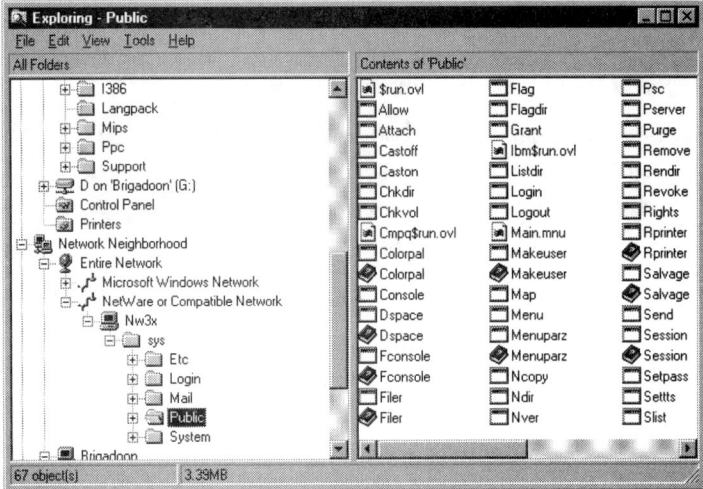

Resource access is managed in much the same way as workgroup or NT Server domain resources. To connect to NetWare resources:

- File resources

    Browse to locate the desired directory through either Network Neighborhood or right-click on the directory and run **Map Network Drive**. The path information will be filled in for you and the suggested local drive ID displayed. Click on **OK** to connect to the NetWare directory.

- Printer resources

    Create the printer using Add Printer in Printers folder. Select Network printer and when prompted, browse to locate the print queue to which you want to attach.

As with Windows networking services, you have the option of having the system attempt to reconnect each time you log on. Your access permissions will be determined by your file and directory trustee rights on the NetWare server.

Exercise 9-1

During this chapter, you will install Client Service for NetWare. This exercise is designed as an introduction to the service only. You are not required to have access to a NetWare server to complete this exercise.

1. Launch Start/Settings/Control Panel.
2. Double-click on the Network utility.
3. Click on the Service tab.
4. Click on **Add**.
5. Click to select Client Service for NetWare if not already selected and click on **OK**.
6. When prompted, verify the path to installation files and press **ENTER**.
7. After the files are copied, click on **Close**.
8. When prompted to restart your system, click on **Yes**.
9. Log on to Windows NT. When prompted for NetWare logon information, click on **Cancel**.
10. If not open, open the Control Panel and double-click on CSNW and review the options settings.
11. Click on **Cancel**.
12. Launch the Network utility and click on the Services tab.
13. If not selected, click to select Client Service for NetWare, then on **Remove**.
14. When prompted to verify your action, click on **Yes**.
15. Click on **Close**.
16. When prompted to restart your system, press **ENTER**.

INTRODUCTION TO REMOTE ACCESS SERVICE

This section will present information on how to connect to network resources from an outside location. Configuration for modems, RAS servers, and protocols will be discussed. The following are topics included in this section:

- Remote Access Service Overview
- RAS Connection Options
- Supported Protocols
- RAS Clients
- Modem Setup
- Modem Detection
- Modem Configuration
- RAS Installation
- Dial-up Networking
- Multiple Connections on RAS

RAS provides users the ability to connect to network resources from a mobile or other remote location. It is important to recognize the differences of connecting through a RAS server as compared to a local connection.

Remote Access Service Overview

Most clients are connected directly to the network. In some cases, however, you are going to need to provide remote connections for your users. Microsoft provides Remote Access Service (RAS) to let you set up and configure client access.

This self study focuses on the RAS client. Keep in mind that you will also need a RAS server.

Users connecting to a RAS server can be limited to accessing that server only or can be given access to the network. Effectively, this is the same as a local connection to the network, expect that any type of data transfers run significantly slower.

RAS Connection Options

You will need to select connection options appropriate to your access requirements, available support, and budgetary constraints. You can select from:

- Modem

    A modem allows connection over a standard phone line. Though transfer rates are limited, this allows connection by nearly any type of client and from nearly any location. Windows NT supports nearly 200 modems. You can also manually configure unsupported modems.

- Null Modem

    A null modem is a direct serial connection between systems. A null modem connection is made by running a cable between serial ports on the server and client.

- ISDN

    Integrated Services Digital Network provides a moderate-speed connection (typically 64 Kbps to 128 Kbps) between stationary remote sites. ISDN requires special digital telephone lines and connection equipment.

- X.25

    A standard packet-switching communication protocol, X.25 is designed to support WAN connectivity. Normally, connection requires Packet Assemblers/Disassemblers (PADs) and X.25 smart cards. Some carriers provide support through standard modems.

In most cases, the best option for connecting a mobile user is through a modem connection.

Supported Protocols

RAS supports the following protocol options:

- TCP/IP

    For TCP/IP connection, you must provide IP addresses for your clients. IP addresses can be managed through a static range at the server. You may also need to provide a name resolution method.

- IPX

    You can integrate RAS servers and clients into an existing IPX-based network. This allows for easy integration with existing NetWare networks. The RAS server can also act as an IPX router for RAS clients. The RAS server can automatically generate IPX network numbers for RAS clients.

- NetBEUI

    The NetBEUI client protocol and NetBIOS gateway are installed by default on all RAS servers and most clients. NetBEUI is required for MS-DOS and MS-DOS based clients, including Windows for Workgroups clients.

- Microsoft RAS

    This is a proprietary protocol supported on older RAS versions and legacy RAS clients. Microsoft RAS provides support for NetBIOS. Older clients must be running NetBEUI, but the RAS server can act as a gateway to networks running other protocols.

RAS server continues to support NetBIOS gateway services. This allows a client to connect using NetBEUI, and then be routed to an IPX or TCP/IP network. The client can then access shared resources, but applications that require IPX or TCP/IP at the client are not supported.

In addition to these, Microsoft supports connectivity through:

- SLIP

    Serial Line Internet Protocol is an access standard most commonly used on UNIX-based servers. Windows NT 3.5 and above RAS clients have the ability to connect to SLIP servers. Windows NT RAS server does not support connection by SLIP clients.

- PPP

    Point-to-Point protocol is a set of framing and authentication protocols. PPP provides flexible and relatively secure connection options. PPP can be used over TCP/IP, IPX, or NetBEUI. In addition to file access, Windows Sockets, NetBIOS, and IPX interface applications are supported.

- PPTP

    The Point-to-Point Tunneling Protocol provides secure client connections over the Internet. Through multiprotocol virtual private networks(VPNs), secure communications are supported over standard Internet connections.

Your protocol selections will be determined by application requirements and client capabilities.

RAS Clients

The following client connections are supported for RAS:

- Windows NT v4.0

    Clients connect using a supported protocol. Microsoft encrypted logon and password validation are supported. NT v4.0 clients can connect to any SLIP or PPP provider. Multilink connections are supported, combining multiple physical links into a single logical link, providing an increased connection bandwidth.

- Windows NT v3.51 and Windows 95

    Windows NT v3.51 and Windows 95 support the same connection features as Windows NT v4.0, except multilink connections. This includes connection to any SLIP or PPP provider.

- Windows NT v3.1

    Windows NT v3.1 clients connect using the Microsoft RAS protocol only. The client must also be running NetBEUI locally.

- Windows, Windows for Workgroups, and LAN Manager clients

  Windows NT Server ships with Microsoft Network Client v3.0 which provides connectivity to RAS servers. Clients can access shared network resources through the RAS NetBIOS gateway.

- Third party PPP clients

  Non-Microsoft PPP clients can connect through IPX, TCP/IP, and NetBEUI. There are no special server configuration requirements.

As mentioned earlier, the most common connection for Microsoft clients is by modem and public carrier.

Modem Setup

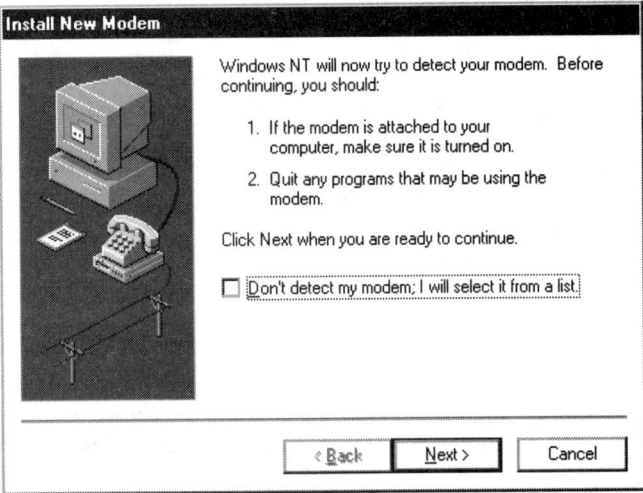

When you install RAS server or client, if you do not already have a connection device (modem, for example) configured on your system, you will be prompted to install one at that time. Since a modem is the most common connection device for RAS, let's step through the configuration procedures as an example.

The first step is to launch the Control Panel Modem utility. If you do not have a modem installed, this will launch the Install New Modem wizard. You have the option of letting Windows NT attempt to detect your modem or select the modem from a list of those supported by Windows NT. Before letting Windows NT detect for the modem, make sure that the modem is turned on and connected, and that there are no applications using the modem.

Modem Detection

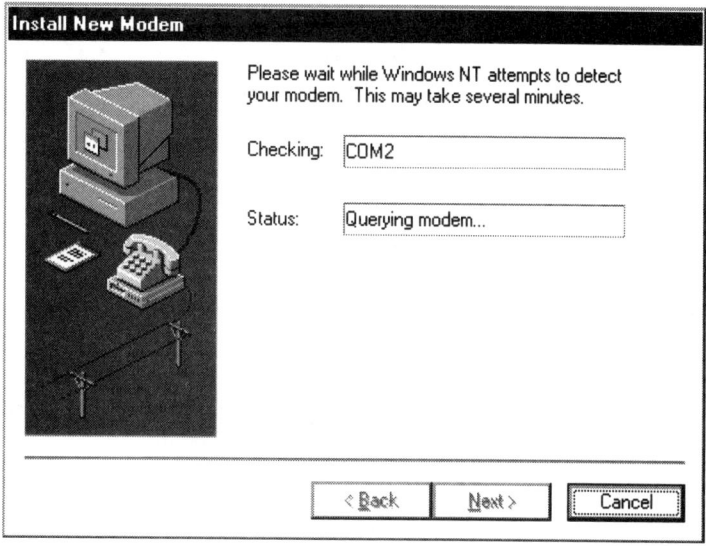

Windows NT will check each available COM (serial) port to see if a modem is attached. If one is found, it will query the modem to try to determine the modem type.

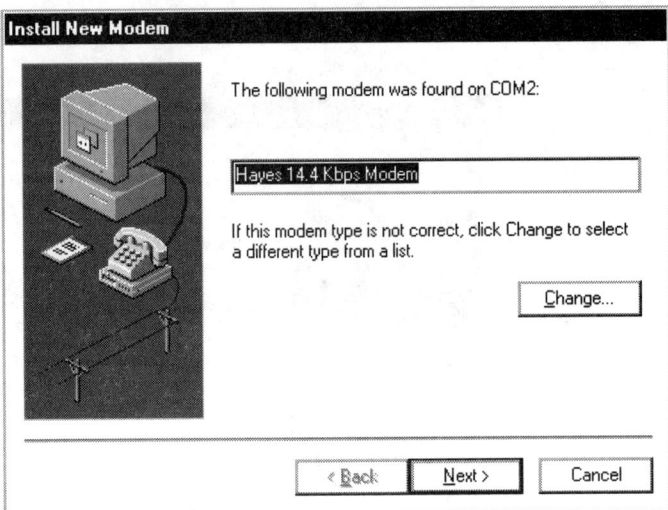

The Wizard will display the detected modem. If this is incorrect, click on **Change** to display a list of supported modems.

Windows NT will install the drivers for the modem. You will next be taken to the modem properties. Once the modem is installed, you can run the Control Panel Modems utility at any time to configure the modem.

Modem Configuration

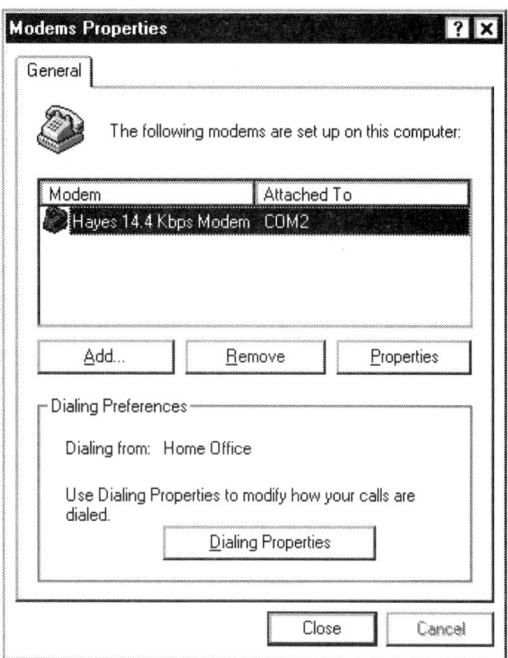

The general modem properties displays the installed modem(s) and the selected dialing preference. Click to select the modem, then on **Properties** to modify modem properties.

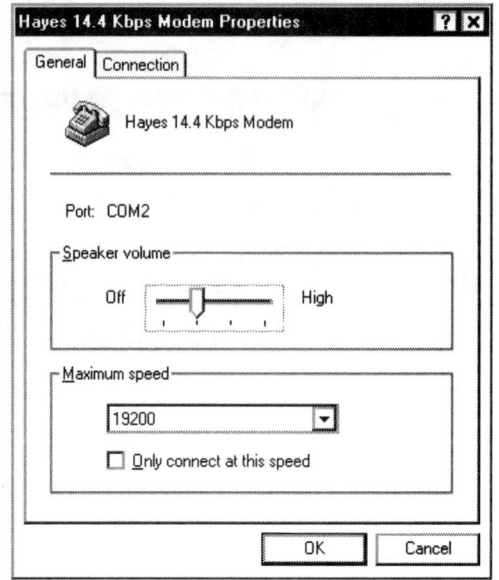

Properties pages are somewhat modem specific. The examples shown here are typical. The General tab lets you set speaker volume and maximum speed.

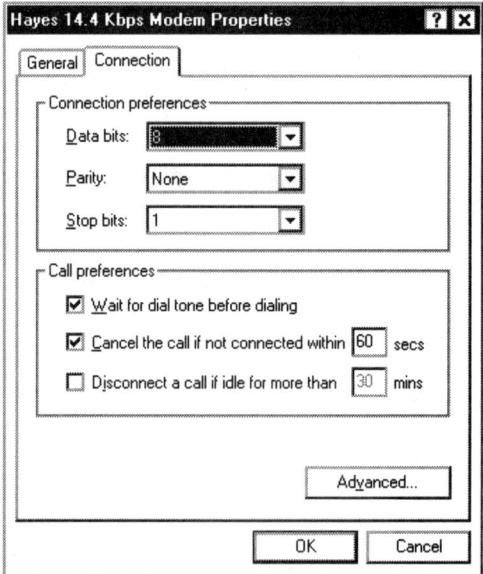

The Connection tab shows default connection properties. Your communications software can override these settings.

RAS Installation

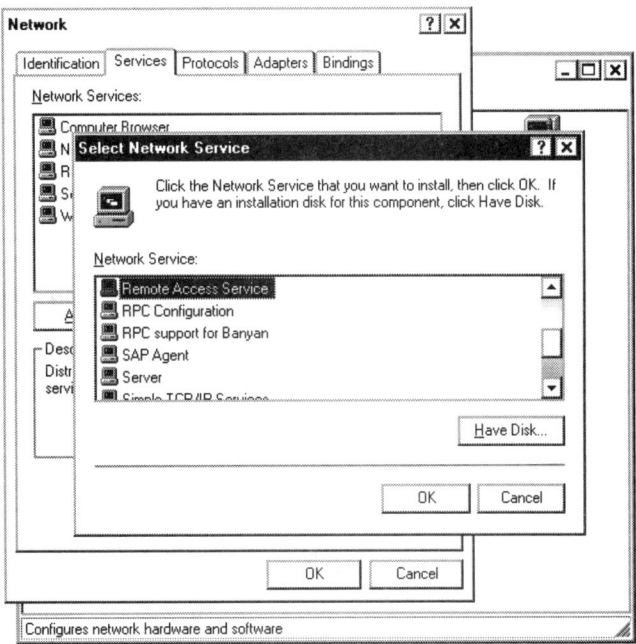

Remote Access Service is installed through the Control Panel Network utility. Launch the Network utility and click on the Services tab. Click on **Add**, select Remote Access Service, and click on **OK**. You will be prompted for a path to the installation files.

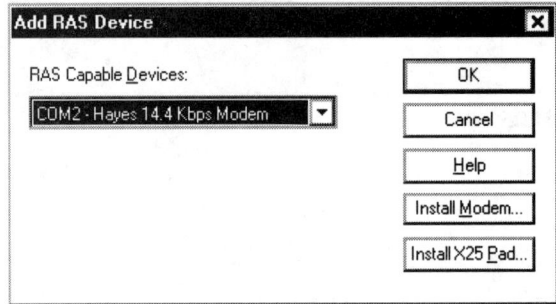

You will be prompted to select a RAS device, defaulting to the first installed communications device. You can also install additional devices at this time. Click on **OK** after making your selection.

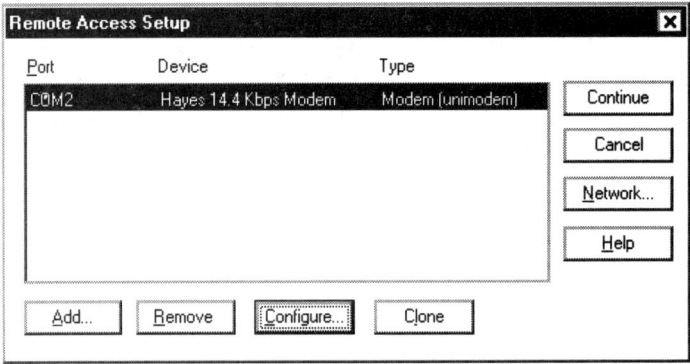

You are finally prompted with the Remote Access Setup screen. This allows you to configure the RAS communication devices. After installation, display the Network utility Services tab, select Remote Access Service, and click on **Properties** to display this dialog.

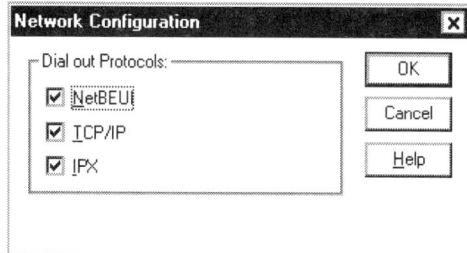

The **Network** button is used to set the Dial-out protocols. Protocol selections will default to all installed protocols.

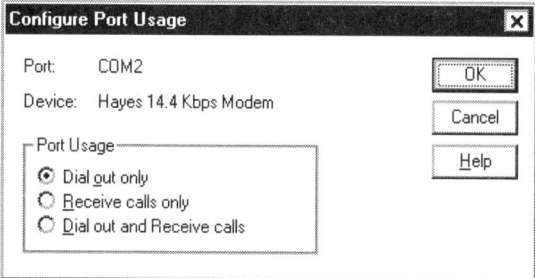

The **Configure** button lets you set the port usage for the selected device. You can set the port for Dial-out only, to Receive calls only, or to both Dial-out and receive calls. Normally, a client will be configured for Dial-out only.

You will need to restart your system after installing RAS for the changes to take effect.

Dial-up Networking

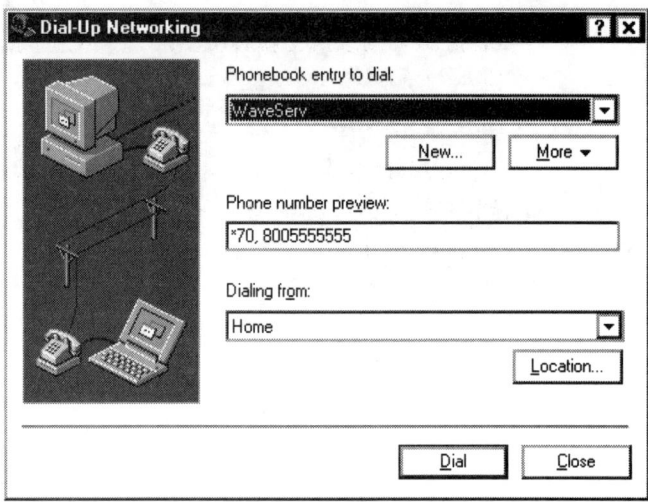

Run **Start/Programs/Accessories/Dial-Up Networking** to launch Dial-up Networking and call out through RAS. Dial-up numbers are managed at phone book entries. Click on **Add** to create a new entry.

Click on **More** to:

- Edit settings for the entry and modem.
- Copy settings for the entry and modem.
- Delete an entry.
- Create a desktop shortcut to the entry.
- Open the monitor.
- Call using operator assistance.
- Set user preferences.
- Set Logon preferences.

You can also configure multiple "Dialing from" locations. This allows a mobile user to simply select the proper location rather than having to fully reconfigure dial-up networking.

Multiple Connections on RAS

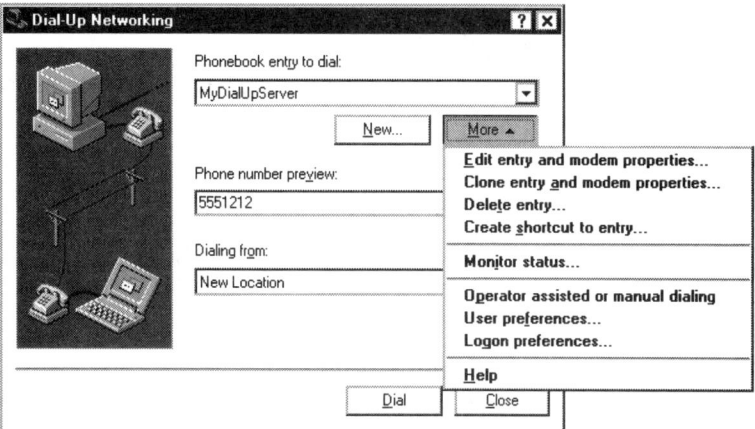

Multilink can also be configured for through the Dial-Up Networking dialog. Select the phonebook entry you want to configure, click on **More**, and run **Edit entry and modem properties**.

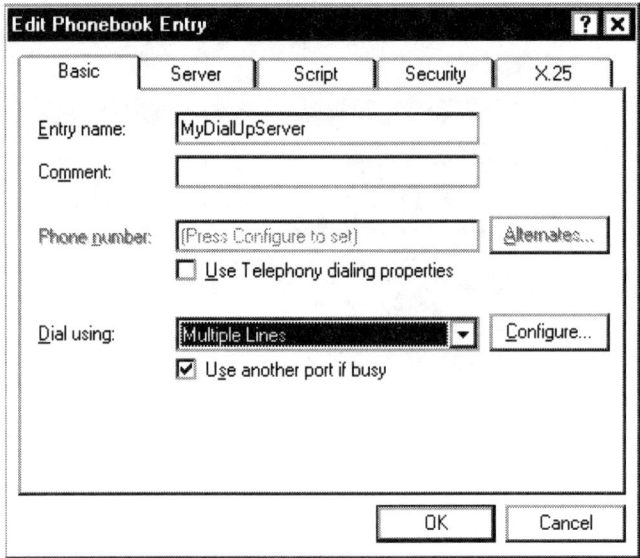

Click on the Dial using drop-down list and select Multiple Lines. Click on **Configure** to display a list of available devices. Enter a phone number for each device to use during dial-in and connection.

Both the server and client must be set up for multilink support. You should also be aware that if you set up call-back security, the server will only call one number back. This is because you can only associate one telephone number with each user.

Exercise 9-2

During this exercise, you will practice the procedures for installing the RAS client. A modem is not required for you to complete this exercise. The primary purpose of the exercise is to help you become more familiar with the RAS client installation screens.

1. Open the Control Panel and launch the Network utility.
2. Click on the Services tab, then click on **Add**.
3. Locate and select Remote Access Service, then click on **OK**.
4. If prompted, type in the path to the installation files, then click on **Continue**.
5. When prompted to invoke the modem installer, click on **Yes**.

   NOTE: You will simulate modem installation. You must have a connection device before you can complete RAS installation.

6. Click to place a check in the "Don't detect my modem; I will select it from a list" check box.
7. Click on **Next**.
8. Select Standard 14400 bps and your modem type and click on **Next**.
9. Select to install on COM2, or any available COM port, and click on **Next**. You must click on the COM port to select.
10. Type in your area code, then click on **Next**.
11. Click on **Finish**.
12. Click on **OK** at the Add RAS Device dialog.
13. Click on **Configure**. This displays the Port Usage dialog.
14. Click on **Cancel**, then click on **Network**.

    This lets you select your dial out protocol. Installed protocols are selected at default.
15. Click on **OK** to close the dialog.
16. Click on **Continue**.
17. Click on **Close**.
18. When prompted to restart your system, click on **Yes**.

INTRODUCTION TO THE INTERNET

This section will present a basic introduction to some general terms relating to the Internet, along with using a workstation as an Internet World Wide Web Server. The following are topics discussed within this section:

- What is the Internet?
- What is an Intranet?
- The Microsoft Internet Information Server
- The Microsoft Internet Explorer

- Peer Server
- Peer Server Services
- Peer Web Server Utilities
- Internet Service Manager (ISM)
- WWW Service Properties
- FTP Service Properties
- Gopher Service Properties

Although the Internet has gained much momentum and popularity in the several of years, it still remains somewhat of a mystery to many. More and more organizations are providing Internet access with the work environment as it provides a great depth of resources and information. An understanding of fundamental terms and technologies is critical.

What is the Internet?

The Internet is the largest computer network in the world. It links computers from every make and operating system together to facilitate the sharing of information. The explosive growth of Internet traffic in recent years can be traced directly to the World Wide Web (WWW).

The Web allows users to access information without having to understand programming or know how the information is stored or transmitted. The use of hypermedia and hypertext enables the user to retrieve information from anywhere on the Web with a mouse click.

The Web provides text, pictures, sounds, and multimedia in a non-linear fashion. Users can examine various sites, depending on their interests. There are more than 34 million people currently exploring the resources on the Web. It is a low-cost method of providing and seeking information.

What is an Intranet?

An Intranet is very similar to the Internet. They both share the same technologies, protocols, and tools. Usually, though, an Intranet has three distinct advantages over the Internet:

- Access is usually limited to employees of the company.

    Less concern is given to worrying about the public image and more concern is given to providing information and services to help employees do their jobs.

- The speed of an Intranet can be much faster and cost much less than Internet access.

    Many times employees access the Intranet using their 10 MBPS internal network and not over phone lines. This faster access enables the Intranet site to use more and bigger graphics than would be useable on the Internet. The files that are available for employee viewing and downloading can also be bigger due to this Intranet speed.

- The company controls all of the clients.

    Since the company owns all of the PCs that will access the Intranet, standard software can be used. If every PC had a copy of Microsoft Word, the Intranet Webmaster would not have to convert company Word documents to HTML. The browser would simply load a copy of Microsoft Word if a user selects a Word document to view.

A corporate Intranet is quickly becoming a method of choice for information sharing. Users can "publish" business information to the Intranet, making it immediately available and easily accessible.

The Microsoft Internet Information Server

The Microsoft Internet Information Server (IIS) is a network file and application server that transmits information in Hypertext Markup Language (HTML) pages using the Hypertext Transport Protocol (HTTP). It receives requests from users and responds with the information on the request. Applications that you can support through IIS include:

- Publish business-specific information on the Internet.
- Publish a catalog and take orders.
- Create interactive programs to provide real time information to site visitors.
- Provide database access for employees and/or customers.
- Allow all members of a company to share business critical information through a private Intranet.

More advanced uses include:

- Creating client server applications using the Microsoft Internet Server Application Programming interface (ISAPI).
- Creating and running Common Gateway Interface (CGI) applications.
- Creating HTML scripts that interface with Microsoft SQL Server.

In many ways, the full potential of IIS has not been explored. It is likely to generate an explosion of new products and applications.

Microsoft Peer Web Services appears to be a scaled down version of IIS that runs under Windows NT Workstation. Installation and configuration is almost identical to that of IIS. Microsoft describes it as designed for a lower volume of traffic and has removed some of the advanced features like IP filtering, which lets you limit access by blocking users by IP address.

The Microsoft Internet Explorer

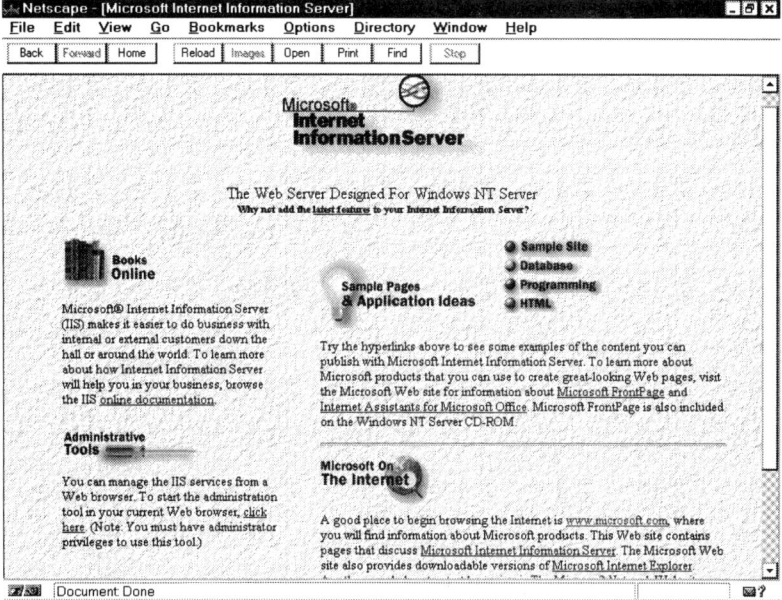

The Microsoft Internet Explorer (IE) Web browser is included on the Windows NT 4.0 installation CD-ROM and is automatically installed on your computer by NT 4.0 Setup. It is a tool for navigating and accessing information on the Web. The version of IE included is not the latest release. The latest version of IE can be downloaded from the Microsoft Web site, *www.microsoft.com*.

> NOTE: *Depending on your Internet connection type and transfer rate, downloading the latest IE version can take a significant amount of time.*

Peer Server

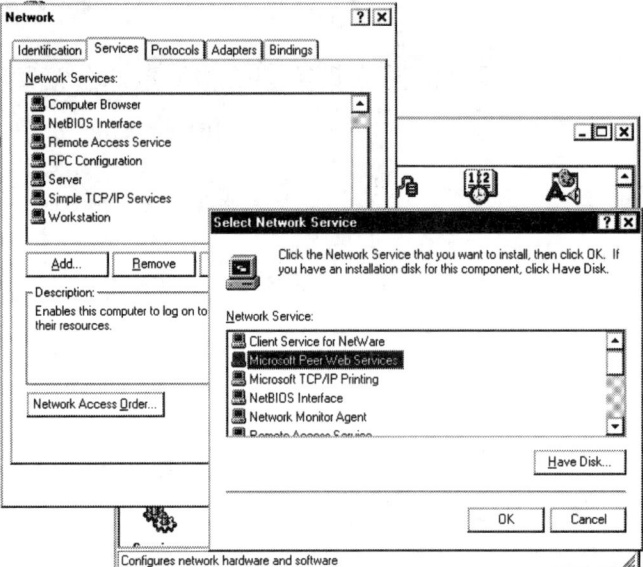

Microsoft's Peer Web services let you use your Windows NT Workstation as an Internet World Wide Web server. Though not as full-featured as NT Server's Internet Information Server, it does give you an easy way of publishing Web pages, running a small corporate intranet, or page development and testing before publication. This is a new feature, released with NT v4.0.

As with other services discussed in this chapter, Microsoft's Peer Web Services are installed through the Services tab of the Control Panel Network utility. Click on **Add** to display the list of services, select the Peer Web Services, then click on **OK**.

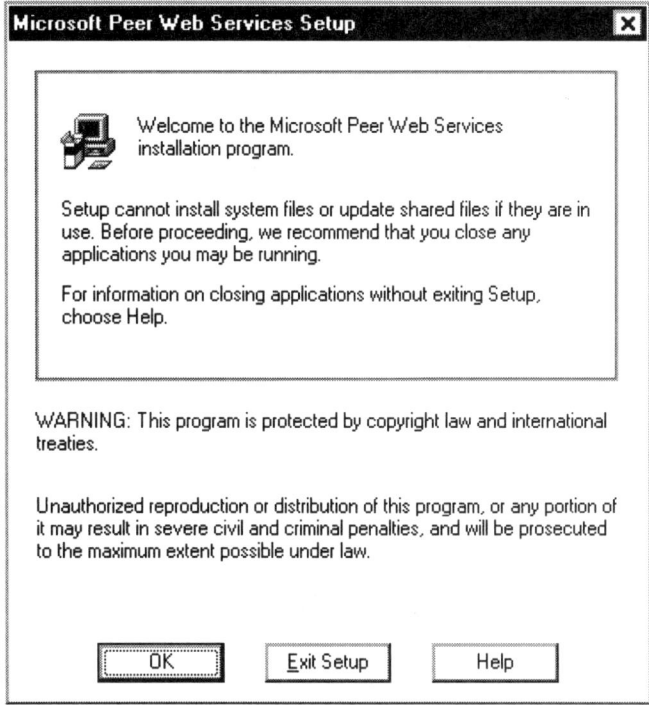

You will be warned to close any applications that may be running on your system before installing Peer Web Services. Click on **OK** to continue.

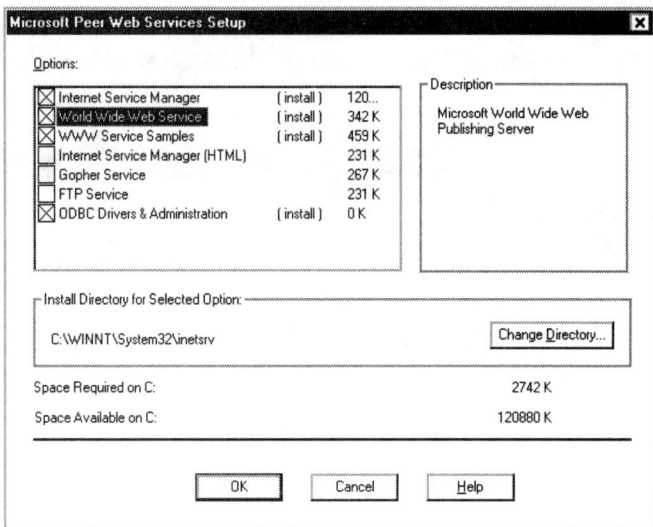

You will be prompted for the services that you want to install. It is suggested that you only install those services which you currently need and plan to support. You can add additional services later, if necessary. Click on **OK** after making your choices.

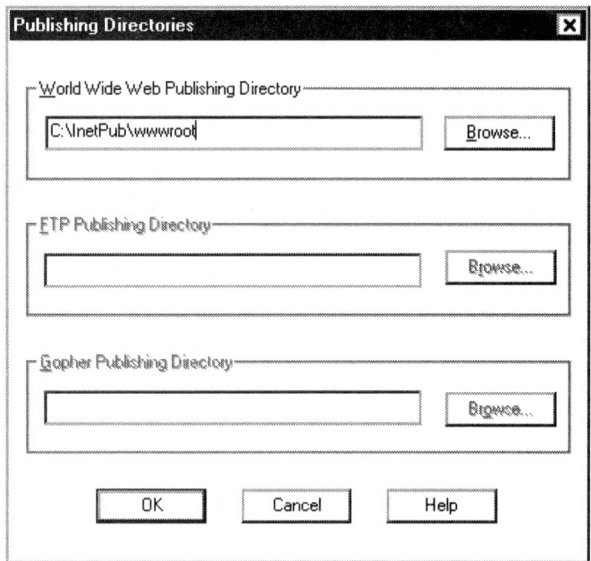

You will be prompted for the publishing directory for each service you are installing. This will act as the home, or root, directory for that service. The default is to install these on drive C:. It is suggested that you install them on an NTFS partition to give you greater access control. Click on **OK** after verifying the directory locations. Setup will install and launch all selected services.

Peer Server Services

You can install the following components during Microsoft Peer Server Setup:

- Internet Service Manager

    This is the Peer Server administration service. You will normally want to install this component.

- World Wide Web

    You must install this component if you want to publish web pages on this server. You will typically want to install this component.

- WWW Service Samples

    This installs sample HTML files. Install only if you want to have the sample files available.

- Internet Service Manager (HTML)

    This is an HTML version of the Internet Service Manager. Install this component if you want to be able to administer the Peer Server through your browser.

- Gopher Server

    This sets your server up as a gopher publishing server. Only install if you have a need for gopher support.

- FTP Service

    This sets your server up as an ftp (File Transfer Protocol) server. Install only if you plan to use the server as a source or destination for ftp file transfers.

- ODBC Drivers and Administration

    The Open database Connectivity drivers are only required if you want to enable database (such as SQL Server) access through the WWW server. You will also need to configure ODBC support through the Control Panel ODBC utility.

You have the option of installing any combination of WWW, gopher, and ftp servers. Only install those that you actually need.

Peer Web Server Utilities

Depending on your Setup choices, some or all of the following utilities will be installed and available through **Start/Microsoft Peer Web Services**:

- Internet Service Manager

    Use this utility to configure installed services, set access restrictions, and to start and stop services.

- Internet Service Manager (HTML)

    This utility lets you manage the server through your browser.

- Key Manager

    The Key Manager is used for setting up secure transmissions and for protection against invalid access.

- Peer Web Services Setup

    This launches the Setup utility, allowing you to add or remove services, reinstall Peer Web Server, or remove the server.

- Product Documentation

    This launches an HTML-based installation and planning guide.

Internet Service Manager (ISM)

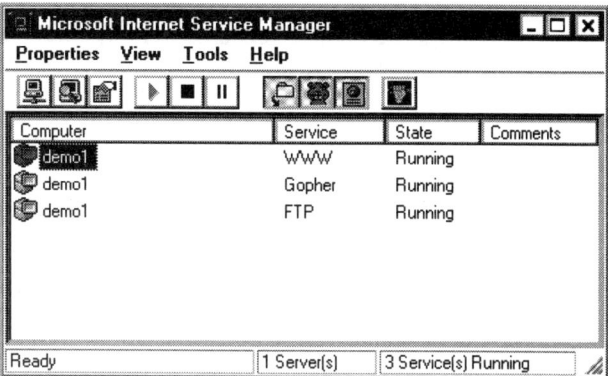

The Internet Service Manager lets you view or modify property settings for installed services. You can also start, stop, pause, or resume services. There are three views supported, Servers, Services, and Report. You manage any installed services from either of the views.

To view or modify properties for a service, double-click on the services, or click to select and run **Service Properties** from the **Properties** menu.

WWW Service Properties

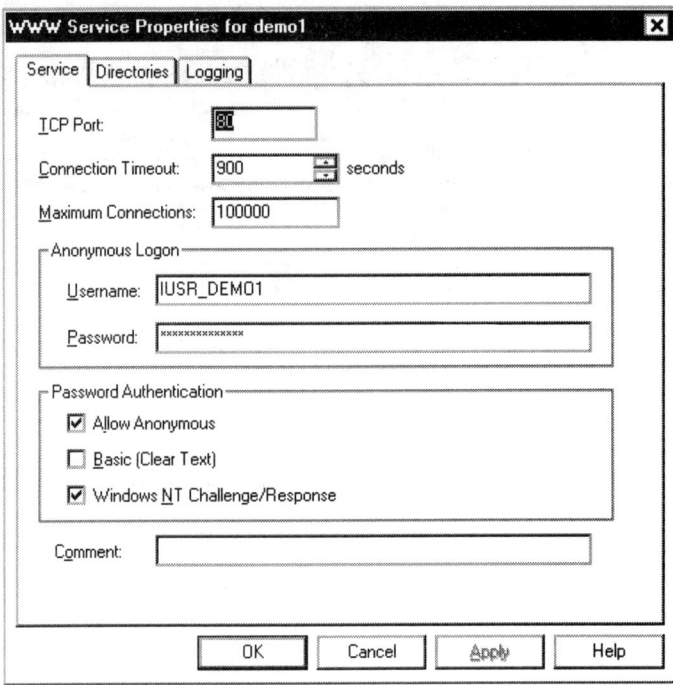

The WWW Service Properties dialog includes three tabs. The Service tab lets you set:

TCP Port	The default port is shown. There is typically no reason to change this.
Connection Timeout	You may want to increase this value if you are dropping connections due to timeout errors.
Maximum Connections	You will typically want to limit the maximum number of connections. The more concurrent connections running, the slower the support for each connection.

The Anonymous Logon allows for anonymous connection to web pages. A default user, IUSER_*servername*, is created during installation and configured for local access.

Password Authentication determines if you will allow anonymous connections and the password authentication method for named connecting by user name. Windows NT Challenge/Response uses encrypted passwords.

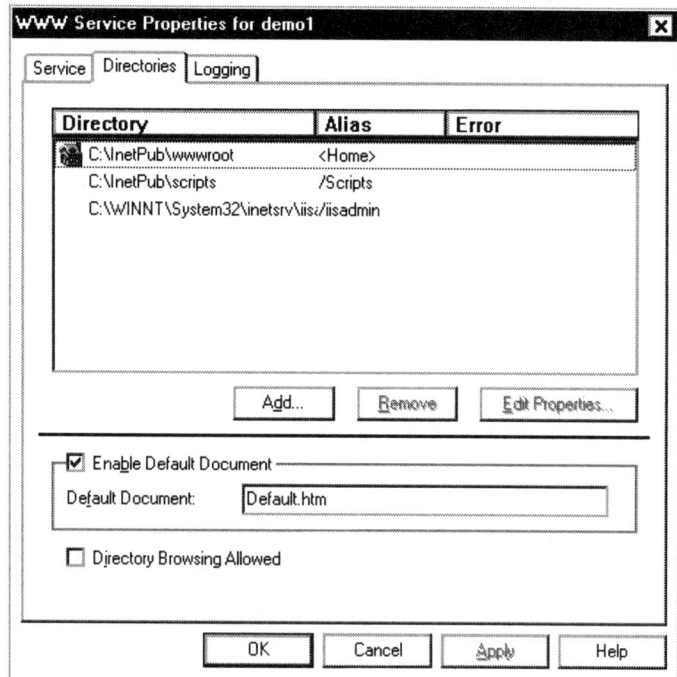

The directories tab lets you set or change the directories the Web server service uses. By default directory browsing is not allowed, which means clients are not allowed to browse through server directories.

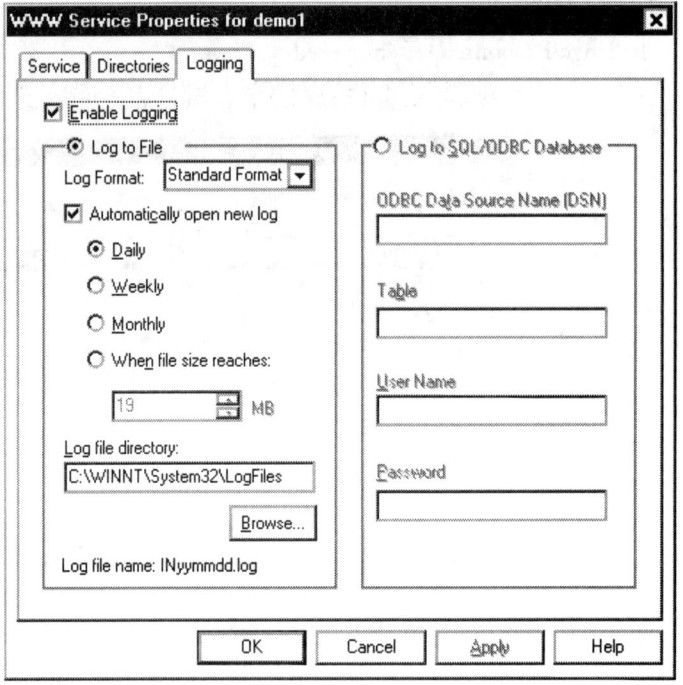

The Logging tab determines if you are going to log WWW server activity, where the log is stored, and when a new log is opened.

FTP Service Properties

![FTP Service Properties dialog for demo1 showing Service tab with TCP Port 21, Connection Timeout 900 seconds, Maximum Connections 1000, Allow Anonymous Connections checked with Username IUSR_DEMO1, and Allow only anonymous connections checked]

The FTP Service Properties dialog has four tabs. The Service tab lets you view or set the TCP Port, Connection Timeout, and Maximum Connections values. As with the WWW service, you will typically want to leave the TCP Port at default.

By default the same user name is used for anonymous connections as is used by the WWW service. It is suggested that you allow anonymous connections only, or set up users specifically for ftp access and not give those users any other file access permisssions.

Passing usernames and passwords for ftp access can be a potential security problem. Passwords for ftp are passed as clear text only.

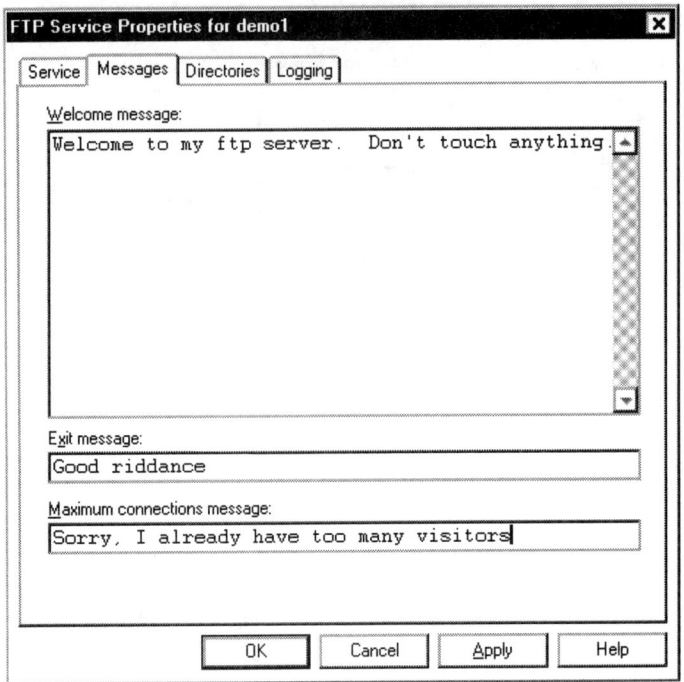

The Messages tab lets you define the connect, disconnection, and maximum connections messages. By default, these are all blank.

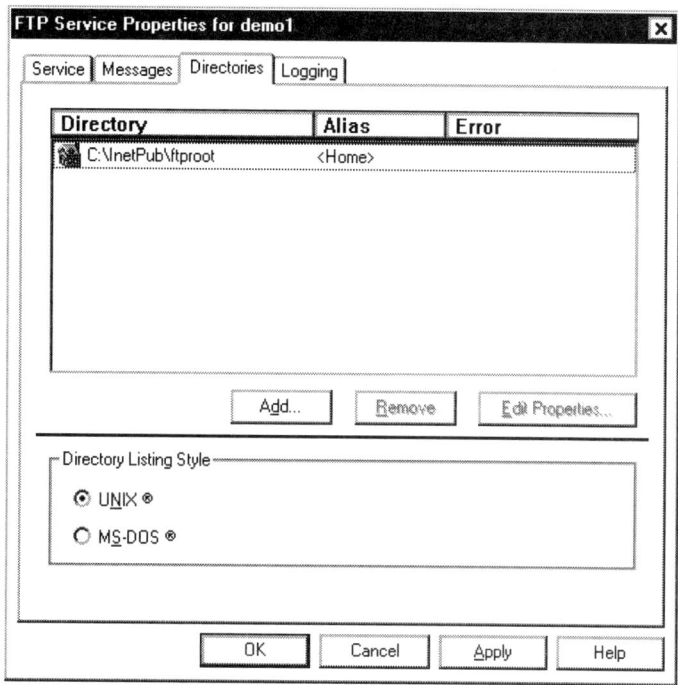

As with the WWW Service, the directories tab lets you manage the directories used for ftp transfers. You can also set the directory listing type as UNIX or MS-DOS format. Most browsers and ftp client utilities expect the server to provide directories in UNIX format.

Not shown here, the Logging tab performs the same function as for the WWW Service, enabling and managing session logging.

Gopher Service Properties

The Gopher service property tabs are very similar to those for the other services. The Service tab supports viewing or modifying the TCP Port, Connection Timeout, and Maximum Connections values. In addition to these and the Anonymous Logon information, you can also manage the Service Administrator name and address.

The Directories tab simply lists the directories set up for the Gopher service. You can also add or remove directories. The Logging tab performs the same function as for the WWW and ftp services.

Exercise 9-3

During this exercise, you will install and test the Microsoft Peer Web Server services. You will need access to the Windows NT Workstation installation files to complete this exercise.

1. Launch the Control Panel Network utility and click on the Services tab.
2. Click on **Add**.
3. Click to select Microsoft Peer Web Services, then click on **OK**.
4. When prompted, verify the path to the Windows NT Workstation installation files and click on **OK**.
5. When the initial Setup dialog is displayed click on **OK** to continue.
6. Click to remove the checks from Gopher Service, FTP Server, and ODBC Drivers & Administration. You are only installing the Internet Service Manager, World Wide Web Service, and WWW Service samples.
7. Click on **OK**.
8. When asked to create directory, click **Yes**.
9. Leave the World Wide Web publishing directory at default and click on **OK**. There will be a short delay while files are copied to your system.

   When you receive the message that the Peer Web Services were successfully set up, click on **OK**.
10. Close Network Dialog box.
11. Launch the Internet Explorer from your desktop.
12. Type your system's machine name in the Open field and press **ENTER**.

SUMMARY

During this chapter, you were introduced to the following:

- Client Service for NetWare (CSNW)
- RAS clients
- RAS protocols
- RAS client installation
- Internet Explorer
- Peer Web Server

POST-TEST QUESTIONS

The answers to these questions are in Appendix A at the end of this manual.

1. Which RAS clients, if any, support multilink connections?

   ....

   ....

2. PPP is supported on what Microsoft RAS clients?

   ....

   ....

3. What information must you provide during CSNW configuration to allow you to access NetWare resources?

   ....

   ....

CHAPTER 10

Ongoing Maintenance

MAJOR TOPICS

Objectives 448

Pre-Test Questions 448

Introduction 449

Review of Windows NT Installation 449

Maintenance Issues 463

Troubleshooting 474

Remote Management 484

Summary 487

Post-Test Questions 488

OBJECTIVES

At the completion of this chapter, you will be able to:

- Describe the Windows NT boot sequence.
- Describe the ARC name format.
- Describe the procedures for creating a Windows NT Boot diskette.
- Update an Emergency Repair diskette.
- Use the Performance Monitor to view selected performance counters.
- List common bottlenecks and list potential solutions.
- Use Windows NT Diagnostics to view system information.
- Identify tools and utilities that support remote management.

PRE-TEST QUESTIONS

The answers to these questions are in Appendix A at the end of this manual.

1. Which Performance Monitor view displays performance data as a line graph for histograph?

   ....

   ....

2. You have a dual-boot system with your startup partition located on an IDE drive. At minimum, what files would you need to copy to a Windows NT boot diskette?

   ....

   ....

3. What must you run before you can collect disk counter statistics through Performance Monitor?

   ....

   ....

4. What do you run to launch the Windows NT diagnostics?

....

....

INTRODUCTION

Most of the information that has been presented in this course relates in some fashion to the ongoing support and maintenance of Windows NT. This chapter focuses on some areas that traditionally fall under that focus.

The chapter opens with a review of Windows NT startup. This includes a look at the procedures for creating a Windows NT boot diskette.

From there, the discussion moves the Performance Monitor. This easy to use monitor gives you the ability to collect data for analysis or view performance counters at near real-time rates.

REVIEW OF WINDOWS NT INSTALLATION

This section will provide you with a review of Windows NT Server installation. Problems that may be encountered during installation will be discussed along with how to make and use a repair diskette for your system. The following are topics discussed within this section:

- About Installation
- Installation Failures
- System Startup
- Windows NT Startup
- Understanding ARC Names
- Can't Find NTLDR

- Recovery Menu
- Configuration Recovery Menu
- Windows NT Boot Diskette
- Using the Boot Diskette
- RISC Boot
- Emergency Repair
- Making Repairs
- Updating the Emergency Repair Diskette

The above outlined topics will explain in detail general thoughts that you may want to consider while installing Windows NT. This also provides a starting point for troubleshooting many system problems.

About Installation

As mentioned at the beginning of the course, one of the keys to a reliable system is a clean installation. Points to keep in mind include:

- Minimum installation requirements

    Make sure that all minimum installation requirements are met before you start installation.

- Hardware compatibility

    While it is true that if a piece of hardware doesn't appear on the Hardware Compatibility List, it still may work with Windows NT. However, you can be more sure of a reliable installation if it is listed.

- Additional hardware requirements

    Remember that minimum hardware requirements are that, the minimum needed to install and run Windows NT Workstation. Actual hardware requirements will depend on the applications your are running.

- Vendor-specific versions

    Some hardware manufacturer's systems require a version of Windows NT matched to that hardware platform. Be sure to use the correct version, and don't use that version on other hardware platforms.

While these guidelines won't guarantee an error-free installation, they will take you in that direction.

Installation Failures

What should you do if an installation fails? Start with the most obvious causes:

- Unsupported hardware/Requirements not met

    Double-check the system and make sure that it meets the minimum hardware requirements and that all of the hardware components are supported.

- Hardware failure

    Keep a good hardware diagnostic on hand. Check the system hardware to verify that it is working correctly. Even new systems can experience hardware failures.

- Hardware conflicts

    Check your expansion cards, such as sound cards and network adapters, to verify that you have not introduced a hardware conflict.

- Media failure

    Sometimes the problem may be with your installation source. If installing from CD-ROM, attempt installation from another copy, if available. If installing from a network source, verify that the files have not been changed and all of the files are present.

- Power failure

    The requirements for recovering from a power failure, such as loss of power or someone accidentally turning off the machine, depends on where you were in the installation. Start by restarting the machine and seeing if installation is able to pick up where it left off by itself. Otherwise, you will need to start the installation over again.

If a failure occurs during installation, there will be files from the installation present on the system. Depending on the disk space available, you may need to manually delete some of these files to give you enough room to restart the installation.

System Startup

If a system won't start, it won't run. With Windows NT, by watching startup, you can often get a good idea when and where it is failing. This can put you well on your way to repairing the problem. Some common causes of startup errors include:

- Improper Setup

    You should see this the first time you try to boot Windows NT. If you just installed Windows NT, and it won't start, it's likely that it either installed improperly, the distribution media is bad, or the system cannot support Windows NT for some reason.

- Configuration changes

    Again, this should be obvious. If you make changes to the system configuration and the system won't start, you probably caused the error. This can also happen when you remove a hardware device, but don't change the system configuration to reflect this.

- Corrupted operating system files

    If files have become corrupted due to a disk error, you may see a message during the initial media check. While you can recover in some circumstances, you may be forced to reinstall Windows NT.

Many types of startup errors are relatively easy to correct.

Windows NT Startup

If a system is having startup problems, it helps to understand the Windows NT startup process. Windows NT boots in a series of steps. While some are platform specific, most are the same for any system. Our description focuses on the startup process on Intel x86 platforms.

Boot record load	During Setup, Windows NT installs a new boot record on your active disk partition. The system BIOS locates the boot device and loads this boot record. This in turn loads the Windows NT bootstrap program which locates and loads the NT loader.
NTLDR	The NT loader file clears the screen, places the processor into 32-bit flat memory mode, and locates the BOOT.INI file. This is a sophisticated loader file that supports the FAT and NTFS file systems.

BOOT.INI   The BOOT.INI file is a text file containing the information used to build the operating system selection menu. It will contain the selection list, optional selections, and timeout value. The file must be located in the root directory of the same drive as NTLDR

A typical BOOT.INI file is shown below:

```
[boot loader]
timeout=30
default=multi(0)disk(0)rdisk(0)partition(1)\WINNT
[operating systems]
multi(0)disk(0)rdisk(0)partition(1)\WINNT="Windows NT
   Server Version 4.00"
multi(0)disk(0)rdisk(0)partition(1)\WINDOWS="Windows NT
   Workstation Version 4.00"
multi(0)disk(0)rdisk(0)partition(1)\WINDOWS="Windows NT
   Workstation Version 4.00 [VGA mode]" /basevideo /sos
multi(0)disk(0)rdisk(0)partition(1)\WINNT="Windows NT
   Server Version 4.00 [VGA mode]" /basevideo /sos
C:\="MS-DOS"
```

The boot loader can contain multiple entries for different versions of Windows NT and one other operating system, either DOS or OS/2. All NT entries follow the ARC naming convention.

Selection menu   The selection menu is built from the information in the BOOT.INI file. The user can make a selection from the menu, or wait the timeout period when the default selection will be loaded.

	If Windows NT is selected, the hardware detection program and Windows NT kernel will be loaded. If a different operating system is selected, a file named BOOTSECT.DOS is loaded into memory and executed. BOOTSECT.DOS contains the boot record for the partition's original operating system. The same filename is used whether booting DOS or OS/2.
Hardware detection	NTDETECT.COM is only used on Intel x86. It builds a hardware list which is then passed back to NTLDR. This information will be written into the registry.
	NTDETECT emulates the hardware information gathered during the ARC POST routine stored in ARC firmware on RISC-based systems.
Kernel load	The Windows NT kernel is loaded into memory and executed. This is the initial Windows NT module. The kernel receives the hardware information collected by NTDETECT or from the ARC firmware.
Low-level loads	The Hardware Abstraction Layer (HAL) is the first operating system module that is loaded by the kernel. It will also load the Registry System hive. The system hive receives the hardware list and contains information on device drivers to load and the order for starting services.
	Information in the System hive allows the kernel to load the low-level device driver files. These are files that are required for system operation. The first drivers loaded will be for the hard and floppy disk drives. If the system has a SCSI controller installed, that driver is also loaded.
Kernel initialization	It is easy to tell when kernel initialization occurs. This is the point when the screen turns blue. If initialization is successful, a CHKDSK is run on all hard disk partitions and the Windows NT signature, the initial logo screen, is displayed.
Driver initialization	The kernel will continue loading device drivers and launching services, using information stored in the System hive. Should errors occur, system recovery is determined by the ErrorControl value stored in the registry with the device driver.

Understanding ARC Names

Initial prompt	The final step is to display the logon dialog. Additional device drivers to be loaded and services to be launched will be determined according to the user account used for logon.

By watching the startup, you can get some idea when and where the error is occurring. This gives you a place to start looking in your troubleshooting.

Understanding ARC Names

Looking back at the startup process, you may wonder about the format used in the BOOT.INI file to identify startup directories. This information is stored in an ARC name format, a generic means of identifying devices in an ARC environment. The general format is:

```
component(x)disk(y)rdisk(z)partition(a)path
```

component	This identifies the device hardware adapter. This will be either scsi, for a SCSI disk controller or multi for a disk interface other than SCSI. SCSI adapters with onboard ROM BIOS are also often identified as multi.
x	This is the adapter number, starting with 0 for the first adapter.
disk(y)	This is the SCSI bus number for multi-bus SCSI adapters. It is always set to 0 for multi-type adapters.
rdisk(z)	This identifies the disk number on the adapter for multi type adapters. For SCSI, this is always set to 0.
partition(a)	This is the partition number for the partition on the disk. MS-DOS extended partitions and unused partitions are not given a number.
path	This identifies the path on the partition to the system files.

Disks are numbered starting with 0. Partitions are numbered starting with 1.

Can't Find NTLDR

One error you are likely to see when you try to start up is:

```
BOOT: Couldn't find NTLDR
Please insert another disk
```

Often, this is due to a procedural error rather than a system failure. If you leave a diskette that was formatted under Windows NT in the diskette drive when you attempt to start up, you will receive this message.

If you receive this error when attempting to start up from the hard disk, you have a more serious problem. The file is actually missing or corrupted.

A similar message you might see is:

```
Windows NT could not start because the following file is
    missing or corrupt: filename
```

In either case, you should attempt the Emergency Repair process to recover the missing or corrupted files. It may be necessary to reinstall Windows NT.

Since this can be caused by the hard disk media, you should check your hard disk for additional errors. It may be an early warning of an impending disk failure.

Recovery Menu

Windows NT provides an automatic recovery feature, known as the Configuration Recovery Menu, to help recover from some types of startup errors. The system must be able to read at least NTLDR, NTDETECT.COM, and BOOT.INI to get to this point.

When you first start Windows NT, the following message is displayed:

```
Press spacebar NOW to invoke the last known good menu
```

The message is only displayed for a very short time, so you have to press the `SPACEBAR` quickly. This displays the Configuration Recovery menu. The menu has three selections:

```
Use Current Startup Configuration
Use Last Known Good Configuration
Restart Computer
```

NOTE: If you have defined multiple hardware configurations on your system, these will be displayed first.

This is helpful when invalid changes have been made to the system configuration that keep the system from starting. This can occur, for example, when you enable startup for a device driver for a device that is not installed on your system.

Configuration Recovery Menu

Below is the Configuration Recovery menu display:

```
Configuration recovery menu (Last Known Good)
This menu allows you to switch to a previous system
    configuration, which may overcome system startup
    problems.
If the system starts correctly now, choose user Current
    Startup Configuration. No changes will occur.
If the system does not start correctly,
    choose Use Last Known Good Configuration.
IMPORTANT: System configuration changes since the last
    successful startup will be discarded.
        Use Current Startup Configuration
        Use Last Known Good Configuration
        Restart computer
Use the up and down arrow keys to make your selection.
Press ENTER when you have made your selection.
```

The configuration data required to launch Windows NT is stored in the Registry, a specialized database that contains all of the system configuration data.

The startup configuration is referred to as a control set. Each system holds multiple control sets, including the set up during the most recent launch. The registry, including control sets, is described in detail later in this manual.

Windows NT Boot Diskette

If the boot record or initial startup files become corrupted on an x86-based machine, it will keep you from starting up Windows NT or any other operating system from the hard disk. One way around this is to create a boot diskette:

- Right-click on drive A: in My Computer and run **Format** to format a floppy diskette, or run FORMAT from a command prompt.
- Remove the hidden, system, and read-only attributes from NTDETECT.COM and NTLDR.
- Remove the system and read-only attributes from BOOT.INI.
- Copy BOOT.INI, NTDETECT.COM, NTLDR, and BOOTSECT.DOS (if you have a dual boot system) to the diskette.
- Return to the hidden, system, and read-only attributes.

If NT is installed on a SCSI drive, you will also need to copy NTBOOTDD.SYS to the diskette.

Obviously, a diskette can only hold a minimal set of startup files. NTDETECT.COM will detect hardware information during execution and load the remaining files from the hard disk. If any of the remaining files are corrupted, you will not be able to launch Windows NT.

BOOT.INI identifies the location of the remaining operating system files. The normal selection menu will be displayed. You still have the option of starting Windows NT or your alternate operating system, if any.

Using the Boot Diskette

The boot diskette gives you a way of getting a system up and running quickly after the load files have been corrupted or accidentally deleted. However, it should not be seen as a permanent solution. Use the boot diskette...

- for quick access to critical files.
- to allow the user to continue working until repairs can be made.
- to back up the Registry files, should it become necessary to recover them separately.
- to boot a mirrored partition if the primary drive should fail.

This should be seen as a temporary solution only. You should replace the load files, either through the Emergency Repair procedure or by reinstalling Windows NT, as soon as possible.

If you wish to have a Windows NT boot diskette available, you will need to prepare the diskette in advance and store it in a safe location.

RISC Boot

The initial boot process is slightly different on RISC-based systems. The system firmware will read boot information from nonvolatile RAM, which will have the name of the operating system boot file (OSLOADER.EXE) and its location. This file will, in turn, load the system kernel. From that point on, the boot process is effectively the same.

Emergency Repair

One way of repairing a damaged system is through the Emergency Repair option of the Windows NT Setup program. To initiate an Emergency Repair:

- Boot from Windows NT Workstation Setup disk #1.
- When prompted, remove disk #1, insert disk #2, and press **ENTER**.
- When the Welcome to Setup screen is displayed, press **R**.

When you press **R**, you are prompted with the Emergency Repair options:

- Inspect registry files

    Setup will let you replace selected registry files from the copies of the files on the Emergency Repair diskette. Any changes made since the diskette was updated are lost.

- Inspect startup environment

    This option is used when Windows NT Server v4.0 does not appear in the list of bootable systems. It also requires the Emergency Repair diskette.

- Verify Windows NT system files

    Setup checks that the system files are present and verifies file integrity. You may select to be prompted before damaged files are replaced or replace the files automatically.

- Inspect boot sector

    This selection copies a new boot sector to the hard disk.

You may select to perform any or all of these tasks.

Making Repairs

After you have made your repair selections, Setup prompts to detect mass storage devices or lets you install device drivers from a manufacturer's diskette. Press **ENTER** for automatic detection or **S** to select device drivers manually. It will be necessary to remove Setup disk #2 and replace it with Setup disk #3 during this process. When the detect phase is complete, press **ENTER** to accept the list as detected, **S** to install additional drivers from a manufacturer's diskette.

If a supported CD-ROM drive is detected, you are prompted to select either CD-ROM or diskette as the source should it be necessary to replace any of the system files. You do not have to choose the same source media as originally used for installation. You cannot, however, select an unsupported CD-ROM or shared network directory.

Setup next prompts for an Emergency Repair diskette (ERD). Press **ENTER** if you have an ERD available. Setup uses the SETUP.LOG file on the diskette to locate Windows NT Server and determine the files copied during installation. Otherwise, press **ESC** and Setup will attempt to locate Windows NT Server on the hard disk.

You are given the option of replacing the registry files. Your selections are:

- SYSTEM (System Configuration)
- SOFTWARE (Software Information)
- DEFAULT (Default User Profile)
- SECURITY and SAM (Security Policy and User Accounts Database)

You may restore any or all registry files from the ERD. Any changes made since the last time the disk was backed up are lost. However, once you get the system started normally, you can recover a more recent copy of the registry from backups, if available.

After copying any selected files, Setup examines the operating system files on the hard disk. You are warned if any files are missing or corrupted and prompted:

- To press **ESC** to skip the file.
- To press **ENTER** to repair the file.
- To press **A** to automatically replace changed or corrupted files.
- To press **-** to exit the Emergency Repair process.

After completing the repairs, you are prompted to remove the Emergency Repair diskette and to press **ENTER** to restart your system.

Updating the Emergency Repair Diskette

The Emergency Repair diskette is an important tool, but must be kept up-to-date. Should it become necessary to recover registry files, your system configuration information, you will want this to be as recent as possible. If not, after recovery from the ERD, it will be necessary to manually recover any configuration changes.

Windows NT provides you with two methods for updating the Emergency Repair diskette:

- RDISK

    The RDISK utility can create or update the Emergency Repair diskette. Not only can the utility keep your Emergency Repair diskette up-to-date, it gives you a way of replacing a damaged or lost diskette.

- Disk Administrator

    The **Configuration** selection in the Disk Administrator **Partition** menu opens an additional submenu. Under this submenu is a selection update the Emergency Repair diskette. One drawback of this method is that it updates disk related configuration information only.

This is not a replacement for regular registry backups.

Exercise 10-1

During this exercise, you will create and test a Windows NT boot diskette. You will need a diskette to complete this exercise.

1. Log on as Administrator.
2. Select the Programs Menu from the **Start** button.
3. Click on **Command Prompt**.
4. Place your scratch diskette in drive A:, type the following, and press **ENTER**:

    FORMAT A:

5. When prompted, press **ENTER**.
6. When prompted for a disk label, press **ENTER**.
7. When asked to format another disk press **N** and **ENTER**
8. Type the following and press **ENTER**:

    CD \

9. Type each of the following lines and press **ENTER** after each:

    ATTRIB NTLDR -S -H -R
    ATTRIB NTDETECT.COM -S -R
    ATTRIB BOOT.INI -S -R
    COPY NTLDR A:\
    COPY NTDETECT.COM A:\
    COPY BOOT.INI A:\
    REN NTLDR ZZZNTLDR

10. Type the following and press **ENTER**:

    EXIT

11. Remove the diskette from drive A:.
12. Press **ALT CTRL DEL**.
13. Click on the radio button next to "Shutdown and Restart" and press **ENTER**. What happens when your system attempts to restart?

    You will receive a message that you cannot find NTLDR. This is the message you will see should NTLDR be accidentally deleted or lost.

14. Place your scratch diskette in drive A: and press **ENTER**. What happens? (Your system should start up normally.)

15. Using the procedures described earlier in the exercise, open a command prompt window.
16. Type the following and press **ENTER**

    CD\

17. Type the following and press **ENTER**

    REN ZZZNTLDR NTLDR

18. Type each of the following lines, press **ENTER** after each.

    ATTRIB NTLDR +S +H +R

    ATTRIB NTDETECT.COM +S +H +R

    ATTRIB BOOT.INI +S + R

19. Type the following and press **ENTER**

    EXIT

20. Remove the diskette from drive A:.
21. Using the procedures described earlier, shut down, then restart your system. The system should now restart normally.

MAINTENANCE ISSUES

This section will introduce some of the utilities and concepts behind maintenance and system diagnostics. As system problems occur, these utilities provide system-specific information about event errors. The following are topics discussed within this section:

- Maintenance
- Management and Maintenance Tools
- Performance Monitor
- Performance Monitor Views
- Chart Views
- Alerts

- Resolving Bottlenecks
- Processor Bottlenecks
- Disk Bottlenecks
- Memory Bottlenecks
- About Printers

These utilities are extremely important to an administrator. As system errors occur, it is important to know which resource to examine.

Maintenance

Monitoring and diagnostics are a vital part of the ongoing support process. Areas of concern include:

- Performance monitoring

    Performance monitoring lets you know how a system is doing, and tells you if configuration or hardware changes have any affect. Performance information can also give you early warning about potential problems.

- Optimization

    Optimization is important on all systems, but can quickly become a critical issue on servers supporting network applications.

- Diagnostics

    The diagnostic provided with Windows NT give you an easy way to collect information about systems.

- Remote Management

    Many management and troubleshooting activities can be completed across the network.

Management and Maintenance Tools

Windows NT includes a suite of tools for monitoring system performance, general management, and aids for troubleshooting. Some of these have already been discussed during the course.

Some of the utilities you are most likely to find helpful in your ongoing management efforts include:

- Event Viewer

    As you have seen, many errors will be logged in the Event Viewer's system log, making it a good first stop when trying to isolate a system failure. It can be especially helpful when trying to find common factors relating to an intermittent failure.

- Control Panel Utilities

    Specifically the Service and Device utilities, the Control Panel utilities can be useful troubleshooting tools. They give you a quick way of checking the Startup status for a device or service, and to see whether or not it started.

- Task Manager

    The Task Manager was introduced earlier in the course. It gives you general performance information, as well as providing a way of end tasks that are hung, failing, or cannot be closed through normal means.

- Performance Monitor

    The Performance Monitor includes a wide array of counters which let you monitor system activity and performance. In addition, some applications and services will add their specific counters to the Performance Monitor. It can also be used to monitor remote systems and for performance comparisons. It is a keep tool for checking results when attempting to optimize and fine tune a systems.

- Windows NT Diagnostic

    The Windows NT diagnostic provides an easy way of reviewing system hardware and configuration settings. The same information can be gathered from the registry, but the format is usually harder to read and it can sometimes take careful investigation to find the values for which you are looking.

- Windows NT Hardware Detection Tool (HDT)

    This tool is especially helpful when diagnosing installation or startup failures. Created as a bootable diskette, you can boot from the HDT to give a list of installed hardware.

In addition, the Windows NT Workstation Resource Kit, available through Microsoft Press and retail outlets, contains a number troubleshooting, monitoring, and management utilities.

Performance Monitor

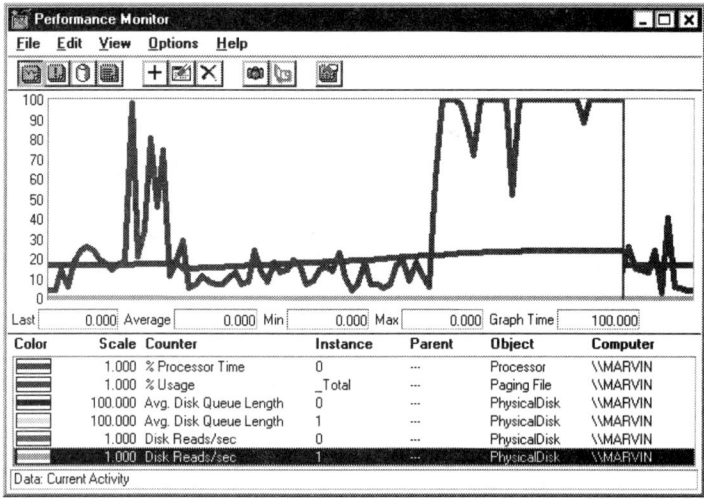

The Performance Monitor is often used to locate and help resolve performance bottlenecks. This is, however, a powerful and flexible utility, and shouldn't be limited to that use only. Performance Monitor can be used to:

- Check performance of system objects.
- Compare the performance of different systems.
- Gather data for more detailed analysis.
- Set alerts to occur when selected object parameters hit specified levels.
- Run executable commands or batch files when alerts occur.
- Create report screens displaying exact values in a timely manner.

Windows NT Server installs a common set of performance counters for objects such as the memory cache, disk usage, processor, processes, and threads. Network counters are installed according to the network software running at the system. Some applications, such as SQL Server for Windows NT, install their own additional counters.

> NOTE: *You can also retrieve performance information through the Task Manager, as described earlier in the course.*

Performance Monitor Views

The Performance Monitor supports four view options so that you can display information in a format that best suits your needs. These are:

- Chart

    In this view, the performance of selected counters is displayed as either a line graph or a histogram. This graphic representation makes it easy to monitor available resources or to see performance bottlenecks. It can become confusing, however, if you try to track too many simultaneous counters.

- Log

    Creating a log file lets you gather data from selected counters over a period of time and perform off-line analysis later. This gives you a way of doing detailed analysis of performance data. Since you can log multiple machines in the same file, you can also do detailed comparative analysis.

- Alerts

    You create an alert log under the Alert view, selecting counters and instances to be monitored, each with an alert threshold value you specify. When the item reaches that threshold, an alert is generated and an entry made in the alert log.

- Report

    The Report view displays the current values for selected counters in a report format. This lets you compare exact values, and makes it relatively easy to simultaneously display a larger number of counters and still keep track of them.

Performance Monitor defaults to the Chart view, displaying data in a line graph format. As you switch between foreground views, those in the background remain active.

Chart View

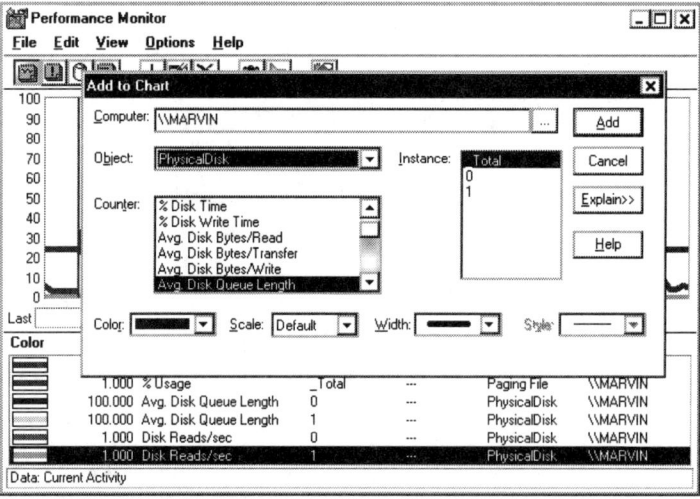

The dialogs for adding counters to the Performance Monitor are all very similar. The Add to Chart dialog is typical:

Computer	This is the system from which data is collected.
Object	The object identifies a set of related counters, such as logical disk, physical disk, NetBEUI, and so on.
Counter	This is a list of individual counters available for the selected object.
Instance	If there is more than one instance of an object running, each instance is listed and may be selected separately.

These settings are common on all of the dialogs used for adding Performance Monitor counters. Each also supports view specific settings. The Color, Scale, Width, and Style selections, for example, let you control the appearance of the chart.

Alerts

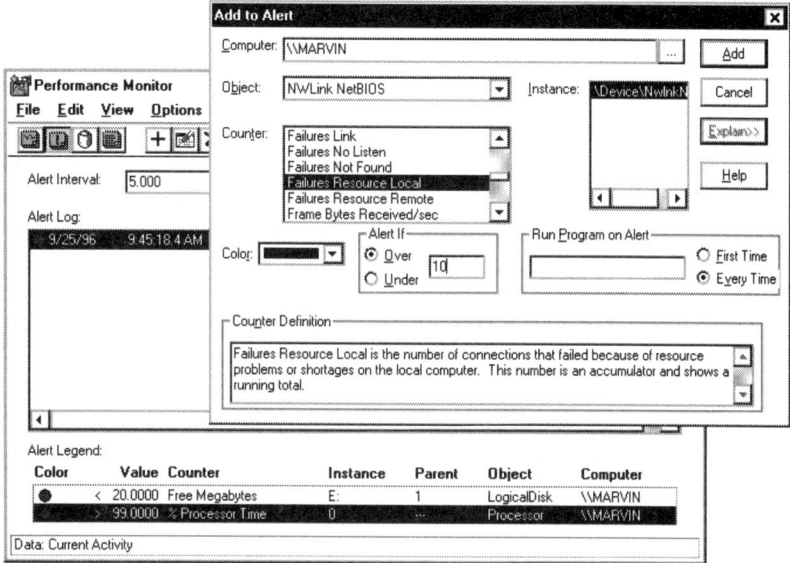

The Alert view lets you monitor system activity and create an entry in the alert log when the alert criteria are met or exceeded. Alerts use the same object, counter, and instance selections as charts. You set the value at which an alert is generated. You can also specify a program to run, either an executable file or a batch, when the alert occurs. This can be set to run only on the first occurrence, or on every occurrence of the alert.

Resolving Bottlenecks

Nearly all computers have at least one bottleneck. If it's something minor, or occurs very intermittently, you might never notice. Then again, it might affect your performance to the point that you have trouble getting anything done.

These bottlenecks often occur in common areas:

- Processor
- Disk
- Memory

The key lies in being able to recognize them when they occur, and then remove the source, if possible. Often, finding the real source requires some detective work. One bottleneck may hide another. It will likely occur only at certain times, so you have to know when to catch it.

You have to fight the urge to make too many changes at a time. Make one change, check the results, then go on to the next.

Also, write down everything you do, or you'll waste time repeating your actions.

Processor Bottlenecks

The simplest test for a processor bottleneck is %Processor Time under the Processor object counters. If this counter commonly hits 90% or above you know that the processor is a limiting factor. On multiprocessor systems, %Total Processor time exceeding 50% indicates a bottleneck. It also helps to monitor active processes, or even active threads, to determine which are placing the greatest load on the processor. The Processor Queue is another good check. If this commonly has a value of 3 or more, you have a bottleneck.

You are somewhat limited in your solutions to a processor bottleneck. Some are obvious, such as run less applications or upgrade to a more powerful processor. If you are using 8-bit adapter cards for network or disk drive access, upgrading to 16 or 32-bit cards will help improve performance. If your system board will support it, you can increase the size of the processor cache.

While adding memory can help improve performance, increasing your RAM without increasing the size of the processor cache may reduce your performance.

Disk Bottlenecks

If you run a number of disk intensive applications, the hard disk is an obvious place to look for a bottleneck. In this case, you want to look at both instantaneous values and averages over a period of time. Neither by itself gives a complete picture of disk performance. You may need to compare some results. For example, to get your average transfer rate, you need to divide the Average Disk Transfer Bytes per transfer by the Average Disk Seconds per Transfer.

In order to activate the disk counters, you will need to execute the command:

```
DISKPERF-Y
```

If running combined disk configurations, including disk mirroring, disk duplexing, disk striping (with or without parity), or disk volumes combining multiple hard disks, run:

```
DISKPERF -YE
```

This can only be run by Administrators, and will generate a performance overhead of about 2%. Restart the system after running diskperf.

Bottlenecks may be indicated by the following counters and values:

- %Disk Time

    85% or higher sustained disk activity is recorded.

- Avg. Disk Queue Length

    A value of 2 or more indicates a bottleneck.

- Page Reads/sec & Page Writes/sec

    An average value of 5 or less per second indicates a bottleneck.

You have a number of options for correcting disk bottlenecks. If you have multiple physical drives, check the performance on each. You may be able to improve your performance by moving a few files around to balance the load. You also need to ensure that the drive is set at the correct interleave.

Another way to balance the load is to use disk striping. This can be done through software, with the Disk Administrator, or by installing a hardware RAID drive array. Whichever method you select, you see your most significant performance increases when working with large data files. A hardware RAID array will give better performance.

Your other options, unfortunately, require investing in additional hardware. Obviously, faster hard disks will improve your performance. So will selecting a controller that uses the widest data path available on your system bus. If the controller supports Direct Memory Access (DMA), this will also help to improve performance, since the controller can write directly to memory.

NOTE: You can run DISKPERF-N to disable collection of disk parameters after analysis.

Memory Bottlenecks

In many cases, memory bottlenecks can be resolved by either of the following:

- Install more memory.
- Run fewer simultaneous processes.
- Avoid programs that use excessive memory.

Memory problems often appear to be other types of problems. Insufficient memory adversely affects disk performance.

Disk usage goes up significantly since the system is unable to cache disk data. You can use Explorer to see the amount of physical memory available to Windows NT Workstation. The Task Manager can give you a snapshot view of memory usage at any point.

Memory is a relatively common cause of poor performance. This is somewhat aggravated in Windows NT by the operating system's memory requirements. The problem becomes especially evident when the system starts paging out to virtual memory. Not only is there time lost while data is moved between RAM and the paging file, but you are also adding to the burden on the hard disk. This is one reason a memory bottleneck may first appear as a disk bottleneck, depending on which you check first.

There are really only two ways to correct a memory bottleneck. The first is to run less simultaneous processes. Only launch those programs that you are actively using, and exit them when you are finished.

Remove any unnecessary drivers and protocols. Even when idle, these will use system memory. Your other option is to install additional memory.

One area of special concern is the size of the virtual memory paging file. Having to increase the size of this file "on the fly" can be somewhat resource intensive. If the file regularly grows beyond the initial size, it should be reset to this value.

To optimize the virtual memory paging file:

- Observe the size of the virtual memory paging file at a representative level of system usage.
- Set the minimum size of the paging file to the current size.

Some other ways to help optimize the paging file:

- Do not keep the paging file on the same drive as the operating system files.
- Put the paging file on the hard disk(s) having the fastest access times and transfer rate.
- Create multiple files on multiple physical hard disks.

About Printers

While talking about optimization, some mention should be made of ways to optimize print processes. While typically not as critical as system performance problems, these are often the most obvious to your users. This means that they are also the type of optimization concerns that are likely to generate the highest number of calls and complaints.

There are a number of things you can do to optimize the print process. One of the best was mentioned earlier in the course, setting up a printer. Some additional ideas include:

- Print time consuming jobs after hours.

    Lengthy jobs can be sent to a print device that only prints after hours. This leaves the printer available during the day for shorter print jobs.

- Use print spooling.

    This will allow you to avoid most device contentions.

- Print while spooling.

    If you allow jobs to print while spooling, they will often be able to finish more quickly.

- Print spooled jobs first.

    By printing the spooled jobs first, you can cut down on lengthy waits for output from the queue. Spooled jobs will print before currently spooling jobs, even if the job being spooled has a higher priority.

In most cases, it will be to your advantage to identify multiple printer operators. This helps to ensure that someone will be alerted if any type of printer fault occurs.

TROUBLESHOOTING

This section will present troubleshooting concepts for network resources. The following are topics discussed within this section:

- Troubleshooting Overview
- Printer Troubleshooting
- Spooler Errors
- System Messages
- Windows NT Diagnostics
- WinMSD Selections
- Combined Configuration List
- Dr. Watson
- Miscellaneous Troubleshooting

As this chapter is the last in this study manual, it is important that you be able to determine which problem you may be encountering, and what be a possible and appropriate solution.

Troubleshooting Overview

Problems are going to occur. Hardware is going to fail. Users are going to make mistakes. A little planning, however, and you can keep minor problems from becoming major headaches.

Some things you should do in advance include:

- Plan on failure.

    Sooner or later, everything breaks. Make sure that you have your maintenance plans in place in advance.

- Plan for worst case scenarios.

    Identify your most critical systems. In case of multiple failures, these are the systems that you must get back up and running first. These will typically include servers and systems running time-critical applications.

- Keep high failure items on hand.

    Some items, such as mice and keyboards, tend to fail on a somewhat regular basis. Keep known high-failure items on hand for quick exchange.

In all cases, keep in mind that you must fix the business problem first. Do what you must to get the most critical operations back on line as quickly as possible.

Printer Troubleshooting

It would not be unusual that you might spend a significant part of your time troubleshooting printer related problems. Printers often receive a great deal of use. In addition, users are likely to notice quickly if a printer is having any kinds of problems.

Start by looking for common failures:

- Printer turned off or off-line
- Printer out of paper or other consumables

- Printer cable disconnected
- Incorrect printer driver
- Incorrect printer cartridge

If the problem is with a shared printer, start by testing the printer locally, if possible. This will let you determine if the printer is working properly. If so, the problem most likely lies in the share (such as inappropriate access permissions) or the remote printer object (such as wrong driver selected).

One common printer problem is not a printer failure, but a failure to understand Windows NT Workstation's limitations. You can have not more than 10 concurrent connections to a shared printer installed on an NT Workstation machine.

Spooler Errors

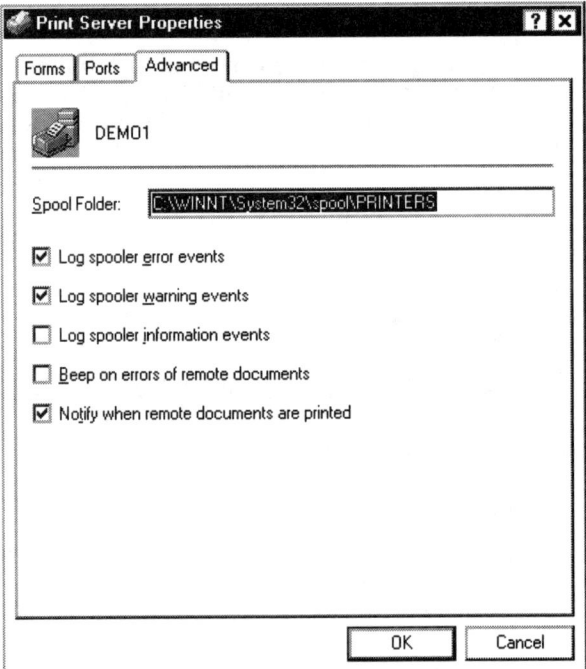

Sometimes your error may be related to the spooler rather than the printer. The spooler is common to all printers defined on a machine. To view of modify spooler information, open the Printers folder and run **Server Properties** from the **File** menu. The Advanced tab displays the spooler settings.

One potential problem is running out of space to spool jobs. You can change the spooler location by overwriting the path from this dialog.

> NOTE: *The directory specified must already exist.*

You can also determine which, if any, spooler events to be logged. By default, error and warning events are logged in the system error log. These are often a good reference source when errors occur.

System Messages

System messages, especially error messages, are one of the best tools available to you for system troubleshooting. You can tell a great deal not only from the message, but even from the type of message you are receiving.

One problem you may encounter on end-user systems is error reporting. Unless fatal errors are occurring, you may never hear about them. Because of this, a relatively minor problem could be masked until it becomes critical.

You should train users to record errors when they occur, possibly passing them along to a central location on an error report form. The error reporting process is especially easy if you have electronic mail in place.

Once you have the error information, you have to evaluate the errors and determine the steps to take for correction. Error information can also be used for trend and failure analysis.

The Windows NT Resource Kit, published by Microsoft Press, is one of your best references for system messages. It contains a full list of error messages and error codes.

Windows NT Diagnostics

The Windows NT Diagnostics, WINMSD.EXE, gives you a safer way of viewing Registry entry values than directly accessing the registry file. Not only that, but the information is formatted in a manner that is much easier to read and understand. You can even generate a report of the information supported by the diagnostic program.

Launch WINMSD from **Start\Run**, or from a Windows NT command prompt.

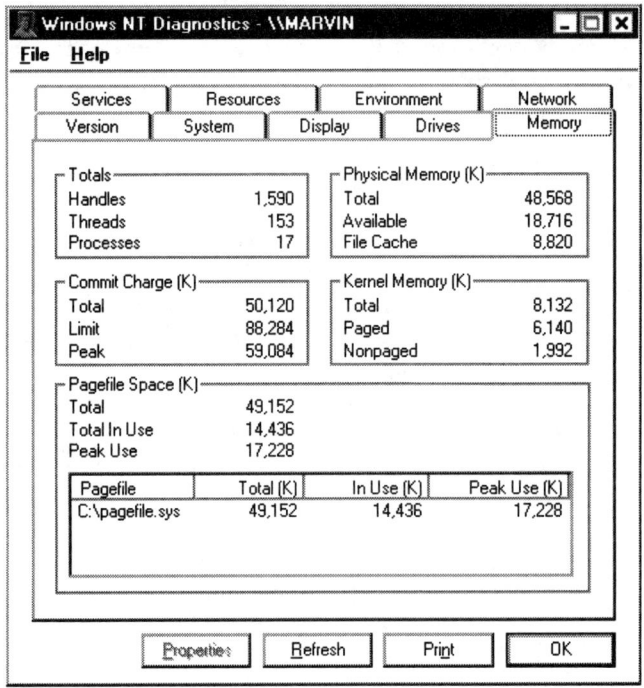

WinMSD Selections

The Windows NT Diagnostic provides information on the following:

Version	This reports the OS version and installation information, such as the installation date and registered owner.
System\Display	The System and Display tabs display System BIOS, Video BIOS, and CPU information.

Drives	The Drives button displays a list of drives recognized by Windows NT. You can select to view additional information, such as cluster information, available space, and the file system type for any drive.
Memory	The Memory button displays information about physical memory (RAM) and virtual memory.
Services	The Services tab consists of two buttons, the Services button and the Devices button. Services lists system services and their status. It also allows you to view detailed information about any selected service. The device button lists device drivers started in the registry and other Windows NT components that are dependent on the device driver or that the device is dependent on.
Resources	The Resources Tab contains five buttons, IRQ, I/O Port, DMA, Memory, and Devices. Each of these displays the resources used by the hardware devices from a different perspective.
IRQ	The IRQ Status lists the supported interrupt values and the usage of each. This includes the interrupt vector, level, and supported device.
I/O Port	The Port Status displays physical address information for device ports.
DMA	The DMA Status displays DMA channels in use and the device assigned to each.
Memory	The Memory Status lists devices with onboard ROM BIOS and the BIOS physical address for each.
Devices	The device button lists hardware devices on your system.

	Shows the System and Local User environment variable settings.
Environment	
Network	The Network Tab gives general information, installed protocol, adapter settings, and network statistics.

You can generate a report including all this information by running **WinMSD Report** from the **File** menu.

Combined Configuration List

The following is a combined list of common devices showing IRQ, DMA, I/O Address, and Memory Address settings for PC/XT and AT systems:

Device	IRQ	DMA	I/O Address	Memory
System Timer	0			
Key Press	1		060 - 06F	
Real Time Clock	8		070 - 07F	
Math Coprocessor	13		0F0 - 0F8	
COM1	4		3F8 - 3FF	
COM2	3		2F8 - 2FF	
COM3	4		3E8 - 3EF	
COM4	3		2E8 - 2EF	
COM5	4		2F0 - 2F7	
COM6	3		2E8 - 2EF	
COM7	4		2E0 - 2E7	
COM8	3		260 - 267	
LPT1 (LPT3 not configured)	7		378 - 37F	
LPT1 (LPT3 configured)	7		3BC - 3BE	
LPT2 (LPT3 not configured)	5		278 - 27F	
LPT2 (LPT3 configured)	5		378 - 37A	
LPT3			278 - 27A	
Floppy controller	6		3F0 - 3F7	
XT Hard disk controller	5	3	320 - 32F	C8000-C8FFF
AT Hard disk controller	14		1F0 - 1F8	

Device	IRQ	DMA	I/O Address	Memory
Monochrome display adapter	0	3B0 - 3BF	B0000-B3FFF	
CGA display adapter		0	3D0 - 3DF	B8000-BBFFF
EGA display adapter	2*	0	3C0 - 3CF	A0000-AFFF
				B0000-BFFFF
				C0000-C3FFF
VGA display adapter	2/9	0	3C0 - 3DA	A0000-AFFF
			3C0 - 3BA	C0000-C7FFF
Hercules Monochrome			3B4 - 3BF	B0000-B7FFF
*EGA will use IRQ 2, or none.				

Dr. Watson

Before leaving the subject of troubleshooting, at least a brief mention should be made of Dr. Watson for Windows NT. Dr. Watson is an application error debugger. It detects, diagnoses, and logs application errors. While you may find few situations where you need to use Dr. Watson yourself, technical support personnel will often request the dumps it produces when working with you on a persistent problem.

The default configuration settings are shown. You will typically want to leave these settings at default. Run DRWATSON.EXE to display this dialog.

Exercise 10-2

The answers to these enxercises are in Appendix A at the end of this manual.

During this exercise, you will work with system monitoring and management tools.

1. Log onto the classroom domain as administrator.
2. Select **Run** from the **Start** menu.
3. Type the following in the Command Line prompt and press **ENTER**:

    WINMSD

4. Click on **Memory**. Record the In Use value for Pagefile.sys below.
5. Launch User Manager and minimize. Click on **Refresh**.
6. Compare the current In Use value with that recorded in step 4.
7. Launch and minimize User Manager for Domains and compare the new In Use value after clicking **Refresh**.
8. Maximize and exit User Manager for Domains and Server Manager.
9. Click on **Services**.
10. Select Directory Replicator and click on **Properties**.
11. Verify the Start Type and click on **OK**.
12. Click on Network to review network statistics. Press **ENTER** or **ALT** to exit Windows NT Diagnostics.

Miscellaneous Troubleshooting

You are not going to have all of the answers. In fact, it's unrealistic to expect any one person to have all of the answers. At some point, you will likely need to get some extra help. Available sources include:

- The Microsoft Support Line
- The Microsoft Resource Kit
- The Microsoft World Wide Web
- Microsoft TechNet

REMOTE MANAGEMENT

This section will introduce tools available to you as an administrator for troubleshooting. Some are already installed with Windows NT Workstation while others are additional software you need to purchase. The following are topics discussed within this section:

- Resource Kit
- Microsoft TechNet
- The Microsoft World Wide Web
- Service Pack Updates

As an administrator, you will want to have these options available to you. Often times, any single source cannot provide the ultimate or best solution for the problem at hand.

Resource Kit

The Microsoft Windows NT Resource Kit is an excellent area for support on Windows NT. The Resource Kit contains a set of books covering areas such as:

- System Optimization and how to effectively use the performance counters in the Performance Monitor Tool.
- Error and message numbers, such as those that display in the Event Viewer.
- Documentation for registry values.

    NOTE: *It is normally suggested that you not change anything in the registry, but sometimes the only way to achieve a result is to modify a registry entry.*

- Tips for networking and integrating Windows NT into a network environment.

Microsoft TechNet

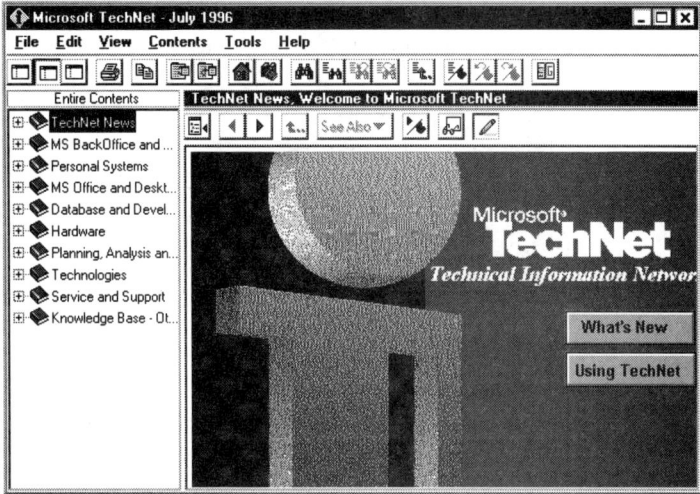

This is perhaps the most valuable tool you could obtain from a troubleshooting perspective. Microsoft TechNet is a monthly CD containing information such as:

- Electronic copies of Microsoft Office and operating system products resource kits.
- A bug list with solutions and workarounds.
- Sample training materials for in-house training.
- Case studies on companies using Microsoft products.
- Extra tools for configuring and managing Windows NT and other Microsoft products.

The Microsoft World Wide Web

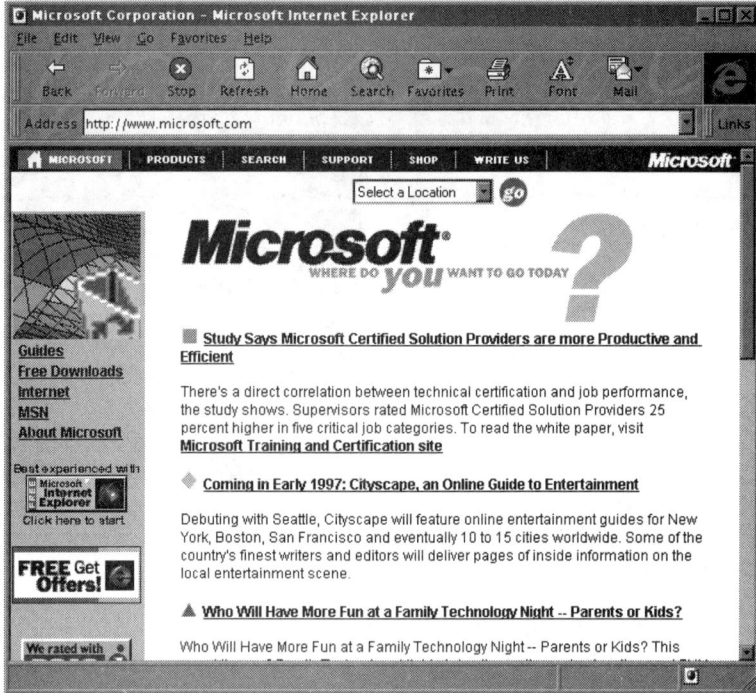

On-line support can also be obtained by connecting to www.microsoft.com. In many ways, this is a one-stop source for Microsoft support. There are also Windows NT discussion forums and the latest bugs found in Windows NT as well as solutions to these bugs posted.

Windows NT ships with Internet Explorer. IE, along with your Internet connection, gives you access to this wealth of information.

Service Pack Updates

Some bugs and problems are incurable and there are no workarounds for them. The only way to fix these is for the Microsoft programmers to reprogram the components so that they work the way they should. Microsoft releases Service Packs with Technet, the Developer's Network, and makes them available over the Internet.

Some guidelines for using Service Packs include:

- Ensure you have backed up your system before using the Service Pack.
- Don't upgrade your system unless the Service Pack updates apply.
- Make sure you have the service pack that applies to your hardware, especially if a vendor-specific version is required.
- Different Back Office components have their own Service Packs which are applied separately.

SUMMARY

During this chapter, you were introduced to the following:

- System startup
- Startup errors
- ARC names
- Recovery menu
- Boot diskette
- Emergency Repair Diskette
- Performance Monitor
- Performance bottlenecks
- Windows NT Diagnostics

POST-TEST QUESTIONS

The answers to these questions are in Appendix A at the end of this manual:

1. What file is used to generate the selection menu during startup?

   ....

   ....

2. Which utility discussed during this chapter will provide you with IRQ usage information for a system?

   ....

   ....

3. What is the first step in running emergency repair procedures?

   ....

   ....

4. You lost the emergency repair diskette for a system. What utility will let you recreate the diskette?

   ....

   ....

5. Which Performance Monitor view lets you gather data for later review?

   ....

   ....

SELF STUDY

Appendix A — Answers to Pre-Test and Post-Test Questions

CHAPTER 1

Pre-Test Answers

1. 12 MB
2. winnt /b
3. FAT
4. TCP/IP, NetBEUI, and NWLink
5. BOOT.INI

Upgrade Scenario One

The five 80386 systems will not support Windows NT. Upgrade the systems to Windows 95, installing Windows 95 to the current Windows directory.

The five 80486 systems will support Windows NT. Upgrade the systems, letting Setup install Windows NT Workstation to the current Windows directory. Inform the users to select to migrate the Windows settings the first time they log on at the workstation.

Upgrade Scenario Two

Install Windows NT normally, letting it install to a different directory.

Unattended Scenario One

Copy the Windows NT Workstation installation files from the \I386 directory on the distribution CD to the network server. Set up a share point (shared directory) giving access to the files.

Create an unattended answer file installing Windows NT Workstation as an NT Server domain client. Create a UDF file with machine name information for all of the systems, setting up a different section for each client in the file.

Connect to the network at each machine and run WINNT, specifying the answer file and UDF file with the appropriate id value.

Unattended Scenario Two

Select one of the systems to use as the model for installing installation. Run SYSDIFF / SNAP to create a snapshot of the system. Install the applications, then run SYSDIFF / DIFF to create the difference file. Copy the snapshot and difference files to an accessible location on the shared directory.

Create a OEM directory at the share point established for installation. Create a $$ subdirectory, and below that subdirectory, a subdirectory for each application's installation files. Copy the files to this directory.

Create a batch file to connect to the shared directory and run SYSDIFF /APPLY to apply the difference file and install the applications. Send an electronic mail message to each user with the batch file attached and instructors for the user to execute the batch file upon receipt.

Implementation Scenario

Assuming that the laptops can support Windows NT Workstation, install each of those systems separately.

For the remaining stations, query the system database to determine which systems can support Windows NT Workstation. Create your shared installation directory, then define SMS PDFs as necessary to install the systems. Run the installations as push installations.

Depending on how remote locations are connected to your mail network, you may need to set up a share point at each of the remote locations. This will keep you from having to copy the installation files for multiple systems across a slow link.

Post-Test Answers

1. [CTRL][ALT][DEL]
2. Run WINNT /B from the CD-ROM.
3. /ox
4. FAT
5. 15
6. NTLDR

CHAPTER 2

Pre-Test Answers

1. C:\WINNT\SYSTEM32\REPL\IMPORT\SCRIPTS
2. Account locked out
3. A workstation local group cannot be designated as a member of another group.
4. It is the length of time a user must wait between password changes.
5. Event Viewer

User Basics Scenario One

First, tell Ed that you cannot set logon time limits on Windows NT Workstation users. Next, run User Manager and connect to the machine. Select all three users and display the user properties dialog. Click on the Profile button and enter the users' home directory as \EdsBrain\TempHome. Save the changes and exit User Manager.

User Basics Scenario Two

Enable auditing and configure the system to track both successful and failed logon attempts. Check the Event Viewer Security log each morning to see if there have been any logon attempts during the evening.

Post-Test Answers

1. Username and password
2. Administrator and guest
3. Add the user to the Administrators group.
4. Disable the account through User Manager, User Properties.
5. Administrators only

CHAPTER 3

Pre-Test Answers

1. Control Panel Network utility
2. Domain global group
3. Roaming
4. NTconfig.pol

Security Management Scenario

Run User Manager for Domains and create two domain global groups. The first group will have EMarsh, JJones, and MWorth as members. At the workstation, add this group as a member of RecRead. The second group will have JSmith and WKemp as members. At the workstation, add the group as a member of RecAll.

User Management Scenario One

You need to implement roaming profiles for all users. Create a directory on either the PDC or BDC and share the directory to the network. Run User Manager for Domains, select all users, and display the user properties dialog. Click on the **Profiles** button and specify the profile location using the format:

```
\\servername\sharename\%USERNAME%
```

The user profiles will be created automatically at this directory location.

User Management Scenario Two

The problem is that the profile isn't being applied when a logon attempt is validated by the BDC. Set up replication with the PDC as exporter and both the PDC and BDC as importers. Copy the profile file to the PDC export directory. It will be automatically replicated to both the PDC and BDC. Make any future changes to the file to the copy in the PDC's export directory.

Post-Test Answers

1. Create a workstation local group with permission to use the printer. Create a domain global group with Wanda, Jorge, and Al as members. Add the domain global group as a member of the workstation local group.
2. Create a roaming profile with your desktop settings.
3. \WINNT\SYSTEM32\REPL\IMPORT\SCRIPTS\NTCONFIG.POL
4. Grayed
5. Administrator (or Server Operator) name and password

CHAPTER 4

Pre-Test Answers

1. General
2. Control Panel SCSI utility
3. 30
4. Load the Windows 95 printer drivers when you install and share the printer.

Printer Implementation Scenario

Starting out with a printer pool was the right idea. Now you need to build from that base. Set up a second printer pool consisting of the same printers. Limit the pool so that it only sends print jobs to the printers after hours. Let everyone know that lengthy, less critical jobs should be to this printer pool.

For your boss, set up a printer definition with just the printer near his office. Give that printer definition a higher priority than either printer pool.

Post-Test Answers

1. Installed components
2. When power is lost
3. Check the Event Viewer System log.
4. They allow supported clients to use the printer without having to manually install printer drivers locally.
5. Administrators
6. The applications may fail in the background when the screen saver becomes active.

CHAPTER 5

Pre-Test Answers

1. Maximum
2. Multimedia
3. Boot
4. REGEDT32 or REGEDIT
5. HKEY_LOCAL_MACHINE

Configuration Scenario

Use the Control Panel System utility to copy the current profile. Boot using the new profile, then install and configure the RAS client. Remove support for LAN devices and drivers.

When you restart your system, you can select between the work and home configurations.

Post-Test Answers

1. That is the control set that was used during the last successful startup.
2. System
3. Set up two hardware configurations for the system and select the appropriate control set when you boot the system.
4. A supported tape drive
5. 0
6. Automatic, Manual, and Disabled

CHAPTER 6

Pre-Test Answers

1. Run **Create** from the **Partition** menu.
2. 2
3. format e: /fs:ntfs
4. NTFS
5. Source

Post-Test Answers

1. 800 MB
2. FAT and NTFS
3. NTFS
4. Full Control to the group Everyone
5. CONVERT
6. No access

CHAPTER 7

Pre-Test Answers

1. Cooperative
2. `CTRL` `ALT` `DEL`
3. The application is controlled through preemptive multitasking rather than coorperative multitasking.
4. Display the application's property dialog and click on the Memory tab.
5. DCOMCNGF

Post-Test Answers

1. WIN32
2. Cooperative
3. cmd.exe
4. >>
5. WIN32C

CHAPTER 8

Pre-Test Answers

1. IP address and subnet mask
2. NWLink
3. Gateway or router
4. DHCP

Quick Checks

1. All machines are probably running IPX/SPX or NWLink. Add TCP/IP to all machines. After verifying that TCP/IP is working correctly, remove NWLink (IPX/SPX).
2. Use NetBEUI as the network transport protocol to keep from changing the existing stations. You will also need to install DLC to support IBM connectivity.
3. Install NWLink.
4. Install TCP/IP on all systems.

Access Scenario

Set up the new drive as a single partition. Format the partition as NTFS. Set the permission at the root so that only Administrators have access permission to the partition and have Windows NT copy the permissions to all subdirectories and files.

Share each of the directories to the network. Create two local groups, one for managing access for Acct and one for all users. Add the domain global group as a member of its local equivalent. Give the local group for Acct Add & Read to Reports and Current. Give the local group for all users (Domain Users) Read access in Reports and Archive.

If not already configured, set up auditing and audit all attempts to delete from Current and all attempts to write to or delete from Archive.

Post-Test Answers

1. End the share name with a dollar sign ($).
2. IP address and subnet mask
3. The user most likely belongs to a group with "No access" assigned.
4. WINS
5. DLC

CHAPTER 9

Pre-Test Answers

1. modem
2. Nothing, that is a default setting.
3. Control Panel Network utility
4. Internet Explorer

Post-Test Answers

1. Windows NT v4.0
2. Windows NT v3.5 and above
3. Preferred server or default tree and context

CHAPTER 10

Pre-Test Answers

1. Chart
2. BOOT.INI, NTDETECT.COM, NTLDR, and BOOTSECT.DOC
3. DISKPERF -Y
4. WINMSD

Post-Test Answers

1. BOOT.INI
2. WINMSD
3. Boot from Windows NT Workstation Setup disk #1.
4. RDISK
5. Log

Appendix B — Sample Answer File

The following is a sample Setup answer file.

```
[Unattended]
OemPreinstall = yes
NoWaitAfterTextMode = 0
NoWaitAfterGUIMode = 0
FileSystem = LeaveAlone
ExtendOEMPartition = 0
ConfirmHardware = no
NtUpgrade = no
Win31Upgrade = no
TargetPath = *
OverwriteOemFilesOnUpgrade = no

[UserData]
FullName = "Frank Miller"
OrgName = "Wave Technologies"
ComputerName = WAVE32
ProductId = "555-5555555"

[GuiUnattended]
OemSkipWelcome = 1
OEMBlankAdminPassword = 0
TimeZone = "(GMT-06:00) Central Time (US & Canada)"

[Display]
ConfigureAtLogon = 1

[Network]
DetectAdapters = DetectAdaptersSection
InstallProtocols = ProtocolsSection
InstallServices = ServicesSection
JoinDomain = WAVE
CreateComputerAccount = Administrator
```

```
[DetectAdaptersSection]
LimitTo = ELNK16, ELNKII
ELNK16 = ELNK16ParamSection
ELNKII = ELNKIIParamSection

[ELNK16ParamSection]

[ELNKIIParamSection]

[ProtocolsSection]
NBF = NBFParamSection
NWLNKIPX = NWLNKIPXParamSection
TC = TCParamSection

[NBFParamSection]

[NWLNKIPXParamSection]

[TCParamSection]

[ServicesSection]
NWWKSTA = NWWKSTAParamSection
RAS = RASParamSection

[NWWKSTAParamSection]
!DefaultLocation = GEN
!DefaultScriptOptions = 0

[RASParamSection]
PortSections = PortSection1
DialoutProtocols = TCP/IP

[PortSection1]
```

Glossary

16-bit application
Application native to Windows v3.1 or Windows for Workgroups v3.11.

32-bit application
Application native to Windows NT or Windows 95.

56k Line
This is a digital phone-line connection (leased line) that can carry 56,000 bits-per-second. At this speed, a Megabyte will take approximately 3 minutes to transfer, making it four times as fast as a 14,400bps modem.

Access Control List (ACL)
A list of trustees who have been granted rights to an object or rights to the properties of an object. Each object in the NDS contains an Access Control List.

Access Control right
A file system right allows the user to change the Access Control List (ACL) trustee assignments and Inherited Rights Filter for a directory or file.

Access group
(In LAN technology) All stations which have identical rights to make use of computer networks, or data PBX resources.

Access Mask
Value passed describing the privilege requirements for a users access request. This is compared against the users access privileges to determine access.

Access method
1. (In IBM environments) A host program managing the movement of data between the main storage and an input/output device of a computer system. BTAM, TCAM, and VTAM are common data communications access methods. 2. (In LAN technology) A means to allow stations to gain access to make use of the network's transmission medium; classified as shared access (which is further divided into explicit access or contended access) or discrete access method.

Access path
This is the route between two communicating computers. An access path on the Internet is routed through nodes on the network.

Access protection
The ability to protect a block of memory by setting flags that determine how the information stored at that memory location can be used.

Access time
Access time is a measurement of the average time it takes, once the PC issues a command, to get data from a disk drive. This is a combination of several factors. The major determining factor is drive seek time. Moving the read/write heads is the slowest single operation for a hard disk. The faster it can move the head array during seek time, the faster the disk access time.

Glossary

Access Token
: Windows NT object describing a user account and group memberships.

Access Unit
: Electronic mail component responsible for transferring messages between dissimilar mail systems.

Accessories
: Microsoft Windows or Windows NT applets.

Account SID
: Unique value identifying a Windows NT or NT Server user or group account, or object.

ACE (Access Control Entry)
: Access Control Entry. Access privilege assigned to a user or group.

ACF/VTAM
: Advanced Communications Function/Virtual Telecommunications Access Method. The most basic and widespread element in IBM's mainframe networking software.

ACL
: Access Control List. List of all access privileges for users or groups.

Active Monitor
: Any station on a Token Ring network that originates a free token. There can be only one active monitor at a time. The active monitor is also responsible for making sure the same frame doesn't keep circulating around the ring.

Adaptive Bridge
: Sometimes referred to as a "learning bridge" because it learns the node address of workstations on the LAN. This type of bridge builds its own table of address which frees the administrator or installer of this task.

Add-on board
: A circuit board that changes or improves a personal computer's capabilities. For example, a memory board increases the amount of RAM in a computer. A network board, also called an NIC card) lets workstations communicate with each other and with the NetWare server. These boards are connected by cabling or some other transmission medium.

Address
: A unique designation for the location of data, the identity of an intelligent device, or a logical network address; allows each device on a single communications line to respond to its own message.

Address mask
: A bit mask used to select bits from an Internet address for subnet addressing. The mask is 32 bits long and selects the network portion of the Internet address and two or more bits of the local portion. Sometimes called subnet mask.

Address resolution
: A means for mapping logical addresses onto physical addresses.

Address space
: A block of addresses that a process can assign to a particular block of data. The memory allocated from an address space must be backed by physical memory.

Addressing (disk channel)
: The method by which numbers are assigned to identify hardware resources on disk channels. Each controller must have a unique address. The documentation shipped with the controller will list the physical address settings.

Addressing space
: 1. The range of addresses which a processor can access. This usually depends on the width of the processor's address bus and address registers. Address space can be either physical or virtual. 2. This is the total amount of RAM available to a NetWare 4 server operating system. It can be divided into domains. The maximum addressing space is 4 gigabytes (GB) in a NetWare 4 operating system, however practical hardware limits are much lower.

ADSP (AppleTalk Data Stream Protocol)
: ADSP is responsible for providing a simple transport method for data across the network.

AEP (AppleTalk Echo Protocol)
: AEP is responsible for checking for communications between different nodes on the network.

AFP (AppleTalk Filing Protocol)
: Protocols for a network of Macintosh computers. AppleTalk is based on the ISO/OSI Reference Model and incorporates the SPX protocol. AppleTalk networks may be configured in Ethernet and Token Ring topologies. AppleTalk networks use various kinds of cables. The AppleTalk Filing Protocol (AFP), for client server architecture, runs on VAX and other non-Macintosh servers. AppleTalk and AFP are compatible with NetWare and are available as VAPs (v2.x) and NLMs (v3.x and v4.x) in NetWare for Macintosh.

AFP Server Object
: Represents an AppleTalk Filing Protocol file server on the network.

AFP.NLM
: The AFP.NLM is the NetWare Loadable Module which is loaded on the file server to provide AFP services.

Agent
: In the client-server model, the part of the system that performs information preparation and exchange on behalf of a client or server application. See NMS, DUA, MTA.

Alert
: An error message sent to the system control point at the host system.

ALGORITHM
: The steps that must be performed in order to complete a particular action.

Alias Object
: This type of object is used to point to another object located in another branch of NetWare's NDS directory tree.

alloc memory
: An expandable section of memory in NetWare v3.11 which is not required for DOS or the NetWare operating system. Alloc memory is used to store network status information such as drive mappings, loadable module tables, and locked files; and also current operations, including user connections, queue manager tables, service request buffers, and messages to be broadcast on the network.

ALLOCATION
: Associating a memory address with a block of data and setting aside physical memory to back it.

Amplitude modulation
: A method of encoding enabling the frequency of the carrier wave to remain constant while the information it carries changes in strength. This system changes the strength (size) of an analog signal (wave) from the zero line, to a positive peak, then an equal negative peak. The stronger the voltage, the higher the wave. Often abbreviated as AM.

Analog
: The representation of a continuously changing physical variable (sound, for example) by another physical variable (such as electrical current).

Analog Adapter
: On the analog video board, intensity information is transmitted across separate lines for each of the three primary colors (red, green and blue). In theory, the possible number of variations of each of the basic colors could allow for an infinite number of displayed color variations, however, most monitors are limited to no more than 262,144 colors. VGA, Super VGA, MCGA, and 8514/A monitors all require analog adapters.

Analog signal
: A smoothly varying value of voltage or current, i.e. a signal that varies continuously in amplitude and time.

Anonymous FTP (file transfer protocol)
: This Internet utility allows a user to connect to a remote computer as a guest to retrieve documents, files, programs, and other archived data without having a user id or password on the host system. Users identify themselves as anonymous and skip local security checks.

Anonymous pipe
: A data storage buffer that OS/2 maintains in RAM; used for interprocess communications.

ANSI (American National Standards Institute)
: A group of committees formed to establish voluntary commercial and government standards. The committee responsible for computing, data processing, and information technology is ANSI-X3, formerly named USASI (United States of America Standards Institute). ANSI is a member of International Standards Organization, or ISO.

ANSI character set
: The American National Standards Institute 8-bit character set, containing 256 characters.

API (Application Program Interface)
: Used where proprietary application programs have to talk to communications software or conform to protocols from another vendor's product. API also provides a standardized method of "vertical" communications. Apple Macintosh was the first computer to use the API concept.

APPC (Advanced Program-to-Program Communications)
: An Application Program Interface (API) developed by IBM for its Systems Network Architecture (SNA).

AppleShare
: Apple's file server and print server software for use with Macintosh client/server networks.

AppleShare software
: A Macintosh computer can function as a file server in an AppleTalk network using this networking software. As Macintosh workstation software, it allows access to an AppleShare server.

AppleTalk
: Protocols for a network of Macintosh computers. AppleTalk is based on the ISO/OSI Reference Model and incorporates the SPX protocol. AppleTalk networks may be configured in Ethernet and token ring topologies. AppleTalk networks use various kinds of cables. The AppleTalk Filing Protocol (AFP), for client server architecture, runs on VAX and other non- Macintosh servers. AppleTalk and AFP are compatible with NetWare and are available as VAPs (v2.x) and NLMs (v3.x) in NetWare for Macintosh.

AppleTalk Filing Protocol
: (AFP) This is the AppleTalk protocol that allows communication and data transmission between file servers and clients in an AppleShare network. If AFP.NLM is loaded on a NetWare server that is running NetWare for Macintosh, the AFP lets Macintosh users share files by interacting directly with the NetWare file system. It operates on the same level as NetWare Core Protocol (NCP).

AppleTalk Phase I
: AppleTalk Phase I networks are limited to one network number per cable segment as well as 256 nodes.

AppleTalk Phase II
: AppleTalk Phase II networks exceed the 254 device limitation by allowing the assignment of multiple network numbers on the same network segment. Phase II networks allow the creation of larger, more open networks with the introduction of TokenTalk and EtherTalk.

AppleTalk Print Services module
: Macintosh users can print to NetWare queues and non-Macintosh users can print to AppleTalk printers using this NetWare Loadable Module (NLM).

AppleTalk protocols
: These are the forms and rules that regulate communication between nodes on an AppleTalk network. They also control the Apple Talk network, from the network board to the application software. They are: Link Access Protocols (LAPs), Datagram Delivery Protocol (DDP), Routing Table Maintenance Protocol (RTMP), AppleTalk Update-Based Routing Protocol (AURP), Name Binding Protocol (NBP), Printer Access Protocol (PAP), Zone Information Protocol (ZIP).

Application
: The use to which an information processing system is put; for example, a payroll application, an airline reservation application, or a network application.

Application layer
: Highest (seventh) layer in the OSI model, containing all user or application programs.

Architecture
: The specific design and construction of a computer, usually referring to the hardware makeup of the central processing unit and the size of the byte or set of bytes it processes, such as 8-bit, 16- bit, or 32-bit architecture.

Archive
: Storing files on a long-term media, such as optical disks or magnetic tape.

Archive Needed (A) attribute
If a file has been changes since the last time it was backed up, this file attribute will be set by the NetWare operating system.

Archive sites
These are computer sites that provide access to a group of files on the Internet. Many popular sites can be reached using anonymous FTP, providing information, freeware, and shareware that can be transferred to the users' computers.

Argument
Under Visual Basic, an argument is a value passed with a procedure containing values needed for procedure execution.

ARP (Address Resolution Protocol)
A protocol used between routers and nodes to determine the MAC or physical layer address when the Network layer (IP) address is known.

ARPA (Advanced Research Project Agency)
The government agency who first started the Internet.

ARPANET
A packet switched network developed in the early 1970s. The "grandfather" of today's Internet. ARPANET was decommissioned in June 1990.

ARQ
Automatic Request for Retransmission. A type of send/receive procedure in which each message must be either positively or negatively acknowledged. ARQ is a popular form of error control.

Array
1. A collection of like elements that can be accessed serially or by index.
2. A series of variables having the same name and data type.

ASCII (American Standard Code for Information Exchange)
Devised in 1968; a code that changes letters, numbers, and symbols into a 7-bit code, with an eighth bit acting as a check bit. ASCII is used for the purpose of standardizing the transmission of data to achieve hardware and software compatibility. ASCII permits a total of 96 visible characters, including the space, and 32 hardware control characters.

ASCII terminal
A terminal that uses ASCII; usually synonymous with asynchronous terminal and with dumb terminal.

ASMP
Asymmetric multiprocessing. Multiprocessor management method where one processor supports the operating system and any additional processors support process threads.

ASP (AppleTalk Session Protocol)
ASP is responsible for maintaining all sessions between the workstation and the file server. Some of these tasks may include: session initiation, maintenance, and termination.

Asymmetric multiprocessing
See ASMP.

Asynchronous
A form of communication in which each transmitted character is preceded by a start bit and followed by a stop bit. This eliminates the need for a particular spacing or timing scheme between characters. The Macintosh and other personal computers communicate asynchronously via a serial port.

Asynchronous modem
: A modem which cannot supply timing signals, therefore requiring that all the timing information be supplied by the associated data terminal equipment (DTE).

Asynchronous transmission
: In computer communications, data (binary digits) can be transmitted in asynchronous mode or synchronous mode. When the mode is asynchronous, the binary digits are not orderly, meaning they are out of synchronization and sent at irregular intervals in characters, words, or blocks. To ensure that the receiving device is ready, a special "start bit" is sent ahead of each character and a "stop bit" at the end of each character, a process which continues until the final character is sent. In ASCII, where eight bits form a character or byte, ten bits must be sent for each character. Asynchronous transmission is sometimes known as start-stop transmission.

ATP (AppleTalk Transaction Protocol)
: ATP is responsible for handling network messaging. Unlike DDPm, ATP requires an acknowledgement of delivery.

Attribute
: A characteristic describing or distinguishing a piece of hardware or software, such as security attributes or database field character types.

Authentication
: A way to verify that an object sending messages or requests to an NDS is permitted to act on or receive those message or requests.

AUTOEXEC.BAT
: A batch program containing basic startup commands that help configure the system. It is automatically carried out by the DOS operating system whenever the computer is started or restarted.

AUTOEXEC.NCF
: NetWare batch file for v3.x and v4.x, which is loaded into the file server after the operating system, initiating file execution for startup.

AUTOEXEC.NT
: The replacement for AUTOEXEC.BAT for DOS programs in Windows NT.

AUTOEXEC.SYS
: NetWare batch file for v2.x which is loaded into the file server after the operating system, initiating file execution for startup.

Average access time
: The average time between the instant of request and the delivery from a storage device.

Backbone
: The primary connectivity mechanism of a hierarchical distributed system. All systems which have connectivity to an intermediate system on the backbone are assured of connectivity to each other. This does not prevent systems from setting up private arrangements with each other to bypass the backbone for reasons of cost, performance, or security.

Background application
: An application that is running, but cannot receive user input.

Background process
: A process that is not the focus of user input.

Background Task
An active process that is not receiving interactive user input.

Backup
1. Pertaining to a system, device, file, or facility that can be used to recover data in the event of a malfunction or loss of data. 2. To copy information, usually onto diskette or tape, for safekeeping.

Bandwidth
The range of frequencies that can be transmitted through a particular circuit.

Base memory address
The bit where a block of allocated memory begins.

Base priority
The thread priority level within the priority class of the process before any dynamic priority modifiers have been applied.

Baseband
Characteristic of any network technology that uses a single carrier frequency and requires all stations attached to the network to participate in every transmission.

Batch
A method of computer job processing in which input is collected and run through the processing programs all at once, with output produced in the form of files and reports. Batch is the opposite of interactive job processing, in which an operator at a terminal interacts with the processing program directly during data entry. Most personal computers employ interactive processing. Mainframes use batch processing.

Batch program
A text file that contains DOS commands. When you run a batch program, DOS carries out the commands in the file as if you had typed them at the DOS prompt.

Baud
Abbreviation for Baudot, which gets its name from J. M. Emile Baudot (1845-1903), who invented the code. The Baudot code is a special set of binary characters which uses five bits per character, forming 32 combinations, which was increased to 62 through the use of two special shift characters. The Baudot code was mainly used to handle telex messages by common communications carriers such as Western Union. The main disadvantage of the Baudot code is its lack of an error-checking bit.

BBS
Bulletin Board Service. A popular PC network that allows users to dial into a central point and read group messages, copy public-domain information, and leave messages for other users.

BCP
SQL Server bulk copy program used for importing data into or exporting data out of databases.

Binary
Having two components or possible states; usually represented by a code of zeros and ones.

Binary access
File access method used for access of binary data files.

Binary stream
An unstructured series of ones and zeros.

Binary tree
: An efficient method of storing data that will be used in search operations.

Bindery
: NetWare database containing information about a network, such as names of users, devices, and other physical and logical entities or objects; the properties of each object, such as user addresses, passwords, and accounts; and the data sets or values of each property.

Bindery context
: A server's bindery services is enabled in this container object.

Bindery context path
: A path statement that sets bindery context in up to 16 containers. The SET parameter can specify bindery contexts, with multiple contexts separated by semicolons.

Bindery objects
: An object placed in the Directory tree by an upgrade or migration utility is represented by this leaf object. NDS cannot identify the object, and it provides backward compatibility with bindery-oriented utilities.

Bindery Services
: Bindery-based utilities, clients and applications can coexist with NDS on the network due to this NetWare 4 feature. Objects listed in the server's bindery exist in a flat, instead of hierarchical, database. Bindery services creates a flat structure for a server, using the bindery relevant leaf objects in an Organization or Organizational Unit object.

Binding
: Establishment of a communications session between a protocol driver and network adapter card driver.

Binding and unbinding
: Binding assigns a communication protocol to network boards and LAN drivers. Unbinding removes the protocol. Each network board needs at least one communication protocol bound to its LAN driver, or it cannot process packets. Multiple protocols can be bound to the same LAN driver and board. You can also bind the same protocol stack to more than one LAN driver on the server. Workstations with different protocols can be cabled on the same scheme.

BIOS
: Basic Input/Output System; software or firmware embedded in chips on the circuit board which determines compatibility. Examples of these are IBM, Compaq, AMI, Award, and Phoenix.

BISDN
: Broadband ISDN.

Bisync (Binary Synchronous Communications or BSC)
: A type of synchronous communications control procedure set up by IBM as a line control procedure in which the sending and receiving stations are synchronized before a message is sent. The synchronization is checked and adjusted during the transmission, using a defined set of control characters.

Bit
: Abbreviation for binary digit. A bit is the fundamental unit of information and is either a zero or a one; the basic unit for storing data in primary storage (zero for "off," one for "on"). Groups of bits are needed to represent other symbols such as letters of the alphabet.

Bitmap
: A group of bits (binary digits) representing an image, stored in a computer's memory as a pattern of dots.

Block
: The smallest amount of disk space that can be allocated at one time on a NetWare volume. It is set automatically during installation. The default block size is recommended. Block suballocation can subdivide a disk block among several files to better use disk space when a block is large.

Block suballocation
: To better utilize disk space, this function allows part of several files to share one block. Block suballocation divides any partially-used disk block into 512-byte sub blocks. These can be used to share the remaining space on the block with leftover fragments of other files. This is set by default with NetWare 4 is installed.

BOC (Bell Operating Company)
: More commonly referred to as RBOC for Regional Bell Operating Company. The local telephone company in each of the seven U.S. regions.

Boot
: To start or restart your computer, loading the operating system from a disk drive.

Boot files
: These files, which include AUTOEXEC.BAT and CONFIG.SYS start the operating system and its drivers, set the environment variables, load NetWare. AUTOEXEC.NCF and STARTUP.NCF are examples of NetWare boot files. Workstation boot files vary depending on the operating system (DOS, MS Windows, OS/2, Macintosh, or UNIX).

bps (Bits per second)
: Usually the number of bits (binary digits) which can be transmitted or transferred each second.

Bps (Bytes per second)
: Usually the number of bytes which can be transmitted or transferred each second.

Break
: An interruption in program execution or data transmission; a loss of communication between sender and receiver. Also a keyboard key that enables the interruption.

Bridge
: A device that connects two or more physical networks and forwards packets between them. Bridges can usually be made to filter packets, that is, to forward only certain traffic. Related devices are: repeaters which simply forward electrical signals from one cable to another, and full-fledged routers which make routing decisions based on several criteria. In OSI terminology, a bridge is a Data Link Layer intermediate system.

Broadband
: A technique for transmitting analog signals along a medium, such as a radio wave, also called wideband. Broadband signaling works the way radio and television work, by splitting up the available frequencies into different channels. The data is transmitted simultaneously and is represented by changes in amplitude, frequency, or phase of the signal. Broadband transmission can be used to transmit different combinations of data, voice, and video information along one physical cable with multiple communication channels of different frequencies. In LAN technology, broadband is a system in which multiple channels access a medium, usually coaxial cable, that has a large bandwidth (50 Mbps is typical) using radio-frequency modems.

Broadcast
: 1. Transmission of a message intended for general reception rather than for a specific station. 2. (In LAN technology) A transmission method used in bus topology networks that sends all messages to all stations, even though the messages are addressed to specific stations. 3. A NetWare console command that transmits a message to all network nodes or list of nodes.

Browse right
: An object right to view an object in the Directory tree.

Browser
: This client program (software) is used to look at various internet resources and retrieve information.

Browsing
: Allows you to find objects in the Directory, which is arranged in hierarchical order.

BSD (Berkeley Software Distribution)
: Term used when describing different versions of the Berkeley UNIX software, as in "4.3BSD UNIX."

BTAM
: Basic Telecommunications Access Method. An IBM software routine; the basic access method for 3270 data communications controls.

Buffer
: A temporary storage place for information. Many times it is a device used to compensate for a difference in either the rate of data flow or the time of occurrence of events in transmission from one device to another.

Built-In Group
: Windows NT and Windows NT Server default groups.

Bus
: Any of the internal control paths which travel from the central processing unit to the input/output ports, and to the random access memory (RAM) of the computer. A personal computer has four pathways. In LAN (Local Area Network) technology, bus is a linear network topology.

Byte
: Short for "binary digit eight." A unit of information consisting of usually eight bits. A file's size is measured in bytes or potential storage capacity is measured in bytes, but when dealing with very large numbers, the terms kilobyte, megabyte, or gigabyte are used.

Cache
: An area of computer memory set aside for frequently used data to speed operations. Some caches are general purpose, while others are for specific operations.

Cache buffer
: Portable NetWare runs as a process program on the host and uses the host's cache, rather than having one of its own. Portable NetWare has a local or spot cache, containing the file block that comes right after the block that is being used. Cache blocks have the same size as the host's block size, and are assigned by the operating system on an as-needed basis from a cache buffer pool.

Cache memory
: NetWare uses this available RAM to improve server disk access time. It includes memory for the hash table, the FAT, the Turbo FAT, suballocation tables, the directory cache, a temporary data storage area for files, loaded NLM, and available memory for other operations.

Captive thread
: A thread that has been created by a dynlink package and that will stay within the dynlink code, never transferring back to the client process's code. Also, a thread that is used to call a service entry point and that will never return or that will return only if some specific event occurs.

Cartridge Fonts
: Some printers support plug-in ROM cartridges to supply additional fonts during printing.

Cell
: This is a fixed length data element that can be transmitted in asynchronous transfer mode (ATM).

CGI
: Common Gateway Interface.

Channel
: This is a route for electrical transmission between two or more points.

Character set
: A set of acceptable and recognizable characters used by a particular computer system or software package. Character sets are binary-coded and often follow a standard such as ASCII, ANSI, or EBCDIC.

Checksum
: Used in data communications to monitor the number of bits being transmitted between communications devices by means of a simple mathematical algorithm. The checksum is used to ensure that the full complement of bits is received successfully by the receiving device.

Child process
: 1. A process that is created by another process. 2. A dependent process. Contrast with parent process.

Circuit
: 1. (In data communications) A means of bidirectional communication between two points, consisting of transmit and receive channels. 2. (In electronic design) One or more components that act together to perform one or more functions.

Claim Token
: Used by a station to become the active monitor when no active monitor is present on a Token Ring network.

Client
: A client is a workstation that requests services of another computer which is a server.

Client area
The area of a window where user interactions occur.

Client socket
The socket that requests connection to a server socket.

Client-server model
A common way to describe network services and the model user processes (programs) of those services. Examples include the name-server/name-resolver paradigm of the DNS and file-server/file-client relationships such as NFS and diskless hosts.

Client/server applications
Applications that have been designed to operate in a network environment. They usually consist of a front end client application and a back end server application.

Clipboard
In a software application, a temporary storage area or buffer for text and graphics which may have been cut or copied from a file. Information in the clipboard can be moved to another area or to another application. If not saved, the contents of the clipboard will be lost when the power is switched off.

Clipboard function
Function provided to enable the user or application to extract data from one window to another, or from one application to another.

ClipBook
Collection of stored data that may be used as a source for data transfer.

Clock/Calendar
The clock is used to identify the date and time of computer transactions. Certain software programs utilize the date and time functions more than others.

CLS
1. DOS command to clear the screen.
2. NetWare v3.x and v4.x CLear Screen console command. The OFF console command also clears the console's screen.

Cluster
A group of data stored together on one or more sectors of a floppy disk or hard disk. (A sector usually contains 512 bytes of data.) When DOS stores data on a disk, it usually breaks the data into smaller sections which it writes at various places on the disk as appropriate. The location of each cluster is recorded in a file allocation table (FAT).

Cluster control unit
Also called cluster controller; a device that can control the input-output operations of more than one device connected to it. A cluster control unit may be controlled by a program stored and executed in the unit.

CMOS
Complementary Metal Oxide Semiconductor; a specialized memory chip, powered by a small battery, that stores basic system configuration information.

CMOS RAM
This memory stores system configuration data, for example the number of drives, types of drives, and amount of memory. It is battery-powered, so it can retain the data, time, and other information that must be stored when the computer is turned off.

Coax (coaxial cable)
A thick, relatively inflexible cable consisting of an inner cylindrical conductor, usually copper, surrounded by an insulator and then encased in a wire mesh or metal sheath. Coaxial cable is used for baseband and broadband communications networks including LANs (Local Area Networks) and WANs (Wide Area Networks). It is used for cable television and computer networks because the cable is relatively free from external interference and permits very high transmission rates.

Code
A set of rules that specify the way data is represented, such as ASCII or EBCDIC.

Code page
A matrix that assigns graphic and control characters to specific hexadecimal values or code points.

COM port
A connection on the computer where the cable for a serial device is attached. The serial device could be a printer, network interface card, modem, or other device. COM ports are often called serial ports. COM ports are numbered, and generally COM1 through COM4 are supported on most personal computers. It is possible to have more or less than four COM ports.

Command processor
Sometimes shown as COMPROC or CP, a program executed to perform an operation specified by a command. Also, the portion of an operating system that executes commands.

Command prompt
A displayed symbol, such as C>, that informs the user the system is idle.

Command subtree
A process and all its descendants.

COMMAND.COM
The program that interprets and runs DOS commands.

Commercial Internet Exchange (CIX)
CIX is a consortium of companies formed in 1992 to promote commercial use of the Internet.

Commit
To specify that a transaction should be completed at once.

Committed memory
Memory that is blocked by physical memory.

Common carrier
In the U.S., a private business or corporation that offers general communication services to the public such as telephone, teletype, or intercomputer communications. All common carriers operate under FCC guidelines and all services offered are subject to tariff schedules filed with and approved by the FCC.

Communication buffer
An area set aside in the NetWare server's memory to temporarily hold data packets arriving from workstations. It was formerly referred to as packet receive buffer.

Communication protocols
Rules used by a program or operating system to communication between two or more points. It allows information to be packaged, sent, and delivered.

Communications protocol
: For computers engaged in telecommunications, the protocol, i.e., the settings and standards, must be the same for both devices when receiving and transmitting information. A communications program can be used to ensure the baud rate, duplex, parity, data bits, and stop bits are correctly set.

Communications rate
: Also called the transfer rate or the transmission rate. The communications rate cannot exceed the maximum rate that both devices can handle.

Communications Software
: To communicate with the modem, communications software is required. The software helps control the modem and specify what data should be sent where. Communication software is required at both the sending and the receiving computers.

Compile error
: Error occurring while program statements are being typed in the code editor.

Complete Trust Model
: Windows NT Server domain model using a two-way trust relationship between all domains. User, groups, and resources are managed separately on each domain and shared between domains.

Component
: Hardware or software that is part of a functional unit.

Component Object Model
: A binary specification that allows unrelated objects to communicate with each other. Also known as COM, the Component Object Model is the foundation of OLE technology.

Configuration (router)
: The settings and parameters that configure a NetWare v4.x server as a router. They are set through internetwork utilities.

Configuration (server)
: The settings and parameters specified when using INSTALL.NLM to install a new NetWare v4.x server or perform maintenance work on an existing NetWare v4.x server.

Connection-oriented
: The model of interconnection in which communication proceeds through three well-defined phases: connection establishment, data transfer, connection release. Examples: X.25, Internet TCP and OSI TP4, ordinary telephone calls.

Connectionless
: The model of interconnection in which communication takes place without first establishing a connection. Sometimes called datagram. Examples: LANs, Internet IP and OSI CLNP, UDP, ordinary postcards.

Constant
: A name used to refer to a value that does not change during application execution.

Control
: Visible Visual Basic object used to generate an event or display on screen information.

Control character
: Any one of 32 special hardware control characters and symbols available in ASCII which are used to control a communications process or a peripheral device such as a printer. Control characters may be used to instruct the printer to advance paper, or move one line; also can be used to signify the start and finish of a data transmission.

Control Panel
1. This desk accessory provided on the Macintosh, allows you to make changes to your working environment including network connections.   2. Windows-family utility containing management tools.

Controller board
A device, also called a host bus adapter (HBA), that allows a computer to communicate with another device, such as a hard disk or tape drive. It manages input/output and regulates the operating of the other device.

Conventional memory
Up to the first 640 KB of memory in the computer, used by DOS to run applications.

Cooperative multitasking
Multitasking method where an application must release the processor before the next application may be given processor time.

Coprocessor
An auxiliary processor designed to relieve the demand on the main processor by performing a few specific tasks. In general, coprocessors handle tasks that would be performed more slowly by the main processor. Math coprocessors are common in IBM PC and compatible systems. Newer CPUs have built-in coprocessors.

cps
Characters per second (cps) is used to define printing speed.

CRC
Cyclic Redundancy Check; a redundancy check in which the check key is generated by a cyclic algorithm. Also, a system checking or error checking performed at both the sending and receiving station after a block check character has been accumulated.

Crosstalk
The disturbance caused in a circuit by an unwanted transfer of energy from another circuit. Also, interference which occurs when cables are too close to each other, resulting in loss or corruption of data.

Cursor
An indicator that keeps track of the current position in the result set.

Cyberspace
This is a term popularly used to indicate the meeting place of ideas and people using telecommunication technology. It describes the whole range of information resources available through computer networks. Science fiction writer William Gibson coined the term in his novel "Neuromancer." He also called cyberspace the fourth dimension, created out of information.

Cylinder
On a disk drive, a cylinder is the data area that can be accessed by all the drive's read/write heads while they are lined up in a single position. When the "gang-mounted" read/write heads move to a position on one platter, they all move to the same position on every platter. Gang-mounted means that they are moved in unison.

DAC (Digital to Analog Converter)
DAC chips are found on analog adapters. Because the PC operates digitally, it sends digitized information to the adapter. If the monitor accepts analog input only, the DAC on the adapter must convert the digital data from the computer into analog instructions for the display to present data on the screen.

DARPA (Defense Advanced Research Projects Agency)
The U.S. government agency that funded the ARPANET.

Data communication
The transfer of data from one device to another via direct cabling; telecommunications links involving modems, a telephone network, or other connection methods. Transfer of information between functional units by means of data transmission according to a protocol.

Data file
A collection of related data records organized in a specific manner, such as a payroll file or an inventory file.

Data integrity
The data quality that exists as long as accidental or malicious destruction, alteration, or loss of data does not occur.

Data Link Layer
The OSI layer that is responsible for data transfer across a single physical connection, or series of bridged connections, between two Network entities.

Data set
Sometimes shown as DS, the major unit of data storage and retrieval, consisting of a collection of data in one of several prescribed arrangements and described by control information to which the system has access.

Data stream
All data transmitted through a data channel in a single read or write operation. Also, a continuous stream of data elements being transmitted, or intended for transmission, in character or binary-digit form, using a defined format.

Data structure
A custom variable that can contain multiple variables of various types.

Data Transfer Rate
The data transfer rate determines how fast a drive or other peripheral can transfer data with its controller. The data transfer rate is a key measurement in drive performance.

Database
A collection of interrelated data stored together that is fundamental to a system or enterprise. A data structure for accepting, storing, and providing on demand data for multiple independent users.

Datagram
A message.

Datatypes
General term referring to data storage formats supported under SQL Server.

DCE
Data Communications Equipment

DDE (Dynamic Data Exchange)
A process that allows two applications to exchange information.

DDP (Datagram Delivery Protocol)
A layer 3 (routed) protocol used by Apple, between Apple-brand computers. DDP is a "connectionless" protocol which means that it does not require an acknowledgement of delivery.

Debugger
An application that allows a programmer to see the statement that is being executed and the contents of variables or registers to facilitate the location of programming errors.

Default
One of a set of operating conditions that is automatically used when a device such as a printer or computer is turned on or reset. Pertaining to an attribute, value, or option when none is explicitly specified.

Default drive
This is the drive the workstation is currently using. It is identified by a drive prompt, such as A:> or F:>.

Default Profile
User profile called when a user account does not have an assigned profile or the user's personal profile is not available from the server.

Default server
The server which a workstation attaches to when the NetWare Requester is loaded. The default is the server specified in the NET.CFG file.

Delete right
An object right that allows users to delete an object from the Directory tree.

Demodulation
The decoding of modulated analog signals after being received from a carrier wave, so they can be converted back to digital signals; for example, the demodulation or extraction in a television receiver of a video signal from a UHF carrier.

Demultiplexing
Dividing one or more information streams into a larger number of streams.

Dependent service
A service that will not run unless a prerequisite service is loaded.

Desktop
Many Graphical User Interfaces (GUIs) refer to the work area on the computer screen as the desktop. All window items appear and are moved around on this desktop area.

DET
(Directory Entry Table) This is a table that contains basic information about file, directories, directory trustees, or other items on the volume.

Device
Any computer peripheral or hardware component (such as printer, mouse, monitor, or disk drive) capable of receiving and/or sending data.

Device driver
: Hardware-specific software that acts as an interface between the operating system and the hardware attached to a computer. Device drivers allow applications to communicate with hardware in a controlled and orderly fashion. A device driver is installed when the system is initialized, either by the operating system or through an installable device driver. Some examples of installable device drivers are mouse driver, graphical/video monitor driver, communications port driver, printer driver, and network adapter card driver.

Device independence
: The quality of being identical, regardless of the type of monitor or other device that is used to display or print the graphic.

Dial network
: Synonymous with public telephone network.

Dialup connection
: This is a connection between computers that has been established over a standard telephone line.

Digital Adapter
: The digital display adapter inside the PC transmits digitized color and intensity information to the monitor. The monitor must then decode the digitized data to create the displayed image. Most MDA, CGA, and EGA adapters transmit digital code.

Digital data
: Data represented by digits, perhaps together with special characters and the space character.

Digital switch
: A star topology local network. Usually refers to a system that handles only data, but not voice.

Digital transmission
: The transfer of encoded information using on and off pulses; unlike analog transmission which uses a continuous wave form and carries more than one channel at a time.

Directory
: 1. Part of a structure for organizing files on a disk. A directory can contain files and subdirectories. The structure of directories and subdirectories on a disk is called a directory tree. The top-level directory in a directory tree is the root directory. 2. In NetWare, the highest organizational level is the file server. Each server's main directory is called a VOLUME, and subdirectories are called directories.

Directory and file rights
: These rights control what a trustee can do with a directory or file.

Directory caching
: A way to decrease the time it takes to find a file's location on a disk.

Directory entry
: Information on NetWare server directories and files, such as file or directory name, owner, date and time of the last update (for files), and location of the first block of data on the network hard disk, is listed in the directory entry. These are located in a directory table on a network hard disk and list information about all files on the volume. The server uses this information to track file location, changes made to the file, and other related properties.

Directory Entry Table
: (DET) This is a table containing information about files, directories, directory trustees, or other items on the volume.

Directory path
Information including the server name, volume name, and name of each directory connected to the file system directory you need to access.

Directory rights
Rights that specify what a trustee can do with a directory in the file system.

Directory services
Information about every resource on the network is maintained by these built-in NetWare v4.x services.

Directory structure
The NetWare server uses this tree or filing system to organization volumes, directories, files, and data on its hard disks.

Directory Synchronization
A process for automatically transferring user list changes and updates between Microsoft Mail postoffices.

Directory tree
A hierarchical structure of objects, based on a logical or physical organization of objects, in the Directory database.

Disk
A circular object with a magnetic surface that is used to store files (programs and documents) on a computer; floppy disk, hard disk.

Disk drive
A mechanism for moving a disk pack or a magnetic disk and controlling its movements. A device that reads and writes data to and from a disk.

Disk driver
This is an NLM (with a DSK extension) that interfaces between the NetWare server operating system and the hard disk controller. The disk driver communicates with an adapter connected to the disk drives. Depending on the type, one or more disk drives can be connected. Drivers are loaded into the operating system during installation or at the command line.

Disk drivers
NetWare v2.2, v3.x, and v4.x routine that enables communication with a hard disk. In v2.2, disk drivers are configured in the INSTALL.EXE program and are linked into the NetWare operating system. In v3.x and v4.x, disk driver files (extension .DSK) are loadable modules.

Disk Duplexing
A fault tolerance method which keeps identical copies of data on disk partitions located on different physical hard disks and are serviced by separate disk controllers.

Disk Mirroring
A fault tolerance method which keeps identical copies of data on disk partitions located on different physical hard disks but serviced by the same disk controller.

Disk partition
NetWare server hard disks can be divided into these logical units. NetWare v4.x creates a disk partition on each hard disk, and volumes are created from the pool of NetWare partitions.

Disk Striping
Method of spreading data evenly across multiple physical hard disks.

Disk Striping with Parity
: Disk fault tolerance method where data is spread across multiple hard disks with parity information allowing data recovery in case of disk failure.

Display Adapter
: The display adapter is the communications path used for sending data from the computer to the screen. There are two formats with which data may be sent from the adapter to the display: analog or digital.

Distributed architecture
: (In LAN technology) A LAN that uses a shared communications medium; uses shared access methods; used on bus or ring LANs.

Distributed computing
: The name of the trend to move computing resources such as minicomputers, microcomputers, or personal computers closer to individual workstations.

Distributed processing
: A technique for implementing a set of information processing functions within multiple physically separate physical devices.

DLC
: Data Link Control. Windows NT protocol used for communication with mainframe systems and printers directly attached to a network.

DLCI
: Data Link Connection Identifier.

DMA
: Direct Memory Access.

DMI
: Digital Multiplexed Interface. (In LAN technology) One of two voice/data PABX standards for using T1 transmission that involves T1-to-64 Kpbs conversion prior to connection to the computer bus; represents a move toward an open architecture. Compare with CPI.

DNS
: See Domain Name System.

Domain
: 1. A logical grouping for file servers within a network, managed as an integrated whole. 2. In NetWare, using file server memory, this is used as a console command that will create a protected operating system domain for running untested NLMs in Ring 3. This prevents a module from interfering with the core operating system. 3. In the Internet, a domain is a part of the naming hierarchy. The domain name is a sequence of names (separated by periods) that identify host sites; example, galenp@mail.msen.com.

Domain Controller
: Primary server within a domain and primary storage point for domain-wide security information.

Domain Model
: A method of organizing Windows NT Server domains for security and management.

Domain name
: A unique domain name designates a location on the Internet. Domain Names always have 2 or more parts, separated by dots. The part on the left is the most specific, and the part on the right is the most general. A given machine may have more than one Domain Name but a given Domain Name points to only one machine. Usually, all of the machines on a given Network will have the same thing as the right-hand portion of their Domain Names, e.g. www.wavetech.com, ftp.wavetech.com, @wavetech.com and so on. It is also possible for a Domain Name to exist but not be connected to an actual machine. This is often done so that a group or business can have an Internet e-mail address without having to establish a real Internet site. In these cases, some real Internet machine must handle the mail on behalf of the listed Domain Name. Domain names for locations in the US do not have the country segment. The types are educational (.edu), commercial (.com), government (.gov), and so forth. Domains at the JHU Homewood campus have names of the form xxx.hcf.jhu.edu or xxx.jhu.edu. Country designations include: au, Australia; ie, Ireland; be, Belgium; in, India; ca, Canada; is, Iceland; de, Germany; jp, Japan; dk, Denmark; se, Sweden; fi, Finland; su, Russia; fr, France; uk, United Kingdom; For more information, see International Domain Names (Standard ISO 3166) (95/06/08), compiled by Olivier M.J. Crepin-Leblond.

Domain Name System (DNS)
: The Internet naming system that orders a sequence of names to identify host sites. Names are ordered in a hierarchy, from specific to general, separated by periods. Some domains in the Internet are .com (commercial), .edu (educational), .gov (U.S. Government), .mil (U.S. Military), and .net (network). Some countries also have a domain, such as .uk (United Kingdom). Examples: galedsl@msen.com; fredg@uofm.edu; president@whitehouse.gov.

Domain SID
: Unique value imbedded in the SID for all domain servers, workstations, users, and groups. The Domain SID identifies domain ownership of objects.

DOS
: 1. Disk Operating System. The software stored on a disk that represents the software programs that control the operation of the computer and the movement of information throughout the computer system; the medium by which the user communicates with the computer system and manipulates data. 2. In NetWare v2.2, DOS is a console command which allows non-dedicated file servers and routers to function as local DOS stations.

DOS client
: This is a workstation that boots with DOS and accesses the network through the NetWare DOS Requester software (for NetWare 4)or a NetWare shell (for NetWare v2.x and v3.x, and NetWare v4.x with bindery services). While on the network, users can map drives, capture printer ports, and send messages with DOS software. Users can also change contexts using the NetWare Requester in NetWare v4.x.

DOS ODI
Novell Open Data Link Interface software that allows various network protocols to be used on a single network board; and forms a logical network board that emulates various protocol configurations on the installed board. The logical network board operates as if physical boards were being used.

DOS prompt
The character or characters that appear at the beginning of the DOS command line. This indicates that the computer is ready to receive input.

DOS Requester
A software which enables a DOS workstation to communicate on a network.

Dot pitch
On color monitors, the dot pitch is the mask through which the electron beam is focused for each set of red, green, and blue phosphors. The dot pitch is the spacing between the holes. The smaller the spacing, the more dots and phosphors, therefore, a finer (i.e., smaller) dot pitch provides a sharper image.

Dotted decimal notation
The syntactic representation for a 32-bit integer that consists of four 8-bit numbers written in base 10 with periods (dots) separating them. Used to represent IP addresses in the Internet as in: 192.67.67.20.

Download
A process in which a file is transferred from a host computer to a user's computer. Opposite of upload.

Downloadable font
Also known as soft font, an electronically-represented printer font (a graphic design of characters and symbols) which must be installed on the computer and sent to a printer before it can be printed.

dpi
Dots per inch (dpi) is used to define the quality of printing. The more dots per inch, the higher the resolution of the output.

Drive mapping
A letter assigned to a directory path on a volume that refers to a location in the NetWare file system. To locate a file, users follow a path that includes the drive letter and any subdirectories leading to the file. The system can execute a program that is not located in the directory users are working in, due to search drive mappings.

Drive Type
The drive type number is placed in a table stored in the computer's CMOS memory. The table identifies the drive and its characteristics (number of read/write heads, storage capacity, number of cylinders, number of sectors per track, etc.) so that the operating system knows how to access the drive.

Driver
This software interfaces between the operating system and devices, such as hard disks, CD-ROMs, or network interface cards.

Drop
Individual connections (sometimes called nodes) on a multipoint (also called multidrop) circuit.

DTR
: Data Terminal Ready; the signal that indicates to a serial device when the data terminal equipment is ready to begin communications.

Duplex transmission
: A method of transmitting information over a communications channel in which signals may be sent in both directions. Other methods of transmission include half duplex, full duplex, and simplex.

Duplexing
: A method of protecting data by duplicating it onto two hard disks, each on a separate disk channel.

Dynamic link library
: A module that is linked at load time or run time.

Dynamic linking
: By using an update command, ensures that all data changed in one program are automatically changed in another program, thereby keeping the data consistent. Dynamic linking is particularly useful in database management.

Dynamic priority
: The priority assigned to a thread in response to how the user interacts with it.

E-mail (Electronic mail)
: Messages, usually text, sent from one person to another via computer. E-mail can also be used to send documents from a host site to an individuals own mailbox site. E-mail can be sent automatically to a large number of addresses (Mailing List).

Effective rights
: The rights that allow an object to see or modify a particular directory, file, or object. NetWare determines an object's rights to a directory, file or object each time an action is attempted. Effective rights to a file or directory are set by the trustee assignments of the object to the directory, file, or other object; inherited rights from an object's trustee assignments to parent directories; trustee assignments of Group objects to which that a User object belongs; trustee assignments of objects listed in a User object's "Security Equal To" list.

Electronic mail
: The sending and receiving of electronic messages, locally within the computer network or via telephone networks to remote sites. It is also possible for text and graphics to be sent via electronic mail. Sometimes referred to as E-mail or electronic text transfer.

Electronic mail address
: Designation given to an individual or domain that directs messages or other information over computers in general to a specific person or destination.

Embedded object
: Information created in one document and inserted into another document. The two documents usually were created in different applications.

EMS (Expanded memory)
: Expanded Memory Specification. Memory in addition to conventional memory used by some applications. EMS was implemented with add-on boards and is an older standard replaced by extended memory (XMS). Only EMS-compatible software can use expanded memory.

EMSNETx.COM
: NetWare expanded memory shell file that places most of the NetWare shell in a workstation's expanded memory. The x represents the station's version of DOS. For example, EMSNET5.COM is used for DOS v5.x, EMSNET3.COM for DOS v3.x. Novell has also released a "universal" version of this program called EMSNETX.COM. (In this case, the X is the character "X," not representative of a number.) This version of the program works with DOS versions 3.x through 5.x. The file is automatically executed when the filename is included in the AUTOEXEC.BAT file.

Emulation
: The imitation of all or part of one system by another, primarily by hardware, so that the imitating system accepts the same data, executes the same programs, and achieves the same results as the imitated system.

Encapsulation
: In object-oriented programming (OOP), encapsulation defines a data structure of attributes and a group of member functions as a single unit called an object. In networking, encapsulation is the process of enclosing packets of one type of protocol by another.

End system
: An OSI system which contains application processes capable of communicating through all seven layers of OSI protocols. Equivalent to Internet host.

End-to-end
: Governs the interaction from the source computer to the destination device and vice versa; i.e., a program in the source machine exchanges messages with a similar program in the destination machine. The transport layer (fourth layer) of the International Standards Organization (ISO) reference model of open systems interconnection (OSI) is an end-to-end process, as are layers five to seven. In contrast, layers one to three of the ISO model specify intermediate, or subnetwork, interactions between a device and its immediate neighbor. Layers one to three are referred to as chained.

Enhanced mode
: One of two modes of operation for Windows v3.1. If a computer has the minimum configuration, Windows automatically runs in the Enhanced mode. Windows NT supports Enhanced-mode emulation only on x86-based systems.

ENQ/ACK protocol
: A Hewlett-Packard communications protocol. The HP3000 computer follows each transmission block with ENQ to determine if the destination terminal is ready to receive more data; the destination terminal indicates its readiness by responding with ACK.

Entity
: OSI terminology for a layer protocol machine. An entity within a layer performs the functions of the layer within a single computer system, accessing the layer entity below and providing services to the layer entity above at local service access points.

Environmental variables
Environmental information, such as drive, path, or filename, which is associated with a symbolic name that can be used by an operating system.

Error control
An arrangement that combines error detection and error correction.

Error correction
A method used to correct erroneous data produced during data transmission, transfer, or storage.

Error handler
See Error Handling Routine.

Error handling routine
Program code that executes when an error occurs that determines what steps to take to recover from the error or end execution.

Error log
A data set or file in a product or system where error information is stored for later access.

Error rate
The ratio of the total number of errors detected to the total amount of data transmitted or transferred.

Error trap
Statement that enables the error hander.

Error-detecting code
A code in which each coded representation conforms to specific rules of construction so that their violation indicates the presence of errors.

Exclusive Lock
Lock set at the start of a read operation allowing neither read or write access.

Expanded memory
See EMS.

Expansion Slots
Electrical connectors in the system board that allow devices to be added to the computer.

Extended memory
See XMS.

Extended memory manager
A program that prevents different applications from using the same part of extended memory at the same time.

Extension
The period and up to three characters at the end of a FAT format filename. The FAT file system is used by DOS and some other operating systems. Many applications use the extension to designate a particular type of information or data contained in the file.

FAQ (Frequently Asked Questions)
A file posted for many Usegroups, newsgroups, and other services containing questions of general interest or which are commonly asked by new users along with the answers. Such lists have come to be known as FAQs (pronounced "faks"). . There are hundreds of FAQs on subjects as diverse as Pet Groooming and Cryptography. Lists of FAQs can be found at Oxford and at Ohio State. Subject FAQs are usually written by people who have tired of answering the same question over and over. Internet users are encouraged to read FAQ files before asking questions.

Fault tolerance
Operating systems features designed to accommodate failures, thus improving disk reliability. Related terms: Disk Mirroring, Disk Duplexing, and Disk Striping.

File
: A collection of records each stored on a secondary storage medium such as a floppy disk or hard disk. Generally, a computer file contains either a program or data. Program files contain instructions or commands which are to be executed by the computer. Data files which contain only ASCII characters are text files, while files containing binary data, i.e., data other than ASCII characters, are called binary files.

File Allocation Table(FAT)
: This is an index table that shows the way to the disk areas where a file is located. Because the file may be in several blocks spread over the disk, the FAT links the file together.

File caching
: This improves file access time by using the NetWare server RAM.

File compression
: More data can be stored on server hard disks by compressing files that are not being used. The NetWare operating system manages file compression internally. Users can flag, or mark, their files or directories for compression after use or to indicate they should not be compressed. After compression is enabled, files marked Immediate Compress (Ic) are compressed immediately; others files are compressed when they have not been used for a specific amount of time. When the user accesses them again, they are decompressed. In case of disk error or power failure during compression, the original file is retained.

File indexing
: Allows faster access to large files by the indexing of FAT entries.

File lock
: A file lock prevents more than one user from using a file at the same time. Locks can be put into place for security purposes, or to prevent users from making changes to a file simultaneously. A lock can be placed on part of a file, if supported in the application being used.

File rights
: Rights which specify what a trustee can do with a file.

File server
: A computer that stores files and provides access to them for workstations. If a computer is used exclusively as a file server, it is a dedicated file server. If used as a workstation and a file server simultaneously, it is a non-dedicated file server. The NOS (Network Operating System) runs on the file server and controls access to files, printers, and other network resources.

File server protocol
: (In LAN technology) A communications protocol that allows application programs to share files.

File Sharing
: The ability for more than one person to use the same file at the same time.

Fill pattern
: In a Token Ring network, a specified bit pattern that a transmitting data station sends before or after frames, tokens, or abort sequences to avoid what would otherwise be interpreted as an inactive or indeterminate transmitter state.

Filter
: A device or program that separates data, signals, or material in accordance with specified criteria.

Finder
: The finder allows a user to maintain the Macintosh Desktop and to manage documents and various applications.

Fire Wall
: A combination of hardware and software that separates a LAN into two or more parts for security purposes. It prevents unauthorized access from the Internet.

Flag
: A variable indicating that a certain condition holds.

Flicker
: The noticeable flashes seen while viewing a screen display. The rate at which the screen is scanned and refreshed, and the persistence of the phosphor coating on the monitor to hold the light, both have an affect on flicker. When monitors are designed to operate at different refresh rates, slower rates produce a significant flicker. Flicker is a result of too much time elapsing before the image is refreshed, therefore, the image begins to decay.

Focus
: Term used to refer to the active screen object or control.

Font
: In typography, a complete set of characters of one particular size, style, and weight, including punctuation marks, symbols, and numbers. The term font is often confused with typeface, which refers to a particular style of character, or type family to which the font belongs.

Foreground category
: A classification of processes that consists of those associated with the currently active screen group.

Foreground process
: A process that can receive user input.

Foreground Task
: A task that is able to receive interactive input from a user.

Fragment
: Part of an IP message.

Fragmentation
: The process in which an IP datagram is broken into smaller pieces to fit the requirements of a given physical network. The reverse process is termed reassembly.

Frame
: In IEEE (Institute of Electrical and Electronics Engineers) terminology, the unit of data transferred at the OSI (Open Systems Interconnection) data link layer.

Frame relay
: Commonly referred to as "bandwidth on demand." Unlike other transmission protocols or processes, frame relay offers users significant benefits over other transmission services, such as T1, by eliminating the processing overhead associated with packets of data moving between packet-forwarding devices.

Frequency
: The number of times one complete incident or function occurs. In electronics, frequency usually refers to the number of waveforms that are repeated per second, measured in hertz.

FTP (File Transfer Protocol)
: The Internet protocol (and program) used to transfer files between hosts.

Full-duplex transmission
: A method of transmitting information over an asynchronous communications channel, in which signals may be sent in both directions simultaneously. This technique makes the best use of line time but substantially increases the amount of logic required in the primary and secondary stations.

Full-height
: Full-height describes the size, in height, of the drive. Full-height drives originated in the IBM PC and XT models. They are roughly three inches in height.

Gateway
: A device that connects two or more dissimilar networks/systems which are normally incompatible. A gateway has its own processor and memory to perform complex functions such as interpreting between two computer networks with different network architectures.

Gateway List
: List of Microsoft Mail gateways available to a local postoffice.

Global Group
: A group definition allowing permission assignments to local machines or other domains through local group membership of the global group.

Gopher
: A hierarchical menu-based information service, developed at the University of Minnesota, that provides access to information collections across the Internet, by taking file directories and turning them into easily navigable menus. It also makes file transfer convenient. Gopher functions as a client server that connects the user to the menu item(s) selected from the gopher server menu. The user must have a Gopher Client program. Although Gopher spread rapidly across the globe in only a couple of years, it is being largely supplanted to Hypertext, also known as WWW (World Wide Web). There are still thousands of Gopher Servers on the Internet and they will remain for a while.

gov
: A governmental organization is identified by this Internet address suffix. For example: whitehouse.gov.

Graphics mode
: The mode enabling applications to display graphics in addition to text. GUI-based applications always run in a graphics mode. DOS applications can run either in graphics or text mode.

Group
: A collection of users. A user with Supervisory rights can create new groups and assign users to them, add users to existing groups, and change the rights granted to a group. All members get these implicit rights.

Group object
: A leaf object that represents several User objects; it provides collective, rather than individual, network administration. Create Group objects based on the use of applications, printers, or print queues. Group objects may also be created based on users who perform similar tasks or need similar information, or to simplify trustee assignments.

Guard band
: The unused bandwidth separating channels to prevent crosstalk in an FDM system.

Guest
: A network device controlled by another network device, or a host device, during data transmission. GUEST, in NetWare v3.x, is a temporary user of the network, assigned to the default group EVERYONE and granted group rights. GUEST is also a Windows NT user with minimal rghts.

GUI
: Graphical User Interface; a collection of graphical icons, menus, clipboards, desk accessories, alert boxes, etc., each accessible by using a mouse. The graphical user interface makes using a computer easier, especially for the beginner. Microsoft Windows, OS/2, and the Macintosh operating system are examples of graphical user interfaces.

HAL
: Windows NT module that isolates the operating system kernal from the hardware platform.

Half duplex
: A method of transmitting information over a communications channel, in which signals may be sent in both directions, but only one way at a time. This is sometimes referred to as local echo.

Half Duplex (HDX)
: Transmission link that allows two-way communication, although transmission is possible only one way at a time. When the communications device at one end has completed its transmission, it must advise the device at the other end that it has finished and is ready to receive. Half-Duplex transmission is analogous to a single-lane bridge on a two-way road.

Half-height
: Half-height describes the size, in height, of the drive. Drives that are half-height are half the height of full-height drives. Half-height drives are about one and one-half inches in height. Two half-height drives can fit in a full-height slot.

Handle
: In draw programs and similar object-oriented graphics programs, handles are the small black squares which appear around a selected object so the object can be resized, moved, copied, or scaled by using a mouse or similar pointing device.

Handshake
: Used in communications technology to define the exchange of data when connection is achieved.

Handshaking
: Before data is transmitted serially, certain communications conditions, or protocols, must be met. Handshaking allows both the sending and receiving computers to understand the required signals, i.e. the method of transmission.

Hard disk
: A peripheral secondary mass-storage device which uses hermetically sealed, rotating, non-flexible disks, magnetically coated to store data and programs. The storage capacity of the hard disk may vary from 5 to more than 1,000 megabytes.

Hard Disk Controller
: The board that communicates with and controls the hard (fixed) disk drive.

Hard Disk Encoding
: A method of compression of data within the hard disk drive. An example is MFM or RLL. Hard disk encoding is mostly used in older devices.

Hard Disk Interface
: The communication device which allows the hard disk drive to interact with the hard disk controller. There are many different types which will affect the speed of data transfers. Examples of hard disk interfaces are ST506, SCSI, ESDI, and IDE.

Hardcopy
: Sending computer data out to the printer and printing the information on paper is referred to as producing hardcopy, or a copy on paper which can be physically handled.

Hardware
: All electronic components of a computer system, including peripherals, circuit boards, and input and output devices. Hardware is the physical equipment, as opposed to software consisting of programs, data procedures, rules, and associated documentation.

Hardware Abstraction Layer
: See HAL.

Hayes
: The company, Hayes Microcomputer Products, developed a special synchronizing compression technique to allow fast line turn-around making a half-duplex modem simulate full-duplex transmission speeds. Hayes patented their method and allow other vendors to utilize the method through licensing fees and royalties. Hayes and Hayes-compatible modems are the de facto standard for PC communications.

Head Crash
: The read/write heads fly across the surface of the disk drive's platters, traveling on a cushion of air. If the head comes in contact with the platter, a head crash occurs. Head crashes damage the platter and corrupts the data; and often the data is rendered inaccessible.

Header
: A header contains identifying information: electronic mail message headers contain the message originator's name and address, receiver, subject, date, etc.; a packet header carries the source and destination addresses and other information.

Heads (disk drive)
: The read/write head on a fixed disk drive is similar to the read/write head on a tape drive. Data is stored as changes in magnetic flux on the disk platters. Read/write heads sweep across the surface travelling on a cushion of air. Read/write heads can perform both functions, reading and writing data. The drive will ususally also have an additional servo head (read only) that is used for disk positioning.

Heap
: A block of memory that is set aside for dynamic allocation.

Hertz (Hz)
The International System of Units unit of frequency so named for German physicist Heinrich Hertz; often abbreviated as hz. One hertz is one complete cycle per second. A cycle may relate to light, heat, radio waves, or other vibrations.

Hexadecimal
A base-16 numeric notation system that specifies addresses in computer memory. In hexadecimal notation, the decimal numbers 0 through 15 are represented by the decimal digits 0 through 9 and the characters A through F (A=decimal 10, B=decimal 11, and so on.)

Hidden file
A file that is not visible in a directory listing.

High memory area (HMA)
In DOS systems, the first 64K above 1 MB of memory.

HIMEM.SYS
An extended memory manager. It coordinates the use of the computer's extended memory. This prevents two applications from using the same block of memory at the same time.

History List
A list of Document Titles and URLs Mosaic keeps in memory that represents the visited URLs during a given Mosaic session.

Hive files
Component files making up the Windows NT Registry.

Home directory
On Local Area Networks, a directory which belongs to a single user for storage of data. Normally, the user is the only person with access to this directory. On most networks, the Supervisor or Administrator can also access any user's home directory.

Home folder
The NetWare for Macintosh's equivalent of a Home directory.

Home page
A document coded in HTML (Hypertext Markup Language) that acts as a top level document for an organization or on a topic. A home page contains hypertext links to related documents.

Hookswitch
The switch that activates to connect a device to a phone line.

Hop
Describes routing through a network. A hop is a data packet moving through routers from the point of origination to the destination.

Hop count
The number of cable segments a message packet passes through between its source and network or internetwork destination. The destination can be no more than 16 hops from the source.

Host
A computer that is remotely accessible and provides information or services for users on the network. It is quite common to have one host machine provide several services, such as WWW and USENET. A host computer on the Internet can be accessed by using an application program such as electronic mail, telnet, or FTP; a host computer may also be a bulletin board.

Hostname
: The name given to a computer that identifies it as an Internet or other site.

Hotlist
: This is a user defined list of preferred URLs to a given World Wide Web document.

Hotspot
: A region of the screen that is associated with some action.

HTML (Hypertext Markup Language)
: This is a set of specifications for tags that tell Web browsers how to format text, and what function each piece of text has in a Web document. HTML looks a lot like old-fashioned typesetting code, where you surround a block of text with codes that indicate how it should appear, additionally, in HTML you can specify that a block of text, or a word, is "linked " to another file on the Internet. It allows users to create documents so they can be read by a WWW Browser. Most documents that are displayed by Mosaic are HTML documents. On UNIX machines, the extension .html designates an HTML file, that is, a text file that contains HTML tags and that is meant to be read by a Web browser. On Windows machines, the extension htm serves the same purpose. For example: homepage.html or homepage.htm.

HTML Editor
: This is a tool that automates and simplifies HTML document preparation.

HTTP (Hypertext Transfer Protocol)
: This protocol is a set of directions for Web servers telling them how to respond to various events initiated by users. The simplest example is clicking on a link to another part of the same file. The server receives the information that the link has been activated, and sends back the designated part of the file, which will then be displayed. An HTTP client program is required on one end, and an HTTP server program on the other end. HTTP is the most important protocol used in the World Wide Web (WWW).

Hub
: 1. In disk drives, it is the central mechanism within the drive that causes the disk to rotate and keeps it centered during the rotation. On floppy diskettes, the hub fits into the hole in the center of the diskette to keep it level and balanced during rotation. 2. In networking, a central connecting point for network wiring.

Hue
: A value between 0 and 239 that indicates whether a color is more red, yellow, or blue. Both 0 and 239 are shades of red, with numbers greater than 0 becoming increasingly yellow and numbers less than 239 becoming increasingly blue. Cyan has a hue of approximately 120.

Huge segments
: A software technique that allows the creation and use of pseudo segments larger than 65 KB.

Hyperlink
: Words, phrases, images, or characters highlighted in bold indicate connections in a given document to information within another document. The user also has the option to underline these hyperlinks.

Hypermedia
: These are richly formatted documents containing a variety of information types, such as textual, image, movie, and audio. These information types are easily found through hyperlinks.

Hypertext
: This feature allows users to move from one site to another. Hypertext links in World Wide Web documents link the user from terms in one document to the actual site referenced in the original document.

Hypertext Markup Language
: See HTML.

Hypertext Transfer Protocol
: See HTTP.

Hyplus
: An on-line guide that provides examples of types of library systems and companion resources, identifies directories and other sources for locating currently available systems, and relates strategies used by experienced searchers to make the most of exploring new resources.

Hytelnet
: Identifies, through hypertext links, Internet sites and services accessible through telnet.

Hz (Hertz)
: See Hertz.

I/O
: I/O (Input/Output) refers to the sending and receiving of data from the central processing unit (CPU) to other peripheral devices such as disk drives. The input/output channel carries out all the transfer of data so as to free up the CPU. The keyboard is the most common input device and the monitor is the most common output device.

I/O address
: I/O address is space that is used to access I/O hardware such as I/O adapters, buses, and special registers used by I/O devices, known as control status registers (CSR). I/O address space is one of two equal parts of primary memory, or addressable memory. The other equal part is memory address space.

I/O privilege mechanism
: A facility that allows a process to ask a device driver for direct access to the device's I/O ports and any dedicated or mapped memory locations it has. The I/O privilege mechanism can be used directly by an application or indirectly by a dynamic link package.

IAB (Internet Activities Board)
: The technical body that oversees the development of the Internet suite of protocols (commonly referred to as "TCP/IP"). It has two task forces (the IRTF and the IETF) each charged with investigating a particular area.

IBM PC network
: A CSMA/CD network introduced by IBM in 1984 that uses a star or bus topology. It was originally a broadband network using coaxial cable, but lower-cost twisted pair wire was subsequently introduced by IBM.

IBM Token Ring network
: A baseband star-wired ring network developed by IBM, using the token-passing access method and running at 4 or 16 megabits per second (Mbps).

ICMP (Internet Control Message Protocol)
: Protocol used for error reporting and recovery. ICMP is a required component of any IP implementation.

Icon
: A small pictorial representation of a file, disk, menu, option, or other object or feature; an image that graphically represents an object, a concept, or a message.

IDE
: A standard hard disk interface.

IEEE (Institute of Electrical and Electronics Engineers)
: A professional ANSI-accredited body of scientists and engineers based in the U.S. IEEE promotes standardization, and consults to the American National Standards Institute on matters relating to electrical and electronic development. The IEEE 802 Standards Committee is the leading official standard organization for LAN (Local Area Networks).

IFS
: Installable File System. A body of code that OS/2 loads at boot time and provides the software to manage a file system on a storage device, including the ability to create and maintain directories, allocate disk space, and so on.

IIS
: Microsoft Internet Information Server is a network file and application server that transmits information in Hypertext Markup Language.

IMHO (In My Humble Opinion)
: A shorthand appended to a comment written in an on-line forum, IMHO indicates that the writer is aware that they are expressing a debatable view, probably on a subject already under discussion. One of many such shorthands in common use on-line, especially in discussion forums.

Importer
: System receiving data during replication.

Index Hole
: On 5-1/4" floppy diskettes, the drive had to identify the starting position of the diskette. During rotation, the drive had to know when that starting position reappeared, thus indicating completion of one full rotation of the diskette. Most drives have a light sensor that reads the index hole rotations and sees the index hole in the floppy diskette when it lines up with the hole in the floppy diskette's outer jacket.

Inheritance
: The means by which a child process can get information from its parent.

Initialization files
: Files with the extension .INI that contain information that define your setup and various other parameters which are needed by a program. This is used extensively in Microsoft Windows and OS/2 for storing environmental or other device information.

Instance
: An occurrence of an object in memory.

INTAP
: Interoperability Technology Association for Information Processing. The technical organization which has the official charter to develop Japanese OSI profiles and conformance tests.

Integrated Drive Electronics (IDE)
: This is standard interface for a hard disk drive. Controller electronics are integrated onto the drive by the IDE. The controller connects to a paddleboard that may be external to, or on, the system board. The paddleboard then interfaces with the bus to the CPU. An IDE bus can be identified by its 40-pin connector, as opposed to the 50-pin connector of a SCSI bus.

Integrated Login Security
: Validation method where members of a Windows NT domain are automatically logged in for SQL Server access.

Interactive
: Pertaining to the exchange of information and control between the user and a computer process. Interactive also refers to time-dependent (real-time) data communications, typically one in which a user enters data and then awaits a response message from the destination before continuing.

Interface
: 1. A shared boundary between two functional units, defined by functional characteristics, signal characteristics, and other characteristics, as appropriate. Also, any of the electrical and logical devices that permit computers and peripherals to be interconnected. 2. A contract between an object and its users.

Interlaced
: In monitors, interlaced is often implemented because it is less expensive. Interlaced monitors allow lower-cost circuitry to be used to display higher resolutions (scan rate) than it would otherwise be capable of producing.

Interleave
: Interleave is a method of arranging disk sectors to compensate for relatively slow computers. It attempts to minimize the amount of time required to read consecutive sectors from a single track on the fixed disk. By numbering every other sector it encounters as though it were the next consecutive sector, the controller is effectively able to slow the spin rate of the fixed disk drive so that it can issue a command to read the next consecutively numbered sector. An interleave ratio that is set to read every other sector as consecutive is said to run at a 2-to-1 rate. (For example, it would start with Sector 1, skip a sector, number the next sector 2, skip a sector, number the next sector 3, skip a sector, etc.) If set to read every third sector, the interleave is 3-to-1. Ideally, interleave should be set to the lowest number that the computer, the disk drive, and the disk controller can support. Virtually all new computers and disk controllers support 1-to-1 interleave rate.

Intermediate system
: An OSI system which is not an end system, but which serves instead to relay communications between end systems.

Internet
: An international computer network of networks that connect government, academic and business institutions. Networks on the Internet include MILNET, NSFnet, and other backbone networks, as well as mid-level networks and stub (local) networks. Internet networks communicate using TCP/IP (Transmission Control Protocol/Internet Protocol). The Internet connects colleges, universities, military organizations and contractors, corporations, government research laboratories, and individuals. Although parts of the Internet operate under single administrative domains, the Internet as a whole reaches around the globe, connects computers from personal computers to supercomputers, and is not administered by any single authority. The Internet in July of 1995 roughly connected 60,000 independent networks into a vast global Internet; Used as a descriptive term, an Internet is a collection of interconnected packet-switching networks. Any time you connect two or more networks together, you have an Internet - as in inter-national or inter-state.

Internet Address
: A 32-bit value written displayed in numbers that specifies a particular network and a particular node on that network.

Internet Information Server (Microsoft)
: See IIS.

Internet Protocol (IP)
: The layer 3 (routed) protocol used to transmit packetized information on a TCP/IP network.

Internet relay chat (IRC)
: An Internet protocol that supports real-time conversations between Internet users worldwide.

Internet service provider (ISP)
: Companies that provide an Internet connection for educational institutions, individuals, companies, and organizations.

Internetwork
: Two or more networks connected by a router.

InterNIC
: Developed in 1993 by General Atomics, AT&T, and NSI to provide information services to Internet users. Offers a reference desk that provides networking information, referrals to other resources, and associate users with their local NICs; coordination to share information and coordinate activities with U.S. and international organizations; and education services to train midlevel and campus NICs and end users and to promote Internet use.

Interoperability
: The ability to use products from different vendors in the same system. Communication protocols, such as IP or AFP, can be used in ODI to process information from the network. The user does not have to know each protocol's required method of packet transmission. Interoperability also means an application can share files, even when running on different platforms, such as Macintosh or UNIX.

Interprocess communication
: The exchange of information between processes by means of messages.

Interrupt request lines
: See IRQ.

Intranet
: A private Internet, usually inside a company, for facilitating information sharing. Looks and acts just like the public Internet.

IP
: Internet Protocol.

IP address
: The dotted decimal notation address that is used to communicate over TCP/IP.

IP datagram
: The fundamental unit of information passed across the Internet. Contains source and destination addresses along with data and a number of fields which define such things as the length of the datagram, the header checksum, and flags to say whether the datagram can be (or has been) fragmented.

IP Number
: Sometimes called a "dotted quad". A unique number consisting of 4 parts separated by dots, e.g. 109.123.451.2. Every machine that is on the Internet has a unique IP number - if a machine does not have an IP number, it is not really on the Internet. Most machines also have one or more Domain Names that are easier for people to remember.

IPX
: NetWare Internetwork Packet eXchange protocol, used along with SPX as the resident protocol in NetWare. In v2.x and 3.x, IPX is the name of the command line utility used to see the versions and options of IPX.COM. It can also be used to install the network board's configuration number without using DCONFIG. This was used prior to the introduction of ODI drivers.

IPX external network number
: A network number that uniquely identifies a network cable segment. An IPX external network number is a hexadecimal number, one to eight digits (1 to FFFFFFFE). When the IPX protocol is bound to a network board in the server, the number is assigned. IPX can be bound with multiple frame types or protocols to the same network board. Network number and network address are two terms used to refer to the IPX external network number.

IPX internal network number
: A logical network number that identifies an individual NetWare server. During installation, the service is assigned an IPX internal network number. It is a hexadecimal number, one to eight digits (1 to FFFFFFFE), that is unique to each server on a network. The IPX internal network number must also be different from any IPX external network number on the internetwork.

IPX internetwork address
: A 12-byte number (represented by 24 hexadecimal characters) divided into three parts: the 4-byte (8-character) IPX external network number, the 6-byte (12-character) node number, and the 2-byte (4-character) socket number.

IPXODI (Internetwork Packet Exchange Open Data-Link Interface)
: This is a module that takes the workstation requests, determined to be for the network by the NetWare DOS Requester, packages them with transmission information (such as their destination), and transfers them to the LSL. IPXODI requires each packet have an initialized header, specifying information targeting network delivery and announcing where the packet came from, where it is going, and what happens after delivery.

IRC (Internet Relay Chat)
: Basically a huge multi-user live chat facility. There are a number of major IRC servers around the world which are linked to each other. Anyone can create a "channel" and anything that anyone types in a given channel is seen by all others in the channel. Private channels can (and are) created for multi-person "conference calls".

IRQ line (Interrupt request lines)
: Hardware lines over which devices can send signals indicating that the device is ready to accept or send information. Each device connected to the computer typically uses a separate IRQ line.

IRTF (Internet Research Task Force)
: One of the task forces of the IAB. The group responsible for research and development of the Internet protocol suite.

ISAPI
: Microsoft Internet Server Application Programming Interface

ISDN (Integrated Services Digital Network)
: A special kind of telecommunications network designed to handle more than just data. Using existing telephone lines and computer networks, integrated networks can handle video, text, voice, data, facsimile images, graphics, etc.

ISO (International Standards Organization)
: A worldwide federation of national standards bodies whose objective is to promote the development of standardization and related activities in over 90 countries, with a view to facilitating international exchange of goods and services.

ISP
: See Internet Service Provider.

IXC
: Inter-exchange Carrier.

Java
: A programming language for distributed applications. Small applets (programs) are downloaded when a Java object is encountered with browsers that support Java.

Jpeg (Joint Photographic Experts Group)
: Jpeg, like gif, is a format for storing a graphics file in digital format; like GIF, it is a standard for images on the Web. The names of jpeg-formatted files often end in ".jpg". The main differences between gif and jpeg are the manner in which data is compressed (lossless in gif, lossy in jpeg), and the bit depth (8-bit for gif, up to 24-bit for jpeg. Read the JPEG FAQ to learn more.

Jughead
: A server that maintains a database of menu items at a gopher site and allows users to search them. Jughead is an acronym for Jonzy's Universal Gopher Hierarchy Excavation and Display.

JUNET
: Japan UNIX Network.

Kb (Kilobit)
: In computing, it refers to 1024 bits. (A bit is the basic unit for storing data in primary storage.) Kilobit is used mainly to express the speed of data transmission.

KB (Kilobyte)
: In computing, it refers to 1024 bytes. (A byte is a unit of information consisting of 8 bits.) Kilobyte is mainly used to express the capacity of primary storage.

Kbps (Kilobits per second)
: Thousands of bits per second.

KBps (Kilobytes per second)
: Thousands of bytes per second.

Kermit
: A popular file transfer and terminal emulation program.

Kernel
: A set of essential operating routines used by the operating system (usually hidden from the user) to perform important system tasks such as managing the system memory or controlling disk operations.

Kernel Mode
: Lower level Windows NT or Windows 95 operating system functions.

Keyboard
: The device which allows the user to input data into the computer or to execute commands. Most keyboards resemble a typewriter. The standard is a 101-key keyboard.

Knowbot
: A computer program that automates the searching and gathering of data from distributed databases. The general term is sometimes shortened to bot.

LAN (Local Area Network)
: A collection of computers and other devices, such as printers, connected to each other by wire (coaxial cable or fiber optics) or radio frequency devices, which usually cover a small geographical area. Computers or workstations in a LAN can communicate with each other. One of the benefits of a LAN is the ability for all users to share the same software, printers, mass storage, and other devices.

LAN driver
: Software that establishes communication between a file server's network board and the NetWare operating system.

LAN Requester
: The term used to refer to a workstation on a LAN Server network. It is also the name of LAN Server's primary management utility.

Landing Zone
: On fixed disk drives, the read/write heads must return to a specific position when the drive is not operating (or when the system is powered off). This position is referred to as the landing zone. Early fixed disk drives (for instance those introduced in the IBM XT systems) had problems with the heads falling on the surface of the disk drive platters when the systems lost power, causing a head crash. The landing zone is a portion of the disk where no data is read or written, thereby ensuring no damage to the data if the heads accidentally touched the disk platter surface.

Landscape
: A document orientation that has a vertical dimension that is greater than its horizontal dimension.

LAPS
: LAN Adapter and Protocol Support. This is the program that provides LAN adapter and protocol device drivers for OS/2.

LATA (Local Access and Transport Area)
: Within a LATA, a local exchange common carrier provides connections, service, and a dial tone to all telephone subscribers. A LATA typically includes all of the local exchanges and inter-office trunks and toll offices required to service a metropolitan area which may include several small cities and towns. The U.S. has been divided into more than two hundred Local Access and Transport Areas, in order to define areas of responsibility.

Leased line
: A telephone line reserved for the exclusive use of leasing customers, without interexchange switching arrangements. Also called a Private Line.

Library
: A group of programs in a file.

Link
: Any part of a Web page that is connected to something else. Clicking on or selecting a link will make that something else appear. (This is one major difference between virtual reality and real reality.) The first part of the URL named in a link denotes the method or kind of link. The methods include: file (for local files), ftp, gopher, http, mailto, news, and wais (for some kinds of search).

Linked list
: A dynamic series of objects, each of which contains a pointer to the next object in the list.

Listserv
: Electronic mail-based discussion forums organized around topics of interest to subscribers. Internet users may subscribe to a listserv; a listserv program maintains the list of subscribers and routes all messages to subscribers electronic mailboxes. Responses sent by subscribers are sent to all other subscribers. The most common kind of mail list, Listservs originated on BITNET but they are now common on the Internet.

LLAP (LocalTalk Link Access Protocol)
: LLAP provides the physical connection of LocalTalk and to various hardware including EtherTalk (ELAP) and TokenTalk (TLAP).

Loading and unloading
: The process of linking and unlinking NLM programs to the NetWare operating system. NLM programs can be loaded and unloaded while NetWare is running.

Local Account
: A Windows NT Server user account not authorized interactive logon, but supporting resource access.

Local Area Networks (LAN)
: This is a network of computers located in a common environment, such as in a building or building complex.

Local Caching
: Storage of a copy of a user's personal profile on a local hard disk.

Local drive
: The common name for a physical drive attached to a workstation.

Local Group (Domain)
: Group definition supporting local domain resource management.

Local Group (Workstation)
Group definition supporting local management of a Windows NT workstation.

Local printer
A printer directly connected to one of the ports on the computer. The opposite is one connected through a network, which would be a remote printer.

Local Profile
User profile stored on and specific to a particular Windows NT workstation.

Locked files
Files that were in use during an installation or software removal. The files will be processed the next time the system is restarted.

Login restrictions
These control access to the network by requiring a password, setting account limits, limiting disk space, limiting the number of connections, setting time restrictions. If a user violated login restrictions, NetWare can disable the account, allowing no logins using that username, preventing unauthorized users from logging in.

Login scripts
There are files containing commands that set up users' workstation environments on login. They are similar to batch files and are executed by the LOGIN utility. Login scripts can be used to map drives and search drives to directories, display messages, set environment variables, execute programs or menus.

Logon Script
DOS batch, NT batch, or executable that may run when a user logs on.

LPT port
Also known as a parallel port. A connection on the computer, usually LPT1, where the cable for a parallel printer is connected. Generally, LPT1 through LPT3 can exist on a personal computer. Special equipment can be added to extend this capability.

MAC
See Media Access Control.

MAC address
The hardware address of a device connected to a channel, such as the address of a terminal connected to an Ethernet.

Mailbox
An area on a computer used to receive and store electronic mail messages.

Mandatory Profile
Server-based profile defined for the user by the domain administrator. Users cannot store changes made to a mandatory profile.

MAPI
Messaging API set which allows creation of mail enabled applications and utilities.

Mapping
The transferring of data between a disk and a computer's RAM. In NetWare, mapping is assigning a drive letter to a path from a station to a volume or directory on a file server. The volume or directory path is automatically active when the drive letter is entered at the command line.

Master Database
SQL Server database controlling all user databases and the SQL Server program.

Master Domain Model
Windows NT SERVER domain model when one domain provides user and global group management for a set of trusting domains. Resources and local groups are managed individually at the trusting domains.

Master replica
The Directory replica that is used to create a new Directory partition in the Directory database. It also allows users to read and update Directory information. Although many Directory replicas of the same partition can exist, only one can be the master replica.

Math Co-Processor
A specialized chip that supplements the mathematical operations of the CPU or microprocessor. Older systems had a separate chip for this purpose, while newer systems incorporate it into the microprocessor.

Mb (Megabit)
1,048,576 bits.

MB (Megabyte)
1,048,576 bytes.

Mbps (Megabits per second)
Millions of bits per second (bps).

MBps (Megabytes per second)
Millions of bytes per second (Bps).

MCGA
The Multi-Color Gate Array or Memory Controller Gate Array (MCGA) adapter was introduced by IBM to support CGA and some VGA modes.

Media
Media is a generic term for the medium that is used to record data. Media can be a floppy diskette, a hard disk, or other similar recording surface (an audio tape for instance).

Media Access Control (MAC) Sublayer
The level of the IEEE 802 data station that controls and mediates access to media.

Megahertz
A million cycles per second; abbreviated as MHz.

Memory
A hardware component of a computer system that can store information and applications for later retrieval. Types of memory are RAM (Random Access Memory), ROM (Read Only Memory), conventional, expanded, and extended memory.

Memory manager
The section of OS/2 that allocates both physical memory and virtual memory.

Memory model
A compiler setting for 16-bit application development that determines various memory allocation variables, such as the number of bits in a particular data type.

Memory overcommit
Allocating more memory to the running program than physically exists.

Memory segmentation
The requirement on 16-bit platforms to allocate memory as either near or far.

Memory suballocation
The OS/2 facility that allocates pieces of memory from within an application's segment.

Menu
1. A displayed list of items from which a user can make a selection. 2. A NetWare menu utility in v3.x that allows for the use of customized menus created as ASCII text files.

Message
A notification from one object to another that some event has occurred.

Method
A defined behavior for a particular interface. An object that owns an interface must implement its methods.

Micro-to mainframe link
The connection of personal computers to mainframe-based networks.

MIDI (Musical Instrument Digital Interface)
Musical Instrument Digital Interface; a standard communications protocol for the connection of a computer to a musical synthesizer. MIDI enables musicians to compose complex music on a piano-style keyboard and then capture that information using a computer which can be used to automatically write the score.

mil
Used as part of an Internet address to identify a military domain. For example: cop@army.mil.

Minicomputer
A legacy computer that is capable of multitasking, but can support fewer users than a mainframe. An AS/400 is a minicomputer.

Mirroring
The duplication of data from one NetWare partition to the NetWare partition on another hard disk.

Modem
Abbreviation for modulator/demodulator; a peripheral device that permits a personal computer, microcomputer, or mainframe to receive and transmit data in digital format across voice-oriented communications links such as telephone lines.

Modem eliminator, modem emulator
A device used to connect a local terminal and a computer port in lieu of the pair of modems that would be expected to connect these. Allows DTE-to-DTE data and control signal connections otherwise not easily achieved by standard cables or connectors. Modified cables (crossover cables) or connectors (adapters) can also perform this function.

Modulation
The process of changing the amplitude, frequency, or phase of a carrier wave in a periodic or intermittent way from a digital signal to an analog signal for the purpose of transmitting information.

ms
Used to represent Milliseconds, a thousandth of a second. Access rates are expressed in milliseconds.

MS Windows client
A workstation that boots with DOS and accesses the network through the NetWare DOS Requester and its VLM programs (for NetWare v4.x), or a NetWare shell (for NetWare versions earlier than NetWare v4.x). While on the network, users can map drives, capture printer ports, send messages, and change context with MS Windows software.

MS-DOS
MS-DOS is Microsoft's version of the DOS operating system.

Multi-homed host
A computer connected to more than one physical data link. The data links may or may not be attached to the same network.

Multidrop
: Referring to a circuit in a communications line which is a multipoint link where the telephone company "drops" several sets of local-loops into various customer sites at secondary stations. Multidrop is in contrast to a standard multipoint link where there is only one set of local-loop connections at each end of the telephone network.

Multilink
: Windows NT RAS connection method whereby multiple serial lines are treated as a single virtual connection.

Multimedia
: In computing, multimedia refers to the presentation of information on a computer using sound, graphics, animation, and text.

Multiple Document Interface (MDI)
: An application that allows the user to have more than one document open at a time.

Multiple Link Interface Driver (MLID)
: This is a device driver written to the ODI specification that sends and receives packets from a physical or logical LAN medium.

Multiple Master Domain Model
: Windows NT Server domain model when multiple trusted domains provide user and global group administration for a set of trusting domains. Resources and local groups are managed individually at the trusting domains.

Multiplexer
: A device that takes several input signals and combines them into a single output signal in such a manner that each of the input signals can be recovered. A device used to transmit information more efficiently and economically across a network. A multiplexer combines a number of low-speed inputs into a smaller number of high-speed outputs. Some multiplexers temporarily store information in buffers, so the information can be sent all at once when the line becomes free.

Multiplexing
: In data transmission, a function that permits two or more data sources to share a common transmission medium in such a way that each data source has its own channel.

Multipoint line
: A circuit established between one primary station and multiple secondary stations simultaneously. This type of network groups devices together so they can share the same communications line.

Multiprocessing
: The ability to execute more than one thread simultaneously.

Multiprogramming
: A mode of operation that provides for the interleaved execution of two or more computer programs by a single processor.

Multisynch
: Multiscanning or multisynch monitors adapt to the incoming horizontal and vertical frequency signal sent by the computer. By adapting rather than being fixed at a particular setting, multisynch monitors earn their name and can work with almost any other video standard. Multisynch monitors were first introduced as EGA displays.

Multitasking
: A mode of operation that provides for the concurrent performance or interleaved execution of two or more tasks.

Multithreaded application
: An executable that activates more than one thread of execution. For example, a thread to handle user input and one to perform background operations.

Multiuser
: The ability of a computer to support several interactive terminals at the same time.

Name resolution
: The process of mapping a name into the corresponding address.

Named pipe
: An Application Program Interface for LAN Manager which allows an unlimited number of sessions on the network. Named pipe is a much higher-level interface than NetBIOS (Network Basic Input/Output System); a single named pipe function is equal to many NetBIOS calls. With named pipes, LAN Manager handles all the low-level details of communications.

NCP
: 1. Network Control Point. 2. NetWare Core Protocols used to provide file, print, and other services.

Near Letter Quality (NLQ)
: By striking the paper several times to create a character, dot matrix printers can give the impression of non-dot matrix quality output.

Net
: An Internet domain designated for networks that includes network service centers, network information centers, and others. An example is nyser.net.

NetBEUI
: NetBIOS Extended User Interface. This is a transport protocol written to the NetBIOS interface.

NetBIOS
: Standard programming interface for the development of distributed applications.

NetBIOS name
: The computer name of a machine running NetBIOS.

NetWare volume
: A fixed physical amount of hard disk storage space. A NetWare volume is the highest level in the directory structure.

Network
: A group of computers and other devices connected together so they can communicate with each other.

Network adapter
: The card that allows a computer to interface with the network.

Network address
: A network number which uniquely identifies a network cable segment. It may also be referred to as the IPX external network number.

Network backbone
NetWare servers and routers are attached to this central cabling system, which provides connection to other cable segments. The central cable handles all internetwork traffic, decreasing packet transmission time and traffic on the network.

Network board
Workstations communicate with each other and the NetWare server via this circuit board which is installed in each computer. Printers that contain their own network boards can attach directly to the network cabling. NetWare documentation uses the term network board, it can also be referred to as an NIC, LAN card, or network card.

Network drive
The common name for a logical drive.

Network File System (NFS)
Software developed by Sun Microsystems that allows you to use files on another network as if they were on your local computer.

Network Information Center (NIC)
A resource providing network administrative support as well as information services and support to users. The most famous of these on the Internet is the InterNIC, which is where new domain names are registered.

Network Layer
The OSI layer that is responsible for routing, switching, and subnetwork access across the entire OSI environment.

Network news
An electronic news service divided into newsgroups concerned with a variety of topics. Users of network news can post messages to an electronic forum and read messages posted by others.

Network News Transfer Protocol (NNTP)
A protocol that defines the distribution, inquiry, and retrieval of news articles on the Internet (TCP/IP sites).

Network node
A server, workstation, router, printer, or fax machine connected to a network by a network board and a LAN driver.

Network number
A number which uniquely identifies a network cable segment. It is also referred to as the IPX external network number.

Network numbering
A system of numbers, including IPX external network number, IPX internal network number, and node number, identifying servers, network boards, and cable segments.

Network Operations Center (NOC)
The authority for monitoring network or Internet operations. Each Internet service provider (organization providing Internet connections) maintains its own network operations center and is responsible for users connectivity.

Network printer
A printer shared by multiple computers over a network.

Network server
A network node that provides file management, printing, or other services to other nodes or workstations. A node can function as a file server exclusively, or as both a file server and a workstation.

Network Time Protocol (NTP)
A protocol that assures accurate local timekeeping with reference to radio and atomic clocks located on the Internet.

NFS
(Networked File System) This allows UNIX systems to integrate with NetWare v4.x file systems.

NFS (Network File System)
A distributed file system developed by Sun Microsystems which allows a set of computers to cooperatively access each other's files in a transparent manner.

NIC
1. Network Interface Card. 2. Also, with TCP/IP, it is used to reference the Network Information Center. Originally there was only one, located at SRI International, and tasked to serve the ARPANET (and later DDN) community. Today, there are many NICs, operated by local, regional, and national networks all over the world. Such centers provide user assistance, document service, training, and much more.

Node
1. A device at a physical location that performs a control function and influences the flow of data in a network 2. The points of connection in the links of a network. 3. Any single computer connected to a network.

Node address
A number which uniquely identifies a network board. It is also referred to as the node number.

Node number
A number which uniquely identifies a network board. It may also be referred to as a station address, physical node address, or node address. Every node must have at least one network board connecting it to the network. Each board must have a unique node number to distinguish it from other network boards on the network.

Noise
In data transmission, any unwanted electrical signal which interferes with a communications channel. Noise is often a random transmission of varying frequency, amplitude, and phase. Such noise may radiate from fluorescent lights and electric motors, and can also be caused by static, temperature changes, electric or magnetic fields, or from the sun and the stars.

Non-Priority Scheme
A Token Ring can be used on a priority or non-priority basis. When a station receives a free token it transmits the data units it needs to send. Opposite of Priority Scheme.

Non-Windows application
An application designed to run with DOS, but not specifically with Microsoft Windows. The application may not be able to take full advantage of all Windows features, such as memory management.

Nonpreemptive multitasking
See cooperative multitasking.

NT
Short for Windows NT. NT is an acronym for New Technology.

Null modem
A device that connects two DTE devices directly by emulating the physical connections of a DCE device.

Null variable
A variable set specifically to a value of null.

Numeric variable
A variable used to store numeric values, such as integer or real.

Object
1. Program component having an interface and properties. 2. In Novell networking, information about network resources, for example, user, group, printer, or volume, is stored in this NDS structure. An object is made up of categories of information, called properties, and the data in those properties. Information about an entity is stored in an object. It is not the actual entity. The information is kept in the NetWare Directory database. Some objects represent physical entities, like a user or printer. Others represent logical entities, like groups and print queues. The Organizational Unit object helps you organize and manage other objects.

Object Linking and Embedding
Microsoft open object model for programming.

Object-oriented programming
Component-based application development. C++ is a popular object-oriented language, providing classes that combine data and functionality in a single object.

Octet
A set of 8 bits or one byte.

OLE
See Object Linking and Embedding

OLE (Object Linking and Embedding)
Microsoft's specification which allows applications to transfer and share data.

On-line access
Refers to direct interaction with a host computer through local or long-distance telecommunications links.

Orientation
A setting that indicates whether the vertical or horizontal dimension is longer.

OS/2 Client
An OS/2 computer that connects to the network and can store and retrieve data from the network and run executable network files using NetWare Client for OS/2 software. OS/2 client workstations support IPX/SPX, NetBIOS, and Named Pipes, allowing users access to OS/2-based applications such as SQL Server.

OSI
Open Systems Interconnection; a set of universally-accepted standards published by the International Standards Organization, the Institute of Electrical and Electronic Engineers, and other standards organizations. The OSI reference model lists seven layers which define the activities that must take place when devices communicate on a network. The goal of OSI is to enable computerized systems in multi-vendor environments to share information more easily.

OSI (Open Systems Interconnection)
To support international standardization of network terminology and protocols, the International Standards Organization (ISO) proposed a reference model of open systems interconnection. Currently under development, OSI ensures that any open system will communicate with any other OSI-compliant system.

OSI layer 1 (physical layer)
The lowest of the seven defined layers of the generalized network architecture. It defines the transmission of bits over a communication channel, ensuring that 1s and 0s are recognized as such. The physical layer accepts and transmits a bit stream without recognizing or defining any structure or meaning.

OSI layer 2 (data link layer)
: Provides methodologies for transforming the new physical layer link into a channel that appears free of errors to the network layer (the next higher layer). The data link layer accomplishes this by splitting the input or data stream provided in the physical layer into data frames that are transmitted sequentially as messages, and by processing the acknowledgment (ACK) frames sent back over the channel by the receiver.

OSI layer 3 (network layer)
: Accepts messages of data frames from the transmitting host, converts the messages to packets, and routes the packets to their destination.

OSI layer 4 (transport layer)
: Accepts data from the session layer (the next layer up, which is the human user's interface to the network), splits this data into smaller units, passes these units down to the network layer, and ensures that all the pieces arrive at the destination in the correct order. The transport layer is a true end-to-end process: a program on the source transmitter carries on a conversation with a similar program at the end receiver. This end-to-end consideration in layers 4 to 7 is different from the protocols in layers 1 to 3, which regulates subnetworks at intermediate stages of a true end-to-end transmission.

OSI layer 5 (session layer)
: The user's interface into the network through which the user establishes a connection with a process on another distant machine. Once the connection is established, the session layer manages the end-to-end dialog in an orderly manner, supplementing the application-oriented user functions to the data units provided by the transport layer. Establishing the session layer connection is typically a multistep operation, involving addressing the host, authenticating password access, stating communications options to be used, and billing arrangements. Once the session is underway, the session layer manages the interaction.

OSI layer 6 (presentation layer)
: The presentation layer protocols format the data to meet the needs of different computers, terminals, or presentation media in the user s end-to-end communications. The protocols at this layer may also provide data encryption for security purposes in transmission over networks, or data compression for efficiency and economy.

OSI layer 7 (application layer)
: Specifies the protocols for the user's intended interaction with the distant computer, including such applications as database access, document interchange, or financial transactions. Certain industry-specific end-to-end application protocols, such as in banking or airline reservations, enable computers and terminals of connection created by a physical link.

OSI Network Address
The address, consisting of up to 20 octets, used to locate an OSI Transport entity. The address is formatted into an Initial Domain Part which is standardized for each of several addressing domains, and a Domain Specific Part which is the responsibility of the addressing authority for that domain.

OSI Presentation Address
The address used to locate an OSI Application entity. It consists of an OSI Network Address and up to three selectors, one each for use by the Transport, Session, and Presentation entities.

OSI reference model
The International Standards Organization (ISO) has promulgated a reference model of open systems interconnection (OSI) to support international standardization of network terminology and protocols. The OSI model has seven levels or layers, each of which performs a well-defined function for passing data through them.

Owner
An object that creates and/or manages some other object. For example, a dialog box is the owner of the controls that appear on it.

Packet
A unit of data transmitted at the OSI network layer; or any addressed segment of data transmitted on a network.

Page
1. Basic SQL Server I/O unit, 2 KB in size. 2. A Web "page" isn't literally a page, but an entire document, however long. A home page (often called "home.html" or "index.html") is the first page called up when you enter a Web site, or if the URL doesn't give a filename.

Page File
Dedicated hard disk space used to emulate RAM for virtual memory.

Paging File
A portion of the hard disk used to hold nonpersistent information associated with running applications.

Palette
A set of colors that can be displayed on a particular device. Applications can use the Windows default palette or define their own logical palette.

Parallel interface
A connection between a parallel device, such as a printer, and a computer. The computer sends multiple bits of information to the device simultaneously. This is also known as a Centronics interface.

Parallel multitasking
The process whereby programs execute simultaneously.

Parallel port
An input/output port that sends and receives information synchronously in lots of 8-bits at high speeds along parallel lines to peripheral devices, typically printers. Most personal computers are configured with three parallel ports, called LPT1, LPT2, and LPT3. LPT is an abbreviation for line printer.

Parallel transmission
In computer communications, parallel transmission is the transmission of data (binary digits) simultaneously (in parallel with each other) using separate lines. In contrast, serial transmission sends only one bit after the other using only one communications line.

Parameter
A variable that is given a constant value for a specified application and that may denote the application; or a variable that is given a constant value for a specific document processing program instruction.

Parent directory
This is the term for the directory immediately above any subdirectory. For example, SYS:SALES would be the parent of the SYS:SALES/NEW.

Parent object
Container objects which hold other objects.

Parity check
A technique used to quickly check the integrity of data received after a transmission, or from memory. Parity checking can apply to bytes, words, longwords, and other units of information.

Partition
1. An area of storage on a fixed disk that contains a particular operating system or a logical drive where data and programs can be stored.   2. In NetWare v4.x, it is a division of the NetWare Directory Services.

Partition (disk)
NetWare server hard disks can be divided into these logical units.

Partition management
A method of management which allows users to divide the Directory into partitions and manage various Directory replicas of these Directory partitions.

Pass-through validation
A process where a logon attempt that cannot be validated by the local domain is passed to trusted domains for validation.

Password
A word or set of letters and numbers allowing access to a facility, computer, or network. A password may be accompanied by some other unique identifier before the user is allowed to login.

Path
1. In hierarchical data structures, such as operating system directories, the path is the chain from a root directory, as in MS-DOS, or volume, as in NetWare, to a specific subdirectory or file.   2. In data communications, the path is the transmission route from sending node to receiving node.

PCI (Protocol Control Information)
The protocol information added by an OSI entity to the service data unit passed down from the layer above, all together forming a Protocol Data Unit (PDU).

PCL (Printer Control Language)
Hewlett Packard developed PCL for its own LaserJet printers. PCL instructs the printer on how to construct the output on a page. A large number of other manufacturers also support the HP PCL language.

Peer
A Windows Socket application that functions as both a server and a client.

Peer-to-peer
: Communication in which two communications systems communicate as equal partners sharing the processing and control of the exchange, as opposed to host-terminal communication in which the host does most of the processing and controls the exchange.

Personal Profile
: Server-based, user specific profile applied when a user logs in from any domain workstation. Users are allowed to make changes to local profiles.

Physical Layer
: The OSI layer that provides the means to activate and use physical connections for bit transmission. In plain terms, the Physical Layer provides the procedures for transferring a single bit across a Physical Media.

Physical Media
: Any means in the physical world for transferring signals between OSI systems. Considered to be outside the OSI Model, and therefore sometimes referred to as "Layer 0." The physical connector to the media can be considered as defining the bottom interface of the Physical Layer, i.e., the bottom of the OSI Reference Model.

PIF (Program Information File)
: A file used by Microsoft Windows and Windows NT to provide parameters necessary for running non-Windows applications.

Ping (Packet internet groper)
: A program used to test reachability of destinations by sending them an ICMP echo request and waiting for a reply. The term is used as a verb: "Ping host X to see if it is up!"

Pipe
: To start execution of an instruction sequence before the previous instruction sequence is completed to increase processing speed.

Pitch
: In printing, pitch refers to the number of characters per horizontal inch, and is related to the character point size. Some fonts use a fixed pitch, where the spacing is the same for each character. Many fonts use a variable or proportional pitch, where each character has a different width. Overall, controlling the pitch makes for a better document appearance.

Pixel
: A pixel, or pel, is an individual picture element. This is the smallest single element that can be displayed on the screen. Screen resolution is given in horizontal and vertical pixel counts. The more pixels, the greater the resolution.

Platters
: In hard disks, platters are rigid aluminum disks covered with metal particles that are magnetized. When read/write heads sweep across the platter, the magnetized particles form patterns that represent stored data. Platters are similar to floppy diskettes, except that there are multiple platters in each hard disk. Data can be written to both sides of the platters' surface. The term platters refers specifically to hard (fixed) disk drives. Most drives have at least four platters; some have as many as ten.

Point size
: In printing, characters are measured in points. There are 72 points per inch. The point size refers to the maximum size for any character, measured top-to-bottom.

Point-to-point
: Data communications links are divided into two main categories, depending on how the line is structured: either point-to-point or multipoint. Point-to-point describes a channel that is established between two, and only two, stations. The link may be a dedicated or a dial-up line connecting a processor and a terminal, two processors, or two terminals.

Point-to-Point Protocol (PPP)
: Provides router-to-router and host-to-network connection over both synchronous and asynchronous circuits. The successor of SLIP.

Point-to-Point Tunneling Protocol
: See PPTP.

Polling
: The process by which a computer periodically asks each terminal or device on a LAN if it has a message to send, and then allows each to send data in turn. On a multipoint connection or a point-to-point connection, polling is the process whereby data stations are invited one at a time to transmit.

Port
: 1. A place where information goes into or out of a computer, such as the "serial port" on a person computer is where a modem would be connected. 2. On the Internet, "port" often refers to a number that is part of a URL, appearing after a colon (:), right after the domain name. Every service on an Internet server "listens" on a particular port number on that server. Most services have standard port numbers, e.g. Web servers normally listen on port 80. Services can also listen on non-standard ports, in which case the port number must be specified in a URL when accessing the server, so you might see a URL of the form: gopher://peg.cwis.uci.edu:7000/ which shows a gopher server running on a non-standard port (the standard gopher port is 70). 3. Port also refers to translating a piece of software to bring it from one type of computer system to another, e.g. to translate a Windows program so that will run on a Macintosh.

Posting
: A single message entered into a network communications system. eg: A single message "posted" to a newsgroup or message board.

Postoffice
: Microsoft Mail message store element.

PostScript
: PostScript is a registered trademark of Adobe Corporation, and is the accepted standard for high resolution printing on laser printers. PostScript is a language used to tell the printer how to print a character on the page. PostScript uses vector information to define graphics. Some printers, such as Apple LaserWriter printers, are true PostScript printers. Some printers use PostScript emulation, either at the system or in the printer.

POTS (Plain Old Telephone Service)
: A term used by the telecom industry to denote the service has not been upgraded to support higher-level data transmissions.

Power Supply
: A device that takes the electricity from the wall (AC, or alternating current) and converts it into the type of electricity required by the computer (DC, or direct current).

PPP (Point-to-Point Protocol)
: The successor to SLIP, PPP provides router-to-router and host-to-network connections over both synchronous and asynchronous circuits.

PPTP
: The Point-to-Point Tunneling Protocol provides secure client connections over the Internet.

Preemptive multitasking
: Multitasking method where the operating system allocates processor time to tasks according to their relative priority.

Presentation Layer
: The OSI layer that determines how Application information is represented (i.e., encoded) while in transit between two end systems.

Print queue
: A network directory which stores print jobs. The print server takes the print job out of the queue and sends it when the printer is ready. It can hold as many print jobs as disk space allows.

Print server
: A network computer, either dedicated or nondedicated, used to handle the printing needs of workstations.

Printer
: Peripheral hardware which produces printed material.

Printer driver
: A program that translates the file that is printed into the language the printer understands. A printer cannot be used unless the correct driver is installed on the current startup disk.

Printer fonts
: May be downloadable soft fonts or fonts which are built into the printer.

Printer languages
: In addition to simple control characters, more advanced printers (such as laser printers) support a command and control language, allowing even greater applications support. PCL (Hewlett-Packard) and PostScript (Adobe) are two primary, de facto industry standards for printer languages.

Priority
: Sometimes abbreviated as PRI, PRIO, or PRTY; a rank assigned to a task that determines its precedence in receiving system resources.

Priority class
: A priority setting for an entire process.

Priority level
: A priority setting for a thread within a process.

Problem determination
The process of identifying the source of a problem, such as machine failure, power loss, or user error.

Procedure
1. A block of program code with or without formal parameters, the execution of which is invoked by means of a procedure call. 2. A set of executable Visual Basic program steps.

Process
To perform operations on data in a process; or a course of events defined by its purpose or by its effect, achieved under given conditions. A course of events occurring according to an intended purpose or effect.

Processor
In a computer, a functional unit that interprets and executes instructions. A processor contains at least an instruction control unit and an arithmetic and logic unit.

Project
Visual Basic application and all of its components while under development.

Properties
Values related to a Visual Basic object.

Property
A variable containing information about a particular object. Properties can be exposed or private.

Protected mode
The operating mode of the 80286 microprocessor that allows the operating system to use features that protect one application from another; also called Protect Mode.

Protocol
A set of strict rules (usually developed by a standards committee) that governs the exchange of information between computer devices. Also, a set of semantic and syntactic rules that determines the behavior of hardware and software in achieving communication.

Protocols
Programs and operating systems used these conventions or rules to communicate between two or more endpoints.

Proxy
The mechanism whereby one system "fronts for" another system in responding to protocol requests. Proxy systems are used in network management to avoid having to implement full protocol stacks in simple devices, such as modems.

Proxy ARP
The technique in which one machine, usually a router, answers ARP requests intended for another machine. By "faking" its identity, the router accepts responsibility for routing packets to the "real" destination. Proxy ARP allows a site to use a single IP address with two physical networks. Subnetting would normally be a better solution.

Public Switched Network
Any switching communications system - such as Telex, TWX or public telephone networks - that provides circuit switched connections to many customers.

Pulse dialing
Older form of phone dialing, utilizing breaks in DC current to indicate the number being dialed.

Qualifier
A word or words that further defines a help topic.

Query
: The process by which a master station asks a slave station to identify itself and to give its status. In interactive systems, query is an operation at a terminal that elicits a response from the system.

Queue
: A holding area in which items are removed in a first in, first out (FIFO) manner. In contrast, a stack removes items in a last in, first out (LIFO) manner. Also, a queue is a list that is constructed and maintained so that the next data element to be retrieved is the one stored first. This is the first in, first out method.

RAID
: Redundant Arrays of Inexpensive Disks.

RAM (Random Access Memory)
: RAM is the computer's storage area to write, store, and retrieve information and program instructions so they can be used by the central processing unit. The contents of RAM are not permanent.

RAM drive
: Also known as a virtual drive. A portion of memory used as if it were a hard disk drive. RAM drives are faster than hard disks because the memory access time is much faster than the access time of a hard disk. Information on a RAM drive is lost when the computer is turned off.

Random access
: File access method where data can be read from the file in any order.

RAS
: Service that provides network access to remote Windows NT, Windows for Workgroups, and DOS workstations in a Windows NT Server domain environment.

RAS programs
: Reliability, Availability, and Serviceability programs. These programs monitor the operating system and facilitate problem determination.

RBOC
: Regional Bell Operating Company.

Read right
: A file system right which allows users to open and read files. It is also a property right that allows the reading of values of the property.

Read-after-write verification
: A way to assure that data written to the hard disk is the same as the original data still in memory. If it matches, the data in memory is released. If it does not match, the block location is recognized as bad, and Hot Fix send the data to a good block location within the Hot Fix Redirection Area.

Read/write heads
: In a fixed disk drive, there is one read/write head for each side of each platter. The read/write heads are said to be "gang mounted" because they move together in unison across multiple platters.

Real mode
: The operating mode of the 80286 microprocessor that runs programs designed for the 8086/8088 microprocessor.

Redundancy check
: A check made with redundant hardware or information that can provide an indication that certain errors have occurred.

Region
: An area of the screen that responds to user input. It may be non-rectangular.

Registry
Windows NT combined configuration database.

REM or REMARK
A non-executable statement in a computer program, entered as documentation or as a reminder to the programmer. In a NetWare login script, REM or REMARK, an asterisk, or a semicolon at the beginning of a line indicates that what follows is not to be executed.

Remote Access Service
See RAS.

Remote Client
Remote Microsoft Mail user.

Remote Management
Use of a remote console by a network supervisor or by a remote console operator to perform file server tasks.

Remote Procedure Call (RPC)
A protocol that standardizes initiation and control processes on remote computers.

Remote workstation
A terminal or personal computer that is connected to the LAN by a remote asynchronous connection.

Repeater
A device which propagates electrical signals from one cable to another without making routing decisions or providing packet filtering. In OSI terminology, a repeater is a Physical Layer intermediate system.

Replication
Process whereby data directories are dynamically copied between selected file servers.

Requester
NetWare program on the REQUESTER diskette that allows a workstation running under OS/2 to communicate through a NetWare network by attaching to a file server.

Resolution
In monitors, this refers to the sharpness of the displayed image or text on a monitor, and is a direct function of the number of pixels in the display area. Resolution is the number of pixels across one line of the monitor by the number of lines down the screen (for example, 800x480). The greater the pixel count, the higher the resolution and the clearer the screen image.

Resources
Objects an application needs, such as icons, cursors, and regions.

Restore
To bring back computer data or files that have been lost through tampering or other corruption or through hardware malfunction. Files should be backed up frequently to protect against such loss.

Reverse Address Resolution Protocol (RARP)
A protocol used primarily by diskless hosts to find their Internet address at startup. RARP maps a hardware address to an Internet address.

Ring 3
The privilege level that is used to run applications. Code executing at this level cannot modify critical system structures.

RIP (Routing Information Protocol)
The routing protocol used by routers to share network information in a TCP/IP or IPX network. Note that TCP/IP RIP and IPX RIP are 2 different protocols.

ROM
: Read Only Memory is used to store permanent instructions for the computer's general housekeeping operations. A user can read and use, but not change, the data stored in the computer's ROM. ROM is stored on a non-volatile memory chip, enabling the information to be retained, even after the computer's power has been turned off.

Root directory
: The first-level directory of a disk, created when the user first formats a disk and then is able to create files and subdirectories in it.

Router
: 1. A connection between two networks that specifies message paths and may perform other functions, such as data compression. 2. In early versions of NetWare, the term bridge was sometimes used interchangeably with the term router.

Router Information Protocol(RIP)
: This protocol allows routers to exchange routing details on a NetWare internetwork. Using RIP, NetWare routers can crate and maintain a database, or routing table, of current information. Workstations can query the nearest router to determine the fastest route to a distant network by broadcasting a RIP request packet. Routers send periodic RIP broadcast packets with current information to keep all routers on the internetwork synchronized. They also send RIP update broadcasts when a change is detected in the internetwork configuration.

RPC (Remote Procedure Call)
: An easy and popular paradigm for implementing the client-server model of distributed computing. A request is sent to a remote system to execute a designated procedure, using arguments supplied, and the result returned to the caller. There are many variations and subtleties, resulting in a variety of different RPC protocols.

RS-232-C
: A low-speed serial interface used to connect data communications equipment (such as modems and terminals) defined as a standard by the Electronic Industries Association. All standards recommended by the EIA have an RS prefix.

SAA
: Systems Application Architecture. SAA was created by IBM in 1987 to help developers standardize applications so that software can function in different operating environments with minimal program modifications and retraining of users. SAA provides a common programming interface, common user access, and a common communications support for IBM operating systems.

SAPS
: Number of service access point stations for Token Ring. This parameter may be required on a Novell network in the shell.cfg file depending on the network interface card.

Scan mode
When a monitor screen is refreshed by the electron gun and beam, there are two modes of scanning that may be used. With sequential scanning, all lines are scanned in order from the top left corner, across and then down the screen. This is sometimes referred to as non-interlaced scanning. With interlaced scanning, the lines are divided into an odd and an even group. First one (the odd) and then the other (the even) group is scanned each time the screen is refreshed. As a result, interlaced scanning takes more time and the image on the display begins to deteriorate. Because it takes longer for the electron beam to return to the top corner after the odd and even scan to start scanning the odd group again, flicker is produced as the electron gun refreshes and excites the phosphor elements on the screen. Non-interlaced scanning is considered preferable over interlaced.

Scan rate
Screens must be refreshed several times per second to continue displaying data. This is called their refresh rate or the frame rate. This rate is expressed in Hertz (Hz). Standard rates vary from 50 to 72 Hz (or more), which means that the screen is scanned 50 to 72 times per second. The more times a refresh occurs per second, the sharper the image, the less the image decays between scans, and the less flicker can be seen.

Scanning frequency
The number of lines scanned per second on a monitor. The formula for frequency is the number of pixels scanned per second divided by the number of pixels per line. The higher the frequency, the higher the resolution.

Scheduler
The part of OS/2 that decides which thread to run and how long to run it before assigning the CPU to another thread, also, the part of OS/2 that determines the priority value for each thread.

Scheduler (dispatcher)
The part of the operating system that determines which thread should run and the relative priority of each executing thread.

Screen font
The font displayed on the computer screen. It may or may not approximate a printer font.

SCSI
(Small Computer Systems Interface) This is an industry standard with guidelines for connecting peripheral devices (such as hard drives and tape backup systems) and their controllers to a microprocessor. The SCSI, commonly pronounced "scuzzy," interface defines standards for hardware and software to communicate between a host computer and a peripheral device. Computers and peripheral devices designed to meet SCSI specifications are normally compatible.

SCSI bus
This is an interface that connects HBAs to controllers and hard disks.

Search drive
The operating system searches this drive when a requested file is not found in the current directory. Search drives are supported only from DOS workstations. They allow a user working in one directory to use an application or data file in another directory.

Sector
: In disk drives, each track is divided into sectors. Sectors resemble pieces of a pie.

Sector Sparing
: Disk fault tolerance feature which allows remapping of bad sectors to an alternate sector when disk I/O errors occur.

Secure Sockets Layer
: See SSL.

Security descriptor
: A structure that contains information about which users can access an object and for what purpose. Only objects created under Windows NT can have security descriptors.

Security Token
: See Access Token.

Segment
: 1. A self-contained portion of a computer program that may be executed without the entire computer program necessarily being maintained in internal storage at any one time. 2. In computer graphics, a segment is a collection of display elements that can be manipulated as a unit. A segment may consist of several and separate dots, line segments, or other display elements. 3. In TCP/IP, a message block.

Selector
: The identifier used by an OSI entity to distinguish among multiple SAPs at which it provides services to the layer above.

Semaphore
: A variable that is used to enforce mutual exclusion.

Serial interface
: A connection point through which information is transferred one digital bit at a time. The term serial interface is sometimes applied to interfaces in which the data is transferred serially via one path, but some control signals can be transferred simultaneously via parallel paths.

Serial multitasking
: The process by which multiple programs execute, but only one at a time.

Serial port
: A connector for peripheral devices that receive data in a serial format, that is, one bit at a time. See COM port.

Serial transmission
: Transmission in which data (binary digits) can be transmitted only one bit at a time using only one communications line. In contrast, parallel transmission sends each byte simultaneously using separate lines. Connections exceeding one meter in distance typically use serial transmission.

Server
: A node on a network, usually a Local Area Network, that provides service to the terminals on the network through managing an expensive shared resource. File server, printer server, and communication server are examples.

Server Manager
: Windows NT Server and Workstation management utility.

Server-based Profile
: A user profile that is stored on a domain server.

Service Advertising Protocol (SAP)
: A protocol which allows servers to advertise their services on a NetWare internetwork. This allows routers to create and maintain a database of current internetwork server information. Routers also send SAP broadcasts to synchronize all routers on the internetwork. They also send SAP update broadcasts when a internetworking configuration change is detected.

Service provider
: A DLL that interfaces with a device or third-party application. A service provider is generally developed by the developer of the device or application it supports.

Session
: 1. That group of processes or tasks associated with an application. 2. A NetWare v3.1x menu utility used to change a user's environment while logged into the server. It can be used to change file servers, logout, view a list of network groups or users, or send a message to a group or user. It can display, add, delete, or modify drive mappings.

Session Layer
: The OSI layer that provides means for dialogue control between end systems.

Share name
: The name give to a shared resource. The universal naming convention references machine name and share name.

Shared memory
: The use of the same portion of memory by two distinct processes, or the memory so shared. Shared memory is used for interprocess communication and for purposes that lead to compactness of memory, such as common subroutines.

Shareware
: Software publicly available for downloading. If the shareware is copied and used, the author of the software is expected to receive compensation.

Shell
: A portion of a program that responds to user commands, also called user interface. The shell is loaded as a terminate and stay resident program (TSR).

Signaling
: Using semaphores to notify threads that certain events or activities have taken place.

Signals
: Notification mechanisms implemented in software that operate in a fashion analogous to hardware interrupts.

Signature
: The three- or four-line message at the bottom of a piece of electronic mail or a USENET article identifying the sender.

Simple Mail Transfer Protocol (SMTP)
: The Internet standard protocol for transferring electronic mail messages between computers.

Simple Network Management Protocol (SNMP)
: A network architecture designed in 1988 by the U.S. Department of Defense and companies using TCP/IP. It is used to manage nodes that join TCP/IP networks as well as other network types.

Single Domain Model
: Simplest Windows NT Server domain model where only one domain exists on the network.

SLIP (Serial Line IP)
: An Internet protocol used to run IP over serial lines such as telephone circuits or RS-232 cables interconnecting two systems. SLIP is now being replaced by PPP.

Smart
: Containing microprocessor intelligence. A modem or adapter is smart if it has its own computer chip. A dumb device is limited in functions and features, and takes processing power from a high-level system.

SNMP (Simple Network Management Protocol)
: The network management protocol of choice for TCP/IP-based internets.

Socket
: The destination of an IPX packet is represented by this part of an IPX internetwork address in a network node. Some sockets are reserved by Novell for specific applications, all NCP request packets are delivered to socket 451h. By registering those numbers with Novell, third-party developers can reserve socket numbers for specific purposes.

Software
: A computer program, or a set of instructions written in a specific language that commands the computer to perform various operations on data contained in the program or supplied by the user. Programs, procedures, rules, and any associated documentation pertaining to the operation of a data processing system, independent of the carrier used for transport.

Source code
: Textual program statements.

Source routing
: A means IBM uses to route data across source-routing bridges. NetWare source-routing programs enable IBM token ring network bridges to forward NetWare packets (or frame).

SQL
: Structured Query Language; an ISO data definition and data manipulation language for relational databases. Variations of SQL are offered by most major vendors for their relational database products. SQL is consistent with IBM's Systems Application Architecture and has been standardized by the American National Standards Institute (ANSI).

SSL
: Secure Sockets Layer is a transmission scheme proposed by Netscape Communications Corporation. It is a low-level encryption scheme used to encrypt transactions in higher-level protocols such as HTTP and FTP.

Standard mode
: A mode of operation used by Microsoft Windows 3.x which can be used with an 80286 or higher processor. Standard mode provides access to extended memory and also enables the user to switch between non-Windows applications. It does not provide virtual memory, or non-Windows applications to be run in a window or in the background.

Start/stop bits
: Additional bits inserted to mark the beginning and the end of transmitted characters. Start bits and stop bits are used in asynchronous communications.

Start/stop transmission
: See asynchronous transmission.

Station
: A term used as a shortened form of workstation, but can also refer to a server, router, printer, fax machine, or any computer device connected to a network by a network board and communication medium.

Station address
: A number which uniquely identifies a network board. It is also referred to as a node number.

Stored Procedures
: Custom SQL Server procedures that have been compiled, an execution plan created, and the procedure stored in the current database.

Stream transmission
: A connection-oriented transfer of data between two sockets.

Stream-oriented
: A type of transport service that allows its client to send data in a continuous stream in the same order as sent and without duplicates.

Subdirectory
: This is a directory that lies below another in the file system structure. For example, In SYS:SALES/NEW, NEW is a subdirectory of SYS:SALES.

Subnet
: A portion of a network that shares a network address with other portions of the network and is identified by a subnet number. A subnet is to a network what a network is to an Internet.

Subnet Mask
: A filter which separates subnetted addresses into network and local entities. Local systems have subnet masks so they can restrict the broadcast to be received on the local network only.

Subnetting
: When a complex network is recognized as a single address from outside of the network.

Subnetwork
: A collection of OSI end systems and intermediate systems under the control of a single administrative domain and utilizing a single network access protocol. Examples: private X.25 networks, collection of bridged LANs.

Super VGA
: Also known as VGA Plus, Extended VGA, and abbreviated SVGA. Super VGA provides analog output by varying intensity of the three primary colors. SVGA provides higher resolutions than VGA.

Suspend
: An action that causes an active program to become temporarily inactive. In effect, the suspended program is waiting for the user to reactivate it.

Swap file
: A file that contains temporarily data moved out of main storage to the swap file on disk. Sometimes known as a paging file.

Swapping
: A process that interchanges the contents of an area of main storage with the contents of an area of auxiliary storage. Sometimes known as Paging.

Switched line
: A communications link for which the physical path may vary with each usage, such as the public telephone network.

Synchronization
: Replica synchronization is a way to ensure that replicas of a Directory partition have the same information as other replicas of the same partition. Time synchronization is a way to ensure all servers in a Directory tree register the same time.

Synchronous
: Pertaining to two or more processes that depend upon the occurrence of a specific event such as a common timing signal.

Synchronous modem
: Modem that carries timing information with data.

Synchronous terminal
: A data terminal that operates at a fixed rate with transmitter and receiver in synchronization.

Synchronous transmission
: In computer communications, data (binary digits) can be transmitted in synchronous or asynchronous mode. When data is transmitted in synchronous mode, both the sending and receiving devices must be precisely timed with each other, to ensure that data is sent speedily, with control signals used only when there is a major break in transmission.

System configuration
: A process that specifies the devices and programs that form a particular data processing system.

System Default Profile
: Windows NT profile defining background color, screen saver, and wallpaper settings when no user is logged on.

System dump
: A dump of all active programs and their associated data after an error stops the system.

Tape backup device
: This internal or external tape drive backs up data from hard disks.

Target
: Any server, workstation, or service on the network that has a Target Service Agent loaded. The data can be backed up or restored on a target. When backing up and restoring to the host server, the target and host become the same.

Task
: In a multiprogramming or multiprocessing environment, one or more sequences of instructions created by a control program as an element of work to be accomplished by a computer.

Task bar
: The Windows 95 user interface element that shows the running applications and open windows.

Terminal emulation
: The use of hardware and software on a personal computer to duplicate the operation of a terminal device at both the operator and communications interface sides of the connection, so that a mainframe computer capable of supporting the emulated terminal will also support the PC.

Terminal emulator
: A program that allows a computer to act like a terminal when logged in to a remote host. The VT100 terminal is emulated by many popular communications packages.

Termination
: Placement of a connector on a cable.

Thread
    The object of a process that is responsible for executing a block of code. A process can have one or multiple threads.

Time Out
    When two computers are talking and, for whatever reason, one of the computer fails to respond.

Time sharing
    The interleaved use of time on a computer system enabling two or more users to execute computer programs concurrently. Also, a mode of operation of a data processing system that provides for the interleaving in time of two or more processes in one processor.

Time slice
    An interval of time on the processing unit allocated for use in performing a task. After the interval has expired, processing unit time is allocated to another task. Therefore, a task cannot monopolize processing unit time beyond a fixed limit. In systems with time sharing, time slice is a segment of time allocated to a terminal job.

Time synchronization
    A way to ensure all servers in a Directory tree report the same time. Clocks in computers can lose or gain time, resulting in different times on various servers. Time synchronization corrects these differences so all servers report the same time and provide a valid time stamp to arrange NDS events.

Time to Live (TTL)
    The amount of time between when a packet of data leaves its point of origin and when it reaches its destination. The TTL is encoded in the IP header, and is used as a hop count (to measure the route to the packet's destination).

Time-critical priority
    A classification of processes that may be interactive or noninteractive, in the foreground or background screen group, which have a higher priority than any non-time critical thread in the system.

Topology
    Refers to the physical layout of network components (such as cables, stations, gateways, and hubs).

Tracks
    On a disk, data is organized into concentric circles, or tracks on the disk medium. One complete circle represents one track. Tracks on disks are analogous to the tracks you might see on a record used in a record player (curving lines on the record surface). Tracks are typically numbered from the outermost track to the innermost, or from the outer edge of the media to the inner hub area. To figure out the number of tracks on a fixed disk drive, multiply the number of cylinders by the number of heads.

Traffic
    The total information flow in a communications system.

Transmission rate
    The transmission rate is stated in baud or bps. If the connection cannot be made at the selected transmission rate, most modems and communications software will automatically attempt to connect at a slower speed.

Transmit
    To send data from one place for reception elsewhere. Also, to move an entity from one place to another, as in broadcasting radio waves, dispatching data via a transmission medium, or transferring data from one data station to another via a line.

Transport Layer
The OSI layer that is responsible for reliable end-to-end data transfer between end systems.

TrueType fonts
Fonts conforming to a specification developed by Microsoft and Apple. TrueType fonts can be scaled to any height, and will print exactly as they appear on the screen, to the highest resolution available to the output device. The fonts may be generated as bitmaps or soft fonts, depending on the output device's capabilities.

Trust Relationship
Security link between Windows NT Server domains, allowing the establishment of NT Server domain models.

Trusted Domain
A domain receiving security rights and permissions from another (trusting) domain.

Trusted Users
Users from a trusted domain.

Trustee
In NetWare, a user or group eligible to be granted rights in a directory or file. For any specific directory or file, the trustee can be granted all, some, or none of the rights available. Trustee rights in a directory or file are called trustee assignments.

Trusting Domain
The domain granting security rights and permissions to another (trusted) domain.

Two-Way Trust
A trust relationship where there is mutual trust between two domains.

Typeface
The typeface is the style or appearance of the set of characters. Typeface examples include Times Roman, Helvetica, Script, etc. Many font names are trademarked and may be called by different names when coming from different sources.

UDP (User Datagram Protocol)
A transport protocol in the Internet suite of protocols. UDP, like TCP, uses IP for delivery. However, unlike TCP, UDP provides for exchange of datagrams without acknowledgements or guaranteed delivery.

UMBs (Upper Memory Blocks)
Areas of the upper memory that contain general-purpose memory. These areas can be used to hold device drivers or other memory-resident programs. This will free conventional memory for use by applications.

Uniform Resource Locator
See URL.

Uninterruptible power supply (UPS)
A backup power unit that supplies uninterruptible power if a commercial power outage occurs.

UNIX
A computer operating system originally developed at AT&T's Bell Research Laboratories and later at the University of California Berkeley. It is implemented in a growing number of minicomputer and microcomputer systems. UNIX is designed to be used by many people at the same time (it is "multi-user") and has TCP/IP built-in. It is the most common operating system for servers on the Internet.

Upload
A process where a user copies a file "up" to a host computer. Opposite of Download.

Upper memory area
: The area of the computer's memory usually reserved for running the system's hardware, such as the monitor. Upper memory is the 384 KB area of address space adjacent to the 640 KB of conventional memory. Upper memory is not considered part of the total memory because applications normally cannot store information in this area. Some programs, such as Microsoft Windows, can access unused portions of upper memory.

Upper Memory Blocks
: See UMBs.

UPS
: Uninterruptible Power Supply; an auxiliary power supply, usually battery operated, that provides reliable electricity to a file server, workstation, bridge, router, or other network device when normal electrical supply is interrupted or fails.

Upstream Neighbor Address
: The address of the network station that is physically and immediately upstream from another specific node. The upstream neighbor is the location from which the signal is being received. (Token Ring networks.)

URL (Uniform Resource Locator)
: A pathname of a document on the Internet. When you click on a link, your browser will inspect the URL to determine what action should be taken - loading a new page, retrieving a file directory, sending email, submitting information from a form [...]. URLs can be absolute or relative. An absolute URL consists of: a prefix denoting a method ('http' for Web sites, 'gopher' for gophers, and so forth), followed by a colon and two slashes (://); an address, which in turn consists of a domain name followed by a slash and a pathname (or 'username@domain name' for mailto), and finally an (optional) anchor, preceded by a #, which points to a place within a web page. A complete URL looks like this: http://www.jhu.edu/~phil/guidefold/webgloss.html#here. The method here is the Hypertext Transfer Protocol, which is used to transfer Web pages, the domain is www.jhu.edu, better known as "JHUniverse", and the address is the pathname of the page you are looking at together with a reference to an anchor in the page. All together the components of a URL tell a Web browser where to look for an item (the address), what to do once it finds the item (the method). Like email addresses, URLs must be completely correct in order to work. One trick, however, is worth knowing. If you are looking at a page and you want to find out more about its site, or if a URL turns out to be wrong, you can try lopping off segments of the pathname and linking to the address that remains (try, for example, truncating the address above to "http://www.jhu.edu/"). Sometimes you will need the slash at the end, sometimes not. Accessing the truncated address will sometimes take

you to a home page or index page. That page will usually contain information about the site. A relative URL designates an item relative to the item in which the designation is made. Here's an analogy: if you are in Baltimore and you give someone a local phone number, you don't include the area code, but only the seven digits of the number itself. That seven-digit number uniquely identifies something (someone's home or business) only when it is understood that the area code is 410. Likewise when you mention to someone a mutual acquaintance, you can often just say "Jane" instead of "Jane Doe from Baltimore, MD, USA". The first name is all you need; the rest will be supplied by the listener. So too a browser reading a relative URL supplies the pathname to the page you are looking at, and adds it to the front of the relative designation. Instead of having to designate the top of this page by "http://www.jhu.edu/~phil/guidefold/webguide.html#theTop", on this page I can call it simply "#theTop". The difference between absolute and relative URLs matters if you save a page to your own computer. Absolute URLs will still work, but relative URLs, which will now point to (presumably) nonexistent documents on your computer, will not work.

Usenet
A world-wide system of discussion groups, with comments passed among hundreds of thousands of machines. Not all Usenet machines are on the Internet, maybe half. Usenet is completely decentralized, with over 10,000 discussion areas, called newsgroups.

User
An individual permitted to access a Local Area Network. In NetWare, the user name can be up to 47 characters.

User Datagram Protocol (UDP)
A connectionless best-effort protocol.

User login script
This login script sets environment specifics for a user. It is optional, but most often used for items that cannot be included in a system or profile login script. If used, it will run after container and profile login scripts.

User Manager
Windows NT user and group administration utility.

User Manager for Domains
Windows NT Server user and group administration utility.

User Mode
Higher level Windows NT or Windows 95 operating system functions. The user mode includes the protected subsystems and application sessions.

User Profile
Environment configuration settings applied when a user logs on from a Windows NT workstation to Windows NT Server domain. Each user is given either a personal or a mandatory profile. See also Local Profile, Default Profile, Personal Profile, and Mandatory Profile.

User template
A file which contains default information that can be applied to new User objects to give them default property values. If you are creating many users who need the same property values, this is useful.

Utilities
In NetWare, utilities are programs that add functions to the operating system by being added to the file server, workstation, or router. Utilities can be in the form of console commands, including screen commands, installation, maintenance, and configuration commands.

Utility
The capability of a system, program, or device to perform the functions for which it is designed.

UUCP
UNIX-to-UNIX copy. A file transfer utility. Also used with UNIX electronic mail.

Variable
Memory identified by a unique name and used to store data.

Vector font
Generally used to refer to any font that is defined mathematically, and which supports scaling to any size. Vector fonts provide a smooth appearance at large font sizes.

Vertical spacing
Though not actually a font characteristic, the vertical spacing is also set to match the font appearance. This may be set in lines per inch, or as points of space to be inserted before and after each line.

VGA (Video Graphics Array)
VGA uses a DAC chip and sends analog signals at varying intensities to alter the three primary colors. By varying the intensity, a seemingly infinite number of color variations can be produced and displayed on the monitor.

Virtual circuit
A network service that acts like a dedicated line between a user's computer and a host. Data are processed through a virtual circuit in the order in which they are sent, regardless of the underlying network structure.

Virtual memory
A technique whereby a computer offloads some of the data or program from its primary memory onto disk, thereby giving the impression that primary memory can continue to accept or store almost unlimited amounts of data. The process is done through segmentation, dividing a program into manageable blocks and placing them in the most convenient locations on a disk.

Virtual Memory Manager (VMM)
The portion of the operating system that is responsible for swapping pages between RAM and the paging file and for keeping track of how an address in a virtual address space maps to physical memory.

Virus
A program that can change and destroy data. A virus can move into other computer systems by incorporating itself into programs that are shared among computer systems.

Voice-frequency
Frequency in part of the audio frequency range essential for the transmission of commercial quality speech.

Voice-Grade-Line
A channel that is capable of carrying voice frequency signals.

Volume
NetWare name for amount of named storage space on a hard disk, allocated when the network is installed.

WAN (Wide Area Network)
: A communications network similar in operation to a local area network (LAN) that can cover hundreds or thousands of kilometers, using public or private telephone lines, or microwaves. The public telephone system is an example of a WAN. A WAN usually consists of data terminal equipment owned or controlled by the user, and data communication equipment provided by a common carrier.

Web browser
: A client program that serves as the interface between the user and the resources of the World Wide Web.

Wide Area Network(WAN)
: This network communicates beyond a local area. A local area network can become part of a WAN when a link is created, using modems, remote routers, phone lines, satellite, or a microwave connection, to a mainframe system, a public data network, or another local area network.

WIN32S
: A set of APIs that allow 32-bit applications to run on Windows v3.1. Some of the functions are implemented as stubs.

Windowing
: In routing terms, windowing refers to flow control technique to send multiple message packets before requiring an acknowledgment from the receiver.

Windows (Microsoft)
: A graphical shell operating environment which runs on top of DOS. It contains many accessories and features which access DOS functions such as file, program, and printer management. Windows is referred to as a GUI (Graphical User Interface).

Windows Internet Naming Service (WINS)
: A Windows NT utility that translates a NetBIOS name into an IP address. It is designed for use in a routed network.

Workgroup
: A defined set of Windows for Workgroups or NT stations that are able to communicate and share file and print resources.

Workgroup manager
: Person appointed by a NetWare network supervisor to manage data and users belonging to a group.

Workstation
: A personal computer that is connected to a NetWare network. It can perform tasks through application program or utilities. The term client or station may also be used.

World Wide Web (WWW)
: A public domain document retrieval system that extensively uses hypertext links to connect a document to a series of relevant documents. Created by the network of the European Laboratory for Particle Physics (CERN) in Switzerland, WWW is a front-end program based on client/server architecture that allows Internet users to create, edit, or browse hypertext documents. The user can, in a Windows, X-Windows, NeXT, and MAC environment, click on specific (highlighted) terms and be transparently connected to the site of the related document. Mosaic, available from the National Center for Supercomputing Applications, can be used to access the Web.

Worm
: A computer program that replicates itself infinitely, filling up memory space. It can pass from one network to another.

WOW
Term used to describe DOS Windows running under Windows NT.

Write right
A file system right which allows users to open and write to files. As a property right, it allows the adding, changing or removing of any values of the property.

WYSIWYG
An acronym that stands for What You See is What You Get. A word processing term meaning that what is seen on the computer screen will correspond to what prints out on paper, including typeface, layout, and size.

X.25
A CCITT standard that defines the accessing protocol for public packet-switching networks. X.25 is a dynamic standard with many variations in the U.S. and abroad. The X.25 recommendation specifies a three-level structure for the transmission of data between data terminal equipment and data circuit equipment and outlines three levels of operation: the physical level, the link level, and the packet level.

X.25 Pad
A device that permits communication between non-X.25 devices and the devices in an X.25 network.

x86
Term used to refer to Intel-family processors such as the 80386 and 80486.

XMS memory
Memory beyond 1 MB in 80286 or higher processor computers. XMS memory is used by operating systems such as Windows for managing and running applications. Also known as extended memory.

Zone
A grouping of logical devices on one or more networks.

Zone List
A list of zones (up to 255).

Index

Symbols

OEM	49
$Unique$.udf	51

Numerics

16-bit Windows Application Restrictions	314
16-Bit Windows Applications	312
16-bit Windows Support	315

A

Account Policies	102
Account SID	124
Administrator	76
Alerts	467, 469
Answer File	52
answer file	50
API	231
Application Errors	316
ARP/RARP (Address Resolution Protocol/Reverse Address Resolution Protocol)	369
Asymmetric Multiprocessing (ASMP)	296
Attaching to Shared Printers	396
Audit Events	108
Audit Trails	107
AUTOEXEC.NT	332

B

Bindings	382
Boot record load	58, 452
BOOT.INI	59, 453, 456
Browsing	380

C

C-2 Level Security	79
Can´t Find NTLDR	456
Chart	467
Chart View	468
Client Licensing	33
Client Service for NetWare (CSNW)	406
Combined Configuration List	480
Command Prompt	306
Command Symbols	307
CONFIG.NT	329
Configuration changes	452
Control Panel	159
Control Sets	242
Cooperative Multitasking	293
Corrupted operating system files	452
Course Purpose	1
Creating Users	83
CSNW Configuration	408
Custom Configuration Files	328

D

Date/Time	219
DCOM	339
DCOM Configuration	346
Defining Profile Location	138
Destination	34
Detail Entries	113
Detail Event Information	181
Device/Service Errors	182
Devices	223
Dialin	88
Dial-Up Networking	424
Difference Files	55
Directory Sharing	387
Disk Administrator	256, 461
Disk Administrator Menu	257
Disk Bottleneck Indicators	471
Disk Bottlenecks	471
Disk partition	259
Disk Sets	260
DISKPERF -YE	471
DISKPERF-Y	471

D (cont.)

Display Settings 173
DLC 363
DNS 376
DNS (Domain Name System) 370
Domain 42
Domain Clients 125
Domain Global Group 133
Domain global group 130
Domain Local Group 132
Domain local group 130
Domain SID 124
Domains 122
DOS Applications 317
DOS Program Properties 321
Dr. Watson 482
Driver initialization 60, 454
Dual-Boot After Install 26
Dual-boot Configuration 25

E

Emergency Repair 459
Emergency Repair diskette (ERD) 460
Environment 213
ERD 461
Event Viewer 110, 179
Exercise 10-1 462
Exercise 10-2 483
Exercise 1-1 44
Exercise 1-2 68
Exercise 2-1 91
Exercise 2-2 100
Exercise 2-3 115
Exercise 3-1 127
Exercise 3-2 151
Exercise 4-1 178
Exercise 4-2 201
Exercise 5-1 228
Exercise 5-2 248
Exercise 7-1 299
Exercise 7-2 305
Exercise 9-1 411
Exercise 9-2 426

F

FAT 18
Font Settings 325
FTP (File Transfer Protocol) 369

G

General Settings 322
GPF (General Protection Fault) 316
Graphic Mode 36
Graphics mode 30
Group Accounts 130
Group Members 96
Guest 76

H

HAL 21, 60
Hardware detection 59
Hardware Profiles 216
Hardware Recognizer 236
HOSTS file 376
Hung applications 316
Hypertext Markup Language (HTML .. 430
Hypertext Transport Protocol (HTTP) 430

I

ICMP (Internet Control Message
   Protocol) 369
IIS 430
Improper Setup 452
INF file 56
Initial prompt 455
Install 162
Installation Requirements 17
Installation Troubleshooting 43
Internet Explorer 431
Internet Information Server 430
Internetworks 370
IP (Internet Protocol) 368
IP Address 374
IP Addresses 371
IPX 414
ISDN 413

Index

K

Kernel 236
Kernel initialization 60, 454
Kernel load 59, 454
Keyboard Properties 165

L

Launching Programs 297
LMHOSTS 377
LMHOSTS file 376
Local Groups 94
Log 467
Logging Off 65
Logging On 61
Logon 139
Logon Failures 62
Logon validation 129
Low-level loads 454

M

Maintenance 464
Making Repairs 460
Managing Local Groups 95
Managing Profiles 140
Mandatory profile 138
Mapping Keys 246
Memory Bottlenecks 472
Memory Optimization 473
Memory Settings 326
Microsoft Data Link Control (DLC) 361
Microsoft Internet Information Server .. 430
Microsoft RAS 414
Microsoft Technet 485
Microsoft World Wide Web 486
Miscellaneous Settings 328
Miscellaneous Troubleshooting 484
Modem 413
Modem Configuration 419
Modem Detection 417
Modem Setup 416
Mouse Properties 163
MS-DOS Restrictions 318
MS-DOS Support 319
Multimedia 221

Multiple Printer Definitions 198
Multiprocessing 296
Multitasking 293
Multitasking Applications 292
Multitasking Priority 294
Multithreading 296

N

Name Resolution 376
NDIS Interface 356
NetBEUI 361-362, 414
NetBIOS broadcasts 376
Network Installation 49
Network Installation Source 49
Network Properties 358
Network Selections 40
Network Services 379
Networking Model 355
NFS (Network File Services) 370
No Windows 95 Upgrade 25
NT Server domain 122
NTDETECT.COM 59, 456
NTFS 19
NTLDR 59, 452, 456
NTUser.dat 138
NTUser.man 138
Null Modem 413
NWLink 362-363
NWLink IPX/SPX Properties 367
NWLink NetBIOS 368

O

Object Embedding 335
Object Linking 335
OEM$ 49
OEM$$ 54
OEM$_id 49
OS/2 Applications 309

P

Package Definitions File 57
Partition 257
Passwords 78
PDF 57

Peer Print Server 197
Performance Monitor 466-467
Performance Settings 211
Policies 136
policy (.POL) 141
Policy File 142
Policy Settings 149
Pop-up menus 13
Ports 220
PPP 415
PPTP 415
Preemptive Multitasking 293
Primary Domain Controller (PDC) 123
Print Spooler 200
Printer drivers 187
Printer Failures 475
Printer Management 398
Printer Optimization 473
Printer pooling 185
Printer pools 199
Printer Property Sheet 185
Printer scheduling 191
Printer Security 194
Printer Sharing 193
Printer Troubleshooting 475
Printers 183
Processor Bottleneck Indicators 470
Processor Bottlenecks 470
Profile 86
Profile Locations 137
Profiles 136
Property sheets 13
Protected Subsystems 291
Protocol Installation 365

R

RAID and performance 472
RAS 231
RAS Clients 415
RAS Connection 413
RAS Installation 421
RDISK 461
Recovery 215
Recovery Menu 456
Regional Settings 230

Registry 142, 235-236, 246
Registry Backup 247
Registry Key 240
Registry Keys 238
Registry Logical Organization 237
Registry Mode 143
Registry Recovery 248
Remote Access Service 412
Removing Windows NT 68
Replicator 99
Report 468
Resolving Bottlenecks 470
Resource Access 386, 410
Resource Kit 484
RISC 23
RISC Installation 18

S

Screen Settings 327
SCSI Properties 167
Security ID 77
Security IDs 124
Security Log Entries 112
Security Management 129
Selection menu 59, 453
Server 209
Server Installation 43
Server Roles 123
Service Configuration 226
Service Pack Updates 486
Services 225
Setup 236
SETUPLDR 20
Share Parameters 388
Share Permissions 389
Shared Resources 193
Sharing Printers 395
Shortcut 298
Shut Down 66
SID 77
SLIP 414
SMS 57
SMTP (Simple Mail Transfer Protocol) 369
SNMP (Simple Network Management
 Protocol) 370

Index

Sounds 222
Spooler 200
Spooler Errors 476
Standard File Systems 259
Standard Rights 105
START 295
Start Menu 298
Start menu 12
Startup/Shutdown 214
Static Data Exchange 334
Static versus Dynamic Exchange 334
Supported Protocols 414
Symmetric Multiprocessing (SMP) 296
Sysdiff 55
System 210
System Components 236
System Policies 141, 145
System Policy Editor 142

T

Tape Drives 169
TAPI 231
Taskbar 12
TCP (Transmission Control Protocol) . 368
TCP/IP 362, 364, 368, 414
TCP/IP Properties Sheet 372
Telephony 231
TELNET 369
Text mode 30
Tools 258
Transport Protocols 361
Triple-boot 28
Troubleshooting 475
Trust Relationships 131

U

UDF 50
UDF File 54
UDF id 51
UDP (User Datagram Protocol) 369
UNATTEND.TXT 50
Unattended Application Setup 54
Unattended Installation 50
Understanding ARC Names 455
Uninstall 162
Uniqueness database file 50
Updating the Emergency Repair
  Diskette 461
Upgrade Notes 24
Upgrading Windows v3.x 26
UPS 170
User and Group Management 81
User Manager 82
User Policies 147
User Profiles 217
User Rights Policy 104
Users and Groups 93
Using DHCP 375
Using Policy File Mode 144

V

Value Entries 239
VDM Support 318
Viewing Audit Trails 109
Volume sets 260

W

Windows 9
Windows 95 9
Windows 95 Applications 317
Windows 95 User Interface 12
Windows Explorer 13
Windows Family 9
Windows for Workgroups 9
Windows NT Applications 309
Windows NT Boot Diskette 458
Windows NT Client 126
Windows NT Diagnostics 478
Windows NT Features 10
Windows NT Security 79
Windows NT Server 10
Windows NT Server Features 11
Windows NT Settings 324
Windows NT Setup 160
Windows NT Task Manager 302
Windows NT v3.1 415
Windows NT v3.51 and Windows 95 .. 415
Windows NT v4.0 415
Windows NT Workstation 10
WinMSD 478

WINNT 20, 22
WINNT /B 23
WINNT/WINNT32 Without Diskettes 23
WINNT32 .... 20, 22
WINNT32 /B 23
WINS 377-378
Workgroup 42, 122
Working With Drivers 224
Workstation 34
Workstation Information 37
Workstation local 130
Workstation Local Group 131
Workstation Local Groups 94
Workstation Networking 39
WOW Errors 316

X

X.25 413